Message and Medium

Topics in English Linguistics

Editors
Susan M. Fitzmaurice
Bernd Kortmann
Elizabeth Closs Traugott

Volume 105

Message and Medium

English Language Practices Across Old and New Media

Edited by
Caroline Tagg, Mel Evans

DE GRUYTER
MOUTON

ISBN 978-3-11-077715-4
e-ISBN (PDF) 978-3-11-067083-7
e-ISBN (EPUB) 978-3-11-067089-9

Library of Congress Control Number: 2019955473

Bibliographic information published by the Deutsche Nationalbibliothek
The Deutsche Nationalbibliothek lists this publication in the Deutsche Nationalbibliografie;
detailed bibliographic data are available on the Internet at http://dnb.dnb.de.

© 2021 Walter de Gruyter GmbH, Berlin/Boston
This volume is text- and page-identical with the hardback published in 2020.
Typesetting: Integra Software Services Pvt. Ltd.
Printing and binding: CPI books GmbH, Leck

www.degruyter.com

Acknowledgments

Like many textual artefacts – medieval, print or digital – this volume is the product of an elaborate process involving multiple actors. We'd like to thank the British Association of Applied Linguistics (BAAL) for funding the seminar *Historicising the Digital: language practices in new and old media* (University of Leicester, June 2016) from which this book emerged. We are indebted to the seminar participants for their inspiring discussions and debates, as well as to all the contributors to the book for putting a compelling range of transhistorical approaches into practice, and to our anonymous external reviewers. Our particular thanks go to the series editors, Elizabeth Closs Traugott and Bernd Kortmann, for their continued support, enthusiasm and insightful feedback.

Contents

Acknowledgments —— V

List of contributors —— XI

Mel Evans and Caroline Tagg
Introducing transhistorical approaches to digital language practices —— 1

Section 1: Rethinking Perspectives

Introduction to rethinking perspectives —— 14

Rodney H. Jones
1   The rise of the Pragmatic Web: Implications for rethinking meaning and interaction —— 17

Dániel Z. Kádár
2   Interpreting "historicisation" in the digital context: On the interface of diachronic and synchronic pragmatics —— 38

Caroline Tagg and Mel Evans
3   Spelling in context: A transhistorical pragmatic perspective on orthographic practices in English —— 55

Susan Fitzmaurice
4   Reflections on historicity, technology and the implications for method in (historical) pragmatics —— 80

Section 2: Historicizing Discourses

Introduction to historicising discourses —— 86

Agnieszka Lyons and Samia Ounoughi
5   Towards a transhistorical approach to analysing discourse *about* and *in* motion —— 89

Philip Seargeant
6 "New" media and self-fashioning: The construction of a political persona by Elizabeth I and Donald Trump —— 112

Korina Giaxoglou
7 From *Rest in Peace* to *#RIP*: Tracing shifts in the language of mourning —— 129

David Barton
8 Digital literacies and the long history of the academic article —— 149

Alison Sealey
9 Reflections on historicizing discourses: Connections, linkages, continuities —— 164

Section 3: Media Trajectories

Introduction to media trajectories —— 170

Joanna Kopaczyk
10 Unstable content, remediated layout: Urban laws in Scotland through manuscript and print —— 173

Hanna Rutkowska
11 Visual pragmatics of an early modern book: Printers' paratextual choices in the editions of *The School of Vertue* —— 199

Mari-Liisa Varila, Sirkku Ruokkeinen, Aino Liira and Matti Peikola
12 Paratextual presentation of Christopher St German's *Doctor and Student* 1528–1886 —— 232

Claudia Claridge
13 Reflections on visuality and textual reception —— 253

Section 4: **New to Old**

Introduction to new to old —— 258

Colette Moore
14 Information design and information structure in the Middle English prose *Brut* —— 261

Riki Thompson and Matthew Collins
15 Disruptive practice: Multimodality, innovation and standardisation from the medieval to the digital text —— 281

Martine van Driel
16 "It makes it more real": A comparative analysis of Twitter use in live blogs and quotations in older news media from a reader response perspective —— 306

Emma Moreton and Chris Culy
17 New methods, old data: Using digital technologies to explore nineteenth century letter writing practices —— 329

Elisabetta Adami
18 Transhistoricizing multimodality: Reflections on the how-to —— 359

Ana Deumert
Postscript: You say you want a revolution? Histories and futures of researching the digital, a view from the south —— 363

Index —— 377

List of contributors

Caroline Tagg is Senior Lecturer in Applied Linguistics at The Open University, UK. Her research into language and digital technologies rests on the understanding that digital communication practices are deeply embedded into individuals' wider social, economic and political lives. She is author of *The Discourse of Text Messaging*, 2012, and *Taking Offence on Social Media*, with Philip Seargeant and Amy Aisha Brown, 2017.

Mel Evans is a Lecturer in English Language and Linguistics at the University of Leicester. Her research explores the relationship between language and identity, particularly in early modern English. She draws on sociolinguistic and pragmatic frameworks for interpretation, and experiments with interdisciplinary methods from linguistic, digital humanities and literary fields. Her most recent book, *Royal Voices: Language and power in Tudor England* is published with Cambridge University Press, 2020.

Elisabetta Adami is Associate Professor in Multimodal Communication at the University of Leeds (UK) and is editor of *Visual Communication*. Her research and publications use and develop a social semiotic approach to understand sign-making practices in digital environments, in place and in face-to-face interaction, with a recent focus on inter-, cross- and trans-cultural dynamics of meaning making and re-making.

David Barton is Professor Emeritus in the Department of Linguistics at Lancaster University, England and erstwhile Director of the Lancaster Literacy Research Centre. His most recent books, both co-authored and published by Routledge, are *Language Online*, 2013, *Researching Language and Social Media*, 2014, and *Academics Writing*, 2019.

Claudia Claridge is Professor of English Linguistics at the University of Augsburg, Germany. Her research interests include the history of English, text and discourse linguistics, (historical) pragmatics, intensification, and figurative language.

Matthew Collins is currently a PhD student and Research Assistant at the University of Birmingham, where he explores how linguistic and digital methodologies can inform our understanding of literary and creative texts.

Chris Culy has been a professor of linguistics and computational linguistics in the United States and Germany, where he also taught visualisation of linguistic data. In addition, he has developed linguistic and visualisation software for research projects ranging from ancient Latin to machine translation to a social history of early women professional photographers.

Ana Deumert is Professor of Linguistics at the University of Cape Town. Her research program is located within the broad field of sociolinguistics and has a strong transdisciplinary focus. In addition to publishing widely on a range of topics in sociolinguistics, she is a regular columnist for Diggit magazine.

Susan Fitzmaurice is a historical linguist interested in computational approaches to the investigation of semantic change and the lexicalisation of conceptual structures in English. She is currently Vice President and Head of the Faculty of Arts and Humanities at the University of Sheffield.

Korina Giaxoglou is Lecturer in Applied Linguistics and English Language at the Open University, UK, where she leads the Health Discourse Research Group. Her research on the sociolinguistics of mourning, narrative, and affect has appeared in edited volumes, special issues, and peer-reviewed journals including *Pragmatics, Applied Linguistics Review, Discourse, Context and Social Media*. She is a member of the steering group member for the International Death Online Research Network and Secretary for BAAL Language and New Media Special Interest Group.

Rodney H. Jones is Professor of Sociolinguistics and New Media at the University of Reading. His research interests include algorithms, online surveillance, and the pragmatic dimensions of human-computer interaction.

Dániel Z. Kádár is Chair Professor and Director of the Center for Pragmatic Research at Dalian University of Foreign Languages, China. He is also Research Professor and Head of Research Centre at the Research Institute for Linguistics, Hungarian Academy of Sciences. He is author of 23 books and edited volumes, published with publishing houses of international standing such as Cambridge University Press. He is co-editor of *Contrastive Pragmatics: A Cross-Disciplinary Journal*. His research interests include the pragmatics of ritual, linguistic (im)politeness research, language aggression, contrastive pragmatics and historical pragmatics. He is particularly keen on the research of Chinese language use. His most recent book is *Politeness, Impoliteness and Ritual: Maintaining the moral order in interpersonal interaction* (Cambridge University Press, 2017).

Joanna Kopaczyk is Senior Lecturer in Scots and English at the University of Glasgow. She is a historical linguist with an interest in corpus methods, formulaic language, the history of Scots and historical multilingualism. Her most recent co-edited collections include *Historical Dialectology in the Digital Age* (Edinburgh University Press, 2019) and *Applications of Pattern-Driven Methods in Corpus Linguistics* (John Benjamins, 2018). She has also published on *The Legal Language of Scottish Burghs* (Oxford University Press, 2013) and co-edited *Binomials in the History of English* (Cambridge University Press, 2017) and *Communities of Practice in the History of English* (John Benjamins, 2013).

Aino Liira is a doctoral candidate at the Department of English, University of Turku. Her research interests include medieval and early modern paratextuality, metadiscourse, and material philology, particularly the layout and design of manuscripts and early printed books.

Agnieszka Lyons is Senior Lecturer in applied linguistics at Queen Mary University of London, UK. Her research employs multimodal and mediated discourse analytic as well as ethnographic approaches to explore the discursive construction of embodied identity in polycentric migrant environments. She has published in *Language in Society, Journal of Pragmatics* and *Social Semiotics*, among others.

Colette Moore is Associate Professor of English at the University of Washington. She teaches and writes about the English language and its history, particularly in the fields of historical pragmatics, historical sociolinguistics, historical stylistics, and the history of standardization.

Emma Moreton is a Lecturer in Applied Linguistics in the Department of English at the University of Liverpool. Her current research uses corpus and computational methods of analysis to examine the language of historical correspondence data, with a particular focus on nineteenth century letters of migration.

Samia Ounoughi is a Senior Lecturer of English studies at Université Grenoble Alpes (France). She specialises in discourse analysis in corpora of mountain travel narratives.

Matti Peikola is Professor of English at the Department of English, University of Turku. He specialises in philology, textual scholarship and book studies in the late medieval and early modern periods.

Sirkku Ruokkeinen is a doctoral candidate at the Department of English, University of Turku. Ruokkeinen's research focuses on the linguistics of evaluation, paratextuality, and book history, and she is currently working on a dissertation on the evaluation of the sixteenth-century book.

Hanna Rutkowska is University Professor at the Faculty of English, Adam Mickiewicz University in Poznań (Poland). She has published books such as *Orthographic Systems in Thirteen Editions of the* Kalender of Shepherdes *(1506–1656)*, *Graphemics and Morphosyntax in the* Cely *letters (1472–88)*, and (co-edited with Jacob Thaisen) *Scribes, Printers, and the Accidentals of their Texts*. She is also the author of several articles and chapters on various aspects of historical orthography and historical sociolinguistics as well as on late medieval English morphosyntax.

Alison Sealey is Professor Emerita of Applied Linguistics at Lancaster University, UK. She has published extensively on the role of discourse in representations of the social world, often using corpus-assisted methods. Two current research interests are parliamentary discourse and discursive representations of the non-human.

Philip Seargeant is Senior Lecturer in Applied Linguistics at the Open University. His work focuses on language, politics and social media. His recent books include *The Art of Political Storytelling*, and *The Emoji Revolution*.

Riki Thompson is an Associate Professor of Rhetoric & Writing Studies at the University of Washington Tacoma. Her current research employs critical multimodal discourse studies to examine storytelling, identity construction, and how people find connection and belonging through digitally-mediated spaces.

Martine van Driel is a linguist affiliated with the University of Birmingham. Her research investigates reader response to new media such as online news reporting and podcasting.

Mari-Liisa Varila is a Lecturer at the Department of English, University of Turku. Her research focuses on late medieval and early modern English books and book producers from the perspective of book studies, material philology, and textual scholarship.

Mel Evans and Caroline Tagg
Introducing transhistorical approaches to digital language practices

1 Introduction

In 1964, the Canadian philosopher Marshall McLuhan famously declared that "the medium is the message", arguing that the media through which something is said can carry more meaning than the content itself: in the case of print, to take one of his examples, its actual content (the written word) has been less consequential for society than the principles it ushered in; namely textual uniformity, continuity and linearity. Central to his argument is the understanding that human communication is shaped and altered by the technologies through which it is mediated. Although this argument has been critiqued as oversimplistic, and as technologically deterministic (e.g. Winston 1986: 126–127), McLuhan's work remains a starting point for much social analysis of new media technologies (Jones & Hafner 2012; Danesi 2018). In this book, we invert the central premise of the widely cited phrase by adopting what we call a *transhistorical* approach to data analysis. The approach explores the extent to which elements of human communication endure across time despite the different technologies that shape how a message is conveyed, and unpicks the complex and multiple relationships between message and medium.

Three texts, written at distinct points in the development of communication technologies in the western world, can be used to illustrate changes and continuities over time.

Text 1
Thankyou for ditchin me i had been invited out but said no coz u were cumin and u said we would do something on the sat now i have nothing to do all weekend i am a billy no mates i really hate being single

Text 2
A P.C. from you this mg. is it tomorrow or next Sat. the opening. if tomorrow it is decidedly off with me. & I am afraid it would be the same next week. I should very much like to come to you for Easter but I am afraid unless your are very busy (as we were) I shan't manage it. I am just in the middle of a big wash & I have already filled up every line & hedge. M. is not so well again today.

Mel Evans, University of Leicester, Leicester, e-mail: mel.evans@leicester.ac.uk
Caroline Tagg, The Open University, Milton Keynes, e-mail: caroline.tagg@open.ac.uk

https://doi.org/10.1515/9783110670837-001

> Text 3
> Deare Daught^r Margaret Knight, I rec~ yor dolefull l~r, but not till after the Carrier was gone, & so, by that meanes I could not send you an answere the next returne, & so I hope you will not take unkindly, that I did not answere you as you desired. For I could not answere that which I never knew of, & I wish that I might never have heard so much of him, as you writ to me of, for the ill newes of my sons death doth very much trouble & distemper me

All three texts were written and sent in England. Text 1 is a text message, sent by an 18-year-old woman to her sister around 2005 (Tagg 2012: 2); Text 2 is a postcard sent in 1905 to Mrs Rowarth of 'The Lamb Inn', Chinley, Derbyshire (Gillen & Hall 2009: 6); and Text 3 is an extract from a letter sent by William Knight in November 1649 (MS1095/115 Birmingham Library Archives).

Looking at these snippets of informal written communication side-by-side enables us to explore the similarities and differences in writing over time. On the one hand, the extracts point to the different effects of the changing technologies on literacy practices. For example, while the letter opens with the conventional greeting "Deare Daught^r Margaret Knight", the postcard begins more abruptly with "A P.C. from you this mg" ('a postcard from you this morning') and the text message – like many others of this mode (Spilioti 2011) – has no greeting and is instead framed as a contribution to an ongoing conversation (cf. Ito & Okabe 2005: 264). These differences are indicative of the respective writing conventions and practices of each text and its medium, all of which were shaped in part by the speed at which the correspondence could take place (this is not always the speed we might expect: Gillen and Hall (2009) note that Edwardians could expect up to ten postal deliveries a day). Yet the comparison also highlights plausible continuities in practice across the three periods, including the use of abbreviations – e.g. <coz>, <mg> and <rec> ('received') – and the fact that, to differing degrees, each writer might be seen to be writing-as-speaking, with the text message and the seventeenth-century letter stringing sentences together in a way that evokes spoken language (Chafe 1982) – and, consequentially, thinking (spontaneously) as they write. More fundamentally, each writer is using (one of) the media available to them at the time in order to reach out and convey a message to someone close to them and, in these particular cases, to express and share their dissatisfaction or grief. Whilst the medium changes and so does the social context, the expression of emotion through the written word echoes through the centuries.

This book builds on these initial observations by exploring the possibilities for a *transhistorical* perspective on English language practices as mediated through different technologies; an approach to the study of digital media that situates recent technological and social developments within the longer history of technologically mediated change. Key to our transhistorical approach is the argument that certain elements of human communication – including both communicative practices and the ideologies or values that sustain them – can be seen to endure across time and are remediated through new technologies; the argument is neatly captured in Thompson and Collins' (this volume) assertion that "writing and reading practices transcend time". A central aim of our transhistorical approach (and this book) is to *historicise* contemporary digital language practices in order to better understand what Lyons and Ounoughi (this volume) call "human communication across time and place".

Such a venture is key for studies of English language practices, both past and present. For studies of English prior to the late nineteenth century, all linguistic evidence is mediated by writing technologies, from papyrus and parchment to the postcard. Researchers are increasingly attending to the mediated nature of their material, engaging with the verbal and visual practices of historical English usage, rather than treating it as a proxy for speech (e.g. Peikola et al. 2017). This relates to the use of visual features alongside linguistic forms, such as marking-out sections of reported speech (e.g. Moore 2011) or in signalling the authority of a text through intertextual continuity, such as the illustrated initials used in printed royal proclamations and English Bible publications (Evans 2020; Stallybrass 2011). In understanding contemporary uses of English, and its continued online dominance and diversification, we need to consider digitally mediated language change. Over the last two decades, language and new media research has explored how digital technologies afford a unique set of multimodal resources and encourage highly innovative linguistic strategies for the performance of mediatised identities and the maintenance of online social networks, alongside studies of how the internet facilitates the global circulation, appropriation and entextualisation of cultural resources. Research in this field is predicated to some extent on the endeavour to identify changes in practice between pre-digital and digital contexts, often by applying analytical frameworks developed for the understanding of pre-digital texts onto digital contexts. At the same time, digital technologies have provided new tools for data analysis and apparently new online phenomena have prompted discussion around the need for similarly original analytical frameworks and theories. However, what is often missing from such discussions is an interrogation of earlier practices and phenomena against which claims about digital linguistic novelty can be made.

The collective purpose of the chapters in this edited volume is to interrogate and refine these assumptions regarding the novelty of digitally mediated English language practices by bringing together linguistic experts from disciplines ranging from historical pragmatics to present-day sociolinguistics and rhetoric to explore the possibilities for developing a transhistorical approach to the study of written language and "new" media. The book as a whole is exploratory and seeks not to establish a fixed framework, but rather to highlight the many ways in which an awareness of what came before – and what is to come after – can inform English language scholarship.

2 Existing work: Familiar, reconfigured, remediated and new

Our transhistorical approach draws on and extends a body of work seeking to consider the use of communication technologies as part of wider histories of technologically mediated change. Importantly, researchers have sought to historicise the understanding of contemporary "new media" by reconceptualising what we would now see as "old media" as once having been experienced as new, and exploring their situated uses as new media within sociohistorical contexts and wider media ecologies (for example, Gitelman 2006; Marvin 1988; and edited collections by Gershon & Bell 2013 and Gitelman & Pingree 2003). Such treatments show how "new" media both disrupt or reconfigure and yet are subsumed into existing media ecologies, and encourage us to identify similarities in how evolving media are experienced and used across time. Similarly, histories of particular technologies, genres and communicative phenomena serve to place sociocultural specificities in a broader timeline and identify continuities in practice across periods. These histories vary in scope. Baron (2000) takes a broad-brush approach to trace the development of writing over time, from the emergence of the alphabet to email in the late twentieth-century, in order to argue for the role of digital media in the increasing informality of written English. Similarly, Fischer (1994) traces the social history of the telephone before 1940, showing how communication technologies are neither a cause nor symptom of wider social change; instead, technological and social factors intertwine in complex and integrated ways (see Williams' 1989 [1974] discussion of television; and Lipset's 2013 exploration of mobile phone use in Papua New Guinea). Discussions of the history of English often consider particular aspects of the medium and the message, such as Claridge (2012) on genre, or Cameron (2012) on the commodification of English in a global (and digital) context. Shortis (2007, 2016) shows that, although respelling in early twenty-first century text messaging reflects and extends existing orthographic patterns across a range of texts from nineteenth-century trade names to song lyrics, the mass popularity of text messaging and its salience in the popular imagination have instigated a shift in perceptions regarding the communicative possibilities of spelling. These and other accounts highlight the value of historical depth in explaining and contextualising apparently "new" phenomena, and provide the historical backdrop against which a systematic approach to the study of mediated English language practices can be developed.

We draw particularly on an approach developed to explain the development of the internet, and use it to explore the wider history of social and linguistic change. The history of the internet has long been conceptualised as a move from publishing and user consumption towards user-generated content and user participation, a shift captured in the terms Web 1.0 and Web 2.0 (DiNucci 1999; O'Reilly 2012) – compare, for example, a store's online shopping service, which makes products available to consumers, with either Amazon (shaped by user reviews) or eBay (formed through user transactions). The terms should be seen as representing sets of gravitational principles (O'Reilly 2012: 33) rather than a hard-and-fast distinction, although Berners-Lee (2006) has criticised the distinction, arguing that the web had always been conceived as a place for collaboration. Nonetheless, the perceived shift has proved useful in contextualising changing usage patterns and language practices and linking them to technological developments (e.g. Herring 2013, 2019). Drawing on Crowston and Williams (2000), Herring (2013) adopts a three-part categorisation of Web 2.0 discourse phenomena as features *familiar* from older Web 1.0 platforms; features *reconfigured* by Web 2.0 environments; and new *emergent* phenomena. Perhaps Herring's most relevant insight, for the purposes of this book, is that most (if not all) online practices are familiar or reconfigured from earlier practices, even if they appear at first to be new. The act of retweeting on the microblogging site Twitter, to take one of Herring's examples, can be seen as a reconfiguration of "quoting" in older asynchronous forms of computer-mediated communication such as Usenet (Severinson Eklundh 2010). Herring (2013: 15) points to "the need to abstract common structures, functions and/or social dynamics across different media affordances in order to identify what they are reconfigured from and the reasons for the reconfigurations". This book responds to this challenge, whilst broadening the perspective to the wider history of technologically mediated communicative change. Gardner and Allsop (2016) observe a broad distinction between texts that are truly "born digital" and those (the majority) that were once offline but have now "achieve[d] digitality" and online status (often with some reconfiguration; see e.g. Johnson 2011 on the evolution of the personal diary from the sixteenth century to the blog).

A key concept in understanding why familiar practices persist while others are reconfigured is Bolter and Grusin's (2000) theory of *remediation*. Remediation describes the uptake of new technologies in terms of how texts repurpose and translate (that is, *remediate*) existing technologies (Bolter & Grusin 2000). As Thompson and Collins (this volume) point out, this is often evident when new technologies take up terminology – such as *scroll* or *page* – associated with their predecessors. Technological change from this perspective is not transformational but often incremental, and deeply embedded in (changing) historical and cultural contexts. One example is the online news site which, as Herring (2013) points out, has moved from simply reproducing print content towards incorporating online affordances in the form of user comments, multimedia and hyperlinks (Eriksen & Ihlström 2000). Other researchers have used remediation to explain how social and communicative practices shift over time in response to changes in technologies. In applying remediation to their understanding of how Trinidadians use internet technologies, Madianou and Miller (2012: 177) show how Trinidadians initially saw email as "computer-based letters" and only later began to use email for shorter, more spontaneous and less carefully crafted messages. In Fisher's (2013) study of radio as new media in aboriginal Australia, he noted how programme directors saw digital audio media technologies as a potential threat to the intimate relationships constructed on air, but came to see their potential for extending this kinship to new audiences. There are examples from earlier historical periods, too. Early English printers tried to replicate manuscript practices e.g. typeface appearance, or the placement of the printer's impression (equivalent to a scribe's signature) at the end of the document, before developing a set of more distinct strategies that capitalised on the particular affordances of print, transforming the mechanisms of marketisation (see Eisenstein 2005; Gaskell 1972). In early telephone communications, subscribers were identified by name until the lines were depersonalised and the more flexible numerical system was introduced (Tanaka 2001).

Remediation thus enables us to reconceptualise communication technologies as part of a wider integrated communicative environment that shifts in response to technological developments and changes in user practices (see Gershon & Bell 2013). Madianou and Miller's (2012) theory of *polymedia* is useful here. According to polymedia, new technologies inhabit – or carve out – niches in people's communicative repertoires depending on how users perceive their affordances (Madianou 2015: 2). People's prior experiences of technologies are central to how a current technology is perceived and exploited, and each technology is thus defined in part by its perceived relationship to other technologies, past and present. In the present-day, for example, text messaging or instant messaging may be seen in some contexts as more intimate and private than Facebook (Jones, Schiefflin & Smith 2011) and may be considered more appropriate for many communicative functions – including ending a relationship – than handwritten letters, which are described by one individual in Gershon's (2010: 392) study of break-ups as cold and distancing. In the pre-digital era, with its different configuration of technological options, a letter physically written in the hand of the named author was deemed more intimate than one produced (handwritten or, later, typed) by a professional scribe, even if that named author had little involvement in composing the words to be used in the text (Daybell 2012: 23; for other examples, see Andersen 2013; Hinkson 2013).

As these examples show, the choice of technology can itself become communicatively meaningful; in Madianou's (2014: 672) words, "users are held responsible for their choices" by their interlocutors. Choice of technology therefore becomes ideological, in the sense that the positioning of that technology within the communicative repertoire of users is bound up with their internalisation of media ideologies. Technologies accrue their own social meanings and significance through use, which in turn shape how individuals go on to use them; one might consider the indirect (negative) indexicalities of the *comic sans* font (Jones 2012; Tushnet 2012), which have likely arisen through social attitudes towards its iconic representation of a "simple" and "child-like" hand, and which determines the contexts in which people are likely to use it. From this perspective, any contemporary linguistic practice should be appreciated as one that occurs at a moment in time within the unfolding technological and social history of the wider mediascape.

Understood through the lens of remediation and polymedia, we might return to Herring's (2013) three-way model (familiar, reconfigured and emergent) and question whether any new media practice can be defined as *emergent*: that is, new and without precedent – although they may be experienced as such (Gershon & Bell 2003). Herring (2013: 23) puts forward suggestions of contemporary practices that have not "previously existed as *common* communicative practices online or offline" [our emphasis] – including the collaborative text production which takes place on wikis and the carrying out of exchanges solely through visual resources such as YouTube videos (Pihlaja 2011) and we might add the human-algorithm interactions explored by Rodney Jones (this volume) – but with the caveat that other researchers working in related disciplines may well be able to identify antecedent practices. In line with this, the transhistorical approaches adopted throughout this book look for the familiar and assume continuities as much as they seek to isolate, describe and explain innovation. This approach also highlights methodological implications, which chapters in this volume also explore, including the need for descriptive analysis of truly new practices (a point made by Herring 2013) and questions over whether existing methods and theories can be applied to new data or must themselves be reconfigured or replaced (see Deumert 2014; Hogan & Quan-Haase 2010; and for studies which apply existing frameworks to new media see e.g. Jones' 2016 study of spelling on Twitter using methods developed for the analysis of Vulgar Latin graffiti).

3 The contributions

The chapters in this volume build on the above research by focusing explicitly on the question of how to establish and develop a transhistorical approach to the study of mediated English language use, and the many forms such an enterprise might take. Our interest is in written (mediated) English, and the continuities in text-based communication, which distinguishes our work from much of contemporary pragmatics and sociolinguistics, to the extent that they continue to prioritise spoken language (Lillis 2013). Our focus in this volume on a *trans*historical rather than a historical perspective reflects our attempt not only to explore language practices as lived experiences grounded in historical contexts but also to identify and explain those elements of human behaviour that transcend historical boundaries, and therefore to look beyond particular developments in communication technologies to understand the enduring motivations, stances, relationships and identity performances that drive human communication. A transhistorical approach seeks to explore the potential for communicative continuities within and among the developments and diversification of English language practices, with the chapters engaging with historical periods from medieval manuscripts to twenty-first century social media platforms, looking both narrowly (e.g. a period of a year or two) and expansively (e.g. over centuries), continuously (such as a century of evolving practice) and in contrastive temporal snapshots (such as sixteenth-century and present-day) to identify consistencies, reconfigurations, and the implications for ideologies and identities constructed through language-in-use. Taken together, the work suggests that whilst the medium may be the message, as posited by McLuhan, the message is always grounded in human experience and practice, informed by antecedents in the communicative histories of both the individual and the community. Message and medium, in this view, is thus a circular, bi-directional phenomenon with human interaction at its heart.

The volume is divided into four sections which engage with the transhistorical approach in distinct but related ways. Each section is introduced by the editors and concluded with a personal reflective piece by a leading scholar, in which they consider how the themes and approaches raised relate to and inform their own work.

- The first section, **Rethinking perspectives**, lays out new approaches to the pragmatic study of digitally mediated language which enable scholars to think transhistorically and to identify evidence not only of change but also of continuity in practice.
- The second section, **Historicising discourses**, focuses on the extent to which individual practices and social actions endure over time as they are remediated through new communication technologies. The chapters draw variously on ideas of self-fashioning, citizen sociolinguistics and socio-cultural theory to explore discourses ranging from mourning to political leadership.
- The third section, **Media trajectories**, develops this focus by exploring how visual and verbal resources are repeated across iterations of the "same" text in varying media environments. Drawing variously on visual pragmatics and paratext theory, they show how handwritten manuscripts including legal texts and conduct books are reproduced in subsequent editions and in print.
- The last section, **New to old**, considers the insights that can be obtained through contrastive analysis of "old" and "new" texts – such as traditional news texts and online live blogs – as well as through the application of "new" methodological frameworks, including corpus analysis, digital humanities, information structure and information design, to "old" texts such as Middle English prose and nineteenth-century migrant letters.

Evident across these sections are three approaches which characterise transhistorical investigations: contrastive or comparative work, which in some cases involves co-authorship by scholars working on different periods; a diachronic approach in tracing the development of an English language practice or genre; and the application of new concepts to old data and vice versa.

Two themes emerge from this volume: firstly, that analysis of historical textual practices in many cases reveals longer-term patterns in the indexical functions of seemingly innovative digital resources and – significantly – in the ideologies that underpin them, highlighting precedents to the apparent complexity of current online practices; and, secondly, that methods are not necessarily contingent on their datasets: historical analytic frameworks can be applied to digital data and newer approaches used to understand historical data. These insights present exciting opportunities for English language researchers, both historical and modern, which are only appreciable when data is approached from a transhistorical perspective.

References

Andersen, Barbara. 2013. Tricks, lies, and mobile phones: "phone friend" stories in Papua New Guinea. *Culture, Theory and Critique* 54 (3). 318–334.

Baron, Naomi. 2000. *From alphabet to email: How written language evolved and where it's heading*. Abingdon: Routledge.

Berners-Lee, Tim. 2006. DeveloperWorks Interviews: Tim Berners-Lee. https://www.ibm.com/developerworks/podcast/dwi/cm-int082206txt.html (accessed 29 May 2019).

Bolter, Jay D. & Richard Grusin. 2000. *Remediation: Understanding new media*. Cambridge, MA: MIT Press.

Cameron, Deborah. 2012. The commodification of language: English as a global commodity. In Terttu Nevalainen & Elizabeth Closs Traugott (eds.), *The Oxford handbook of the history of English*, 352–262. Oxford: Oxford University Press.

Chafe, Wallace L. 1982. Integration and involvement in speaking, writing, and oral literature. In Deborah Tannen (ed.), *Spoken and written language: Exploring orality and literacy*, 35–53. Norwood: Ablex.

Claridge, Claudia. 2012. From manuscript to printing: Transformations of genres in the history of English. In Terttu Nevalainen & Elizabeth Closs Traugott (eds.), *The Oxford handbook of the history of English*, 304–13. Oxford: Oxford University Press.

Crowston, Kevin & Michelle Williams. 2000. Reproduced and emergent genres of communication on the world-wide web. *The Information Society* 16 (3). 201–216.

Danesi, Marcel. 2018. *Understanding media semiotics*, 2nd edn. London: Bloomsbury.

Daybell, James. 2012. *The material letter in Early Modern England*. Basingstoke: Palgrave Macmillan.

Deumert, Ana. 2014. *Sociolinguistics of mobile communication*. Edinburgh: Edinburgh University Press.

DiNucci, Darcy. 1999. Fragmented future. *Print* 53 (4). 32.

Eisenstein, Elizabeth L. 2005. *The printing revolution in Early Modern Europe*, 2nd edn. Cambridge, UK: Cambridge University Press.

Eriksen, Lars B. & Carina Ihlström. 2000. Evolution of the web news genre: The slow move beyond the print metaphor. Proceedings of the Thirty-Third Hawaii International Conference on System Sciences. Los Alamitos, CA: IEEE.

Evans, Mel. 2020. *Royal voices: Language and power in Tudor England*. Cambridge, UK: Cambridge University Press.

Fischer, Claude S. 1994. *America calling: A social history of the telephone to 1940*. Oakland: University of California Press.

Fisher, Daniel. 2013. Intimacy and self-abstraction: Radio as new media in Aboriginal Australia. *Culture, Theory and Critique* 54 (3). 372–393.

Gardner, Sheena & Siân Alsop. 2016. *Systemic functional linguistics in the digital age*. London: Equinox.

Gaskell, Philip. 1972. *A new introduction to bibliography*. New York: Oxford University Press.

Gershon, Ilana. 2010. Breaking up is hard to do: Media switching and media ideologies. *Journal of Linguistic Anthropology* 20. 389–405.

Gershon, Ilana & Allan Bell. 2013. Introduction: The newness of new media. *Culture, Theory and Critique* 54 (3). 259–264.

Gillen, Julia. 2014. *Digital literacies*. Abingdon: Routledge.

Gillen, Julia & Nigel Hall. 2009. The Edwardian postcard: A revolutionary moment in rapid multimodal communications. Paper presented at the British Education Research Association Annual Conference, Manchester, 2–5 September.

Gitelman, Lisa. 2006. *Always already new: Media, history, and the data of culture*. Cambridge, MA: MIT Press.

Gitelman, Lisa & Geoffrey B. Pingree. 2003. *New Media, 1740–1915*. Cambridge, MA: MIT Press.

Herring, Susan C. 2013. Discourse in web 2.0: Familiar, reconfigured, and emergent. In Deborah Tannen & Anna M. Trester (eds.), *Georgetown University Round Table on Languages and Linguistics 2011: Discourse 2.0: Language and new media*. Washington D.C.: Georgetown University Press.

Herring, Susan C. 2019. The coevolution of computer-mediated communication and computer-mediated discourse analysis. In Patricia Bou-Franch & Pilar Garcés-Conejos Blitvich (eds.), *Analyzing digital discourse*, 25–67. Basingstoke: Palgrave Macmillan.

Hinkson, Melinda. 2013. Back to the future: Warlpiri encounters with drawings, country and others in the digital age. *Culture, Theory and Critique* 54 (3). 301–317.

Hogan, Bernie & Anabel Quan-Haase. 2010. Persistence and change in social media. *Bulletin of Science, Technology & Society* 30 (5). 309–315.

Ito, Mizuko & Daisuke Okabe. 2005. Technosocial situations: Emergent structurings of mobile email use. In Mizuko Ito, Daisuke Okabe & Misa Matsuda (eds.), *Personal, portable, intimate: Mobile phones in Japanese life*, 257–276. Cambridge, MA: MIT Press.

Johnson, Alexandra. 2011. *A brief history of diaries: From Pepys to blogs*. London: Hesperus Press.

Jones, Graham M., Bambi B. Schiefflin & Rachel E. Smith. 2011. When friends who talk together stalk together: Online gossip as metacommunication. In Crispin Thurlow & Kristine Mroczek (eds.), *Digital discourse: Language in the new media*, 26–47. Oxford: Oxford University Press.

Jones, John. 2015. Information graphics and intuition: Heuristics as a techne for visualization. *Journal of Business and Technical Communication* 29 (3). 284–313.

Jones, Rodney & Christoph A. Hafner. 2012. *Understanding digital literacies: A practical introduction*. Abingdon: Routledge.

Jones, Taylor. 2016. Tweets as graffiti: What the reconstruction of Vulgar Latin can tell us about Black Twitter. In Lauren Squires (ed.), *English in computer-mediated communication: Variation, representation and change*, 43–68. Berlin: De Gruyter Mouton.

Lillis, Theresa. 2013. *Sociolinguistics of writing*. Edinburgh: Edinburgh University Press.

Lipset, David. 2013. Mobail: Moral ambivalence and the domestication of mobile telephones in peri-urban Papua New Guinea. *Culture, Theory and Critique* 54 (3). 335–354.

Madianou, Mirca. 2014. Smartphones as polymedia. *Journal of Computer-Mediated Communication* 19. 667–680.

Madianou, Mirca. 2015. Polymedia and ethnography. *Social Media + Society*. 1–3.

Madianou, Mirca & Daniel Miller. 2012. Polymedia: Towards a new theory of digital media in interpersonal communication. *International Journal of Cultural Studies* 16 (2). 169–187.

Marvin, Carolyn. 1988. *When old technologies were new: Thinking about electric communication in the late nineteenth century*. Oxford: Oxford University Press.

McLuhan, Marshall. 1964. *Understanding media: The extensions of man*. New York: Mentor.

Moore, Colette. 2011. *Quoting Speech in Early English*. Cambridge: Cambridge University Press.

O'Reilly, Tim. 2005. What is Web 2.0? Design patterns and business models for the next generation of software. O'Reilly Network [website], September 30. http://oreilly.com/web2/archive/what-is-web-20.html.

O'Reilly, Tim. 2012. What is Web 2.0? Design patterns and business models for the next generation of software. In Michael Mandiberg (ed.), *The social media reader*, 32–52. New York: New York University Press.

Peikola, Matti, Aleksi Mäkilähde, Hanna Salmi, Mari-Liisa Varila & Janne Skaffari (eds.). 2017. *Verbal and visual communication in Early English texts*. Turnhout: Brepols.

Pihlaja, Stephen. 2011. Cops, Popes, and garbage collectors: Metaphor and antagonism in an atheist/Christian YouTube video thread. *Language@Internet* 8, article 1.

Severinson Eklundh, Kerstin. 2010. To quote or not to quote: Setting the context for computer-mediated dialogues. *Language@Internet* 7, article 5.

Shortis, Tim. 2007. Revoicing Txt: spelling, vernacular orthography and "unregimented writing". In Santiago Posteguillo, María J. Esteve & M. Lluïsa Gea (eds.), *The texture of internet: Netlinguistics*, 2–21. Cambridge, UK: Cambridge Scholar Press.

Shortis, Tim. 2016. Texting and other messaging: Written system in digitally mediated vernaculars. In Vivian Cook & Des Ryan (eds.), *The Routledge handbook of the English writing system*, 487–511. Abingdon: Routledge.

Spilioti, Tereza. 2011. Beyond genre: Closings and relational work in text messaging. In Crispin Thurlow & Kristine Mroczek (eds.), *Digital discourse: Language in the new media*, 67–85. Oxford: Oxford University Press.

Stallybrass, Peter. 2011. Visible and invisible letters: Text versus image in Renaissance England and Europe. In Marija Dalbello & Peter Shaw (eds.), *Visible writings: Cultures, forms, reading*, 77–98. Piscataway: Rutgers University Press.

Tagg, Caroline. 2012. *The Discourse of Text Messaging*. London: Continuum.

Tanaka, Keiko. 2001. Early telephone use in Seattle, 1880s–1920s. *The Pacific Northwest Quarterly* 92 (4). 190–202.

Tushnet, Rebecca. 2012. Worth a thousand words: The images of copyright. *Harvard Law Review*. 125 (3). 683–759.

Williams, Raymond. [1974] 1989. *Television: Technology and cultural form*, 2nd edn. Abingdon: Routledge.

Winston, Brian. 1986. *Misunderstanding media*. Cambridge, MA: Harvard University Press.

Section 1: **Rethinking Perspectives**

Introduction to rethinking perspectives

A key debate in the field of digital language research concerns the extent to which scholarly understanding of "new" media practices requires similarly "new" theories of language, communication and society. The argument for developing novel theoretical approaches presupposes that digitally mediated interactions are characterised – perhaps even defined – by their novelty and constitute a break from past practices. In seeking to historicise new media practices – to situate them as the latest developments in a complex and ongoing history of technologically mediated social change – we call instead for the rethinking of existing theoretical and methodological frameworks in the light of contemporary practices, based on the assumption that what is already known about social interaction remains of relevance in understanding how and why humans take up and use new technologies (Brooks 2007: 10). This approach is widely adopted elsewhere in linguistics and has resulted in the emergence of hybrid "old-new" methodologies such as MOOD, the microanalysis of online data, a digital version of conversation analysis (Giles et al. 2015; Giles, Stommel & Paulus 2017). The approach also enables frameworks developed for understanding early internet interactions to be re-evaluated in the light of newer media practices (Herring 2019). The particular concern of the current volume is the extent to which this approach truly enables scholars to think transhistorically – to look beyond the technology at enduring features of human communication – and to identify evidence not only of change but also of continuity in practice.

This first section lays down the groundwork for subsequent chapters by exploring the extent to which existing theories of communication are fit for a dual purpose – that of analysing new media practices and doing so from a transhistorical perspective. In his opening chapter on the pragmatic web, Rodney Jones considers the continuing relevance and analytical utility of pragmatic principles for understanding human-algorithm interaction in technologically mediated contexts. Although he calls for a new way of approaching pragmatics ("algorithmic pragmatics"), his main argument is that contemporary online communication – and, specifically, "how algorithms 'do things' with people" – can only be fully understood from a pragmatic perspective, and with reference to established pragmatic concepts including implicature, context and the speech act. His chapter contributes to a transhistorical approach by interrogating the extent to which key pragmatic principles guiding human communication remain relevant in new mediated contexts. In chapter two, Dániel Z. Kádár also starts from existing pragmatic frameworks, both synchronic and diachronic, and draws out the various contributions that each can be said to have made to a "historicisation" agenda (which we would see as a crucial element of a "transhistorical" approach), highlighting for example the reinterpretation of historical constructs such as "courtesie" through a modern lens and comparisons between contemporary pragmatic behaviour such as politeness and its historical antecedents. In illustrating what he identifies as a historically grounded interpersonal interactional approach, Kádár's analysis of online shaming practices draws on a ritual interactional framework to explore similarities in practice between medieval ritual shaming and its twenty-first century equivalent. The final chapter by Caroline Tagg and Mel Evans proposes a transhistorical pragmatic approach that aligns with, and complements, existing pragmatic frameworks. Our framework focuses on enabling comparative pragmatic analysis of communicative practices in different historical periods by drawing on the uniformitarian principle commonly associated with sociolinguistic research – the assumption that linguistic data from the past is equivalent to that of contemporary data – whilst foregrounding the importance of contextual understanding. Our transhistorical analysis of spelling in Tudor correspondence and twenty-first century SMS feeds into and refines existing pragmatic accounts of new media spelling practices.

The theoretical focus of this section highlights the important role of evidence in transhistorical research, and the difficulties that can arise in sourcing comparative old data: while study of new media spelling can draw on participant interview, analysis of the motivations behind sixteenth-century orthographic practices must rely on metacommentary in the texts themselves, and on published writing manuals. Kádár's study of medieval shaming rests necessarily on later commentaries around the practice, rather than actual interactional data or contemporary accounts (such as those provided elsewhere by the Old Bailey records, for example). Jones' algorithmic pragmatics raises wider questions about methods, and how current analytical approaches to digital communication can be adapted to collect data on human-algorithm interaction and what form that data might take. Despite the limitations of evidence, the three theoretical chapters in this section go some way to showing how a sensitivity to continuities in practice and changing technological and social contexts can strengthen existing pragmatic frameworks and enable analysts to build on existing insights. These points are identified by Susan Fitzmaurice in her reflective conclusion, who cautions against presentism when dealing with historical data, and argues for the importance of refining methodologies to explore the language and societies of both past and present on their own, inter-connected but distinct terms.

References

Brooks, JoAnn. 2007. Understanding virtuality: Contributions from Goffman's frame analysis. School of Information Studies: Faculty Scholarship, 87. Syracuse University. https://surface.syr.edu/istpub/87/ (accessed 26 April 2019).

Herring, Susan C. 2019. The coevolution of computer-mediated communication and discourse analysis. In Patricia Bou-Franch & Pilar Garcés-Conejos Blitvich (eds.), *Analyzing digital discourse: New insights and future directions*, 25–67. Basingstoke: Palgrave Macmillan.

Giles, David, Wyke Stommel, Trena Paulus, Jessica Lester & Darren Reed. 2015. Microanalysis of online data: The methodological development of "digital CA". *Discourse, Context and Media* 7. 45–51.

Giles, David, Wyke Stommel & Trena M. Paulus. 2017. Introduction: The microanalysis of online data: the next stage. *Journal of Pragmatics* 115. 37–41.

Rodney H. Jones
1 The rise of the Pragmatic Web: Implications for rethinking meaning and interaction

1.1 "This is your digital life"

At the time I was writing this chapter, social media was going through a bit of a hard time. It had just been revealed that a firm called Cambridge Analytica had harvested the data of millions of Facebook users and their friends by convincing them to take a "personality test" called "This is your digital life". The quiz was like so many of those that circulate through social media promising users to reveal to them what character they would be in Shakespeare or how they would die in *Game of Thrones* in exchange for granting access to their data. In the end, Facebook had to admit that the data of over 87 million users was used by Cambridge Analytica to support the political campaigns of right-wing American candidates, including Donald Trump, as well as to influence the British Brexit vote. The scandal ignited debates not just about online privacy and ethics, but about the fundamental business model of social media.

In most of these debates, however, the key focus was "information" in a very conventional sense – what the media referred to as a "data breach". And most people assumed that "the data" that had been "breached" consisted chiefly of the content of their profiles – information such as where they lived, the university they had attended, their five favourite movies, and who their friends were. In truth, however, this "explicit" information was the least useful information for Cambridge Analytica. What they were really after was the *implicit* information, the record of seemingly trivial actions people took when interacting with their friends – what they were really after was the "likes". By combining a person's history of "likes" (or what were subsequently reframed as "reactions") with their profile information and the kinds of people they interact with, Cambridge Analytica was able to infer a great deal about people without having to delve into things like personal messages, status updates, photos, or all of the other information Facebook holds (Cadwalladr & Graham-Harrison 2018; Grassegger & Krogerus 2017).

Rodney H. Jones, Department of English Language and Applied Linguistics, University of Reading, Whiteknights Campus, Reading, UK, email: r.h.jones@reading.ac.uk

https://doi.org/10.1515/9783110670837-003

Obviously, the issue here was not just "information", but also the kinds of meanings that could be *inferred* from the information collected. For this, Cambridge Analytica used a sophisticated algorithm which it developed based on the research of Michal Kosinski and his colleagues (Kosinski, Stillwell & Graepel 2013), who had come up with a model that was able to predict users' personality traits based on the posts they had "liked" on Facebook. They found that on the basis of only 68 "likes" it was possible to predict, with a high degree of accuracy, a user's skin colour, political affiliation, sexuality, religion, alcohol, cigarette and drug use, and even whether their parents were divorced. The predictive power of this algorithm was then combined with the communicative power of thousands of "bots", which were able to react instantly to trending topics and produce targeted posts for particular "microcategories" of people.

There are at least four things about this incident that are of interest to scholars of English language and discourse analysts. The first is the fact that the most valuable source of information for Cambridge Analytica came not so much from things that people said about themselves or others, but from things that they *did*, specifically the "speech act" of clicking the "like" button underneath a post in their Newsfeed. The second is that the important "meaning" of these "likes" was not the fact that someone liked something, but rather "deeper meanings" that could be inferred from these acts of liking. Of course, many of us have the experience of trying to infer what people mean when they "like" certain things on social media (see Maíz-Arévalo 2017). The difference here was that the inferences that were drawn by Cambridge Analytica's powerful algorithm were not formed based on individual reactions, but on the *trail* of reactions users created over time, correlated with the reactions of thousands of other users. Finally, it is notable that the main thing these inferences were used to do was to generate "membership categories" (Antaki & Widdincombe 1998; Sacks 1992), similar to the kinds of membership categories people use to make sense of others, predict their behaviour and tailor their communication to them. But again, these membership categories were different from the recognizable "social" categories that people use to negotiate their identities and make judgements about others. They were sophisticated aggregates of "measureable types" (Cheney-Lippold 2017), "microcategories" (like "straight male smoking vegetarian heavy metal fan who had grown up in a single parent family and made less than $50K a year"), identities that combined hundreds of data points to predict what sort of messages users would respond to.

From the point of view of linguistics, then, the "meaning" of the information harvested by Cambridge Analytica was not so much a matter of the meanings of the words people wrote on their profiles or in their status updates, but of the meanings that could be *inferred* based on people's actions, the informational contexts in which those actions were produced, and the kinds of identities that were associated with them. In other words, "meaning" here was not so much a matter of *semantics* as a matter of *pragmatics*. But what Cambridge Analytica's algorithm was engaged in was no ordinary brand of pragmatics. It was, we might say, "pragmatics on steroids".

This chapter is about the relationship between meaning and action in digitally mediated communication in the first decades of the early twenty-first century, and how that relationship is increasingly governed by non-human participants in our interactions. It argues that understanding how people interact with technologies (and how technologies interact with people) requires that we look beyond notions of "data" and "information" to the pragmatic dimensions of digitally mediated communication. I am less interested in what Yus (2011) calls "cyberpragmatics", the term he uses to refer to the ways "different applications for Internet communication (chatrooms, Messenger, e-mail, Web pages, etc.) affect the quality and quantity of contextual information accessed by users" and the "inferential strategies that people engage in while processing information exchanged with other people using digital technology", and more interested in how meanings are made and inferred in the kinds of complex sociotechnical assemblages such as the one described above. These are environments in which communication is not just a matter of people talking to people "through" applications, but also of people talking to applications, and applications talking to one another, environments that don't just involve multiple media, with different affordances for inferring context, or different platforms with different norms for how information is shared and interpreted, but environments which link together different platforms and media as information is shared and processed by algorithms which shape the kinds of information human actors are exposed to and the kinds of interactions they can have in real time. The question I wish to address then is to what extent the repertoire of concepts and tools developed in "analogue pragmatics" (the pragmatics of unmediated human-to-human communication) since the mid-twentieth century, or even the "cyberpragmatics" (the pragmatics of "computer-mediated communication") of the twenty-first, are adequate for understanding the pragmatics of human-algorithm communication, what I have elsewhere referred to as "algorithmic pragmatics" (Jones 2016a).

1.2 Historicizing the "pragmatic web"

The history of the internet is in many ways a history of human engagement with different ways of understanding meaning – how meaning is created and what can be done with it. The earliest way of seeing the internet was in terms of syntax – a model in which information derives meaning from its relationship to other information. The "syntactic web" is basically a web of interrelated static information linked together with hyperlinks. The way information is connected to other information and the "grammar" of those connections is what makes it possible for us to navigate through it in a meaningful way. But the problem with this vision is that it offers a very narrow range of meaning making options and makes processes of information retrieval and interpretation sometimes cumbersome and time consuming. The syntactic web has improved significantly over the years, Google's Page Rank algorithm, which exploits the hyperlinking structure of the web as a means of ranking some information as more important than other information, being a notable example. But the way we have come to experience Google (and, more importantly, the way Google *experiences us*) goes far beyond this initial syntactic vision of information.

A more ambitious way of approaching the web, and the one that has dominated most discourse around software development in the last decade, is the vision of the "Semantic Web", originally articulated by Tim Berners-Lee (Berners-Lee & Hendler 2001). The idea of the Semantic Web sees the internet as a networks of concepts, relations, and rules which can be used by different platforms and agents to "talk to" each other. As Berners-Lee (2000: 191) put it, "The first step is putting data on the Web in a form that machines can naturally understand, or converting it to that form. This creates...a Semantic Web – a web of data that can be processed directly or indirectly by machines".

Rather than just a collection of linked documents, the Semantic Web is potentially a collection of linked *ontologies*, that is, sets of different concepts about reality and relations between them. Initial advances toward the vision of a Semantic Web were made possible through the development of "metadata" (Greenberg, Sutton & Campbell 2003), machine-readable descriptions of data and documents which has allowed static information resources to be transformed into dynamic resources that interact with and respond to one other. This is what allows, for example, highly customised web content to be delivered to different users (Cardoso 2007). The development of machine learning technologies, data mining, advanced statistics, and predictive analytics has given a boost to this vision of a Semantic Web, making the extraction of meaning from unstructured and semi-structured data, text, images and videos much easier. As Cabeda (2017) puts it, "instead of rewriting the web so that the computers could understand, we are making the computers smarter and are slowly empowering them to aggregat(e) information...and learn what it means".

For many, however, the vision of a Semantic Web, even a super-powered version fueled by big data, has proven unsatisfactory, particularly when it comes to getting computers to interact with humans in ways in which meaning might be less ontological and more experiential. For them, the key problem with the notion of the Semantic Web lies in its underlying assumptions about meaning itself, specifically the assumption that meaning is a matter of "context free facts and logical rules" (Schoop, de Moor & Dietz 2006: 75; see also McCool 2005). It fails to take into account the way meaning is shaped by the way people and machines use information *together* in "the context of the informational moment" (Casagrande 1999: 4). "The human factor in the Semantic Web", wrote Di Maio in 2008 "is still a largely unresolved issue, prompting central questions that...have been left behind in technical debates" (Di Maio 2008: 1).

This dissatisfaction with the model of meaning offered by the Semantic Web has led to what Casanovas and his colleagues (Casanovas, Rodríguez-Doncel & González-Conejero 2017) describe as a "pragmatic turn" in web development, an increased interest in how user behaviour and the contexts in which information is used can be represented in ways that machines can understand and respond to. What has come to be called the "Pragmatic Web" is a vision of the internet as a network of tools, protocols and agents (both human and algorithmic) that interact to make and interpret meaning through actions. Whereas meaning in the Semantic Web is a matter of relations between signs, meaning in the Pragmatic Web is created through relations between *actions* and the *contexts* within which those actions take place.

For many computer scientists and digital strategists (e.g. de Moor 2005; Leonard-Hansen 2009), the "real" Pragmatic Web is a vision for the future – what Weigand and Paschke (2012: 190) call "Web 4.0". But in many ways the web is *already* implicated in a wide range of pragmatic processes, a fact seen most clearly in the ways algorithms regularly monitor the actions of users (such as "likes") and transform them into inferences about the kinds of content they wish to be fed or the kinds of products they wish to buy. At the time of writing, search engines like Google, for example, serve users results not just based on the syntactic technology of the original PageRank algorithm, but on inferences its algorithm forms about what users "want" based on thousands of previous actions of searching and clicking on particular results, as well as where that user is and what they might be doing when they search. Recommender systems like that used by Amazon.com similarly are becoming better and better at inferring what kinds of products people might buy based on the "footprints" they leave as they transverse both digital and physical spaces. Finally, filtering systems like Facebook's EdgeRank, which determines the order in which updates appear on users' newsfeeds, are getting better at predicting what kinds of posts will trigger "reactions", not just because Facebook the company wishes to do a better job at connecting people to the people they care about but because the more users react to posts, the better Facebook's algorithms get at making future inferences about them. In all of these systems, meaning is created not just through the syntactic relationship between different bits of data, or the semantic relationship between different concepts represented through metadata, but through the ways algorithms have become adept at inferring meaning from the actions people perform and in enticing them to act in particular ways that make their intentions, desire and goals more legible to these algorithms.

The Pragmatic Web, then, at least the way I am treating it in this chapter, is not so much a "thing" as it is a *perspective* on the way human-computer interaction has developed in the early twenty-first century. As Weigand and Paschke (2012: 183) put it:

> The Pragmatic Web is a perspective. It is not a web besides the WWW or Semantic Web. Considering the Internet as a platform of communication and coordination means that messages are not viewed in isolation but in the context of an interaction. Although messages can be interpreted to some extent in a context-free manner (the "literal" meaning), this does never exhaust their meaning. We also need to know (or design) its relationship with other messages, and actions, in the context of use.

The question I would like to consider then, is not the degree to which the Pragmatic Web is achievable as a technological reality, but rather the degree to which the Pragmatic Web is achievable *as an analytical perspective* given our current understanding of pragmatics, or what I am calling "analogue pragmatics", the set of tools developed to explain how humans create meaning and make inferences. We have already seen how the introduction of new technologies (such as the telephone) alter the way people create implicature and form inferences, requiring linguists to rethink the tools they use to understand these strategies (Hutchby 2001). What is different about the internet is that the medium does not just provide a new architecture within which humans exchange information, but that the medium itself has become a participant in the exchange of information, a participant which brings to interactions inferential processes that are very different than those used by humans. As Kitchin and Dodge (2011) argue, algorithms don't just mediate but also function to *constitute* social interactions and associations. Hayles (2010: 96) similarly characterises the environment created by digital media as an environment "that senses the environment, creates a context for...information, communicates internally among components, draws inferences from the data, and comes to conclusions that, in scope if not complexity, far exceed what an unaided human could achieve".

Of course, when I speak of human-algorithm communication, I am not implying that algorithms are free-agents. They are created by humans and designed to advance the individual or institutional goals of their creators, whether those goals are to stoke the flames of political tribalism or to sell books. But, although the overall goals of algorithmic systems broadly reflect the intentions of their human programmers, the actual micro-mechanics of data-gathering, aggregation, inference and response are largely automated, and sometimes end up advancing broader goals in specific ways that programmers may not have anticipated. For example, YouTube's recommender system favoured pro-Trump videos nearly 4 to 1 over pro-Clinton videos during the 2016 US elections, not because the creators of the algorithms favoured Trump, but because the algorithms were programmed to maximize engagement, and the algorithms figured out quite quickly that pro-Trump videos resulted in more responses (both negative and positive) from viewers (Lewis 2018). In another example, Microsoft's machine-learning chatbot, Tay, had to be taken offline within 24 hours of its launch on Twitter after its conversation and language patterns became disturbingly racist, not because of the racist biases of its creators, but because that is how the algorithm learned to interact from human users of Twitter (Vincent 2016). In other words, what is programmed into algorithms is the directive to pursue a goal as efficiently as possible, and with newer systems, enhanced with machine learning capacities, to learn how to increase efficiency using the data that is made available to them. Rather than seeing algorithms, then, as simple, unitary interactants, it is better to view them them as socio-technical assemblages (Latour, 1990) that both embody the plans and goals of human creators and adapt to the behavior of the humans with which they interact.

Problems of algorithmic biases versus the intentions of their creators, as well as problems of privacy and surveillance, as illustrated in the Cambridge Analytical scandal discussed above, are not so much problems about information as about the algorithmic *processing* of information and the way inferences about information are put to use; not so much problems of texts as problems of context; not so much problems of the Semantic Web as problems of the Pragmatic Web.

1.3 Pragmatics: Analogue and algorithmic

Just as a pragmatic approach to digital communication involves looking at the web in a new way, as a web of actions and inferences, it also involves approaching pragmatics in a new way. Analogue pragmatics gives us a toolkit for understanding how people manipulate features of text and context to design interactions in ways that influence the direction and outcomes of communication. Algorithmic pragmatics, rather than focusing on closed systems of usually dyadic communication, sees pragmatic norms as operating within open complex systems in which information circulates and inferences are formed on multiple levels, in multiple contexts, based on multiple logics that both exploit and defy the forms of reasoning characteristic of human-to-human communication. Understanding it requires asking how algorithms form inferences based on people's actions, how they create context and construct identities for people, and how they coerce behavioral change (Gorayska & Mey 2002). Whereas analogue pragmatics is about how people "do things with words", algorithmic pragmatics is about how algorithms "do things" with people.

I do not mean to imply that the insights of analogue pragmatics are obsolete when it comes to understanding the interaction between humans and algorithms. Humans are still humans, and the processes of meaning making and interpretation that they have developed with human interlocutors naturally affect their actions with and inferences about the workings of algorithms (Jones forthcoming). In fact, many of the strategies internet companies use to entice people into making information about themselves available to algorithms by, for example, completing online quizzes or clicking on "Agree" in the dialogue boxes that pop up on their screens, are based on cleverly exploiting the principles and conventions of analogue pragmatics (such as the "Cooperative Principle" and expectations about the conditional relevance of sequential actions in communication; see Jones 2016b). Furthermore, the interfaces through which algorithms gather and respond to information are usually based on traditional assumptions about how human communication takes place (Galloway 2012), creating situations in which communication with an algorithm is made to resemble communication with a human, or in which certain types of human-to-human communication (such as "liking") is encouraged because it provides data that is more "legible" to algorithms and more easily processed by them.

Similarly, it might be argued that human pragmatic reasoning is also essentially "algorithmic", that the whole idea of pragmatics is that people (and machines) produce and infer meanings by following processual logics, "recipes" for figuring out what is going on. The main difference between analogue and algorithmic pragmatics has to do with the underlying epistemological bases for these processual logics and the relative affordances for information processing of the human brain and the computer, two differences which I will elaborate on in the remainder of this chapter.

Although pragmatics, as it has evolved over the past half a century, comes in many flavours, from more socially informed approaches (e.g. Culpepper 2011; Jaspers, Östman & Verscheuren 2010; Mey 2001) to more cognitive approaches (e.g. Beaver & Clark 2008; Bara 2010; Nuyts 1991), what all scholars of pragmatics have in common is a concern with how people communicate and discern intentions below the level of explicit meaning. Much has been made of the "black box" nature of communicating with and through algorithms, what DeNicola (2012: 266) calls the "iceberg quality" of digital communication. For students of pragmatics, however, the "black box" nature of communication is nothing new, nor is it the sole provenance of technologically mediated communication. The central premise of pragmatics is that *all* communication is mediated through the "black box" of the human mind, and the only way communicators can discern the content of the minds of their interlocutors is through processes of inference formed through analyzing the relationship between "output" and the circumstances within which output is produced.

The topics that have traditionally been of interest to students of pragmatics are 1) deixis, the ways language "indexes" people, objects or concepts in the external world; 2) conversational implicature, how it is possible for people to mean more (or less) than what they say; 3) pragmatic inference, how people figure out what people mean; 4) speech acts, how words can be used to perform various actions and the social conventions that make this possible; 5) discourse structure, how the sequence of utterances can affect what they mean; 6) participation, the different kinds of roles speakers and hearers can play in conversation and how those roles affect what they can say, do and understand; and 7) identity, how who we are or who we are taken to be affects how we communicate and how people interpret what we say (Jones 2016c; Levinson 1983; Mey 2001). While all of these aspects of analogue pragmatics are somehow implicated in algorithmic pragmatics, I will limit my discussion here to four main areas where I see the need for students of pragmatics to refine their tools or redefine their concepts to cope with the new analytical challenges posed by digitally-mediated communication. These are: 1) speech acts, 2) inference and implicature, 3) context, and 4) identity.

1.3.1 Speech acts

According to Austin (1976: 76), whenever we communicate we are engaged in a "field of actions", and we must distinguish what words "mean" from the way they operate within this field. Austin referred to this mode of operation as "force", the effect words have on the situated experiences of interlocutors; in other words, what words "do". In formulating an algorithmic pragmatics, then, the first question that must be asked is what the difference is between how people use language to do things and how algorithms do things.

The most obvious difference between people and algorithms is in the arena of what Austin called *performativity*. In natural language, certain utterances have the ability to materially change the contexts in which they are uttered, but only if they meet certain conditions. "I now pronounce you husband and wife", for instance, only results in two people being married if it is uttered by a particular kind of person at a particular time and in a particular place. The language of algorithms, on the other hand, is *purely performative*; a performativity that presupposes its own felicity. If code can be considered a language, Galloway says, it is a special kind of language: it is "the only language that is *executable*...the first language that actually *does what it says*" (Galloway 2004: 165–6; emphasis mine).

How does this feature of code affect us when we interact with algorithms? The most important way is that is imposes a kind of "tyranny of performativity". We cannot help but "act" whenever we interact through digital media, because algorithms automatically turn our utterances into actions – when we type a word on our keyboards, we set into motion a chain of operations within our own devices and other devices connected to ours over a network; when we react to or comment on a friend's post, we set into motion a series of algorithmically orchestrated operations that can affect the order of information on other people's newsfeeds as well as our own and may, when aggregated with other actions, eventually be interpreted as a "request" to receive certain political advertisements, news stories, or "memes", even if that was not our intention.

At the same time, just as algorithms automatically turn words into actions, they also automatically turn actions into "words" (or, rather, code), not only making those actions "legible" in particular ways to computers, but also preserving them for future reference. As Andrejevic (2009: 53) puts it, the internet is a "realm wherein every action, interaction, and transaction generates information about itself". Clicks, steps, purchases, even the speed and rhythm with which one navigates websites or types on their keyboard (e.g. Epp, Lippold & Mandryk 2011) become information that is relentlessly recorded. Algorithmically extextualised actions are then turned back on users in feedback loops that are often designed to reinforce the same actions or re-engineer these actions in ways more amiable to the algorithm's agenda. Algorithmically coerced actions are coerced based on what we have already done, and what the algorithm wants us to do next can change moment by moment based on our responses. Perhaps this is what Google's Michael Schmidt meant when he said, half-jokingly, that people don't want Google to give them information; they want Google "to tell them what they should be doing next" (Jenkins 2010).

The first step to formulating an algorithmic pragmatics, then, is to regard digital systems not as "information systems", but as "action systems", systems designed to act on our information and compel us to act in particular ways. Goldkuhl and Ågerfalk (2002: 85) argue that the key to understanding and designing computer systems is not "usability", but *"actability"*, which they define as "an information system's ability to perform actions, and to permit, promote and facilitate the performance of actions by users, both through the system and based on information from the system". Of course, this view of information systems as action systems is, in some ways, not so different from Austin's insistence that human communication takes place within a field of actions. The difference is the speed and efficiency with which computer systems transform information into actions and actions into information.

1.3.2 Inferences and implicature

The central focus of pragmatics is the "guesswork" involved in social interaction: how people interpret the intentions of others, and how people communicate meanings and perform actions without making their intentions explicit. Understanding language is more than just decoding words; it involves exquisitely sensitive processes of inferential reasoning. The only way the "guesswork" of communication works is because of a tacit agreement between speakers and hearers about the logical principles that should govern this "guesswork". If nothing else, Grice (1989) argued, talking is a form of "rational behaviour". The rational basis of human communication, however, is not just a matter of agreeing upon a set of principles or "maxims"; it is a matter of committing to a particular epistemology. The epistemological stance outlined by Grice and his followers (e.g. Horn 1984; Levinson 2000) is basically that knowledge is the result of deductive "if...then" reasoning: It is a "causal" epistemology in which hearers form hypothesis about meaning based on testing input against a mutually agreed upon "theory" of communication.

Algorithms, on the other hand, while also engaging in guesswork, do so based on a very different epistemology: knowledge is a matter not of causation but of *correlation*. No underlying set of rules or "theory" of communication is necessary. Meaning is constructed mathematically, probabilistically, based on correlations between pieces of input. That is why Google can translate languages without actually "knowing" the rules of grammar or the meanings of words, simply by calculating the probability of a particular word in a particular context having a particular meaning based on billions of other occurrences of the use of that word in context. The probabilistic induction of algorithmic inferencing can tell retailers what book you might buy by correlating your past purchase with that of other readers, and political operatives can tell what candidate you might vote for based on your supermarket purchases or whether or not you shared posts related to Hello Kitty on Facebook (Cadwalladr &

Graham-Harrison 2018), as well as how these behaviors might be altered with just the right algorithmically-informed nudge at the right time.

There are risks related to all inferencing, whether algorithmic or analogue. One or both of the participants, for example, may be in possession of too little, too much, or the wrong kind of information with which to make inferences, or one of the participants may have access to resources for interpreting information not available to the other, making control of the personal information that is "given" and "given off" more difficult (Goffman 1959). When it comes to human-algorithm communication, these potential asymmetries are an inevitable feature of the interaction. The ability of algorithms to infer information from seemingly unrelated information makes it harder for people to control what can be known about them, and far exceeds humans' ability to infer information about algorithms. Furthermore, algorithmic inferencing is much harder to challenge. A good example is the way police officers "profile" suspects. Sacks (1972) describes the analogue process by which police decide whether or not to stop and search a potential suspect, noting that the "propriety" of the inference is based on an agreed upon set of expectations about what sort of behaviour would rouse an "ordinary person" to suspicion, and it is only if the officer is able to convince a judge or jury that the inference has been properly arrived at that the person is convictable. Nowadays, however, many police forces make use of what is known as "predictive policing", which uses algorithms to, for example, deploy police officers to neighbourhoods where there is a higher probability of a crime being carried out. What arouses suspicion, then, is simply being present in the neighbourhood. This, of course, results in more crimes being discovered in these neighbourhoods, which can snowball into what Ensign and her colleagues (Ensign et al. 2017) call a "runaway feedback loop" that makes the algorithm's prediction a self-fulfilling prophesy. In such cases, contrary to the well-known warning of scientists, correlation *is* causation, since it causes what it predicts (see also Brayne 2017; Krasmann 2007).

1.3.3 Context

Although people and algorithms use very different kinds of epistemologies when making inferences, they both depend on the same sorts of information, including the *content* of the language that has been produced, the *contexts* in which this language may later appear, and the *identities* of the speakers and hearers. But what "context" and "identity" mean to algorithms is dramatically different from what they mean for humans. In one sense, algorithms' understanding of "context" and "identity" is extremely reductive, limited to information that can be digitised and made *legible* to computers. On the other hand, their ability to laminate different contexts onto one another, to rapidly create new contexts within which to interpret information, and to construct very precise "identity types" based on very specific goals, allows them to use these kinds of information in ways that are not available to humans.

Understanding context and how we use it to communicate in the analogue world is already a rich and contested topic (e.g. Duranti & Goodwin 1992; van Dijk 2008). Linguists and discourse analysts have debated whether context in communication should be approached as a micro-social phenomenon or a macro-social one, and how much context is fixed or emergent. One thing that most scholars concur on, however, is that human communication depends a great deal on the degree to which people are able to negotiate and, to some extent, agree upon the "definition" of the particular communicative situations in which they find themselves. Goffman (1972) argued that all situations have their own properties that follow from the fact of co-presence between two or more people, and that this co-presence and the "mutual monitoring possibilities" it affords makes it possible for people to negotiate "what's going on here". While pragmatic contexts naturally consist of individual contexts, communication requires that some common context be defined, often based on community norms and/or joint goals. In other words, there must be some alignment regarding what aspect of the situation "matters" when people create implicature and form inferences. More cognitively oriented linguists see this negotiation about what matters in terms of "relevance" (Sperber & Wilson 1986), arguing that communication is not so much a matter of shared social norms, but a matter of shared biologically determined cognitive imperatives to filter out potentially irrelevant information and to focus on information more likely to provide informational rewards.

The rise of technologies like social media and mobile communication has problematized both social and cognitive understandings of context, making it more difficult for people both to negotiate shared understandings of context with others and to determine what information is more likely to be relevant in particular situations. This is because, as Weigand and Paschke (2012) point out, the Pragmatic Web is not a web of texts, but a web of contexts, which are exceedingly difficult to keep separate from one another. For humans, this has resulted in new challenges around juggling multiple contexts online and negotiating what they wish their interlocutors to take as relevant (boyd 2010; Tagg, Seargeant & Brown 2017).

What is sometimes problematic for people is, for algorithms, rich with opportunities. For algorithms, the network of linked contexts that make up the internet is really a rich array of circumstances for forming inferences about our actions and utterances, and for seeing meaning in multiple text-context combinations *simultaneously*. Because algorithms have at their disposal informational horizons that exceed human perception, they are able to make relevant aspects of context about which people may not even be aware. While for humans, for example, the context of a web search might be a particular goal or activity, such as a school assignment, for Google, the context stretches back to all of the other searches this individual has performed, and may even include their email conversations about related topics.

Much has been made of algorithms' ability to design the contexts in which people consume and share information, such as one's Facebook Newsfeed, an ability that was particularly evident in the 2016 US election and the UK Brexit vote, and much has also been made of the ability of algorithms to *recontextualise* information in ways that create new contexts that affect the ways we interpret texts and what we do with them, as when information from that web search suddenly becomes part of the context of another site in the form of a "clickbait" headline related to what was being searched for. Maybe what is most challenging about communicating with algorithms, though, is not that their tools for determining what is *relevant* in a given context or set of contexts is so different from ours, but that the "reasoning" behind these determinations are opaque to us.

Humans still have some advantages over computers when it comes to contextualization in their ability to mutually monitor signals from interlocutors that are illegible to computers, and to adapt to subtle changes in the physical and social environment, framing and reframing their understanding and "design" of contexts as they go along (Tagg, Seargeant & Brown 2017). As digital media increasingly weave themselves into the fabrics of human physical lives, however, embedded in watches, refrigerators, thermostats, and even clothing, not to mention the mobile phones that are carried everywhere, algorithms will become more adept at sensing patterns in human behaviour: where we go, who we interact with, even what we say, and be able to use this information to design more efficient contexts for interpreting our actions.

1.3.4 Identities

In interaction between humans, the social identities of interlocutors is an important ingredient for sense making. We use the social identities of interlocutors to interpret their words, and we use words to construct or alter aspects of our identities. In other words, like context, identity is both "fixed", based on a certain set of "membership categories" available in our social worlds and relevant to whatever we happen to be doing, and "emergent", negotiated and co-constructed with our interlocutors in accordance with certain strategic goals (Bucholtz & Hall 2005; Jones 2016c; Sacks 1992). The "fixed" and "emergent" aspects of identity are not separate, but rather intertwined: we use membership categories strategically, appropriating and discarding them, making some more relevant in certain instances than others, and mixing them together to form hybrid identities.

Similarly, when it comes to algorithms, much of the way they operate on us and affect our textual and interactional options is based on "who they think we are". Much has been written about the "data doubles" (Haggerty & Ericson 2000) that algorithms cobble out of our incremental actions and utterances, and how these digital shadows follow us, both online and off, determining what sorts of discounts we are offered at shops and whether or not we are able to get loans from banks. In his book *We are data*, Cheney-Lippold (2017) argues that algorithms make sense of us by turning us into "measurable types". The worst thing about these "types", he believes, is that they somehow obscure our "true selves". "Who we are in the face of algorithmic interpretation", he writes, "is who we are computationally calculated to be...and when our embodied individualities get ignored, we increasingly lose control not just over life but over how life itself is defined" (Cheney-Lippold 2017: 5). He suggests that "[w]hen data defines us, the complexities of our emotional and psychological lives online are flattened out for purposes of mass-scale, approximate data analysis" (Cheney-Lippold 2017: 53).

While this is no doubt true to some degree, the ways algorithms construct our identities and reflect them back to us is more complicated, and potentially more problematic. First of all, the processing of people into "recognizable types" that algorithms engage in is not entirely different from the way humans use "the recognizability of people as certain sorts of people or, more specifically, people as certain sorts of members of society" (Day n.d.: 1) as a resource for dealing with others. It is just that the categories available to algorithms are potentially more complex, and the ways they group different categories together (based on correlation rather than causation, see above), provides them with different kinds of resources for judging "who we are" and acting accordingly. What characterises algorithmically constructed identities is, first, their precision – we are not just men or gay or caucasian, but members of complex "micro-categories" consisting of bundles of inferences that algorithms have formed about us, and second, their flexibility; we are not the same from one moment to the next or from one site to the next. Algorithms adjust their assessments of us with every click or swipe, aggregating and processing these quotidian actions in ways that can reveal not just our personality traits, but our momentary moods. The problem might not be, as Cheney-Lippold suggests, that algorithms ignore our emotional complexities, but just the opposite, that they get revealed and explained in ways that we ourselves are not even aware of. In other words, the problem with data doubles is not that they don't reflect our "true selves", but that they *do*, robbing us of the opportunity to engage in the kinds of self-presentation and impression management that is central to social life.

The most important thing to remember about algorithmic identity projects, though, is that, like all identity projects, they are "goal directed". The identities that algorithms imagine for us are configured towards certain "category specific activities" (Sacks 1992), in this case, usually shopping. In studies of Membership Categorization Analysis, Jayusi (1984) has highlighted the *moral* and *normative* character of categories and categorization. In the famous example by Sacks (1992), for instance, the fact that the categories of mother and baby are inferred by the action of the mother picking the baby up is predicated on the idea that mothers *should* pick up their babies when they cry. The normalising power of algorithms is even more efficient. Algorithms don't just tell you "who they think you are" but also reward you for acting accordingly by offering you discounts, special offers, and other enticements, so that gradually you become the kind of person (or customer) you are expected to be.

1.4 Conclusion: Pragmatic competence in the age of the algorithm

In pointing out some of the differences between the way humans do pragmatics, and the way algorithms do, I have not intended to demonise algorithms nor to suggest we have become slaves to them. We have not. In fact, as important as the ways algorithms have come to control us are the processes humans have been developing to figure out how to control algorithms and use them for their own purposes. Galloway (2006: 106) argues that video games are "allegories for our contemporary life under the protocological network of continuous informatic control". As much as the code of the game produces the "perimeters for discursive possibility (and) possible actions...and subjective experiences" made available to players (Cheney-Lippold 2017: 218), good players are still able to master the game. "To play the game", Galloway (2006: 91) writes, "means to play the code of the game. To win means to know the system. And thus to interpret a game means to interpret its algorithm".

Some have suggested that the way for us to get good at playing this game is to open up the "black box" (Pasquale 2015), that is, to force tech companies to tell us how their algorithms work, to lay bare their inferential processes. It is an approach that rests on assumptions that being able to *see* a system is the same as being able to know how it works and control it, a deep-seated enlightenment notion that drives many of the attempts by governments to legislate the digital world. Insisting that companies like Facebook and Google tell us how their algorithms work, however, will probably have little effect, not just because big tech companies are not likely to part so easily with their intellectual property, but because even if algorithms *were* made transparent, their real workings would remain opaque to all but the most technologically savvy of us (Ananny & Crawford 2018). But most important, making algorithms transparent would compromise much of the efficiency and convenience we have come to expect from digital communication, just as asking people to make everything they mean explicit would render human communication not just incredibly inefficient but also frequently uncivil.

Coping with the communicative challenges posed by the pragmatic web will require more than just trying to make algorithms more "accountable", because they are just one component of the pragmatic web. As I said above, algorithms do not operate independent of their human interlocuters, nor do they exist independent of the institutional agendas, social practices, and relations of power through which they are created (Annany & Crawford 2018; Crawford 2016). The way to approach the pitfalls of the pragmatic web, therefore, is not just with political or technical solutions, but with a fuller engagement with *pragmatics*. Training in digital literacies must involve helping people to develop the new kinds of *pragmatic competencies* that digital environments demand, helping them to become more sensitive to how algorithms process not just their "information" but also their actions, and helping them to reflect upon not just the inferential processes of algorithms, but also on the inferential processes they themselves develop as they interact with both human and non-human actors within the Pragmatic Web.

After the dust from the Cambridge Analytica scandal has settled, the kinds of algorithms implicated in it will continue their relentless processing of our information. What is perhaps good about the scandal is that it brought the issue of algorithms into the public conversation – it (aided by algorithms) elevated algorithmic pragmatics to the top of our Newsfeeds. And the more algorithms are included in our thinking about how our lives are organized, the better we will become at mastering the game of the Pragmatic Web.

References

Ananny, Mike & Kate Crawford. 2018. Seeing without knowing: Limitations of the transparency ideal and its application to algorithmic accountability. *New Media and Society* 20 (3). 973–989.

Andrejevic, Mark. 2009. Privacy, exploitation, and the digital enclosure. *Amsterdam Law Forum* 1 (4). 47–62.

Antaki, Charles & Sue Widdicombe (eds.), 1998. *Identities in talk*. Thousand Oaks: Sage.

Austin, John L. 1976. *How to do things with words*. Oxford: Oxford University Press.

Bara, Bruno G. 2010. *Cognitive pragmatics: The mental processes of communication*. Cambridge, MA: MIT Press.

Beaver, David I. and Brady Z. Clark. 2008. *Sense and sensitivity: How focus determines meaning*. Chichester: Wiley-Blackwell.

Berners-Lee, Tim 2000. *Weaving the web: The past, present and future of the world wide web by its inventor*. London: Texere.

Berners-Lee, Tim, James Hendler & Ora Lassila. 2001. The semantic web. *Scientific American*. May. https://www-sop.inria.fr/acacia/cours/essi2006/Scientific%20American_%20Feature%20Article_%20The%20Semantic%20Web_%20May%202001.pdf (accessed 10 April 2018).

boyd, danah. 2010. Social network sites as networked publics: Affordances, dynamics and implications. In Zizi Papacharissi (ed.), *A networked self: Identity, community and culture on social network sites*, 39–58. Abingdon: Routledge.

Brayne, Sarah. 2017. Big data surveillance: The case of policing. *American Sociological Review* 82 (5). 977–1008.

Bucholtz, Mary & Kira Hall. 2005. Identity and interaction: a sociocultural linguistic approach. *Discourse Studies* 7 (4–5). 585–614.

Cabeda, José. 2017. Semantic Web is dead, long live the AI!!! https://hackernoon.com/semantic-web-is-dead-long-live-the-ai-2a5ea0cf6423 (accessed 10 April 2018).

Cardoso, Jorge. 2007. The syntactic and Semantic Web. In Jorge Cardoso (ed.), *Semantic web services: Theory, tools and application*, 1–24. Hershey: IGA International.

Cadwalladr, Carole & Emma Graham-Harrison. 2018. How Cambridge Analytica turned Facebook 'likes' into a lucrative political tool. http://www.theguardian.com/technology/2018/mar/17/facebook-cambridge-analytica-kogan-data-algorithm (accessed 8 April 2018).

Casagrande, David G. (1999) Information as Verb: Re-conceptualizing Information for Cognitive and Ecological Models. *Journal of Ecological Anthropology* 3 (1): 4–13.

Casanovas, Pompeu, Victor Rodríguez-Doncel & Jorge González-Conejero. 2017. The role of pragmatics in the web of data. In Francesca Poggi & Alessandro Capone (eds.), *Pragmatics and law. Perspectives in pragmatics, philosophy & psychology*, vol 10. Cham: Springer.

Cheney-Lippold, John. 2017. *We are data: Algorithms and the making of our digital selves*. New York: New York University Press.

Crawford, Kate. 2016. Can an algorithm be agonistic? Ten scenes from life in calculated publics. *Science, Technology and Human Values* 41 (1). 77–92.

Culpeper, Jonathan (ed.). 2011. *Historical sociopragmatics*. Amsterdam: John Benjamins.

Day, Dennis. n.d. Membership categorization analysis. ms. University of Southern Denmark. bit.ly/2ujzWFn (accessed 8 April 2018).

de Moor, Aldo. 2005. Patterns for the Pragmatic Web. In Frithjof Dau, Marie -Laure Mugnier & Gerd Stumme (eds.), *Conceptual structures: Common semantics for sharing knowledge Vol. 3596*, 1–18. Berlin: Springer.

DeNicola, Lane. 2012. EULA, Codec, API: On the opacity of digital culture. In Pelle Snickars & Patrick Vonderau (eds.), *Moving data: The iPhone and the future of media*, 265–277. New York: Columbia University Press.

Di Maio, Paola. 2008. The missing pragmatic link in the Semantic Web. *Business Intelligence Advisory Service* 8 (7). 1–3.

Duranti, Alessandro & Goodwin, Charles G. (eds.). 1992. *Rethinking context: Language as an interactive phenomenon*. Cambridge, UK: Cambridge University Press.

Ensign, Danielle, Sorelle A. Friedler, Scott Neville, Carolos Scheidegger & Suresh Venkatasubramanian. 2017. Runaway feedback loops in predictive policing. *ArXiv:1706.09847 [Cs, Stat]*. http://arxiv.org/abs/1706.09847 (accessed 17 July 2019).

Epp, Clayton, Michael Lippold & Regan L. Mandryk. 2011. Identifying emotional states using keystroke dynamics. *Proceedings of the SIGCHI Conference on Human Factors in Computing Systems*, 715–724. New York: ACM.

Galloway, Alexander R. 2004. *Protocol: How control exists after decentralization*. Cambridge, MA: MIT Press.

Galloway, Alexander. 2006. *Gaming: Essays on algorithmic culture*. Minneapolis: University of Minnesota Press.

Galloway, Alexander 2012. *The interface effect*. Cambridge, UK: Polity Press.

Goffman, Erving. 1959. *The presentation of self in everyday life*. New York: Doubleday.

Goffman, Erving. 1972. *Relations in public: Microstudies of the public order*. New York: Harper & Row.

Goldkuhl, Gören & Pär J. Ågerfalk. 2002. Actability: A way to understand information systems pragmatics. In Kecheng Liu, Rodney J. Clarke, Peter Bøgh Andersen, Ronald K. Stamper & Al-Sayed Abou-Zeid (eds.), *Coordination and communication using signs: Studies in organisational semiotics*, vol. 2, 85–113. Boston: Kluwer Academic Publishers.

Gorayska, Barbara & Jacob L. Mey. 2002. Introduction: Pragmatics of technology. *International Journal of Cognition and Technology* 1 (1). 1–20.

Grasseger, Hannes & Mikael Krogerus. Jan. 28, 2017. The data that turned the world upside down. *Motherboard*. https://motherboard.vice.com/en_us/article/mg9vvn/how-our-likes-helped-trump-win) (accessed 30 March 2018).

Greenberg, Jane, Stuart Sutton & D. Grant Campbell. 2003. Metadata: A fundamental component of the semantic web. *Bulletin of the American Society for Information Science and Technology* April–May. 16–18.

Grice, Herbert Paul. 1989. *Studies in the way of words*. Cambridge, MA: Harvard University Press.

Haggerty, Kevin D. & Ericson, Richard V. 2000. The surveillant assemblage. *British Journal of Sociology* 51 (4). 605–622.

Hayles, N. Katherine. 2010. RFID: Human agency and meaning in information intensive environments. In Jörgen Schäfer & Peter Gendolla (eds.), *Beyond the screen: Transformations of literary structures, interfaces and genres*, 95–122. Bielefeld: Transcript-Verlag.

Horn, Laurence R. 1984. Toward a new taxonomy for pragmatic inference: Q-based and R-based implicature. In Deborah Schiffrin (ed.), *Georgetown University Round Table on Languages and Linguistics*, 11–42. Washington, D.C.: Georgetown University Press.

Hutchby, Ian. 2001. *Conversation and technology: From the telephone to the Internet*. Cambridge, UK: Polity Press.

Jayusi, Lena. 1984. *Categorization and the moral order*. Abingdon: Routledge.

Jaspers, Jürgen, Jan-Ola Östman & Jef Verschueren (eds.), 2010. *Society and language use*. Amsterdam: John Benjamins.

Jenkins, Holman W. Jr. 2010, August 14. Google and the search for the future. *Wall Street Journal*. https://www.wsj.com/articles/SB10001424052748704901104575423294099527212 (accessed 8 April 2018).

Jones, Rodney H. 2016a. Surveillance. In Alexandra Georgakopoulou & Tereza Spilloti (eds.), *The Routledge handbook of language and digital communication*, 408–411. Abingdon: Routledge.

Jones, Rodney H. 2016b. Linguistics and the study of online surveillance. Paper presented at the 17th Annual Conference of the Association of Internet Researchers (AoIR), Berlin, October 5–8.

Jones, Rodney H. 2016c. *Spoken discourse*. London: Bloomsbury.

Jones, Rodney H. 2016d. 'Have you swiped your nectar card?' Pretextuality and practices of surveillance. A lecture at the Lancaster Literacy Research Centre, University of Lancaster, January 25. https://www.lancaster.ac.uk/linguistics/news-and-events/events-archive-to-aug-2016/5494 (accessed 31 May 2019).

Jones, Rodney H. Forthcoming. 'Folk algorithmics': Reading and writing in the age of the algorithm. *Linguistics and Education*.

Kitchin, Rob & Martin Dodge. 2011. *Code/space: Software and everyday life*. Cambridge, MA: MIT Press.

Kosinski, Michal, David Stillwell & Graepel, Thore. 2013. Private traits and attributes are predictable from digital records of human behavior. *Proceedings of the National Academy of Sciences*, 110 (15). 5802–5805. https://doi.org/10.1073/pnas.1218772110

Krasmann, Suzanne, 2007. The enemy on the border: Critique of a programme in favour of a preventive state. *Punishment & Society* 9 (3). 301–318.

Latour, Bruno. 1990. Technology is society made durable. *The Sociological Review* 38 (1 suppl). 103–131.

Leonard-Hansen, Alisa. 2009, November 20. The future is all about context: The Pragmatic Web. https://readwrite.com/2009/11/20/future_all_about_context_the_pragmatic_web/ (accessed 11 February 2019).

Levinson, Stephen C. 1983. *Pragmatics*. Cambridge, UK: Cambridge University Press.

Levinson, Stephen C. 2000. *Presumptive meanings: The theory of generalized conversational implicature*. Cambridge, MA: MIT Press.

Lewis, Paul. 2018. Fiction is outperforming reality: How YouTube's algorithm distorts truth. *The Guardian*. https://www.theguardian.com/technology/2018/feb/02/how-youtubes-algorithm-distorts-truth (accessed 31 May 2019).

Maíz-Arévalo, Carmen. 2017. Getting 'liked'. In Christian Hoffmann & Wolfram Bublitz (eds.), *Pragmatics of social media*, 575–606. Berlin: De Gruyter Mouton.

McCool, Rob. 2005. Rethinking the Semantic Web, Part 1. *IEEE Internet Computing*, 86–88.

Mey, Jacob L. 2001. *Pragmatics: An introduction*, 2nd edn. Malden: Wiley-Blackwell.

Nuyts, Jan. 1991. *Aspects of a cognitive-pragmatic theory of language: On cognition, functionalism, and grammar*. Amsterdam: John Benjamins.
Pasquale, Frank. 2015. *The black box society: The secret algorithms that control money and information*. Cambridge, MA: Harvard University Press.
Sacks, Harvey. 1972. Notes on police assessment of moral character. In David Sudnow (ed.), *Studies in social interaction*, 280–293. New York: Free Press.
Sacks, Harvey. 1992. *Lectures on conversation* (vol. 2), Gail Jefferson (ed.). Oxford: Blackwell.
Schoop, Mareike, Aldo de Moor & Jan L.G. Dietz, 2006. The Pragmatic Web: A manifesto. *Communication of the ACM* 49 (5). 75–6.
Sperber, Dan & Deirdre Wilson. 1986. *Relevance: Communication and cognition*. London: Blackwell.
Tagg, Caroline, Philip Seargeant & Amy Aisha Brown. 2017. *Taking offence on social media: Conviviality and communication on Facebook*. Basingstoke: Palgrave Macmillan.
van Dijk, Tuen A. 2008. *Discourse and context: A sociocognitive approach*. Cambridge, UK: Cambridge University Press.
Vincent, James. 2016, March 24. Twitter taught Microsoft's friendly AI chatbot to be a racist asshole in less than a day. *The Verge*. https://www.theverge.com/2016/3/24/11297050/tay-microsoft-chatbot-racist (accessed 11 February 11 2019).
Weigand, Hans & Adrian Paschke. 2012. The Pragmatic Web: Putting rules in context. In Antonis Bikakis & Adrian Giurca (eds.), *Rules on the Web: Research and applications*, 182–192. Berlin: Springer.
Yus, Francisco. 2011. *Cyberpragmatics: Internet-mediated communication in context*. Amsterdam: John Benjamins.

Dániel Z. Kádár
2 Interpreting "historicisation" in the digital context: On the interface of diachronic and synchronic pragmatics

2.1 Introduction

This chapter provides a predominantly theoretical and pragmatics-driven contribution to the present volume. It explores the ways in which "historicisation" – which is the focus of the present collection of studies – can enrich understandings of both historical and modern interactional phenomena. The chapter will:
1. Provide an overview of "historicisation" as a principle for cross-fertilising diachronic and synchronic research.
2. Introduce a particular way of historicising modern interactional phenomena – labelled as the "historically-grounded interpersonal interactional" approach – which provides a powerful avenue to study interactional digital data. Essentially, this approach includes the use of historically-grounded frameworks – in combination with pragmatics – to analyse present-day interactional data.

Historicisation encompasses all forms of cross-overs between diachronic and synchronic research on pragmatic phenomena. In such cross-overs, many experts follow a from-synchronic-to-diachronic conceptualisation schema. That is, they deploy frameworks developed for the analysis of synchronic language use to examine interaction in historical pragmatic data, and/or contrast historical data with its modern counterparts. For example, Haggis and Holmes (2011), amongst others, have used modern pragmatics and communication theory to explain similarities between modern emails and historical epistles in order to provide a developmental

---

Notes: I would like to thank the MTA Hungarian Academy of Sciences Momentum/Lendulet Research Grant (LP2017/5) for funding my research on ritual which has also been featured in this chapter. I would also like to extend my gratitude to the Dalian University of Foreign Languages for supporting my research. It is perhaps needless to say that all remaining errors are my responsibility.

Dániel Z. Kádár, Dalian University of Foreign Languages, Dalian, China, Research Professor, Research Institute for Linguistics, Hungarian Academy of Sciences, Budapest, Hungary, e-mail: dannier@dlufl.edu.cn

theory of emails. Such an approach to historicisation has a clear explanatory power: pragmatics provides a significantly more rigorous way to study historical sources from an interactional point of view than other – more conventional – methodologies such as philology or stylistics. Yet, approaches to historicisation also include uptakes of a reversed logic: one may just as well deploy historically-grounded analytic methodologies to historicise modern interactional data.

A prime example of an approach that follows this reversed logic is the "historically-grounded interpersonal interactional" approach, which is in the centre of the current research. To illustrate the operation of this approach, this chapter will examine a dataset of online shaming incidents in the U.S. media, by adopting an interactional ritual framework. While interactional ritual research is not a fully-fledged historical approach in that a body of studies on interactional ritual has focused on ritual behaviour in modern industrialised societies, the field has roots in the exploration of spatially/diachronically distant cultures. Due to this, ritual research provides a prime example for an analytic approach that – unlike pragmatics – often follows a from-diachronic-to-synchronic logic. As a core of this logic, the interactional ritual theorist often explains the operation of present-day phenomena from a historical developmental angle and uses technical terms such as "liminality" that have originally been developed for the study of diachronic data. Note that ritual is only a case study here: arguably, there are a variety of historically-grounded methodologies that can be cross-fertilised with pragmatics and communication studies, such as religious studies (e.g. Richerson & Christiansen 2013) and rhetoric (Jucker, Fritz & Lebsanft 1999). The use of such frameworks does not at all preclude the use of pragmatics; rather, they should preferably be used in combination with the latter.

It is important to emphasise at this point that historicisation is a research principle that prompts us to move outside of our standard diachronic or synchronic "comfort zones" of research. What binds approaches of historicisation together is the belief that – as far as one engages in historicisation – making divides between "historical" and "modern" becomes redundant and counterproductive. While historicisation as a principle is relatively new to the field of pragmatics (see section 2.2), what validates this principle is that diachronic and synchronic research have always influenced each other both conceptually and in terms of research methodologies.

Historicisation not only helps us to reinterpret sociopragmatic phenomena from innovative angles, but also it raises various self-reflexive ontological questions, such as whether there are *any* digital (or other modern) phenomena without roots in history, as well as epistemological questions, such as whether it is worth engaging in modern pragmatics without a certain sense of historical self-reflexivity, and vice versa. While there may always be boundaries between historical and synchronic pragmatics simply due to the different data types these areas examine (e.g. Shakespeare v. trolling), historicisation can help us to increase critical self-awareness, and also enrich academic methodologies by bringing historically situated frameworks and concepts into synchronic research.

2.2 Historicisation: An overview

"Historicisation" as a research principle has rarely been adopted in pragmatics,[1] and it has been only relatively recently that pragmaticians have started to investigate the ways in which modern and historical pragmatics interrelate (e.g. Herring 2003). Some studies have used the Heideggerian concept of "historicity", by arguing that various modern interactional concepts and phenomena are historically situated (Ehlich 1992; and Kádár & Haugh 2013). However, such research has not adopted "historicisation" beyond mentioning it in passing (e.g. Ehlich 1992: 104).

The beauty of historicisation as a principle, however, is that it evokes various – significantly different – approaches to interactional data. Such approaches are not of higher or lower-order in any respect: simply, they represent (potentially interconnected) ways through which to historicise modern data and/or concepts. The following overview of approaches also helps to position the case study discussed in section 2.3.

There are at least three major types of approaches to interactional data evoked by the principle of historicisation:
 – Lexical historicisation
 – Historicisation of data
 – Interactional historicisation

Note that these approach types cannot be strictly separated from each other, as the subsequent discussion will illustrate, but rather they represent research directions with a different academic focus (on words, data and interaction) on the one hand, and with many overlaps, on the other. In what follows, I provide an overview of these approaches.

---

[1] It is also relevant to note in passing that in Hungarian - which is the native tongue of the author - there is no equivalent for "historicisation". While one can attempt to translate this English analytic construct to various languages, such as Chinese (*lishihua* 历史化), even speakers of English may not necessarily agree about the scope of this term.

2.2.1 Lexical historicisation

As part of cross-fertilising historical and synchronic pragmatics, previous research has shown that many modern analytic constructs can be reinterpreted through historical lenses; and, vice versa, many historical concepts can and should be revisited from a modern angle (for examples, see table 2.1).

Table 2.1: Approaches to lexical historicisation.

Modern analytic construct reinterpreted from a historical angle	Historical analytic construct reinterpreted from a modern angle
Example: Ide's (1989) notion of "discernment": Kádár and Paternoster (2015) have pointed out the problems of using "discernment" for historical research, since during the Renaissance and later *discernere* and other equivalents of "discernment" had been broadly used in European metadiscourses, with a different meaning from how Ide (1989) operationalises this term.	*Example:* The examination of historical metalexical items such as "courtesie": Various scholars such as Jucker (2010) have engaged in the analysis of historical analytic constructs, by interpreting them with the aid of modern frameworks and understandings of politeness.
Use: Such research reinterprets a modern analytic construct – that is, an analytic term with a seeming self-evident agreed meaning in modern pragmatics – from the historian's point of view.	*Use:* Such research reinterprets a historical analytic/intellectual construct from the modern analyst's point of view, hence making such diachronically distant terms – and the sociopragmatic norms such terms cover – accessible for academics working outside of the historical field.

Both examples of lexical historicisation shown in table 2.1 represent historical pragmatics-based contributions to sociopragmatics, and as such they are examples of historicisation in operandi. They illustrate that any type of historicisation (in this case, lexical historicisation) can be bidirectional, involving approaches that move from-synchronic-to-diachronic and the other way around.

2.2.2 Historicisation of data

A body of research has engaged in historicisation by exploring cross-overs between historical and modern data. In a similar way to other types of historicisation, this type of research – which I define here as "historicisation of data" – is a two-way street. That is, one can examine the pragmatic characteristics of modern data by looking into its historical counterpart and, vice versa, one may attempt to reconstruct the characteristics of historical data (provided that a historical data type is somehow scarce) by using modern data as a starting point.

The former line of research has been far more popular than the latter. For instance, in the context of digital communication, various pragmatic studies have engaged in exploring digital data by comparing it with historical datatypes; some representative works in this area include Carey (2005), Giltrow and Stein (2009), and Herring, Stein and Virtanen (2013). At the same time, studies working on historical behaviour in languages with no written history unavoidably need to follow a from-synchronic-to-diachronic route to reconstruct how historical data might have looked like by using modern data as a departure point (see a detailed discussion on this problem in Basso 1996).

What interconnects all such studies is that academics who have pursued an interest in historicisation by somehow contrasting data types (including digital pragmatic phenomena) share an interest in the *evolution* of a mode of interaction. This body of research represents an important contribution to the area of contrastive pragmatics (e.g. House 1993). Furthermore, this evolutionary take is particularly relevant to digital communication in that it reveals that many seemingly "modern" (digital) phenomena have historical antecedents, and interpersonal communication in the digital age cannot be fetishised as saliently different from other realms of interpersonal interaction across space and time.

2.2.3 Interactional historicisation

Table 2.2 summarises the two major approaches to interpersonal interactional historicisation.

"Interactional pragmatic approaches adopted for historical data" represent the from-synchronic-to-diachronic part of interactional historicisation. Previous research has demonstrated the power of synchronic frameworks in the study of historical interactional phenomena, such as politeness (including studies that have tested Brown and Levinson 1987 on historical English, e.g. Jucker 2012), disputes (e.g. Blum-Kulka, Blondheim & Haconen 2002), and humour (Attardo 1994).

"Historically-grounded interpersonal interactional approaches" encompass cross-disciplinary research that merge pragmatics with approaches grounded in the study of historical data. The key rationale behind engaging in such cross-disciplinary work is that the use of historically-grounded frameworks in the study of synchronic data provides alternative analytic insights to those which

Table 2.2: Approaches to interpersonal interactional historicisation.

Interactional approaches adopted for the study of historical data	Historically-grounded interpersonal interactional approaches
Example: Using Brown and Levinson's (1987) seminal work to examine Middle English (im)politeness behaviour (e.g. Jucker 2010)	*Example:* The examination of modern interaction through a historically-grounded framework, such as research on etiquette (e.g. Paternoster 2015)
Use: Explains the dynamics of interaction in historical data through modern lenses	*Use:* Brings historically-grounded concepts into the analysis of modern data

one would achieve by using synchronic-focused frameworks. Importantly, to date very little work has been done either to systematically summarise such research that I am introducing here as "historically-grounded interpersonal interactional approaches" to historicisation, or to exploit the implications of such research to historicisation per se. Thus, the present chapter in a sense refocuses or reintroduces such research from the perspective of historicisation, by using ritual research as a case study (section 2.3). Ritual in my view covers morally-loaded interactional practices in contexts in which rights and obligations prevail. Ritual tends to operate with a complex participation structure, and is deployed by groups of language users to reinforce rights and obligations in a theatrical morally-loaded fashion (Kádár 2017).[2] Note that the "group" of persons who perform a ritual may be a loose one, i.e. it is often the case that ritual engagement somehow brings together the people on the street. An important aspect of ritual as an analytic concept is that it is grounded in historical research. While ritual researchers have interconnected ritual with modern urban life (cf. Goffman's 1967 seminal work), ritual as a core concept has remained very much historical, and all attempts to interconnect it with modernity have set out from the assumption that ritual is predominantly historically-grounded.[3] Importantly, many analytic constructs of ritual research – such as "liminality" – need often to be "reinterpreted" for synchronic research

---

[2] Note that this definition refers to "ritual" in a conventional sense, and it does not cover "contact rituals" in ordinary life.
[3] This assumption has been particularly salient in historical pragmatics, in which it has often been argued that historical communication is "more" ritual than its modern counterpart, and interpersonal communication across languages and cultures has gone through a process of "deritualisation" in modernity (Bax 2004, 2010).

(Kádár 2017). This also illustrates that the field essentially follows a from-historical-to-modern approach. Note that ritual theory provides an example par excellence for a historically-grounded interpersonal interactional analysis for two reasons:
- Its academic train of thought: By essence, ritualists unvoidably approach the object of their study from a historical angle to a certain degree, i.e. they capture ritual through its interrelatedness (or the lack of such interrelatedness) with history. This trend is valid even to ritual theory such as Goffman's (1967) seminal work, which focuses on ritual in secular urban settings. For instance, by developing "face" as a sacred concept to describe the operation of ritual and thus introducing the historical concept of sacredness into urban sociology, Goffman implicitly interconnected urban rituals with their historical tribal counterparts.
- Its moral focus: Ritual research operates with a focus on concepts of morality that are prevalent in historical data. For instance, Kádár and Márquez Reiter (2015) point out that rites of bystander intervention in many secular modern Euro-Atlantic cultures are centred on the ancient moral concept of being a "Good Samaritan", and follow schemas of chivalrous challenges.

The present chapter will provide a case study of the operationalisation of ritual theory in the historicisation of interactional phenomena, by examining online shaming in the early twenty-first century. I will argue that the ways in which the computer-mediated practice of shaming works is not essentially different from the historical practice of public shaming. The main difference between this analysis and that of research categorised above as "historicising data" is that I do not pursue an interest in parallels between datatypes that record shaming or attempt to look into the diachronic development of shaming, but rather explore the dynamics of this practice from an interactional ritual point of view, and by this means reveal similarities between modern online shaming incidents and historically recorded events.

Note that ritual is only one of many directions through which historically grounded theory can be brought into the analysis of contemporary interpersonal interaction (see also section 2.1). For example, it is worthwhile to examine modern politeness through the concept of "etiquette" (see Paternoster 2015). In a similar way to ritual, "etiquette" is a phenomenon that tends to be approached predominantly from a historical angle, and which involves various technical terms that have been developed for the analysis of historical data (in a similar fashion with "liminality").

The present section has attempted to overview the diverse ways through which historicisation can operate. In what follows I illustrate how interpersonal interactional historicisation – in particular, its historically grounded version – can be operationalised, with the aid of a case study.

2.3 The case study

As a case study, I analyse online shaming practices, which include practices through which a group of internet users jointly target a person who has, or is claimed to have, committed a major moral trespass. Shaming is a supreme example of historicising the digital: outside of pragmatics, various scholars have insightfully demonstrated that the practice of shaming is deeply embedded in human history (see e.g. Webb 2015; Suler 2016; and Stroud 2018). Such previous research has astutely manifested the key similarities that exist between archaic and modern practices of public punishment of shaming, and as such they have successfully historicised a seemingly brand-new internet practice of shaming within the broader history of shaming as a form of social punishment. Previous research has thus covered a mainstream form of "historicisation of data"; for instance, it has pointed out that:
- Both modern and historical forms of shaming inflicted significant emotional and potentially physical damage on the target (Suler 2016);
- Historical and modern forms of shaming are both communal practices (Webb 2015);
- From an interactional rhetorical perspective, there is relatively little difference between historical and modern (online) forms of shaming (Stroud 2018).

Whilst these findings are clearly important, from the pragmatician's perspective they do not capture the interactional dynamics that interconnects historical and modern practices of shaming. Previous research has left the pragmatic aspect of shaming relatively untouched, in the sense that relatively little has been said on the pragmatic features through which shaming conventionally operates. To fill this knowledge gap, it is interesting to test the applicability of ritual research to the cross-diachronic analysis of shaming.

As data, I have collected a small set of 30 randomly selected narratives on online shaming, from North American internet sources, selected from a Google search of "online shaming" (henceforth referred to as the 'dataset').[4] I have

---

[4] Data (re)search presented in this chapter was carried out between 5/10/2017 and 9/10/2017.

also collected and observed what I define as "metalexemes", i.e. recurring expressions through which the shamers and the shamed persons are evaluated. There are of course abundant evaluations within narratives on shaming – such as the ones found in the database – made either by the author of these texts or participants/observers of the shaming incident whose voices the texts animate in the form of quotes. In the dataset I found altogether 172 metalexemes made by the perpetrators about the victim and 117 made by the narrator of the event (i.e. author of the report) and members of the public commenting on the incident. The narratives are written by journalists, and they represent various evaluative layers of reports of shaming incidents in that they feature both the voices of the narrator (journalists), and those who experience/witness shaming incidents (in the form of in-text quotes).

I studied this dataset from a historical angle, by approaching it through what historians such as Muir (2005 [1997]) observe of historical shaming practices, in particular historical equivalents of the modern practice of ritual "slut shaming" performed by the Youth Abbeys of late medieval towns. As Muir explains, members of the Youth Abbeys identified and publicly punished "lewd" women and "adulterous" couples, often by gang-raping the former and publicly shaming and occasionally beating up the latter. As Muir insightfully points out, shaming as a practice of "public justice (making)" operated with the following event features:

- Attacks committed by the Youth Abbeys often started in a playful fashion: a group of abbey members surrounded the target and made teasing remarks about her/their perceived immorality; such attacks were often communally and/or religiously justified.
- This "game" became excessively aggressive, often ending in a serious emotional and even physical injury of the targeted person.
- Youth Abbeys had their own "code of behavior": they avoided targeting "moral" women such as "chaste widows" (or, at least, they claimed that they avoid such attacks).
- Town communities initially tolerated the existence of these communities, mainly out of fear of their power; however, with the strengthening of town authority alongside the development of the social regulation of towns, people in charge soon penalised the activity of Youth Abbeys, and there were some serious showdowns between town authorities and Youth Abbeys. Importantly, authorities outlawed Youth Abbey through public notices that denounced the activity of the Abbeys.

These observations help us to examine modern practices of online shaming from an interactional ritual point of view. As Muir (2005 [1997]) reveals, historical narratives on the activities of Youth Abbeys are rather limited in scope, in the respect that they do not record the *actual* language use of these groups. Thus, the historical pragmatician who studies manuscripts may not be able to gather significantly more information on the practices of these groups than the bullet point list above summarises. However, such pieces of information are invaluable in the respect that they help us to theorise a modern form of behaviour from an alternative ritual angle, provided that we accept the fact that modern practices of online shaming are not significantly different from such historical forms of ritual behaviour. A power of this explanation is that it de-fetishises the view that the internet has created unprecedented forms of (aggressive) behaviour (see also section 2.4).

It is worth here to briefly revisit the previously mentioned interactional definition of ritual, which is an interactionally salient and morally-loaded practice (Wuthnow 1989), by which groups of people reinforce rights and obligations (Kádár 2017). There are ritual practices – typically rites of aggression – which reinforce rights and obligations and the related moral order of a community in a violent way. Considering these feature points, it is obvious that shaming is a typical form of aggressive ritual. While such forms of ritual behaviour are usually condoned by the broader society, they tend to be represented through a "moral" lens as "acceptable" or even "appropriate" by the particular group – which is again a key feature of rites of aggression, as the following section will also demonstrate.

2.4 Analysis

The internet has often been regarded as a source of "unprecedented" aggression due to the technological affordances it provides (Kumar et al. 2018). In extreme cases, people can stigmatise a person and drive them to suicide by bombarding them with nasty comments, as recurring incidents have shown. The internet has also become a source of school and workplace abuse. Although it is tempting to exoticise such behaviour as something very new (Herring 2008), the power of historicisation is that it can reveal fundamental pragmatic similarities between online behaviour and its historical antecedents on the one hand, and on the other show that seemingly new forms of interactional behaviour represent ancient quasi-tribal traits.

Interactional ritual analysis of the dataset reveals the following two joint interactional features between the online shaming dataset and narratives on medieval shaming practices:

Firstly, the participants and the observers of a shaming ritual tend to engage in conflictive moralising metadiscourse. Not surprisingly, members of the public frequently use negative metalexemes to morally condemn those who engage in shaming. While of course not everyone condemns shaming, usually those who hear about it or observe it (e.g. as news article authors) feel repelled by shaming events. More surprisingly, the shamers themselves tend to use metalexemes to attack the shamed person, and if the validity of their action is questioned, they frame it through moral lenses. This discursive moral conflict accords with what the author of this chapter has found on online bullying (Kádár 2013, 2017): shaming, as with many other forms of ritual aggression, triggers moral conflict between the perpetrators and the broader public. This tension becomes evident if one looks into the metapragmatics of such events (cf. Kádár & Márquez Reiter 2015). In the 30 online narratives studied, one can identify the following groups of metalexemes.

Table 2.3: Metalexemes in the data studied.

Made by the perpetrators	Frequency of occurrence (out of 172 metalexemes)	Made by the narrator/members of public	Frequency of occurrence (out of 117 metalexemes)
sexual metalexemes ("slut", "perv", "twat", etc.)	53.4% (92)	behavioural metalexemes ("cruel", "vicious", "antisocial")	66.6% (78)
physical metalexemes ("ugly", "slutty", "look like shit", etc.)	33.2% (57)	social metalexemes ("mob", "gang", etc.)	33.4% (39)
behavioural metalexemes ("bully", "evil", "sociopath", etc.)	13.4% (23)		

Considering the modest size of the data, these figures are of course only of illustrative value here. If one looks into the proportion of metalexeme categories in table 2.3, it reveals surprising similarities with what historians like Muir (2005 [1997]) have found about medieval practices of shaming. The most significant metalexeme that the perpetrators of shaming incidents use is sexual, followed by metalexemes of physical characteristics, and only after this come those words that re-enact higher-order moral values. Note that sexuality and imperfect physical values are closely interrelated in moral conflicts (e.g. Omansky Gordon & Rosenblaum 2010): they represent the attacked person as a deviant who is a "misfit" in society, and they often co-occur. These results are thought-provoking if one considers that most of the present-day shaming incidents take place in contexts in which the shamers seem to fight for a justifiable cause, such as stopping animal cruelty (see the case example below). This shows interesting similarity with Muir's discussion of medieval shaming where sexually-loaded shaming was morally cloaked – e.g. the perpetrators often presented themselves as "defenders" of religious values. The metalexemes used by the narrator of these events and members of the public also show similarity with how reactions to the activities of Youth Abbeys are described by historians such as Muir (2005 [1997]).

Secondly, rites of aggression (and shaming is not an exception) tend to become excessively aggressive, basically because ritual as a phenomenon triggers increasingly excessive emotive communal engagement (Collins 2004). In the case of rites of aggression, this excessive engagement manifests itself in the form of verbal and physical threats because the very essence of such rites is to become a form of folk-justice. Again, if one considers descriptions of historical cases of shaming, it is evident that these rites physically threatened and, in many cases, destroyed the shamed person. In modern times an online threat may less easily be a physical one than verbal threats in medieval towns, also because these threats take place in cyberspace and the perpetrators may not be able to form a collaborating group (i.e. coordinate their efforts). Yet, manifestations of shaming show cross-diachronic similarity, in that modern forms seem to follow a from-condemnation-to-threat pattern, similarly to the practices of Youth Abbeys who initially playfully ridiculed their victims, and then resorted to violent physical attacks. In practically all of the 30 narratives studied in the dataset, online shaming is represented as a practice resulting in a sense of physical threat that forces the targeted person to close their social media account, call the police, relocate, and so on.

Due to space limitations, in what follows let us refer to two fragments of a case example from the dataset studied, which reports the digital shaming of Kyle Quinn (wrongly accused of holding white supremist views) and big-game hunter, Kendall Jones; the underlined words in the text refer to metalexemes that have been examined as part of the analysis.

> *Internet shaming: When mob justice goes viral*
>
> *The words FOR SHAME have long been spoken to people accused of offensive behavior. Now, thanks to the Internet, those words (and worse) can be sent, sometimes unjustifiably, to millions around the world. [. . .]*

Last Friday night, Kyle Quinn, an assistant professor at the University of Arkansas, was enjoying a pleasant night out with his wife at Crystal Bridges Museum in Bentonville, Ark. [...]

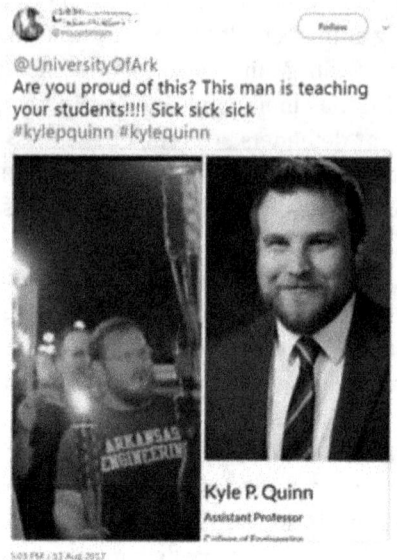

A white nationalist marching in Charlottesville was misidentified on social media as University of Arkansas professor Kyle Quinn. The hate mail started pouring in.

While Quinn was at that museum in Arkansas, white supremacists were gathering in Charlottesville, Virginia – and on the Internet, outraged onlookers misidentified Quinn as one of the participants.

[...]

Quinn felt his personal safety was threatened.

The Internet mob was so aggressive that the real man in the photo – Andrew Dodson – came forward, expressing guilt that attacks were directed at Kyle Quinn.

[...]

If you're a woman, [...] the abuse can go to a whole new level of viciousness.

Kendall Jones was a Texas cheerleader who enjoyed big-game hunting with her father. Her hunts were licensed and legal, and big game hunters routinely take trophy pictures. But Jones' photos went viral.

And the messages poured in: " 'Hi. I am going to find you, and I'm going to rape you, and torture you, and rip each of your limbs off one by one until you have the most painful death.' 'You're disgusting.' 'You're ugly.' 'You're fat.' 'Your hair is ugly.' 'Your eyes are too far apart.' 'You look like a horse.'

"Can you say that to someone? Much less say it to their face?" she laughed.

(CBS News 2017)

The first part of the extract illustrates that what begins as an increasing number of stand-alone attacks ends up with the victim (the university professor) being forced out of his house, not unlike unfortunate "adulterous" couples in medieval towns whose lodgings were raided by the Youth Abbeys. For instance, it is interesting to compare the course of events here with Muir's (2005 [1997]: 110) following account:

> The case of Florie Nallo, the Lyonnaise widow ... who married one of her servants, illustrates how a charivari [the mocking ritual practice of Italian Youth Abbeys] could turn dangerously sour. After parading around the newlyweds' house and raising a racket for about an hour, the journeymen performing the charivari broke in the door. Etienne Tisserand, the servant who had become a master by marrying the mistress, tried to bribe the revelers with a paltry sum that was insufficient to supply drinks for the several dozen men in the group. Dismissing the bribe with contempt, they promised to return in the next evening. The following day Tisserand publically insulted the master of the journeymen who had organized the charivari, and when a small group again showed up outside Tisserand's house that night, he met them armed with a stick and supported by some friends. The journeymen responded by arming themselves with tools and weapons, and in the ensuing exchange Tisserand was mortally wounded from a pistol shot.

While Tisserand's case is different from that of Quinn and Jones – in that the latter do not get hurt – the events show definite similarities. Tisserand is stigmatized just as Quinn and Jones are: he is claimed to inappropriately marry his mistress. In addition, the initially honorous game gradually builds up into a very dangerous course of events. At the beginning, members of the Youth Abbey only shout things outside but, as the narrative explains, due to their large number ("several dozen men") ultimately they feel strong enough to break in and deliver the threat of returning. While we can only speculate about why Tisserand decided to try to fight off the mob when they returned the next day, it is very likely that psychologically he felt equally vulnerable as Quinn and Jones. In an early modern Italian city – in which people were closely interconnected – the public humiliation of charivari must have had a detrimental effect on him.

The second part shows the complexity of the moral conflicts that underlie shaming practices across historical periods. For instance, in the above-cited case, members of the public shame Kendall Jones as a cruel person, while the narrator represent the shamers as a "mob". In addition, the shaming kicks off in the pretext of animal cruelty, but it is centred on sexuality and physical inappropriacy. Note that while describing Jones as "ugly" seems to follow the argumentative line that she is "not more beautiful than the animals she hunts", as social psychologists and sociologists have demonstrated (Omansky Gordon & Rosenblaum 2010), taunts regarding sexuality and physical unattractiveness tend to go hand in hand. Again, if we look into descriptions of how Youth Abbeys behaved, it is clear that in both historical and modern times alleged violations of norms are regarded as pretexts for shaming via sexual aggression:

> The rapists and, unless they had mistakenly chosen their victim without proper sensitivity of public opinion, the rest of the community considered her to be the guilty party. Typically, she had broken or appeared to break the normal rules of sexual behaviour: she was a servant kept as a concubine by her master, the mistress of a priest, an "abandoned" wife. The boys acted, therefore, as enforcers of the habitual misogyny of the community
> (Muir 2005 [1997]: 34)

While such misogyny is definitely more covert in many present-day societies compared with how it used to be in early modern towns, two factors indicate that it has remained a component of public humiliation:
1. the high frequency of sexually-loaded metacomments in modern online data (see table 2.3), and
2. the fact that sexually-loaded threats (in particular, against females) tend to occur in instances that are unrelated to sexual behaviour.

To sum up, the present section has demonstrated how historically-grounded interpersonal approaches to historicisation can be utilised. It is hoped that this brief case study triggers further interest in this approach.

2.5 Conclusion

This chapter has discussed the principle of historicisation and offered an overview of the approaches that allow us to engage with this approach to interactional data. Although the principle of historicisation has been rarely mentioned in pragmatics, it can bring a cluster of new insights into both diachronic and synchronic research. The chapter has illustrated that historicisation involves various analytic procedures: it interconnects a cluster of possible approaches by means of which historical and present-day data can be studied from a pragmatic angle.

There are various tasks for future research on this area. For example, it is important to establish synergies between historical and contrastive pragmatics –

and of course the principle of historicisation is key to such synergies – by examining the historicity of concepts and forms of behaviour across a variety of lingua-cultures. In addition, it remains an important task to develop more historically grounded analytic frameworks to "historicise" modern interactional phenomena, hence increasing the visibility of historical pragmatics. These areas of future research illustrate that "historicisation" is an intriguing concept.

References

Attardo, Salvatore. 1994. *Linguistic theories of humour*. Berlin: De Gruyter Mouton.
Basso, Keith H. 1996. *Wisdom sits in places: Landscape and language among the Western Apache*. Albuquerque: University of New Mexico Press.
Bax, Marcel. 2004. Out of ritual. A semiolinguistic account of the origin and development of indirect language behavior. In Marcel Bax, Barend van Heusden & Wolfgang Wildgen (eds.), *Semiotic evolution and the dynamics of culture*, 155–213. Bern: Peter Lang.
Bax, Marcel. 2010. Epistolary presentation rituals: Face-work, politeness, and ritual display in early-modern Dutch letter writing. In Jonathan Culpeper & Dániel Z. Kádár (eds.), *Historical (im)politeness*, 37–86. Bern: Peter Lang.
Blum-Kulka, Shoshana, Menahem Blondheim & Gonen Haconen. 2002. Traditions of dispute: From negotiations of Talmudic texts to the arena of political discourse in the media. *Journal of Pragmatics* 34 (10/11). 1569–1594.
Brown, Penelope & Stephen Levinson. 1987. *Politeness: Some universals in language usage*. Cambridge, UK: Cambridge University Press.
Carey, James W. 2005. Historical pragmatism and the internet. *New Media & Society* 7 (4). 443–455.
CBS News. 2017. Internet shaming: When mob justice goes virtual. 20 August 2017. https://www.cbsnews.com/news/internet-shaming-when-mob-justice-goes-virtual/ (accessed 17 July 2019).
Collins, Randall. 2004. *Interaction ritual chains*. Princeton: Princeton University Press.
Ehlich, Konrad. 1992. On the historicity of politeness. In Richard J. Watts, Sachiko Ide & Konrad Ehlich (eds.), *Politeness in language: Studies in its history, theory and practice*, 71–108. Berlin: De Gruyter Mouton.
Giltrow, Janet & Dietr Stein. 2009. Genres in the internet: Innovation, evolution, and genre theory. In Janet Giltrow & Dietr Stein (eds.), *Genres in the internet: Issues in the theory of genre*, 1–25. Amsterdam: John Benjamins.
Goffman, Erving. 1967. *Interaction ritual. Essays on face-to-face behavior*. Garden City: Doubleday.
Haggis, Jane & Mary Holmes. 2011. Epistles to emails: Letters, relationship building and the virtual age. *Life Writing* 8 (2). 169–185.
Herring, Susan. 2003. Media and language change: Introduction. *Journal of Historical Pragmatics* 4 (1). 1–17.
Herring, Susan C. 2008. Questioning the generational divide: Technological exoticism and adult constructions of online youth identity. In David Buckingham (ed.), *Youth, identity, and digital media*, 71–92. Cambridge, MA: MIT Press.

Herring, Susan, Dieter Stein & Tuija Virtanen. 2013. *Pragmatics of computer mediated communication*. Berlin: De Gruyter Mouton.

House, Juliane. 1993. Toward a model for the analysis of inappropriate responses in native/nonnative interactions. In Gabriele Kasper & Shoshana Blum-Kulka (eds.), *Interlanguage pragmatics*, 161–182. Oxford: Oxford University Press.

Ide, Sachiko. 1989. Formal forms and 'discernment': Two neglected aspects of linguistic politeness. *Multilingua* 8 (2/3). 223–248.

Jucker, Andreas H. 2010. "In curteisie was set ful muchel hir lest": Politeness in Middle English. In Jonathan Culpeper & Dániel Z. Kádár (eds.), *Historical (im)politeness*, 175–200. Bern: Peter Lang.

Jucker, Andreas H. 2012. Changes in politeness cultures. In Terttu Nevelainen & Elizabeth Closs Traugott (eds.), *The history of English*, 422–433. Oxford: Oxford University Press.

Jucker, Andreas H., Gerd Fritz & Franz Lebsanft. 1999. Historical dialogue analysis: Roots and traditions in the study of the Romance languages, German and English. In Andreas H. Jucker, Gerd Fritz & Franz Lebsanft (eds.), *Historical dialogue analysis*, 1–33. Amsterdam: John Benjamins.

Kádár, Dániel Z. 2013. *In-group ritual and communication: Ritual interaction in groups*. Basingstoke: Palgrave Macmillan.

Kádár, Dániel Z. 2017. *Politeness, impoliteness and ritual: Maintaining the moral order in interpersonal interaction*. Cambridge, UK: Cambridge University Press.

Kádár, Dániel Z. & Michael Haugh. 2013. *Understanding politeness*. Cambridge, UK: Cambridge University Press.

Kádár, Dániel Z. & Rosina Márquez Reiter. 2015. (Im)politeness and (im)morality: Insights from intervention. *Journal of Politeness Research* 11 (2). 139–260.

Kádár, Dániel Z. & Annick Paternoster. 2015. Historicity in metapragmatics: A study on "discernment" in Italian metadiscourse. *Pragmatics* 25 (3). 369–391.

Kumar, Ritesh, Aishwarya N. Reganti, Akshit Bhatia & Tushar Maheshwari. 2018. Aggression-annotated corpus of Hindi-English code-mixed data. https://arxiv.org/abs/1803.09402 (accessed 31 May 2019).

Muir, Edward. 2005 [1997]. *Ritual in early modern Europe*. Cambridge, UK: Cambridge University Press.

Omansky Gordon, Beth & Karen Rosenblaum. 2010. Bringing disability into the sociological frame: A comparison of disability with race, sex, and sexual orientation statuses. *Disability & Society* 16 (1). 5–19.

Paternoster, Annick. 2015. *Cortesi e scortesi. Percorsi di pragmatica storica da Castiglione a Collodi*. Rome: Carocci.

Richerson, Peter J. & Morten H. Christiansen. 2013. *Cultural Evolution: Society, technology, language, and religion*. Cambridge, MA: MIT Press.

Stroud, Scott R. 2018. The Jaina rhetoric of non-violence and the culture of online shaming. In Michele Kennerly & Damien Smith Pfister (eds.), *Ancient rhetorics and digital networks*, 252–273. Tuscaloosa: University of Alabama Press.

Suler, John R. 2016. *Psychology of the digital age*. Cambridge, UK: Cambridge University Press.

Webb, Lewis Mark. 2015. Shame transfigured: Slut-shaming from Rome to cyberspace. *First Monday* 20 (4). http://journals.uic.edu/ojs/index.php/fm/article/view/5464/4419 (accessed 31 May 2019).

Wuthnow, Robert. 1989. *Meaning and moral order: Explorations in cultural analysis*. Berkeley: University of California Press.

Caroline Tagg and Mel Evans
3 Spelling in context: A transhistorical pragmatic perspective on orthographic practices in English

3.1 Introduction

This chapter focuses on new media spelling variation (or "respelling") not only to identify what is "new" about digital orthographic practices, but also as a way of reflecting more widely on a transhistorical analysis of language- and literacy-related practices in English. It considers the implications of a *transhistorical pragmatic* approach for our understanding of processes of technologically mediated language change, identity construction, and the dynamics of social interaction. Drawing on the uniformitarian principle (Bergs 2012; Labov 1972), we argue for the value of a comparative approach which seeks to identify and account for both change and continuity between time periods, whilst also recognising the historically and culturally situated nature of contemporary practices and their apparent historical antecedents.

To illustrate how transhistorical pragmatics might enable a more critical and informed assessment of English language practices, we undertake a comparative analysis of spelling in two datasets: twenty-first century text messages and sixteenth-century correspondence. Unlike other studies of new media spelling, we focus not on identifying re-spelt forms but on writers' orthographic consistency, thus enabling comparisons with spelling in a pre-standardised era (Evans 2012, 2013). Our focus is on the wider ideological contexts in which these materials were produced; particularly the impact of orthographic standardisation and the (potential) social meanings that may result. Differences in cultural context entail differences in social meaning: spelling meant different things to our writers, because of the contrasting language ideologies in the two periods. However, the comparison of the two datasets also reveals commonalities that may not be expected, given the four-century-long temporal gap. The twenty-first century digital media and early modern letter writers show similarities in some aspects of spelling practice, such as their consistency in practice, and in the development of personal idiosyncracies, even if the formal properties are more distinct. More abstractly, the analysis highlights the continuities

Caroline Tagg, The Open University, Milton Keynes, e-mail: caroline.tagg@open.ac.uk
Mel Evans, University of Leicester, Leicester, e-mail: mel.evans@leicester.ac.uk

https://doi.org/10.1515/9783110670837-005

over time in the relationships between technology, ideology, and linguistic and social practices, even if the micro-level linguistic forms and their contextual functions diverge across the datasets from the two periods.

3.2 Introducing transhistorical pragmatics

3.2.1 A comparative approach

Understanding what is new about early twenty-first century spelling practices in digital media – as with any communicative practice – involves an appreciation of what is *not* new; that is, of establishing continuities in practice and enduring elements of human communication which transcend historical boundaries. Our argument is that this understanding can be reached through a transhistorical pragmatic approach which views language practices not only as lived experiences grounded in historical contexts but also as potentially atemporal human endeavours to communicate. Our proposed approach seeks to identify continuities in phenomena across historical periods to the present day, and to explain perceived and real differences. At its heart, then, are the principles of comparison and of continuity: the need to look beyond the immediate social context to other times and spaces in order to appreciate the wider trajectories and cycles from which contemporary practices emerge.

The principal way in which we approach communicative practices transhistorically is through a *comparative or contrastive approach* which explores the realisations of a practice – or how it has been conceptualised by researchers – across multiple points in time. This approach can be carried out *directly*, as demonstrated in Seargeant's study (this volume), and/or through comparative analysis of practices involved across synchronic snapshots (see also Kesseler & Bergs 2003; Lötscher 1981). Transhistorical research can also be conducted *indirectly*, though the application to one time period of a concept developed to describe practices in another, as in Kádár's use of the concept of ritual abuse (this volume), developed to explain medieval data, for understanding online aggression. In this chapter, we adopt elements of both approaches, comparing individuals' spelling practices across two points in time using the concept of consistency, developed for the analysis of pre-standardisation spelling in English (Evans 2012, 2013).

A diachronic comparative method of interrogation relies on the uniformitarian principle (Bergs 2012: 84) for its validity. The principle states that throughout history "the forces operating to produce linguistic changes today are of the same kind and order" (Labov 1972: 275), entailing that all possible or impossible linguistic configurations have (most likely) always had that status, with configurations presumed to remain constant over time (Bergs 2012: 85). The uniformitarian principle is a necessary conceptual step for the examination of the past, underpinning interpretations and theorisations of (linguistic) practices made at a temporal remove. Without it, our incomplete knowledge of the past would subsume the evidence we do have, prohibiting extrapolations and generalisations of the (socio)linguistic system. Traugott (2017: 290) advocates treating "historical records as a benchmark", whilst recognising their incompleteness. Transhistorical pragmatics draws on the uniformitarian principle to interpret the incomplete evidence we have of language and communication from historical periods.

Bergs (2012) cautions against an uncritical interpretation of (historical) linguistic evidence without sufficient contextualisation. Whilst linguistic processes may have remained the same, the social meanings and contexts of use of a particular linguistic form or feature may not (see Traugott 2017: 290–1). In the case of digital media, whilst similarities between modern and historical interaction show persuasively that digital phenomena have historical antecedents and should not be conceived of solely as different and unique, we cannot also assume that what looks the same to us was necessarily experienced or interpreted in the same way by people living in historically and culturally distinct social contexts. To be effective, therefore, analysis of digital phenomena needs to recognise and account for the historically and culturally situated nature of contemporary affordances, practices and ideologies, and attend to how this environment of use may vary across time and space. *Contextual breadth* – meaning the contextual factors that shape how a linguistic feature or practice is used and its social significance – is a critical component of transhistorical pragmatics, as it helps to ensure that, when engaging with *historical depth*, interpretations do not become anachronistic.

3.2.2 Context in transhistorical pragmatics

The contextualisation of linguistic data is a central tenet of pragmatics, as well as other linguistic disciplines, such as sociolinguistics, which seek to understand "language in use". Moving on from the early treatment of language as an abstract construct, linguists now recognise the role of context and its complexity as discursively co-constructed through interaction. As one example of this principle, in his ethnographic research Gumperz (1982) observed how "contextualisation cues" – meaning "any feature of linguistic form that contributes to the signalling of contextual presuppositions" (Gumperz 1982: 131) – index the social framing of an utterance and can indicate shifts in footing: "a change in the alignment we take to ourselves and the others present as expressed in the way we manage the production or reception of an utterance" (Goffman 1981: 128). Importantly, contextualisation cues do not emerge *a priori* from pre-existing or stable associations between context and language, but are part of the process of context and meaning creation.

The pragmalinguistic study of digital media since the late twentieth century, which focusses on "speech-like" written interactions mediated through computers between geographically separated participants, has further problematised understandings of context. This is due in part to the observation that online interactions are characterised by a "doubling of place" (Moore 2004), in the sense that digital media makes relevant virtual as well as physical spaces, entailing complex processes of contextualisation (Androutsopoulos 2014; Tagg, Seargeant & Brown 2017). The fact that interactants do not typically share a physical space, and thus do not have access to the contextualisation cues available in face-to-face interaction (such as prosody), means that people must discursively co-construct shared communicative spaces (Lyons 2014), often through visual and largely text-based resources such as respelling and emoji. This understanding of online context has been shaped by the epistemological stances and data collection methods characteristic of digital media studies, which initially tended to assume a distinction between the "offline" and the "online", approaching the study of the latter through analysis of screen-based digital data, rather than (for example) seeing new media as a communicative tool used by people in real-world contexts (Androusopoulos & Staehr 2018). Whilst "blended data" (whereby screen data is complemented by participants' elicited commentary) is now standard practice (Androutsopoulos & Staehr 2018: 121), some studies go further in exploring the integration of digital media into people's offline lives, and the fluid transitions between offline and online contexts (Cohen 2015; Dovchin, Pennycook and Sultana 2008). Thus transhistorical pragmatics must engage with the challenge of delimiting "context" in digital spaces, and how it might be retrieved.

The difficulty of establishing context is also pertinent to the analysis of historical language practices. Historical pragmatics, a sociologically-based approach which relies on "empirical data in context", focussing "on the joint negotiation of meaning" (Taavitsainen & Jucker 2010: 4), addresses the challenge of historical context by undertaking analysis within three (related) frames. The first, "pragmaphilology", seeks to understand the properties of a text or texts of a particular historical period in the original communicative context; it therefore shares a similar focus on context as digital media studies in the interpretation of language practices. The second, "pragma-historical linguistics", looks at the "communicative causes of language change" (Taavitsainen & Jucker 2010: 14), examining how the requirements of a speaker, and the shape of their communicative context, including technological developments, informs the development of languages across time. A third framework, "diachronic pragmatics", takes the synchronic evidence considered in "pragmaphilogical" approaches, and explores the connections and developments that link such evidence across different time periods. The main challenge of each approach arises from the limited ability to define and understand what constitutes context in the past: "the further removed the period under scrutiny is from our own, the more difficult it is to develop an accurate picture. What looks familiar might have had different meanings [... and] motivations guiding communicators may differ in unpredictable ways" (Taavitsainen & Jucker 2010: 12). Elsewhere, other linguistic disciplines, as they become more fine-grained and therefore contextualised in their approach (e.g. Brinton 2017 on syntactic change), are also grappling with this problem and developing methodologies in response. Corpus-based research, in particular, can provide a useful point of contrast, and a means of checking the validity of interpretative assumptions (Brinton 2017; Hilpert & Gries 2016).

3.2.3 The diachronic aspect

With important exceptions (discussed below), both historical and present-day studies of language-in-use have neglected the *historical* dimensions of context. Recognition that the significance of context cannot be constrained to the immediate setting and situation is evident in Malinowski's (1923) descriptions of the cultural events surrounding the language use of the Tobriand people of Papua. This could only be understood, as Halliday and Hasan (1985: 6) put it, with reference also to "the whole cultural history behind the participants, and behind the kind of practices they were engaging in, determining their significance for the culture". In line with this, central to many studies of language-in-use is the recognition of *habitus* (Bourdieu 1977) or the historical body; the recognition that people bring to interactions a history of personal experience and an understanding of wider cultural and social norms and genres (Scollon & Scollon 2004). This needs to be matched with a foregrounding of concern for other historical aspects of a communicative encounter, such as space or communication technologies. In their study of "metrolingualism", Pennycook and Otsuji (2015: 137) explore "the city as palimpsest as different texts in different languages are written over each other", considering the implications this has for our understanding of present-day communicative practices.

A transhistorical pragmatic approach foregrounds the historical dimensions of context, focussing on the development of technologies and social practices, to enrich our understanding of contemporary language practices. The approach thus examines the historical development of a feature and/or practice diachronically (cf. diachronic form-to-function and function-to-form mapping within historical pragmatics). A *diachronic reading* might consider, for example, the way in which new media spelling in the early twenty-first century is built on existing patterns of non-standard spelling in pre-digital texts like graffiti, and how it diffused from internet chat forums to SMS (e.g. Shortis 2016). The specific temporal range – spanning decades, centuries, or even millennia – should be sensitive to the linguistic feature and associated technologies in question. In this chapter's discussion of historical orthography, diachrony is considered firstly by situating spelling practices in their respective historical contexts, and secondly by tracing the development of individuals' orthographic styles within their lifetimes.

Transhistorical pragmatics is therefore aligned with historical pragmatics proper. A robust historical pragmatic approach should investigate the phenomenon of interest closely, and in context; it should be comparative, between one time-frame and another; and it should also consider the evolution of function and form (Taavitsainen & Jucker 2010: 6–7). Our intention is not to dilute the field, but instead offer an approach with a different emphasis that is compatible with, and complementary to, existing work. Transhistorical pragmatics is aligned explicitly with the practices of a selected context, i.e. twenty-first century digital media, which it seeks to contextualise through comparison with earlier (or later) practices and contexts: to check what is new, how it is new, and why that might be the case. In doing so, it utilises analytic approaches that are comparable with those developed within historical pragmatics: contextualised interpretation; comparison with other time periods; and an attention to both similarities and differences between the datasets. Indeed, transhistorical pragmatics can also be understood as a disciplinary effort to build bridges between scholars of the history of (the English) language and those working with digital media. As this chapter illustrates, the conversations taking place within different parts of English language studies show as many parallels and connections as the orthographic practices identified in old and new texts.

3.3 Digital spelling in context

A transhistorical pragmatics approach to non-standard spelling variants in SMS text messaging in the UK at the turn of the twenty-first century entails that the data be understood within the synchronic social, technological and ideological contexts. The present discussion is inevitably selective, but aims to provide a demonstration of transhistorical pragmatics "in action".

"SMS spelling" can be contextualised within a broad timescale as an orthographic development correlating with the end of the print age, and the corresponding rise of the digital. As a linguistic phenomenon, it is an output of a highly literate and educated society, in which ideas about spelling are implicitly and explicitly shaped by the ideology of standards (Milroy & Milroy 1999); that is, by "a set of beliefs in the need for an unchanging standard, even where this is not evident in actual language practices" (Tagg 2012: 312). Despite the wide scope for variation in spelling, both "licensed" (Sebba 2007) and otherwise, English spelling in late modernity is often associated with "knowing how to write words correctly" (Kress 2000: 1), with "respellings" defined as forms which depart from the standard, codified forms found in formal writing (Androutsopoulos 2000; Sebba 2007). Against this broader backdrop, the turn of the twenty-first century witnessed what was described in contemporaneous academic literature as a "media panic" around SMS spelling (Carrington 2005; Shortis 2016; Thurlow 2006).

At the same time, academic studies sought to identify, categorise and interpret patterns of respelling within and across texting communities, showing how respelling as a meaning-making resource was being exploited in the performance of online identities and expressions of group belonging (e.g. Hård af Segerstad 2002; Tagg 2012; Thurlow 2003). These arguments drew on ideas around the meaning-making potential of spelling (and particularly respelling) as a social practice, as outlined by Sebba (2007) who discusses a wide range of spelling practices from sixteenth-century missionary-led spelling reform to the Ali G websites of the early twenty-first century. However, whilst there was some acknowledgement of the relationship between SMS spelling and orthographic practices in older technological contexts (e.g. Shortis 2007), the focus of these empirical studies was primarily on the new. Whilst understandable, this narrow perspective nevertheless entailed that much of the academic discussion was rather insular and isolated, reaffirming and even exoticising differences (Herring 2008: 75) without necessarily acknowledging continuities. The work tended to foreground non-standard forms, rather than exploring the role that respelling played "as part of the text's orthographic *regularities*" (Androutsopoulos 2000: 517; our emphasis). In this respect, Shortis's (2007: 13–14) metaphor of the "extended orthographic palette" is useful in tracing continuities between a period which prioritised the "normative binary choices of print technology" and the subsequent legitimisation of other orthographic choices through the ubiquity and popularity of text messaging and other informal contexts of digital writing. Academic accounts of SMS text messaging as a language – a "mini-language" or supervernacular, in Blommaert's (2012) terms – also overlooked the intersections and continuities with earlier (including non-print) spelling practices.

Contrary to the dominant media narratives of a "broken" spelling and consequently "broken" society, empirical evidence suggests SMS spelling does not represent a break in practices from those established elsewhere in time and space. Instead, SMS respelling draws "upon a tradition of vernacular spelling" (Shortis 2007: 21) remediated through the material constraints of the new medium; "remade by users in their practices" (Shortis 2007: 23). These older practices are primarily located in creative texts (adverts, trade names, song lyrics, literary fiction, comics) and in what Sebba (2007) calls "unregulated" contexts ranging from graffiti to personal correspondence. Respelling practices are attested in the handful of studies examining older technologically mediated contexts such as telegrams (O'Brien 1904), postcards (Gillen & Hall 2010) and nineteenth-century letter-writing (Kesseler & Bergs 2003). In the late twentieth century, the semiotic constraints of early, text-based, computer-mediated communication – such as internet relay chat, bulletin boards, forums – encouraged users to draw on pre-existing text-based resources (such as spelling) to carry out the pragmatic work accomplished in face-to-face contexts through paralinguistic cues (Georgakopoulou 1997). These early practices – which included the invention of the smiley and adoption of angled brackets to delineate the representation of actions – then entered into public consciousness as a "global mass practice" (Shortis 2016: 489) in text messaging. What appeared to some as alien and unintelligible – and was discursively positioned as such by the media – is in fact part of contextualised and dialogic practice: as Deumert (2014: 142) puts it, "similarities are established with existing forms, and existing patterns are exploited, but at the same time writers are able to break through existing molds and invent forms that are unpredictable and original". SMS spelling arose from the same processes and principles as other kinds of linguistic variation. Texters sought to express themselves by drawing on existing (linguistic) resources, and to manipulate and extend them into forms and practices that in time acquired new and shifting meanings.

Despite the relatively short history of the mobile phone, the SMS spelling practices of the early millennium can be reconceptualised as a technologically motivated phase in its ongoing development. In the second decade of the twenty-first century (with the advent of 4G and smartphone technology), the initial technological constraints driving respelling diminished (Shortis 2016). At the same time, there was growing (academic) recognition that respellings were far less frequent and less "harmful" than initially assumed (Tagg 2012). Studies of children's texting practices suggest that respelling often correlates with high literacy achievements (Plester, Wood & Joshi 2009), showing how respelling in the digital age can constitute a deliberate and principled departure from a standard form, reframing SMS spelling not as ignorant or lazy but as playful, self-aware, and socially meaningful.

Yet our understanding of SMS spelling remains limited and partial; existing accounts lack perspective in terms of how distinctive and innovative digital spelling practices really are. To achieve this, the application of context needs to be expanded from the immediate environment – the context typically focussed on by new media analyses of spelling – to encompass a broader longitudinal view that can provide social, technological and ideological counterpoints; in our case, a transhistorical pragmatic analysis that compares and contrasts digital respellings with spellings used in an earlier, pre-standardisation period.

3.4 A transhistorical pragmatic exploration of spelling variation

Our comparative study of spelling in text messaging and sixteenth-century English correspondence seeks to situate present-day digital practices within the longer timeframe of personal writing in English. We do so by reframing SMS spelling in terms of orthographic consistency, thereby enabling comparisons with personal writing from earlier periods, such as the sixteenth century, a period in which English spelling is (like SMS) highly variable, and yet subject to increasing critique. Sixteenth-century manuscript spelling is a tide-mark in the emergence of the present-day written Standard. In the period, printed texts were regularising around a new norm, although debate continues over whether this was a "top-down" and/or "bottom-up" process (Berg & Aranoff 2017). In manuscripts, such as correspondence, writers continued to show a more idiosyncratic and variable orthographic practice into the eighteenth century and beyond (Osselton 1984). That is, inter-speaker inconsistency, rather than consistency, was the norm, with writers seemingly deploying individualized spelling repertoires rather than converging to (or deviating from) a centralized Standard system.

Like text messages, handwritten correspondence is a (potentially) intimate and personal mode of communication between remote interlocutors (spatially and temporally). From this perspective, the configuration of social, technological and ideological factors in the sixteenth century provides a point of comparison with SMS spelling, in order to identify the extent to which the practices (so decried in the modern press) are, in fact, new, and the specific qualities of the identified innovations or continuities. As our discussion will show, the practices show a considerable degree of continuity. It is how they come to "mean", in their technological context, which proves the point of distinction between sixteenth-century epistolary spelling and twenty-first century SMS spelling.

Using a corpus-based approach to reconstruct "repertoires-in-use" (Androutsopoulos 2014), we focus on the micro-level practices of eight individual English (and English-speaking) writers, comparing and contrasting the written variation in the personal letters of four women writers from the second-half of the sixteenth century (Elizabeth I, Bess of Hardwick, Joan Thynne and Elizabeth D'Oyly) with the WhatsApp and SMS text messages of five women (pseudonyms Laura, Kate, Meg, Alice and Joan) in the twenty-first (2004–2014). The selection of women responds, in part, to a mooted sociolinguistic universal that women (due to gendered social structures) are more attuned to sociolinguistic evaluation of variants, and are often more responsive to processes of language change "from above" (Holmes 1993). This potential continuity may provide richer comparative material from across a large temporal divide. That is not to deny that the life opportunities, such as education, of English women in the sixteenth and twenty-first centuries are very different. The nature of historical material means that the evidence of early modern women's manuscript spelling reflects that of the most literate classes – the upper ranks – for whom written language played a key role in their daily affairs (e.g. household management, business and personal correspondence).

Although the sixteenth-century women are all from the upper social ranks (royalty to upper-gentry), their educational backgrounds range from cutting-edge diversity (Queen Elizabeth I) to a more limited, functional curriculum (Joan Thynne; see Evans & Tagg forthcoming). The five women writing in the twenty-first century are from diverse backgrounds but can be described as middle class, with all but one (the oldest, Joan) educated to university-level. With the exception of Alice, they are older than the usual subjects of SMS spelling research, which tends to focus on university students, teens and young adults (e.g. Thurlow 2003). Each individual claimed to have started texting at around 2000, in accordance with the wider cultural boom in SMS text messaging. Period 1 data was collected and analysed as part of a larger SMS corpus (Tagg 2012, 2016); the second period material was collected for the current research (see also Evans & Tagg forthcoming).

Tables 3.1 and 3.2 list the corpora for the two periods. The corpora, and the sub-files within them, are of varying sizes, but there is sufficient material to undertake a comparative analysis.

Table 3.1: SMS corpus.

Name	D.O.B	Period 1			Period 2		
Laura	1976	801 text msgs	14,786 words	17 recipients	2004–7	1645 WhatsApp msgs	14,660 words	4 recipients (3 from Period 1)	2014–15
Kate	1970	133 text msgs	2492 words	1 recipient	2004–7	114 text msgs	3286 words	1 recipient (same as Period 1)	2014–15
Meg	1976	54 text msgs	1598 words	1 recipient	2006–7	227 WhatsApp msgs	2010 words	1 recipient (same as Period 1)	2015
Alice	1984	61 text msgs	933 words	2 recipients	2005–6	50 text msgs	1360 words	1 recipient (also in Period 1)	2014–15
Joan	1954	58 text msgs	553 words	2 recipients	2004–7	51 text msgs	714 words	1 recipient (also in Period 1)	2014–15

Table 3.2: Sixteenth-century women's epistolary spelling (SWES) corpus.

Name	Lifespan	Period 1				Period 2	
Queen Elizabeth I	1533–1603	7 letters	2844 words	3 recipients	1550–56	13 letters 7501	1 recipient	1590–95
Elizabeth Neville	c.1541–1621	11 letters	2747 words	1 recipient	1576–85	5 letters 1054	1 recipient (same as Period 1)	1594–98
Bess of Hardwick	1527–1608	5 letters	1640 words	2 recipients	1550–60	11 letters 3813	5 recipients	1569–78
Joan Thynne	1558–1612	9 letters	2102 words	1 recipient	1575–90	18 letters 14363	2 recipients (1 also in Period 1)	1595–1603

The analysis focusses on three variables which capture different aspects of spelling consistency:
1) individual consistency: how consistent a writer is in their spellings of the same word;
2) preferential forms: which spellings of a given word occur more frequently and can therefore be considered a preferred spelling;
3) standardness: to what extent does the writer use, or not use, forms associated with the written Standard.

The micro-level focus takes a life-span perspective, tracing the spelling conventions over a decade for each writer, in order to establish how (digital) literacy, social change and technological developments impact on our informants' individual orthographic repertoires, read against larger macro-level trends in English orthography. This entails two diachronic dimensions to the analysis: the comparison of present-day English (PDE) and sixteenth-century English spelling; and the potential development of that spelling across the lifespan of each writer (Period 1 and Period 2), situated within their historical sub-period.

We complement the descriptive analysis with meta-textual insights available for each data set (i.e. "blended data"). This includes interview data for the twenty-first century informants, and embedded meta-linguistic evidence for the sixteenth-century informants. This allows us to ascertain, to some degree, how conscious or marked the identified spelling practices are for these informants. Our study highlights the importance of recognising the situated nature of practices at any time.

3.5 Consistency in transhistorical spelling practices

Spelling consistency provides a quantitative measure of the extent to which present-day users of digital media, such as text messaging, are genuinely irregular and inconsistent, as compared with the consistency of the spelling of their predecessors, writing in a very different context of literacy (Evans & Tagg forthcoming). Consistency is calculated from the number of variant spellings used by a given writer for a headword. For example, one writer may use four spellings of the headword English (e.g. <english><englisch><ynglis><inglis>) across a text or texts, whereas another writer may use only two. The latter writer is considered more consistent, because they use a fewer number of variants. This information provides a baseline from which intra- and inter-speaker practices can be compared, and can contextualise more specific properties.

3.5.1 Individual consistency

Within the personal communication of our informants across the two periods, we found (among other patterns) a relatively high degree of consistency in spelling practice. In tables 3.3 and 3.4, the figures represent the percentage of headwords with that number of spelling variants (e.g. in Laura's data, 85.7% of headwords have just one variant).

In the SMS corpus, between 85% and 99% of all word forms are spelt the same way by any one individual (an average of 92%). Most of the variation arises from words with two variant spellings; only three women spell any one headword more than two ways, with the highest number of variants occurring for the headwords *you* (Laura=5; Alice=4), *tomorrow* (Laura=5) and *brother* (Laura=4). For each individual, this variation makes up less than 2% of the total headwords. These findings suggest SMS spelling does not constitute a "new language" but is, as Shortis (2007: 22) puts it, "a constrained variety of writing with some alterations in spelling and grammar". In SWES, the four women also tend towards a one-variant spelling for the majority of words, with one- and two-variant spellings comprising over 80% of spellings. One-variant spellings are less well-established than in the present-day material, comprising an average of 62%. The most variable spellings have six variants: *there, received, desiring* (all in the letters of Joan Thynne) and *faithful* (Bess of Hardwick's letters). Such findings show how a transhistorical approach can put SMS spelling variation into perspective, by highlighting the continuing (and potentially growing) predominance of consistency in a (female) writer's orthographic style, irrespective (perhaps) of the technological innovations. However, this summary plays down the evidence of inter-speaker variation within both corpora. In the SMS corpus, Laura is the least consistent speller (one-variant forms account for around 85% word types), while Joan is very consistent (>95% one-variant forms). In SWES, Joan Thynne is the least consistent (48% one-variant forms) with Elizabeth I the most consistent (73% one-variant forms).

The variation between contemporaneous informants could be explained on the basis of literacy levels. The early modern informants had differing levels of education and experience in using the written word. Elizabeth I was a student of one of the most comprehensive, multilingual educational curriculums of the Renaissance, and Elizabeth Neville also received an education in languages other than English. By comparison, what is known of Bess of Talbot's and Joan Thynne's education suggests it was more restricted to the basics of (vernacular) reading and writing (Evans & Tagg forthcoming). This implies a rough correlation between educational opportunities and the level of consistency for each woman's spelling which could be investigated through statistical analysis of a larger dataset.

Table 3.3: Individual consistency in SMS.

Informant >	Laura		Alice:		Meg		Kate		Joan	
No. variants	Period 1 (%)	Period 2 (%)	Period 1 (%)	Period 2 (%)	Period 1 (%)	Period 2 (%)	Period 1 (%)	Period 2 (%)	Period 1 (%)	Period 2 (%)
1 variant	85.7	86.3	87	90	91	92	94	97	95	99
2 variants	12.4	12.3	11.4	8.8	8.7	5.7	5.7	2.8	4.6	0.8
3+ variants	1.9	1.4	1.3	1	0	0.7	0	0	0	0
Total headwords	1984	2172	149	193	240	274	300	318	86	118

Although the results across speakers show similar practices, the differences in the sizes of individual datasets – which arise from the availability of data in each case – mean that the compared figures should be treated cautiously.

Table 3.4: Individual consistency in SWES.

Informant	Queen Elizabeth I		Elizabeth Neville		Bess of Hardwick		Joan Thynne	
No. Variants	Period 1 (%)	Period 2 (%)	Period 1 (%)	Period 2 (%)	Period 1 (%)	Period 2 (%)	Period 1 (%)	Period 2 (%)
1 Variant	81.5	69.4	68.6	76.1	67	58.8	48.5	48.3
2 Variants	17.2	27.6	28	23.1	27.4	32.8	37.6	39.6
3 Variants	1	2.4	2.7	0.7	4.5	6.8	8.8	8.9
4 Variants	0.3	0.5	0.8	0	1.1	1.2	2.6	2.2
5 Variants	0	0.2	0	0	0	0.3	2.1	0.7
6 Variants	0	0	0	0	0	0	0.5	0.3
Total headwords	297	656	261	134	179	323	194	598

Education provides a less obvious explanation for the (smaller) inter-speaker differences for the SMS corpus. The four present-day women were recipients of a standardised education system; moreover, all except Joan (the most consistent speller) progressed to higher education. Although the current sample permits only tentative interpretation, in line with studies of respelling and children's literacy achievements (Plester, Wood & Joshi 2009) the results seem to point to an inverse relationship to that in SWES: (higher) education might be seen to promote, rather than curtail, inconsistency. This association likely reflects other aspects of the informants' biographical experiences, including their age (which may explain Joan's higher levels of consistency). The data also point to the possibility of individual preference and the development of personal writing habits. Laura stands out as being the most variable speller, and there is no obvious demographic reason why she should spell differently from Meg, who is the same age and has a similar educational background. In interview in 2014, Laura attributed her respelling practice to what we might call an ideology of "functional efficiency" – i.e. she suggested that few of her re-spellings carried indexical meaning but were an ingrained response to the communicative demands or technological constraints of the medium: "I always felt as though it was an easier way of writing ... it makes more sense to use a shorter version which means the same thing".

Intra-speaker variation – that is, the extent to which each informant's spelling consistency changes over time – provides another means of transhistorical pragmatic comparison. In the SMS corpus (c.2004–7 and 2014–5), the data for each woman shows no statistically significant change in consistency over the course of a decade. This appears to contradict current assumptions that technological developments have led users to abandon respelling and abbreviation practices (Shortis 2016). Instead, the evidence suggests that SMS spelling is (now, at least) as much a response to the communicative demands of text messaging as it is to the technological constraints (Thurlow 2003) and also points to the possible formation of spelling habits. In SWES, the pattern is mixed. Thynne and Neville are more consistent in their later correspondence. Bess of Hardwick and Elizabeth I become less consistent. Whilst differences in word counts could influence these trends, it seems tenable that any coherent community-level step-change toward or away from spelling consistency would be observable.

The analysis thus highlights consistency as an enduring feature of orthographic practice across time, in that, although variation is permitted (pre-standardisation; digital media), people are on the whole remarkably consistent: most words are spelt in one or two ways. This (as well as other evidence, discussed below) suggests there might be more continuity than difference between the spelling practices of the past and the twenty-first century digital age.

3.5.2 Preferential forms

The individual variation identified above suggests that writers in both periods have their own preferences. However, it is important to differentiate truly individualized (idiosyncratic) practices from preferences with a broader, potentially sociolectal, status. For example, in the SMS corpus, both Alice and Laura vary their spelling of the headword *you* in more than two ways, but all variants reflect forms and functions attested elsewhere: the letter homophone <u> is found across datasets (e.g. Thurlow 2003) (as well as in Kate's and Meg's data) while the colloquial respelling <ya> is used by numerous SMS users in an attempt to approximate a speech-like quality (Androutsopoulos 2000; Thurlow 2003). Of more interest is the extent to which an individual's practice departs from that of her interlocutors – something we cannot properly gauge from the one-sided datasets used in this analysis. However, previous analysis of Laura's SMS exchanges reveals a consistent use of the spelling variants <u> and <wot> (Tagg 2016) that are not shared by her interlocutors (nor the four women discussed here). The spellings are part of Laura's distinctive orthographic idiolect, resistant to communication accommodation or local orthographic norms. The high frequency, common-core status of these words perhaps makes them more salient candidates for individual preferential respellings.

Sociolectal and idiolectal orthographic variants are evident in the early modern data, as well. 170 words (6.7%) in SWES have three or more variants, with many of these words showing variation across two or more datasets. This offers evidence of a broader commonality in practice e.g. *been, great, have, loving, might, much, received, sayeth, think, very, with, worshipful, would*. Closer analysis reveals that the 3+ variant words share a co-occurrence of common letter-form substitutions in early-modern English. For example, the omission or inclusion of final <e> accounts for 37% of variant spellings in SWES, and alternations of <u/v>, <i/e/y> and <w/u> are also widespread. These variants are typical of contemporary manuscript (and print) spelling practice in the period (Salmon 1999; Kaislaniemi et al. 2017). This evidence supports the interpretation that spelling variation, as a principle, was the norm for these women. Such spellings constitute the typical "noise" of sixteenth-century epistolary orthography.

However, there are also idiolectal spellings reminiscent of those identified in Laura's SMS messages. This includes words spelled distinctively yet consistently, such as Elizabeth I's preferred spelling of *which* <wiche> and Neville's preferred spelling of *you* <yower>, both of which are rare in contemporaneous print and manuscript materials (Evans & Tagg forthcoming). Other idiosyncracies include words where higher inconsistencies – such as the spelling of proper names and placenames, which were less "fixed" in form in the sixteenth century – are not always found. Thus, whilst Bess of Hardwick spells *Cavendish*, her surname during her second marriage, four different ways in five occurrences, and Elizabeth Neville uses four variants across 11 occurrences for her first name, Elizabeth I spells her name the same way throughout her life; a practice linked both to reasons of security (the spelling was part of an elaborate signature which was difficult to forge) and also status, through an authoritative link between the royal sign manual and the royal prerogative (Evans & Tagg forthcoming; Evans 2020). Notably, in material not included in the SWES corpus, Bess of Hardwick also adopted a fixed onomastic spelling upon her third marriage to George Talbot, Earl of Shrewsbury, in the 1580s (Wiggins 2016). The spelling trends for proper names testifies to the importance of a contextualized reading when exploring variation. In this case, the social meaning of consistent spelling can only be recognized against the contemporary cultural norms.

The survey of spelling in SMS and SWES suggests that, for writers in both time periods, spelling is part of their idiolectal repertoire. What is less clear from the textual evidence is its possible role in identity performance and thus any enduring link between identity and spelling. Metalinguistic evidence can be helpful in shedding light on the potential pragmatic meanings of spelling variation for the present-day and early-modern informants. In interviews with the twenty-first century writers, this involved identity claims. For example, Laura saw some respellings, such as g-dropping, as overtly evaluative and indexical of particular stances including indignation on behalf of a friend, as in: "He cant keep gettin pissed and treatin you like that" (Tagg 2016: 73). Similarly, in her explanation of why she stopped using the homophone <u> between the two phases of data collection, Alice constructed its use as childish and no longer "cool" ("I hate using shorthand like u, c and 4 nowadays, I think I see it as something that a young person or a child does"); beliefs that she claimed to draw on when evaluating a friend's continuing use of the homophone. In short, the metalinguistic evidence suggests that informants saw (some of) their own respelling practices as indexical and evaluated those of their interlocutors in the same way.

In SWES, metalinguistic commentary is fairly limited. Joan Thynne and Elizabeth Neville draw attention to the speed of their letters' composition: e.g. "euen so in haste with my beste Loue to your good selfe I ende" (Thynne), and thus provide an excuse for any shortcomings in the letter's content or stylistic form. Both Bess of Hardwick and Queen Elizabeth I use the noun *scribbling* to characterise their writing: the word denoted careless, hasty or thoughtless written expression in the period (OED Online). Bess of Hardwick also describes her correspondence as *rewde*, meaning "unlearned" or "unrefined" (OED Online), and Queen Elizabeth I apologises for her *tedious* and *long* writing. The remarks indicate that the letter's text is functioning as an intermediary agent, a textual representation of the author's persona, shaping their relationship with the recipient. However, whilst these metalinguistic comments indicate the symbolic capital of epistolary writing for the women, they do not highlight spelling directly. *Scribbling* arguably encompasses multiple facets of writing, which may include spelling, but this is conjectural. No letter-writer in the dataset draws attention specifically to spelling practice. The metalinguistic commentary suggests that spelling was not a sufficiently salient feature for any of the four women to warrant explicit comment in the material included in the corpus.

3.5.3 Standardness

The preceding analysis highlighted points of continuity as well as contrast between the spelling practices and nature of consistency in the SMS and epistolary datasets. However, to conclude our analysis it is necessary to consider these findings in relation to the dominant language ideologies of each period. While some commentators describe the digital age as representing a shift in practice and ideology from the conformity of print age (Thompson & Collins this volume), SMS spelling variation is nonetheless produced in a context in which respellings are interpreted in terms of their deviance from a prescribed Standard form. Early modern correspondence, on the other hand, operates in a pre-Standardised context. The relevance, or lack thereof, of the Standard to each dataset's spelling practices is evident in the proportion of Standard spelling forms used in each corpus. In the SMS corpus, 97.8% of headwords include a variant that uses the Standard spelling. By comparison, only 53.3% of headwords in the early modern correspondence use a form that matches the subsequent Standard spelling. The Standard, in its top-down prescribed form, is not a relevant conceptual construct, nor a formal system, for the sixteenth-century writers. Whilst print spelling was beginning to regularise, there was no widespread agreement or enforcement of a particular set of English spellings: spelling was acquired individually, and shaped through local networks (Kaislaniemi et al. 2017). On this basis, we propose that sixteenth-century spelling variation should be read within an "a-Standard" frame – a term preferred to "pre-standard" because it does not presuppose the later development – given that sixteenth-century English spelling, in manuscript contexts, was not prescribed.

Thus, whilst the spelling practices are similar in the two datasets, and one can find continuities between them, their social meanings and motivations are potentially very different. This has two implications for how we understand spelling consistency and its constituent parts in the SWES and SMS datasets. Firstly, the proportion of two or more variant spellings in the SMS messages may have a greater social and semiotic weight for its reader than, say, the 52% variance identified in the sixteenth-century letters of Joan Thynne. As non-standard spelling is "marked" in PDE, the least consistent forms, even in a text message, would draw the attention of the reader in a way that the persistently variable spelling of a sixteenth-century letter may not have (at least, for its intended readership, see Sönmez 2000). In making this argument, we draw on Androutsopoulos's (2000) distinction between "regular" spellings – those that occur in a patterned manner across a text – and "exceptional" ones that stand out from the surrounding text by departing from the text's regular spelling patterns and thus serve as local contextualisation cues (Gumperz 1982). The potential salience of non-standard spelling in the twenty-first century means it can be used in "exceptional" ways for local functions within a text, such as signalling a change in footing, in a way likely not possible in sixteenth-century writing. For example, Tagg (2016) shows how Laura uses mainly Standard spelling when arranging by text message for a friend to join her for a drink, and then keys a switch into a more colloquial speech-like register with the eye dialect form <wot> alongside other non-standard semiotic resources, as she writes 'Wot can i get in for ya?' (that is, what drink can she buy her friend). By comparison, an "exceptional" use of spelling variation seems a less viable resource for pre-standardisation writers, because the lack of a Standard frame entails a less definitive baseline from which a spelling can depart and thus accrue meaning (cf. Sebba's 2007 "zone of social meaning"). Whilst SWES suggests some points of deviation that may have acquired significance (the consistent spelling of <Elizabeth>, the use of idiosyncratic forms <wich> and <yower>), on the whole the pre-standard context reduces expectations among readers for consistency, and potentially impedes recognition of any attempts to build meaning around such exceptional variation.

Secondly, in relation to the regular use of spelling, while Androutsopoulos (2000) focuses on a community's orientation to spoken language in their spelling practices, our data suggests that spelling regularities can also be indexical of an individual voice. Thus, while for a sixteenth-century reader orthographic inconsistency may not be pragmatically meaningful, the relative consistency of Elizabeth I's manuscript spelling may be recognisable, forming part of the queen's epistolary identity (co-occurring with other epistolary features, such as her distinctive handwriting) and indexing her learning and her social uniqueness when compared with her (female) contemporaries. Conversely, the levels of consistency in the text messages likely signal each writer's participation within an emergent sub-culture of text messaging and their positioning within the immediate participation framework vis-a-vis their interlocutors, as well as their wider media/language ideological stances. Within the social, cultural and ideological context of the twenty-first century, the choice of a Standard rather than non-standard form has meaning potential for interlocutors, whose interpretation will be shaped both by the prevailing ideologies of spelling standards and by their awareness of an "extended orthographic palette" in text messaging, where the Standard form is just one choice among others (see Staehr & Madsen's 2014 study of the use of Standard resources in online rap). In sum, we argue that consistency itself can act as a contextualisation cue (Gumperz 1982), signalling the kind of exchange that is taking place (such as its mode, and authorial stance), when contrasted with the contemporary conventions of other media and genres of the sixteenth- and twenty-first centuries.

3.6 Conclusion

Transhistorical pragmatics seeks to enable a more informed understanding of technologically mediated communication by identifying continuities in practice which transcend cultural and historical particularities. In this chapter we applied the approach to analysis of SMS spelling, situating it in a transitional period between the print and digital age, and comparing it with orthographic practices in the personal correspondence of the pre-standardised era. By adopting an analytical framework developed for analysis of sixteenth-century spelling, we directed attention away from the perceived novelty of respelling in SMS text messaging and foregrounded orthographic consistency as the more significant property of personal writing, both across the individual lifespan and between two historical periods. The fact that writers diverge in their use of Standard forms is unsurprising, given that those in the digital context work within a frame of standardization which is not comparable to that of early modern vernacular letter-writing (Evans & Tagg forthcoming). Before Standardisation, consistency itself can be a marker of exception – signalling for example Elizabeth I's unique social position. Post-Standardisation, the consistent use of Standard or non-standard forms can index the extent of individuals' alignment with an emergent sub-culture, whilst enabling "exceptional" respellings to take on local pragmatic functions. Our analysis suggests that spelling variation has always been a feature of personal correspondence and that it has, albeit in more limited and varying ways, been a resource for identity construction. SMS spelling generated alarmist media accounts in the early twenty-first century not because it represented a radical break in practice, but because of the perceived salience and novelty of the new technology, and a bias against youth culture (Herring 2008). These alarmist accounts were fuelled by a focus on what *appeared* different, rather than on any underlying patterns of inconsistency.

However, our contention is not that digital media spelling continues a pre-standardisation tradition which was disrupted, or interrupted by, the conventions and binary of print (as argued by Thompson & Collins, this volume). Our approach shows how SMS spelling should be understood as a *product* of the print age, and the associated processes of standardisation enabled by the printing press, widening education, and mass technologies of communication. The potential for variation in spelling to "mean" has been enhanced, if not transformed, by the ideology of standards and the "Standard" frame through which readers now interpret texts. When digital writers respell, they are usually playing with Standard forms and the degree and nature of its deviation (Sebba 2007); thus, as suggested by our analysis, the ability or inclination to respell may in fact correlate with higher academic literacy (cf. Plester, Wood & Joshi 2009). This means that, far from being a threat to established orthographic and social conventions, SMS spelling is, in a sense, only made possible because of the conventionalised, literacy-related constraints in which it operates.

In conclusion, a transhistorical pragmatic approach enables us to see how contemporary social, technological and ideological factors have come together to create a context in which spelling variation can take on greater potential for social meaning than was possible in the "a-Standard" context of the sixteenth century. In evaluating respelling's impact, we would do well to recognise both the ongoing influence of the Standard and the enduring pull towards orthographic consistency.

References

Androutsopoulos, Jannis. 2000. Non-standard spellings in media texts: The case of German fanzines. *Journal of Sociolinguistics* 4 (4). 514–533.
Androutsopoulos, Jannis. 2014. Moments of sharing: Entextualisation and linguistic repertoires in social networking. *Journal of Pragmatics* 73. 4–18.
Androutsopoulos, Jannis & Andreas Staehr. 2018. Moving methods online: Researching digital language practices. In Angela Creese & Adrian Blackledge (eds.), *The Routledge handbook of language and superdiversity*, 118–132. Abingdon: Routledge.
Berg, Kristian & Mark Aronoff. 2017. Self-organization in the spelling of English suffixes: The emergence of culture out of anarchy. *Language* 93. 37–64.
Bergs, Alexander. 2012. The uniformatarian principle and the risk of anachronisms in language and social history. In Juan Manuel Hernández-Campoy & Juan Camilo Conde-Silvestre (eds.), *The handbook of historical sociolinguistics*, 83–101. Oxford: Blackwell.
Blommaert, Jan. 2012. Supervernaculars and their dialects. *Dutch Journal of Applied Linguistics* 1 (1). 1–14.
Bourdieu, Pierre. 1977. *Outline of a theory of practice*. Cambridge, UK: Cambridge University Press.
Brinton, Laurel. 2017. *The evolution of pragmatic markers in English: Pathways of change*. Cambridge, UK: Cambridge University Press.
Carrington, Victoria. 2005. Txting: The end of civilization (again)? *Cambridge Journal of Education* 35 (2). 161–175.
Cohen, Leor. 2015. World attending in interaction: Multitasking, spatializing, narrativizing with mobile devices and Tinder. *Discourse, Context and Media* 9. 46–54.
Deumert, Ana. 2014. *Sociolinguistics and mobile communication*. Edinburgh: Edinburgh University Press.
Dovchin, Sender, Alastair Pennycook & Shaila Sultana. 2018 *Popular culture, voice and linguistic diversity: Young adults on- and offline*. Basingstoke: Palgrave Macmillan.
Evans, Mel. 2012. A sociolinguistics of early modern spelling? An account of Queen Elizabeth I's correspondence. *VARIENG 10*.
Evans, Mel. 2013. *The language of Queen Elizabeth I: A sociolinguistic perspective on royal style and identity*. Publications of the Philological Society. Chichester: Wiley-Blackwell.
Evans, Mel. 2020. *Royal voices: Language and power in Tudor England*. Cambridge, UK: Cambridge University Press.
Evans, Mel & Caroline Tagg. Forthcoming. Women's spelling in early modern English: Perspectives from new media. In Marco Condorelli (ed.), *Advances in diachronic orthography, 1500–1700*. Cambridge, UK: Cambridge University Press.
Georgakopulou, Alexandra. 1997. Self-presentation and interactional alliances in e-mail discourse: The style- and code-switches of Greek messages. *International Journal of Applied Linguistics* 7 (2). 141–164.
Gillen, Julia & Nigel Hall. 2010. Edwardian postcards: Illuminating ordinary writing. In David Barton & Uta Papen (eds.), *The anthropology of writing: Understanding textually-mediated worlds*, 169–189. London: Continuum.
Goffman, Erving. 1981. *Forms of talk*. Philadelphia: University of Pennsylvania Press.
Gumperz, John. 1982. *Discourse strategies*. Cambridge, UK: Cambridge University Press.

Halliday, Michael A.K. & Ruqaiya Hasan. 1985. *Language, context and text: Aspects of language in a social-semiotic perspective*. Geelong, Victoria: Deakin University Press.

Hård af Segerstad, Ylva. 2002. *Use and adaptation of the written language to the conditions of computer-mediated communication*. Gotëborg: University of Gotëborg PhD Thesis.

Herring, Susan C. 2008. Questioning the generational divide: Technological exoticism and adult constructions of online youth identity. In David Buckingham (ed.), *Youth, identity, and digital media*, 71–92. Cambridge, MA: MIT Press.

Hilpert, Martin & Stefan Th. Gries. 2016. Quantitative approaches to diachronic corpus linguistics. In Merja Kytö & Päivi Pahta (eds.), *The Cambridge handbook of English historical linguistics*, 36–53. Cambridge, UK: Cambridge University Press.

Holmes, Janet. 1993. Women's talk: The question of sociolinguistic universals. *Australian Journal of Communication* 20 (3). 125–49.

Kaislaniemi, Samuli, Mel Evans, Teo Juvonen & Anni Sairio. 2017. 'A graphic system which leads its own linguistic life'?: Epistolary spelling in English, 1400–1800. In Tanja Säily, Arja Nurmi, Minna Palander-Collin & Anita Auer (eds.), *Advances in historical sociolinguistics*, 187–213. Amsterdam: John Benjamins.

Kesseler, Angela & Alexander Bergs. 2003. Literacy and the new media: Vita brevis, lingua brevis. In Jean Aitchison & Diana Lewis (eds.), *New media discourse*, 75–84. Abingdon: Routledge.

Kress, Gunther. 2000. *Early spelling: Between convention and creativity*. Abingdon: Routledge.

Labov, William. 1972. *Sociolinguistic patterns*. Philadelphia: University of Pennsylvania Press.

Lötscher, Andreas. 1981. Zur Sprachgeschichte des Fluchens und Beschimpfens im Schweizerdeutschen. *Zeitschrift für Dialektologie und Linguistik* 48. 145–160.

Lyons, Agnieszka. 2014. *Self-presentation and self-positioning in text-messages: Embedded multimodality, deixis, and reference frame*. London: Queen Mary University of London PhD Thesis.

Malinowski, Bronislaw. 1923. The problem of meaning in primitive languages. In Charles K. Ogden & Ivor A. Richards (eds.), *The meaning of meaning: A study of the influence of language upon thought and of the science of symbolism*, 296–336. London: Kegan Paul, Trench, Trubner & Co.

Milroy, James & Lesley Milroy. 1999. *Authority in language: Investigating standard English*, 3rd edn. Abingdon: Routledge.

Moore, Shaun. 2004. The doubling of place: Electronic media, time-space arrangements and social relationships. In Nick Couldry & Anna McCarthy (eds.), *MediaSpace: Place, scale and culture in a media age*, 21–36. Abingdon: Routledge.

O'Brien, Robert L. 1904. Machinery and English style. *Atlantic Monthly* 94. 464–472.

Oxford English Dictionary. 2019. http://www.oed.com (accessed 28th February 2019).

Osselton, Noel, 1984. Informal spelling systems in early modern English: 1500–1800. In Norman F. Blake & Charles Jones (eds.), *English historical linguistics: Studies in development*, 123–137. Sheffield: CECTAL, University of Sheffield.

Pennycook, Alastair & Emi Otsuji. 2015. *Metrolingualism: Language in the city*. Abingdon: Routledge.

Plester, Beverly, Clare Wood & Puja Joshi. 2009. Exploring the relationship between children's knowledge of text message abbreviations and school literacy outcomes. *British Journal of Developmental Psychology* 27. 145–161.

Salmon, Vivian. 1999. Orthography and punctuation. In Roger Lass (ed.), *The Cambridge history of the English language volume 3, 1476–1776*, 13–55. Cambridge, UK: Cambridge University Press.

Scollon, Ron & Susie W. Scollon. 2004. *Nexus analysis: Discourse and the emerging internet.* Abingdon: Routledge.

Sebba, Mark. 2007. *Spelling and society.* Cambridge, UK: Cambridge University Press.

Shortis, Tim. 2007. Revoicing Txt: Spelling, vernacular orthography and 'unregimented writing'. In Santiago Posteguillo, María J. Esteve & M. Lluïsa Gea (eds.), *The texture of internet: Netlinguistics*, 2–21. Cambridge, UK: Cambridge Scholar Press.

Shortis, Tim. 2016. Texting and other messaging: written system in digitally mediated vernaculars. In Vivian Cook & Des Ryan (eds.), *The Routledge handbook of the English writing system*, 487–511. Abingdon: Routledge.

Sonmez, Margaret, 2000. Perceived and real differences between men's and women's spellings of the early to mid-seventeenth century. In Dieter Kastovsky & Arthur Mettinger (eds.), *The history of English in a social context: A contribution to historical sociolinguistics*, 405–436. Berlin: De Gruyter Mouton.

Staehr, Andreas & Lian M. Madsen. 2014. Standard language in urban rap: social media, linguistic practice and ethnographic context. *Tilburg Papers in Culture Studies*. Paper 94.

Tagg, Caroline. 2012. *The discourse of text messaging.* London: Continuum.

Tagg, Caroline. 2016. Heteroglossia in text-messaging: Performing identity and negotiating relationships in a digital space. *Journal of Sociolinguistics* 20 (1). 59–85.

Tagg, Caroline, Philip Seargeant & Amy Aisha Brown. 2017. *Taking offence on social media: Communication and conviviality on Facebook.* Basingstoke: Palgrave Macmillan.

Taavitsainen, Irma & Andreas H. Jucker. 2010. Trends and developments in historical pragmatics. In Andreas Jucker and Irma Taavitsainen (eds.), *Historical pragmatics*, 3–32. Berlin: De Gruyter Mouton.

Thurlow, Crispin, with Alex Brown. 2003. Generation txt? The sociolinguistics of young people's text-messaging. *Discourse Analysis Online* 1 (1).

Thurlow, Crispin. 2006. From statistical panic to moral panic: The metadiscursive construction and popular exaggeration of new media language in the print media. *Journal of Computer-Mediated Communication* 11. 667–701.

Traugott, Elizabeth Closs. 2017. "Insubordination" in the light of the uniformitarian principle. *English Language and Linguistics* 21. 289–310.

Wiggins, Alison. 2016. *Bess of Hardwick's letters: Language, materiality, and early modern epistolary culture.* Abingdon: Routledge.

Susan Fitzmaurice
4 Reflections on historicity, technology and the implications for method in (historical) pragmatics

Historical inquiry, the investigation of the past, is a thorny business. The three papers in this section acknowledge this as they address "historicisation" in tackling the matter of the "transhistorical analysis of language- and literacy-related practices in English" (Tagg & Evans). Jones "historicises" the notion of the Pragmatic Web by exploring the manner in which the history of the internet presents as a "history of human engagement with different ways of understanding meaning – how meaning is created and what can be done with it". Kádár conducts what he calls a historically grounded interpersonal interactional analysis of medieval public shaming events and on-line trolling through the lens of ritual theory. Tagg and Evans conduct a comparative analysis of women's spelling variation, practices and preferences in SMS messages and in sixteenth-century letter writing in order to examine continuities and discontinuities in human linguistic practices over time.

These analyses of linguistic practices in the world of digital media are informed by and grounded in the principles that underpin modern linguistics approaches to language change. This grounding affords the analysis of linguistic phenomena or interpersonal interactional behaviour in different historical settings and contexts in the confidence that, as Lass (1997: 25) avers, "there are no miracles". As Labov (1972: 275) elaborates for sociolinguistics: "If there are relatively constant, day-to-day effects of social interaction upon grammar and phonology, the uniformitarian principle asserts that these influences continue to operate today the same way that they have in the past". This principle is a crucial anchor for the historical linguist/pragmatician as they venture into the untrodden terrain of the past.

If we are not very careful, the idea that all changes are known changes or that all behaviours are known behaviours has the potential to make historical inquiry vulnerable to presentism ("there is nothing in the present that hasn't happened in the past"). In other words, the historical investigation of conceptual

---

Note: I am grateful to Seth Mehl for his comments and suggestions.

Susan Fitzmaurice, University of Sheffield, e-mail: s.fitzmaurice@sheffield.ac.uk

https://doi.org/10.1515/9783110670837-006

change is susceptible to the charge of anachronism or present-centredness. Now it is reasonable for the historian to formulate questions informed by and rooted in the present, from their own stance.[1] However, if the historian approaches the (historical) sources in an unmediated and direct way to answer them (Ashplant & Wilson 1988: 267), the result is necessarily ahistorical, or, put another way, not necessarily historical. Equally, it would be naïve to insist that the sources themselves can yield the answers; assuming that the "past can speak for itself" is to miss the point that any investigation of historical materials requires interpretation.

In this context, I am interested in the possibilities for new thinking about language and linguistic theory afforded by new technologies that provide unparalleled opportunities for the discovery of information. A computational historical semantics project (aka. Linguistic DNA[2]) involved the bottom-up querying of a universe of printed discourse in English (1500–1800) in order to discover the key concepts that possibly inaugurated western modernity. Using the linguistic framework of distributional semantics to shape the automated analysis of historical texts to yield key concepts opened up the possibility of challenging received intellectual history regarding the ideas that might be especially salient in a particular historical period.

Intellectual historians such as Quentin Skinner have constructed the early modern English intellectual and political world through the forensic analysis of concepts like LIBERTY or the State (Skinner 1978), and Kosellek (1998) has done the same for European modernity through the structural semantic exploration of concepts such as *marriage* using his method of *Begriffsgeschichte*. For our period, Williams (1976) assembled through his intellectual and political work a set of glosses for highly resonant and salient cultural keywords he identified for mid-twentieth century Britain. The Keywords Project, a collaborative and interdisciplinary group, brings Williams' work up to date in a "21st century vocabulary" of keywords (McCabe & Yanacek 2018). All these projects seek to illuminate the thought, culture and politics of their periods via the in-depth examination of the meanings of what they determine to be paradigmatic terms for those times. This work depends upon the identification of a particular word as paradigmatic – a keyword – in order to analyse its importance in its time and place.

---

[1] This was the method adopted by new historicism.
[2] AHRC AH/M00614X/1. Linguistic DNA: Modelling concepts and semantic change in English 1500–1800 was based at the University of Sheffield (PI Susan Fitzmaurice, Co-I Michael Pidd, Matthew Groves, Iona Hine, Seth Mehl) with collaborating institutions University of Sussex (Co-I Justyna Robinson) and University of Glasgow (Co-I Marc Alexander, Fraser Dallachy, Brian Aitken).

Indeed, the word has been methodologically fundamental to disciplines including corpus linguistics and historical semantics and conceptual and intellectual history. Semantic theory starts with the word not discourse; semasiology focuses upon the lexeme; onomasiology focuses upon the concept; both are coterminous with the word. However, the tantalising possibility of discovering conceptual material before it is lexicalised by a (key)word (given the power of the algorithmic construction of meaning "mathematically, probabilistically, based on correlations between pieces of input" (Jones)), raises the possibility of rethinking the concept as originating in discourse, not the lexical item.

The output of the Linguistic DNA processor consists of constellations of expressions that exhibit a strong attraction to one another within a span of 100 words of text.[3] The presence of highly prevalent constellations such as *life – death – soul* and *body – soul – mind* in early modern English printed discourse allows us to explore the construction of concepts that are discursive rather than tied to the single word. And so we can understand the nuanced meanings associated with that ineffable notion, the *soul*, as more complex concepts, constructed in discourse. A virtue of this method is that because the assignment of discursive meaning to the constellation requires the close, historically embedded reading of the constellations in their discursive contexts, the temptation to reach for a convenient, possibly current, keyword (e.g. spirituality) to capture the historical concept is resistible.

Instead, the constellation *life – death – soul* in a 1616 text[4] invites a complex pragmatic inferential construction informed by a very specific historical context. The construction is that it is the soul that imbues the person (not necessarily the body) with life. So crucially, we make sense of the constellation as a discursive concept through the connection of life and death via the soul. Thus is the life of the devout. This discursive concept is supralexical; it is therefore traceable in the associative relations among words distributed in a text. So in any particular historical moment, a concept might not be encapsulated in any

---

3 The production of highly frequent trios and quads involves the automatic calculation of strength of co-occurrence using our local measure of DPMI (discursive PMI) and supplemented with chi square of pairs of expressions, then a pair with a third expression and then a trio with a fourth expression, to arrive at the most prominent and dominant constellations within the universe of discourse being explored. This output consists, then, of associations between expressions within a given stretch or window, calculated for the whole corpus.
4 A16748 The good and the badde, or Descriptions of the vvorthies, and vnworthies of this age Where the best may see their graces, and the worst discerne their basenesse. (Breton, Nicholas, 1545?–1626?) 1616. EEBO-TCP.

single word; instead it will be observable only via a set of words in relation to each other in discourse.

Linguistic DNA accepts the following principles as uniform: there is a kind of discursive meaning that is indicated in lexical co-occurrence constellations in discourse rather than in the single word. This will be true of all language at any point in history. We eschew the present-centred perspective so that contemporary social and cultural debates cannot be used to identify the salient concepts (much less the keywords) of the past. In sum, the uniformitarian principle is the foundation of the Linguistic DNA method adopted to identify conceptual structure and the historicist principle motivates that method.

One problem with presentism is that it is intuitive rather than systematic, principled and rigorous, and it is intuition that allows Skinner, Koselleck and Williams to identify words as the hinges of their arguments (instead of, say, discourses or lexical constellations, etc.). Words are intuitively salient. However, if Skinner, Koselleck or Williams had somehow managed to discuss constellations rather than keywords, we would still argue that our method is a step change for historical pragmatics because it is inductive and bottom-up (not driven by the keyword), and it is based systematically on what we understand to be uniform about language, rather than what we intuit to be uniform about meaning.

This reflection on historical analysis and the risks of presentism in the interpretation of historical material takes us back to the project of historicism and transhistorical comparative analysis adopted in the papers in this section. In most of our work in historical pragmatics, we are driven by questions about how as well as what verbal interaction means, in past contexts that we must construct from the evidence we have to hand. Critically, as in the Linguistic DNA case, the analysis of that meaning depends upon the proper construction of that historical context so that the result can be immune to the charge of anachronism or worse, presentism.

References

Ashplant, T.G. & Adrian Wilson, 1988. Present-centred history and the problem of historical knowledge. *The Historical Journal* 31 (2). 253–274.
Koselleck, Reinhart. 1998. Social history and *Begriffgeschichte*. In Iain Hampsher-Monk, Karen Tilmans & Frank Van Vree (eds.), *History of concepts: Comparative perspectives*, 23–26. Amsterdam: Amsterdam University Press.
MacCabe, Colin & Holly Yanacek (eds.). 2018. *Keywords for today: A 21st century vocabulary. The Keywords Project*. New York: Oxford University Press.
Labov, William. 1972. *Sociolinguistic patterns*. Philadelphia: University of Pennsylvania Press.

Lass, Roger. 1997. *Historical linguistics and language change*. Cambridge, UK: Cambridge University Press.
Skinner, Quentin. 1978. *The foundations of modern political thought*. Cambridge, UK: Cambridge University Press.
Williams, Raymond. 1976. *Keywords: A vocabulary of culture and society*. Cambridge, UK: Cambridge University Press.

Section 2: **Historicizing Discourses**

Introduction to historicising discourses

This section details various ways in which familiar social actions and discourses endure over time as they are remediated and reconfigured through a diverse range of new communication technologies, and how such processes can manifest in different places and times.

In their chapter, Agnieszka Lyons and Samia Ounoughi show how the enduring need to communicate can transcend technological specificities. They trace the timeless human endeavour to locate oneself in one's physical surroundings and to communicate that information to others, by comparing nineteenth century Alpine narratives to mobile messaging via WhatsApp. While the different affordances of each technology shape the narratives that can be told in each context, both mountain climbers and twenty-first century friends draw on similar discursive and multimodal strategies in conveying both location and motion. Mediated communicative practices of any age are also shaped by overarching political structures and entrenched power relations that transcend technological developments. Philip Seargeant explores how political leaders have harnessed the media of the day in building and wielding power, through a comparative analysis of two leaders: Queen Elizabeth I of England (1558–1603) and US President Donald Trump (2016–). The nature of the media available in each historical period shapes the message that can be conveyed and in both cases, Seargeant argues, the medium becomes part of the message – through Elizabeth's appropriation of imagery and discourses from Classical and religious literature and through Trump's undermining of the mainstream media through social media channels. These broad parallels in the practice of statecraft can be said to transcend the distinct particularities of the early modern and twenty-first century mediascapes, with a transhistorical lens highlighting the continuities in the linguistic strategies of power.

In her investigation of the initialism *R.I.P.* on online memorial sites, Korina Giaxoglou shows how discourse phenomena can break from existing practices although, as she notes, the attitudes surrounding it may be slower to change. She explores the extent to which user perceptions and applications of the initialism are shaped by users' awareness of and orientation towards its religious antecedents. In the case of *R.I.P.*, while its historical religious significance remains relevant in shaping its use, the discourse of mourning is being altered by social media users' appropriation of it as part of emerging online social practices. Finally, in his chapter on the development of the academic article, both over its long history and within the lifetime of contemporary academics around the turn of the century, David Barton shows how academic writing practices

https://doi.org/10.1515/9783110670837-007

have been shaped not only by changing technologies – and, in particular, the proliferation of social media and academic genres in the twenty-first century – but by wider contextual changes in the development and perception of science, in the audiences for and purposes of academic writing, and in the immediate managerial, political and economic climate. The role of material context in human communication is a theme taken up and explored by Alison Sealey who reflects on the extent to which the chapters in this section serve to challenge the anthropocentric nature of much social research, highlighting the ways in which human histories intersect with the non-human – not only with technologies, artefacts and discourses but also with the natural world, other living beings and alternative timespans. Her reflection reminds us that a focus on the human – rather than the technology – is in itself a form of determinism which privileges one aspect of a communicative encounter over others.

Taken together, the chapters show how a focus on continuities, connections and historical precedence can provide a rich understanding of the social and discursive practices in play at any one moment in time.

Agnieszka Lyons and Samia Ounoughi
5 Towards a transhistorical approach to analysing discourse *about* and *in* motion

5.1 Introduction

Location has been found to play an important role in communication, both face-to-face and mobile-mediated, especially in Indo-European cultures, where cognitive relation to space is anthropocentric (Levinson 2003). With the ever-increasing popularisation of mobile devices, attention has been directed to the role mobile technologies play in reconfiguring our relationships with our physical environments (Wilken & Goggin 2012). Analyses of conversations point to the centrality of establishing the participants' whereabouts at the onset of a mobile phone call (Laursen & Szymanski 2013), particularly in situations in which location bears relevance to the content of the conversation (Arminen 2006). Mobile devices are used to micro-coordinate (Ito & Okabe 2005) activities throughout the day and have enabled their remotely located users to remain in a state of perpetual contact. They have also fostered the feeling of remotely located interactants being in each other's proximity and resulted in the continuous state of connected presence (Licoppe 2004). One of the instances of this micro-coordination is linked to what Licoppe (2009: 1925) referred to as "co-proximity events", and described as "the interactional performance of accomplishing mutual co-proximity from a distance (beyond the range of sight and speech, through the use of telecommunication resources)". In these types of interactions, distant participants are able to create unplanned opportunities to meet through what Schlegloff (1972) described as "formulating place", including references to well-known landmarks or other forms of "self-localisation" (Licoppe 2009), aimed at establishing mutual positioning (proximity or distance) in geographical space. It is common practice in mobile phone interactions to also micro-coordinate pre-agreed face-to-face meeting arrangements, including establishing the exact meeting time and place, managing last-minute alterations to earlier set out plans, and aiding locating another in space.

Agnieszka Lyons, Queen Mary University of London, London, UK, e-mail: a.lyons@qmul.ac.uk
Samia Ounoughi, Université Grenoble Alpes, LIDILEM bâtiment Stendhal, France,
e-mail: samia.ounoughi@univ-grenoble-alpes.fr

https://doi.org/10.1515/9783110670837-008

This communication in motion and – by extension – discourse in motion, whose main aim is to enable physical convergence of remotely located participants, is sometimes seen as a welcome benefit of new technologies: portable devices, localisation software, and the internet. Despite its apparent novelty, however, precursors of modern space-and-place-focused communication in motion can be found in travel writing across centuries. In the nineteenth century, for instance, Alpine travellers made face-to-face arrangements to meet to ascend the same summit or to re-converge on their descent after parting from their companions. At the time and in that location, landmarks (e.g., Chamonix, Courmayeur, or certain inns) were so well-known that travellers could mention them only briefly or not mention them at all without risking misunderstanding as to the meeting venue. While ascent or descent progress could be predicted, if unexpected changes happened, travellers managed to obtain information about their companions from a range of sources: drawing on the knowledge of other travellers they encountered on their way, querying local people seeking navigational guidance, and deducing from cues in the environment.

This chapter takes as a starting point the overarching motivations and interest in communication across geographical space to explore the possibility and usefulness of adopting a transhistorical approach to *discourse in motion* (i.e. produced while the interactants are in transit) and *discourse about motion* (i.e. concerning movement or transit) in English. We explore two distinct corpora produced for different purposes, at different times and in different locations, by different sets of writers, who use English as a medium of communication: nineteenth century Alpine travel narratives and twenty-first century mobile messaging exchanges via WhatsApp.

It was during a European exchange between Université Grenoble Alpes and Queen Mary University of London that we had the opportunity to discuss our fields of research. Since narratives on alpinism were a novelty in the nineteenth century, Samia is interested in the discursive and multimodal means British writers used to describe their motion in a specific environment with the aim of rendering this environment more accessible to future travellers and – on a more local level – to find one another more easily when they travelled to the same location. Agnieszka specialises in multimodal mobile conversations, including those aimed at micro-coordination and navigation of self and others. We realised that the travellers' needs remained the same throughout time: self-location, environment description/identification, and helping each other to navigate. Travellers' fundamental needs to constantly redefine their location in space and to keep others updated so as to facilitate meeting or future travel experiences became obvious phenomena to explore.

Adopting a data-driven approach to the analysis in this study enables us to avoid being constrained by established methodologies. Instead, bearing those in mind, we allow the texts, their language features and contexts, to drive our analysis, as we bring attention to both similarities and differences in our disparate datasets. Starting from an interest in the process of self-localisation and the discursive construction of the communicators' surrounding environment that the English language and other semiotic means facilitate, we find that both modern and historical discourse in motion and about motion share important characteristics. These are realised through a range of resources, which came into being in the process of remediation (Bolter & Grusin 2000; Bolter 2011). This study contributes to the growing body of research focused on situating English-language electronically mediated interactions in the wider communicative context and anchoring electronic communication patterns in pre-digital practices with the aim of establishing the level to which claims about novelty can be made in the context of "new" media (e.g. Farman 2012; Gillen 2014).

The following section will explore the nature of the analysed texts. In order to do this, we first establish the definition of text which will be employed in this chapter and lay out the relevant units of analysis. We distinguish between discourse created on-the-go (mobile messaging) and discourse whose creation is delayed until reaching a particular location where typing/ writing is possible (travel narratives) and consider the implication of this formal distinction between our datasets. We briefly identify some common characteristics of writing in motion in both datasets. In the following section, we analyse the data referring to aspects of the discursive construction of the key aspects of discourse-in-motion: the self-in-motion and the environment-in-flux. Finally, we move on to discuss the features of a *transhistorical* approach and its applicability to the investigation of discourse *about* and *in* motion, and the implications of the methodological approach adopted for this study for understanding human communication across time and place, in English and beyond.

5.2 Text, location, and motion

Digital technologies are now conceptualised as part of our ongoing sociability, consisting of varied encounters and exchanges with others, both face-to-face and at a distance. They are employed to foster connections across distance, including to maintain transnational family ties in migrant contexts (e.g. Yu, Huang & Liming 2017; Lyons & Tagg 2019), and feature in co-present interactions, where they can support or become a topic of local conversations between peers (e.g. Brown et al. 2018; Ito 2005). It has been argued that mobile phone exchanges are detached from the physical locations in which they occur and belong instead to what Wellman (2001) describes as person-to-person communication, where interactions are initiated with specific people, rather than locations, as in the case of landline phone calls. They are described as "immune to place" (Wilken 2005: n.p.), serving to insulate their users from the surrounding environment through enabling a shift in engagement from the physical to the virtual environment. At the same time, however, the use of technologies demonstrates an intimate relationship between bodies and the spaces they inhabit, as demonstrated in the way CB radio users engage with others they do not know when en route (Farman 2012). Conversations usually revolve around themes related to "the journey, the landscapes, and the other drivers they encountered" (Farman 2012: 5) and help users alleviate the feeling of isolation. Through engaging with mutually relevant spaces, they invite others to share with them the experience of the journey. This early use of CB radio, as a portable, mobile technology, resembles that of our current use of mobile phones in an ongoing contact throughout the day. In interpersonal communication, the importance of specific physical location – be it fixed or shifting as an interactant moves through physical space – for the content of interactions has been linked to the content of individual turns, either textual or photographic. Villi (2016) demonstrates that when communicating with photographs, an essential connection with the source location is made as users may choose to visually mediate their local presence through "send[ing their] place[s]" (Villi 2016: 107). Farman draws attention to the "seamless connection" that we experience with mobile media and compares this experience to that of a good book or the cinema where the medium itself transports its users beyond their physical locations and into the realm of the narrative (Farman 2012: 7; cf. Lyons 2014). Our bodies are therefore fluidly integrated with the mediated environment and exposed to experience mediated environments first-hand. Far from being disconnected from places, our experience of mobile technologies is – for many people – still embedded in physical locations from where messages originate. Nowhere is this more clearly evident than in mobile messaging, such as that via WhatsApp, where the micro-coordination of meetings is frequently performed with a clear focus on facilitating physical convergence and mediated co-experience of mobility.

The way the experience of spaces and places is shared between remotely located people is characteristic also of travel narratives, analyses of which highlight the need to write about motion and explore the reasons that lead people to produce texts while travelling or shortly after completing their travels (Viviès

2003). It is through such narratives – as in Farman's "good book" – that readers may experience the writers' environment through a verbal account of their observations, sensory experiences, and thoughts. Constructed through a different type of mobile technology (pen and paper), they also document embodied experiences of the travellers' surroundings, for, although travellers may walk the same passes or ascend the same summits, a mountainous environment may vary widely even from hour to hour, depending on the climate, the light, the movement of stones, the quality of the snow or ice.[1] Each experience is therefore unique and needs to be conveyed in displaying both its eternal geophysical stability and its permanent climatic mutability. This entails a need to resort to the most appropriate medium (or media) of space representation and self-location according to the environmental conditions and the stage at which travellers express their motion and/or location. What this demonstrates is that there is a clear connection between media, location, and motion and that, from a functional perspective, embodied location-sharing spans media both vertically (at a single point in time) and horizontally (across time).

One of the questions that remain is what specifically connects these different instantiations of communication-in-motion across centuries: How is our relationship with physical location shaped through media – both digital and pre-digital? Are claims as to the novelty of new media in this regard justified or should we look at modern communication-in-motion in the light of historical evidence of the like? In order to answer these questions, we analyse two types of texts: nineteenth century Alpine travel narratives and twenty-first century mobile messaging via WhatsApp. It is beyond doubt that travel writing can be characterised as both more extended and more carefully constructed than mobile messaging, taking into account its literary value for posterity. At the same time, in both contexts, there is evidence of text production in motion: immediacy and up-to-the-moment updates in mobile messaging and meta-discourse in alpine travel writing, as in the extract below, which documents the process of noting experiences of travel:

> **I find nothing more in my notes about Giornico** except that the people are very handsome, and, as I thought, of a Roman type. (Butler 1882: 75; our emphasis)

Such self-referential comments point to the source of knowledge and experiences conveyed in the text and to the specific stages of text-making, with handwritten notes turned into more carefully constructed printed texts, reflecting

---

[1] "In the snow region of the Alps, again, changes are perpetually occurring from one day, and even from one hour, to another; and it is only those who are unacquainted with the ice-world that require to be told that they may find the condition of a glacier, or a snow-slope, very different from the description of preceding travellers." (Ball, PPG: 1859, XIII).

the process of fixing the final form of a text. This can in turn be compared to the impact of the invention of print on manuscript production (Pahta & Jucker 2011). The metalanguage used in this and similar excerpts across the Alpine dataset indicate the status of the texts and the frames within which they are to be interpreted (Verschueren 2000) and serve to situate the texts presented to the readers as closely connected to the moment-by-moment experiences of the Alpinists. On the other hand, the on-the-go mobile messaging is in itself both an account of motion details situated within the moment of text-production and the final form in which this account reaches the intended audience. As a result, it can be expected that the link between the text and the physical and temporal context it describes will be realised differently through both language and other semiotic resources.

Taking into account the differences between the two corpora, we adopt the understanding of "text" as embedded in a particular context or situation and constituting part of a meaning-making event. Texts are both shaped by the contexts in which they occur and transformative (i.e., context-shaping), in the sense that their mere presence affects the interactants' relationships to each other and the environment. We accept that texts do not exist in a vacuum, highlighting their intertextual potential. Texts therefore are inseparable from the contexts in which they function.

5.3 The data

The corpus of Alpine travel narratives consists of about a million words and gathers narratives written in English by British travellers in the Alps between 1857 and 1900. The Alpine Club (http://www.alpine-club.org.uk), which was founded in 1857, was the world's first mountaineering club, and its members have been pioneers of worldwide mountaineering development and exploration. One of the main objectives of the Club is to promote mountain climbing and exploration and "to develop a better knowledge of the mountains through literature, science and art" as well as other areas of the Club's activity, such as meetings and publications (Alpine Club 2018). There are two major types of texts included in the dataset. Straight after its creation in 1857, the Alpine Club of London issued a yearly journal first entitled *Peaks, Passes and Glaciers* (PPG 1858–1862) and then *The Alpine Club Journal* (AJ 1863 – present). Members of the Club, the Alpine travellers whose work we look at in this chapter, wrote their narratives partly as a contribution to the Club's mission and as a duty towards their fellow alpinists. The aim of this text production was to facilitate way-finding, very much like communication of modern-day digital media users who micro-coordinate their meeting places on-the-go. These texts mainly deal with high mountains exploration. The second major source of narratives is a set of publications at the initiative of individual famous mountain explorers (including Samuel Butler, John Ruskin and Alfred Wills) and published in the same period. This set of publications concerned remote places located at lower altitudes. What all these narratives have in common is the necessity to write about the travellers' motion. It is through their own experience – which involved self-localization – that they depicted places, mapped them, and even named them. They informed future travellers of the local scenery, culture, but also about the potential perils of undertaking mountain travel. These narratives also facilitated future travels by giving practical information concerning means of transportation, local regulations, prices, equipment, accommodation, food and the like.

The corpus of twenty-first century WhatsApp messages includes 609 screenshots collected between November 2016 and the end of December 2017 from a group of five women who met through a South-East London local support group for new and expectant parents. The women live within a 2-mile radius and maintain ongoing contact both through instant messaging (mainly group messaging which forms part of the corpus) and in person, meeting for lunch, coffee, and playdates, with all communication within the group being in English. The corpus consists of messages focused on everyday matters of parenthood, childcare, personal and social life, as well as messages concerned with arranging in-person meetings in local parks and venues. The latter group of messages contains those written on-the-go, aimed at updating each other on the progress of their journey, altering arrangements, and verifying practical information regarding timings and locations of meetings. It is this part of the corpus that is the main focus of this chapter. All the WhatsApp data has been anonymised and is being used with contributors' permission. The names have been changed and all identifying information has been removed. By its nature, this dataset includes a large number of photos of babies. All of these images have been blurred to preserve anonymity of participants.

The main difference between the two corpora is temporal: information in mobile phone communication is delivered instantaneously, compared to the days, weeks or months needed for a message to be delivered to its addressee from the nineteenth century Alps. WhatsApp messages – typed or dictated to the phone while walking – are delivered to their addressees within seconds; travel narratives and correspondence (e.g., Ruskin's *Letters from the Continent*) – produced on a train or coach and posted en route and later published – would take much longer to reach their addressees. Additionally, the delivery channel differs: in current mobile phone exchanges, there is no need for a mediator or a messenger. The phone is the messenger. Alpine travel writers, on the other hand, rely on an intermediary, such as the post or a dispatched rider to facilitate their communication. Finally, it is impossible to ignore the gender difference between the two sets of authors. Our focus on male travel writers in the nineteenth century texts is motivated by the nature of texts produced and our focus on the mapping and description of space. This choice does not mean that women's travel writing was non-existent in this historical period. In fact, while some scholars suggest that women rarely "broke out of the domestic circle in the nineteenth century to venture into the wider world as self-acknowledged travellers" (Worley 1986: 40), others (Mills 1991; Foster 1988, 1990) point to the fact that the amount of women's travel writing is far from negligible. It is, however, markedly different from men's travel writing of this historical period and clearly bound by the circulating discourses of femininity and "more tentative" than men's (Mills 1991: 3). As a result, it has been read mainly as "simple autobiographies" (Mills 1991: 4), rather than as textual artefacts. Taking all this into account, aligning authors' gender across out data sets would necessarily require adopting a gender lens in the analysis. This – while admittedly fascinating – falls beyond the scope of this paper, but would be an interesting focus for a further project.

Despite these differences, both Alpine travellers and WhatsApp communicators completed parts of their text-production on the go and both corpora demonstrate similarities in the way in which the writers self-position themselves within space and inform others of their progress along their journey. The means to achieve this include both verbal and non-verbal discourse, and instances where writers drew on their knowledge of other texts to complete their interactions. Multimodal content was not only frequent but also unavoidable in both contexts, as the aim of both was primarily to render perceptible what the addressees could not see for themselves. Beyond their own productions of text and iconographical documents, they also referred to previous documentation such as other narratives or maps as well as local knowledge. Their accounts therefore permeate with intertextuality and inter-iconicity. The Alpinists made notes in their notebooks as they travelled and stopped to draw the scenery. Depending on their degree of expertise, they carried scientific instruments to take measures and render their mapping as accurately as possible. They then re-wrote and re-arranged their notes into the final travel narratives. The WhatsApp users typed or dictated their messages on their way to the meeting place, signalled their current positioning by sending their locations, and shared images and descriptions of their surroundings. Their "scientific instrument" is their mobile phone, which allows for a precise rendering of location, measurements, and sources of reference. There are evidently similarities, which tend to be missed when first putting these two corpora side-by-side but which become visible when one further engages with the data.

5.4 Analysis: Locating the self and the other

In this section, we focus on the discursive ways in which writers locate themselves and others in the two sets of texts: mobile messaging and Alpine travel narratives. We approach the question focusing on three functionally motivated aspects of communication: linguistic reference at a range of scales, the use of locally available or globally accessible visual resources, and mutual knowledge construction drawing on external writer-accessible expertise.

5.4.1 Linguistic reference at a range of scales

Location in our mobile messaging about motion dataset is marked with references to landmarks and features of the environment at a range of scales, from those globally identifiable, such as place names (Station Road and Burnt Ash road, Half Way Street in figure 5.1), to those of temporary significance and fleeting nature ("a fair few geese" in figure 5.4 below). Coincident location of the Figure to the Ground, i.e., the located and the locating entity (Talmy 1972),

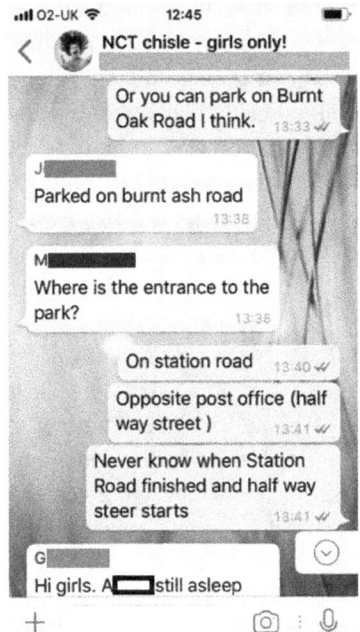

Figure 5.1: Establishing location based on named referents.

is marked in English through a range of prepositions, such as *on*, *at*, and *by*, "the cat is on the mat" and "the car is parked by the entrance". All of these are frequently used in the WhatsApp corpus, alongside a range of linguistic tools marking locations and motion employing coordinate systems with a prominent landmark at the centre (Levinson 2003), e.g. "opposite post office". Linguistic referents to specific locations follow the same general pattern in the Alpine corpus: names of passages, valleys, routes and peaks are juxtaposed with landscape features, such as "rocks on the left" or "the string of ants", which are internally connected to each other forming a mental map of the area:

> **Half-an-hour or so after crossing the string of ants**, one passes from under the pine-trees into a grassy meadow, which **in spring is decked with all manner of Alpine flowers** after crossing this, the old St. Gothard road is reached, which passed by Prato and Dalpe, so as to avoid the gorge of the Monte Piottino. (Butler 1882: 27)

Similar examples of varied referential scales can be found elsewhere in the data, for example, where travellers "[keep] under the rocks on the left" and walk "along a belt of piled and tottering fragments" (PPG 1859: 80). They refer to features of the surrounding landscape, such as "quantities of fresh snow filling the interstices", which are as fleeting as the geese in the WhatsApp exchange reproduced in figure 5.4. The relevance of the fleeting as a way of locating in space serves, in both corpora, a very important function of sharing sensory experiences with others. The aesthetics of what the writers see feature in qualitative comments about the environment, e.g. an ironic comment in one of the WhatsApp exchanges not discussed in detail here: "I'm in Alperton! How stunning!" and in the alpine travel narratives: "Once more I was about to tread the snows of the Alps, and I felt a thrill of delight at the thought" (PPG 1860: 163). This demonstrates that both the Alpine environment and the more local WhatsApp context are shaped within the scope of a personal experience of the writers, rendering their individual experience as perceptible as possible to the reader.

    The discussion highlights the individual and sensory perspective taken by the writers to describe location and motion in both corpora. This is achieved through drawing both on textual means and (as we shall see) on multimodal resources used to situate the writer in space and reflect their personal experiences of the environment (such as the weather, traffic, seasonal features, etc.) and leads us to see space and motion as subjective and discursive constructs. It is then not the corpus or medium themselves that determine the way space and location are constructed throughout centuries. Conversely, the Indo-European human, with their anthropocentric relation to space (Levinson 2003), stands in the centre of discourse in motion and about motion and it is their perspective that should serve as an anchor to the analysis of discourse-in-motion. We return to this argument in our conclusion.

5.4.2 The use of multimodal resources

Apart from being writers, Alpine travellers were also explorers who drew and corrected maps of the area drawn by earlier travellers. Admittedly, they could not have sent audio messages or digitally produced images instantly, but they did try to appeal to the readers' senses using drawings and musical scores to share the experience of hearing a bird's song, or local people singing as they walked. The aim was to show what pleasure could be drawn from rambles beyond a mountain pass (see figure 5.2). Alpine travel writing was then also a way of conveying sensory experiences to readers, and inviting them to experience the remote environment.

Figure 5.2: *Butler's* Alps and sanctuaries*: Musical score.*

High in affordances, facilitating multimodal communication and sharing sensory stimuli, new media is not then the only data set in which multimodal resources are shared. Alpine travel narratives included multimodality which, combined with writing, fulfilled various functions: describing a geographical object never or seldom explored or documented, and defining it as a place contributing to the "conceptualization of spatial relations" (Levinson 2003: 18).

Figures 5.3 and 5.4 demonstrate how similar these media for communication about motion (Alpine writing and mobile messaging) are.

In 1859, E. Weller engraved a map of the area, with a track mapped by Matthews and his fellow alpinists (see figure 5.3). The corresponding text

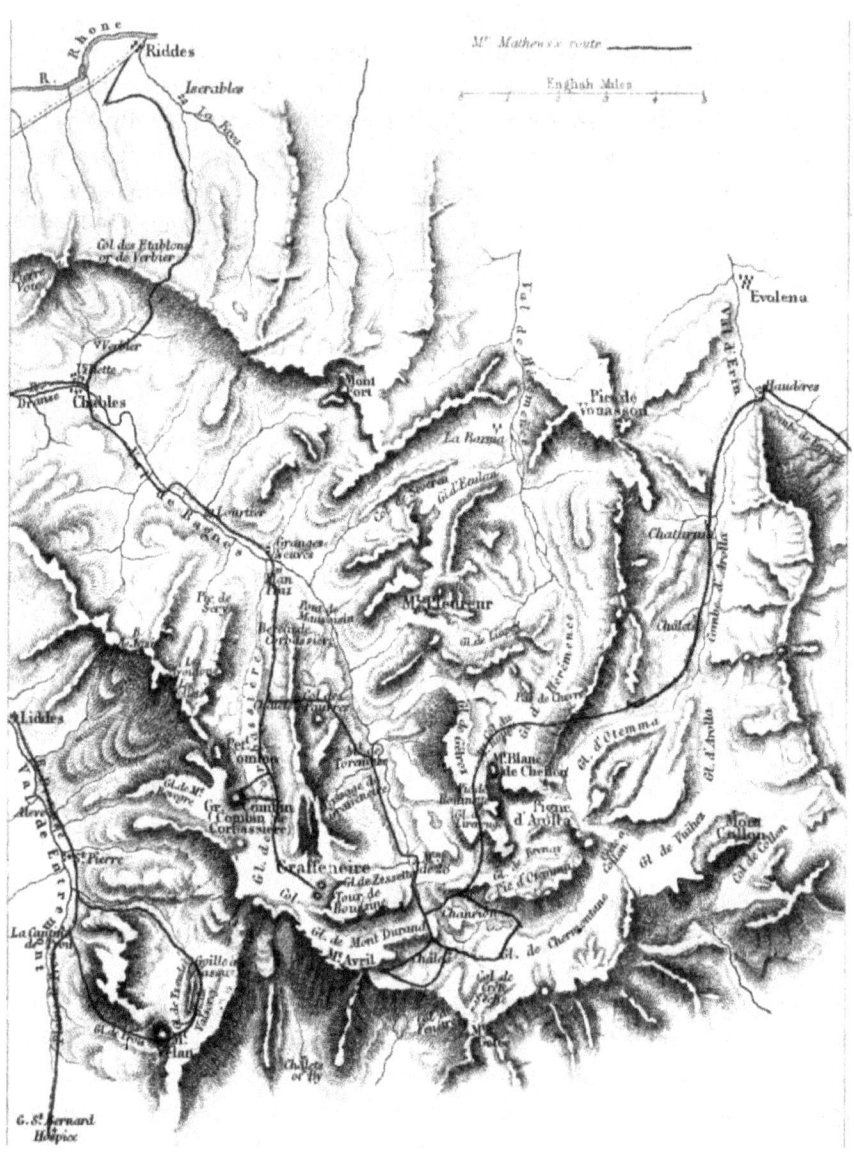

Figure 5.3: E. Weller "Mountains and glacier of Bagnes" (PPG 1859: 74).

from *Peaks, Passes and Glaciers* (PPG 1859: 113) focuses on the details of the environment:

> A track leads across the mountains from Riddes to Chables, over a pass described in some maps as the Col de Verbier, and in others as the Col des Etablons. It ascends in **steep zig-zags up the grassy wall of the Rhone valley**, where every here and there, hundreds of feet above the river, **peep out smooth sheets of rock polished by that wonderful ancient Ice Sea** which reached from the Galenstok to the Lake of Geneva.
>
> (PPG 1859: 113; our emphasis)

In another excerpt, the details of the journey – progress and movement – are foregrounded alongside references to the perceptible surrounding environment, with all its striking features. The traveller's motion and the environmental changes coincide so that the former's experience is rendered possible at a specific moment ("I was now able ... to study the actual summit of the mountain"). From a metadiscursive point of view, the use of the proximal deictic *"now"* encourages the reader's involvement in the narrative (Defour 2008), emphasises the author-centered metadiscourse of the passage (Taavitsainen & Hiltunen 2012) and, in this case, indicates a sensory shift made possible by the change in light conditions along the way. This is something that no map can picture thus explaining the seminal part played by the multimodal nature of the narrative.

> **We started at three, ascended the cliff by lantern light, and walked along the old moraine, having the Graffeneire full in view**, which presently lighted up, and crimsoned by the morning sun, looked magnificent indeed. I was now able, for the first time, to study the actual summit of the mountain: it consisted of two peaks, very near together, and of nearly equal height. **Instead of crossing the glacier towards the Grand Combin, as we had done the year before, we kept under the rocks on the left, walking along a belt of piled and tottering fragments, with quantities of fresh snow filling the interstices.** (PPG 1859: 116; our emphasis)

An investigation of the locative function of new media renders similar results: maps are drawn with a view to mapping one's location in space (in figure 5.4 indicated by the originally blue dot on the map). Here too the sender provides a metacommentary about their location ("This is where we are at [the] moment") and focuses on the direction of further motion and progress. This instance of metalanguage reflects the sender's awareness of how semiotic choices are anchored in the context of the ongoing spatial discourse (Verschueren 2000) and facilitates interpretation of the meanings conveyed through a mix of visual and lexical resources. Interestingly, in digital discourse, maps (or locations) can be shared with no or little preceding commentary: it is understood that their function is to inform of the sender's current location in space. In the Alpine travel narratives, maps fulfilled a more global function of representing whole or parts

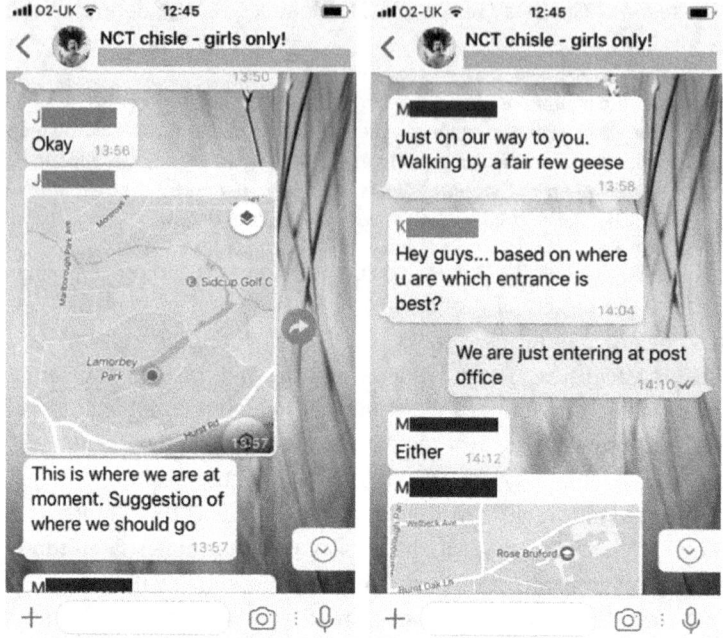

Figure 5.4: Location with metacommentary in WhatsApp.

of ascent or descent, with locations at individual points in time more likely to be represented through drawings.

In figure 5.4, Jade is the first one to arrive at the agreed park and lets all the other group members know where to find her. Others then position themselves in space with respect to each other's earlier indicated location.

Location and self-positioning in the mobile messages are used also in fostering shared sensory experiences: through mapping location and directionality and sharing photographs which illustrate the user's relationship to landmarks and the environment (as in figure 5.5 below). The map in figure 5.5 shows not only the sender's exact positioning in space (the "blue" dot), but also their directionality (the radiating shading, also originally in blue), which helps establish the direction of their spatial progress while in motion. Additionally, this technologically enabled feature and familiarity with the area and its characteristics allows the recipient to imagine the sender's current view. The addressee is invited to share the same visual perspective, including not only direction, but also other visual experiences and associations triggered by them, for example, those triggered by a photo of a particular time of day or season, a view of a pond in a park, or a photo of a sleeping baby taken by a mother directly positioned

5 Discourse about and in motion — 103

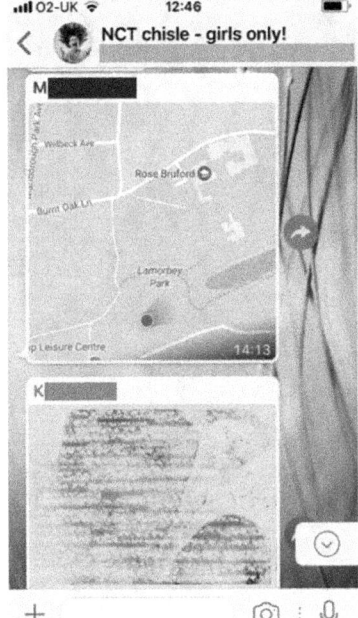

Figure 5.5: Visual resources (maps and images) to illustrate the sender's current perspective.

over the baby's cot (figure 5.5). This is what Villi (2016) referred to when he spoke about "sending places" through camera-enabled mobile phones.

However, we find that location and perspective were shared also in the pre-digital era. Maps – discussed above – were one of the types of location and perspective sharing. Another, which invites sensory alignment, is that made possible through the sharing of drawings, both those of more general landscape features and those of the details of the travellers' environment as they perceived it (figure 5.6). Similarly placed and functionally aligned, these two instantiations of perspective sharing (photographs and drawings) can be seen as differing in their respective truth-values. Photographs were traditionally seen as "perfect *analogon[s]*" of reality[2] (Barthes 1961: 128) and drawings as mediated through the eyes of the artist, whose toolset may have been limited, and were shaped by individual perception or "the *style* of the reproduction"[3]

---

[2] "certes l'image n'est pas le réel; mais elle en est du moins l'*analogon* parfait" (Barthes 1961 :128)
[3] "le *style* de la reproduction" (Barthes 1961: 128)

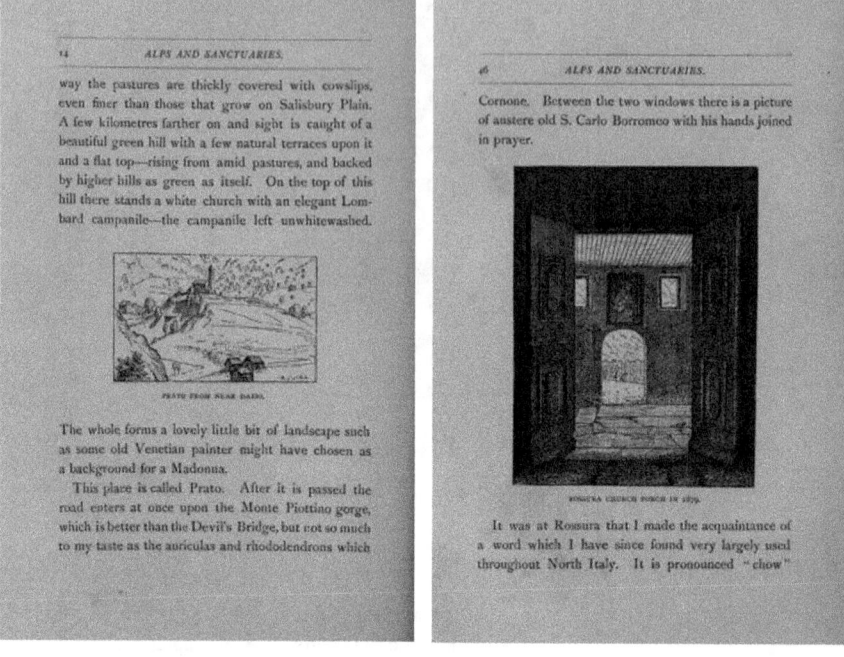

Figure 5.6: Butler's Alps and sanctuaries: The writer's perspective through landscape and detail.

(Barthes 1961: 128). The modern-day availability of a range of technological tools for image alteration means that the potential for modification of "true" or original images is vast, including annotation, the use of filters, and size- and frame-manipulation. While absent from the digital dataset discussed here, image alteration is not uncommon in other images shared digitally, both in mobile messaging and online contexts (e.g. selfies with face filters on Instagram or portraits with affective visual commentary, such as hearts added to a photo, see Poulsen 2018; Schipper 2018). This brings the two types of visual representation closer together, highlighting the anthropocentric nature of spatial representation across centuries.

5.4.3 Identifying locations based on external expertise

The need for communication while travelling and drawing on other travellers' experience en route has remained a feature of communication in motion

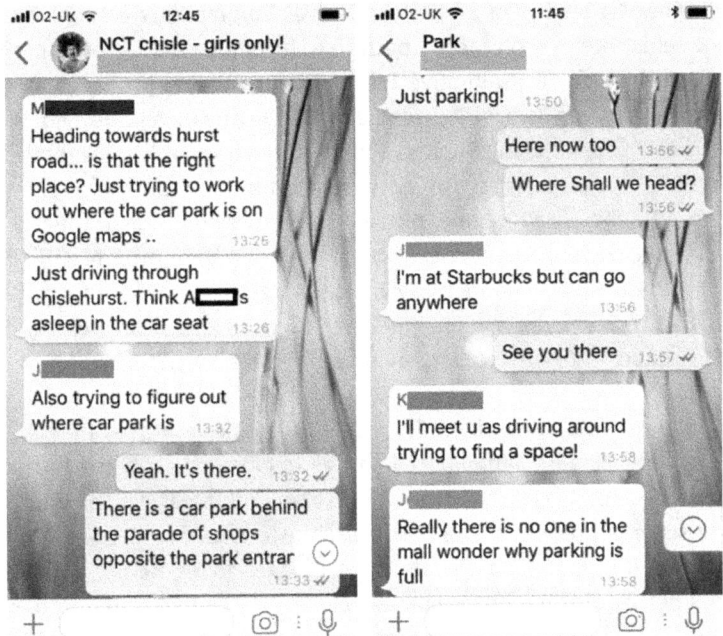

Figure 5.7: Establishing location based on external expertise.

throughout history, particularly in cases where new or unfamiliar territories are being explored. Examples in this section include instances of location and direction enquiries, drawing on the existing experience of others. While new media allows direct real-time communication between the source-informer and enquirer (figure 5.7), older exchanges resort to other means, including, as seen in the quote from *Peaks Passes and Glaciers* below, dispatching a messenger.

> By following the water we got safely down to Verbier, and at three o'clock we were in our old quarters chez Pierre Perrodin. **A messenger was instantly dispatched to Lourtier to bring down the chasseurs, but they did not arrive until ten o'clock the following morning. I questioned them closely about their former expedition, ascertained that they had really reached the summit, and that the ascent was made, as I had anticipated, by the snow slope on the Corbassière side.** (PPG 1860: 79; our emphasis)

This distinction draws attention to the process of meaning-negotiation in the two types of texts as influenced by their respective interactivity-potentials. Eisenlauer and Hoffmann (2008) propose three levels of interactivity: cognitive, structural and productive. On a cognitive level, readers can only respond to a text, but cannot alter it. On a structural level, interactants can ask for clarification or select their own reading path (e.g. through a choice of hyperlinks to follow online). On a productive level, interactants co-produce texts through correcting existing text or supplementing their own. As outlined by Bublitz (2012: 164), instant messaging, both in computer- and mobile-mediated contexts, is characterised by near-immediate reciprocity, which is slightly restricted (if compared to face-to-face communication) due to the limited access to kinetic social context cues. On the other hand, in print texts like the Alpine travel narratives, interactivity in meaning-making can only take place on a cognitive level, as readers interpret texts as they are presented to them, with no access to any structural or productive means of meaning-construction.

For both datasets, this determines the type of semiotic resources that can be drawn upon in the English language to ensure understanding between the writer and the reader and is clearly evident in texts in both datasets. For example, the metadiscourse present in the above excerpt can be compared to the direct enquiry and information in WhatsApp messages in figure 5.7. Mobile messaging does not require carefully planned "close questioning" about former experiences, nor ensuring that users are in possession of all the necessary information prior to departure. Instead, queries can be sent on an ongoing basis, taking advantage of the perpetual contact afforded by mobile phone messaging and the informant's constant availability.

Discursively, the immediate nature of location-focused communication in this dataset is represented through the frequent use of *just* + present participle in "**just trying** to work out where the car park is", "**just driving** through", and "**just parking**", compared to the past simple and past perfect tense used in the meta-commentary in Alpine narratives. Questions in WhatsApp are responded to through deictic terms ("there" and "here") and "there + BE" structures for the discursive construction of space as well as definite articles when referring to clearly identifiable or known locations in space ("**the** car park", "**the** parade of shops" and "**the** park entrance"). In comparison, the nineteenth century narrative recounts meetings, interviews, and location-focused interactions, nonetheless drawing on elements from the writer's existing knowledge demonstrated through the definite articles in "**the** summit" and "**the** snow slope on the Corbassière side". In both cases, we are able to draw conclusions about the writer's positioning based on their use of language: the deictic terms ("there" and "here") and explicit description of motion ("heading towards" and "driving through") in WhatsApp and the use of motion verbs ("get down", "dispatch", and "arrive") in Alpine travel narratives.

5.5 Discussion: A *transhistorical* approach to discourse *about* and *in* motion

Although temporally and formally different, the two corpora permeate with occurrences of self-localisation, location-sharing, and discursive space construction. In both cases, these functions are performed through a combination of multiple verbal and non-verbal modes, such as descriptions, place names, and a range of images, which serve to indicate the writer's position with respect to the environment (or a Figure's positioning with respect to the Ground).

Providing names and descriptions of places, both in the Alps and in the city, means also discursively shaping them (Levinson 2003; Lyons 2015; Ounoughi 2016, 2017), focusing on spatial inter-dependencies anchored around a discursive being – the human – and based not necessarily on reality but on the writer's *perception* of it (Lyons 2015). Conceptualisations of the surrounding environment are evoked by language and originate from the writer's vantage point (cf. Genette's ([1972] 1980) "internal focalization"). They are constructed and assigned meaning through the mere act of text production and just as new discourse emerges, so do new conceptualisations constituted through language (Langacker 1991). Space cannot be conceptualised as a fixed environment, independent of language and action (Lussault & Stock 2010: 16). Rather, just like discourse, it is shaped by the environment in which it is produced, just as physical environments are shaped by discourse, both in its verbal and nonverbal form. Discourse *about* motion and *in* motion consists of a series of performative speech acts through which language users shape space and identify themselves and one another within this constantly changing space.

From identifying a general location in a global space, travellers gradually focus on more detailed descriptions of the environment and their individual viewpoint. Functionally, this discourse moves away from its focus on facilitating convergence in geographical space and enters the sphere of enabling shared sensory experience (Ounoughi 2017). Both in the nineteenth century Alpine travel narratives and in the twenty-first century instant messaging, discourse *about* motion and *in* motion includes personal comments about the changing environment and related emotional and aesthetic responses. Mapping space and shaping it – be it at a local level of immediate mobile exchange or a carefully constructed literary text – involves individual perception of the characteristics of the constantly changing environment and the experience of motion. These factors, among others, contribute to the discursive choices travellers make in communicating *in* and *about* motion. It is these choices that help make sense of the environment as it evolves.

The analysis presented in this chapter has shown that it is not the affordances of the relevant communicative channels that determine the content of communication *in* and *about* motion in the two corpora we analysed. Instead, it is the function of communication and the role of the writer that shape what is conveyed and in what form. It is unquestionable that discourse produced by nineteenth century alpinists and in micro-coordinating everyday activities in the twenty-first century WhatsApp conversation differ. However, the technology-related differences are mainly temporal, which in turn affects the related semiotic choices of the writers. The speed of twenty-first century communication and its ephemeral character do not render the need to map spaces obsolete, just like the crafted character of Alpine travel writing does not mean that the fleeting features of the surrounding environment cannot serve as the sensorily infused referential Ground.

What this suggests is that, as discourse analysts, we should follow the anthropocentric nature of the language of motion (at least in English and other languages which follow this pattern) and start our investigations by considering the human communicative needs across centuries. Communication *in* and *about* motion constitutes one such need, but there are multiple others to consider. Having done that, we can move on to identifying types of texts or communicative channels that foster this type of communication. In our case, wanting to consider the novelty aspects of "new media discourse", the choice of texts will involve a diachronic perspective. The next step of the analysis is to identify the communicative actions taken and processes completed by writers (or speakers, in other types of data) in the context of the functions that are of interest and the types of communicative situations in question. Finally, a microanalysis of discursive means, including multimodal discourse, will demonstrate in what ways the overarching functions are performed across centuries. The starting point, rather than the features of technology, should be the inherent human need to communicate. In our case, it is communication in motion.

Thanks to this approach, we avoid the artificial classification of communication based on the media involved and the technological determinism that this brings. We are also less likely to fall into the trap of separating new media communication or historical communication from the context in which it occurs, a context which, as has been shown, largely determines the content and nature of communication across centuries. This is not to say that the affordances of the medium through which communication is performed should be ignored, but that the oft-marvelled richness of new media exchanges, compared to historical text, is based on superficial analysis of the affordances of the latter and a simplistic one-to-one mapping of multimodal content in both.

5.6 Conclusion

This chapter has demonstrated that the analysis of the co-functioning of space and language is fundamental in increasing our understanding of the ways in which a changing environment is constructed through human perception and its rendering in language. Rather than being dependent on the type of technology used, the time when texts are written or their immediate purpose, communication across centuries is shaped primarily by the human need to exchange and share information and (sensory) experiences, a point that is often obscured by the technologically deterministic discourse of today. A transhistorical approach to discourse *in* and *about* motion helps us strip ourselves of the preconceptions of technological determinism. In its data-driven form, it also allows the researcher to free themselves from the constraints of existing methodologies and approaches, which were designed with a particular data type or research questions in mind. Taking into account the vast differences between potential transhistorical data sets, it is unlikely that a pre-conceived set of methodological tools would allow for a full analysis of communicative features. Starting from the data and placing the exchanging human at the centre of the transhistorical approach to data analysis opens up a window into new layers of discursive possibilities, which help understand the need for communication in a specific context and the human that stands at the centre of this communication. It is this perspective that we need to focus on. In the case of discourse *in* and *about* motion, it is the perspective on the geography of the surrounding environment as people shape and reshape it through their vision, perspective, and representative style that is of central importance.

References

Alpine Club. 2018. http://www.alpine-club.org.uk/ac2/about-the-ac/mission-2 (accessed 11 July 2019).

Arminen, Ilkka. 2006. Social functions of location in mobile telephony. *Personal and Ubiquitous Computing* 10 (5). 319–323.

Barthes, Roland. 1961. Le message photographique. *Communications* 1. 127–138.

Bolter, Jay D. 2011. *Writing Space: Computers, hypertext, and the remediation of print.* New York: Lawrence Erlbaum.

Bolter, Jay D. & Richard Grusin. 2000. *Remediation: Understanding new media.* Cambridge, MA: MIT Press.

Brown, Barry, Kenton O'Hara, Moria McGregor & Donald McMillan. 2018. Text in talk: Lightweight messages in co-present interaction. *ACM Transactions on Computer-Human Interaction* 24 (6). Article 42.

Bublitz, Wolfram. 2012. From speaker and hearer to chatter, blogger and user. In Ulrich Busse & Axel Hübler (eds.), *Investigations into the meta-communicative lexicon of English: A contribution to historical pragmatics*, 151–176. Amsterdam: John Benjamins.

Butler, Samuel. 1882. *Alps and sanctuaries of Piedmont and the Canton Ticino*. London: David Bongue.

Defour, Tine. 2008. The speaker's voice: A diachronic study on the use of *well* and *now* as pragmatic markers. *English Text Construction* 1 (1). 62–82.

Eisenlauer, Volker & Christian Hoffmann. 2008. The metapragmatics of remediated text design. *Information Design Journal* 16 (1). 1–18.

Farman, Jason. 2012. *Mobile interface theory: Embodied space and locative media*. Abingdon: Routledge.

Foster, Shirley. 1988. "Women travellers", a paper to Network feminist theorists, Lancaster, May.

Foster, Shirley. 1990. *Across new worlds: Nineteenth century women travellers and their writings*. Hemel Hempstead: Harvester.

Gillen, Julia. 2014. *Digital literacies*. Abingdon: Routledge.

Genette, Gérard. 1980 [1972]. *Narrative discourse. An essay in method*. Oxford: Blackwell.

Hulme, Peter & Tim Youngs (eds.). 2002. *The Cambridge companion to travel writing*. Cambridge, UK: Cambridge University Press.

Ito, Mizuko. 2005. Mobile phones, Japanese youth, and the re-placement of social contact. http://www.itofisher.com/mito/archives/mobileyouth.pdf (30 Jan 2018).

Langacker, Ronald W. 1991. *Foundations of cognitive grammar. Vol II. Descriptive application*. Stanford: Stanford University Press.

Laursen, Ditte & Margaret H. Szymanski. 2013. Where are you? Location talk in mobile phone conversations. *Mobile Media & Communication* 1 (3). 314–334.

Levinson, Steven C. 2003. *Space in language and cognition*. Cambridge, UK: Cambridge University Press.

Licoppe, Christian. 2004. Connected presence: The emergence of a new repertoire for managing social relationships in a changing communication technoscape. *Environment and Planning D: Society and Space* 22 (1). 135–156.

Licoppe, Christian. 2009. Recognizing mutual "proximity" at a distance: Weaving together mobility, sociality and technology. *Journal of Pragmatics* 41 (10). 1924–1937.

Lussault, Michel & Matthis Stock. 2010. "Doing with space": Towards a pragmatics of space. *Social Geography* 5. 11–19.

Lyons, Agnieszka. 2014. *Self-presentation and self-positioning in text-messages: Embedded multimodality, deixis, and reference frame*. London: Queen Mary University of London PhD thesis.

Lyons, Agnieszka. 2015. Storyworld in text-messages: Sequentiality and spatialisation. In Mari Hatavara, Matti Hyvärinen, Maria Mäkelä & Frans Mäyrä (eds.), *Narrative theory, literature, and new media: Narrative minds and virtual worlds*, 122–143. Abingdon: Routledge.

Lyons, Agnieszka & Caroline Tagg. 2019. The discursive construction of mobile chronotopes in mobile phone messaging. *Language in Society* 48 (5). 657–683.

Mills, Sara. 1991. *Discourses of difference*. Abingdon: Routledge.

Ounoughi, Samia. 2016. La traversée des cols alpins: Analyse d'une poétique de la liminalité, *E-rea: Revue électronique d'études sur le monde anglophone* 14 (1).

Ounoughi, Samia. 2017. Analyse du discours de la liminalité: Butler, de l'autre côté du Saint-Gothard entre passage et ancrage. *ILCEA* 28.

Pahta, Päivi & Andreas H. Jucker (eds.). 2011. *Communicating Early English manuscripts. Studies in English language.* Cambridge, UK: Cambridge University Press.

Poulsen, Søren V. 2018. Becoming a semiotic technology: A historical study of Instagram's tools for making and sharing photos and videos. *Internet Histories* 2 (1–2). 121–139.

Yu, Qian, Peiying Huang & Liu Liming. 2017. From "connected presence" to "panoptic presence": Reframing the parent–child relationship on mobile instant messaging uses in the Chinese translocal context. *Mobile Media & Communication* 5 (2). 123–138.

Schegloff, Emanuel A. 1972. Notes on a conversational practice: formulating place. In David Sudnow (ed.), *Studies in social interaction*, 75–119. New York: Free Press.

Schipper, Meike. 2018. "A whole new way to see yourself(ie)": Exploring how face filters transform the practice of selfie creation. Utrecht: Utrecht University MA dissertation.

Taavitsainen, Irma & Turo Hiltunen. 2012. *Now* as a text deictic feature in Late Medieval and Early Modern English medical writing. In Ulrich Busse & Axel Hübler (eds.), *Investigations into the meta-communicative lexicon of English: A contribution to historical pragmatics*, 179–205. Amsterdam: John Benjamins.

Talmy, Leonard. 1972. *Semantic structures in English and Atsugewi.* Berkeley: University of California PhD thesis.

Verschueren, Jef. 2000. Notes on the role of metapragmatic awareness in language use. *Pragmatics* 10 (4). 439–56.

Viviès, Jean. (ed.). 2003. *Lignes de fuite. Littérature de voyage du monde anglophone.* Aix-en-Provence: Publications de l'Université de Provence.

Villi, Mikko. 2016. Photographs of place in phonespace: Camera phones as a location-aware mobile technology. In Edgar Gómex Cruz & Asko Lehmuskallio (eds.), *Digital photography and everyday life: Empirical studies on material visual practices*, 107–121. Abingdon: Routledge.

Wellman, Barry. 2001. Physical place and cyberplace: The rise of personalized networking. *International Journal of Urban and Regional Research* 25. 227–252.

Wilken, Rowan. 2005. FCJ-036 From stabilitas loci to mobilitas loci: Networked mobility and the transformation of place. *The Fibreculture Journal* 6. n.p.

Wilken, Rowan & Goggin, Gerard. 2012. *Mobile technology and place.* Abingdon: Routledge.

Worley, Linda K. 1986. Through others' eyes: Narratives of German women travelling in nineteenth century America. *Yearbook of German-American Studies* 21. 39–50.

Philip Seargeant
6 "New" media and self-fashioning: The construction of a political persona by Elizabeth I and Donald Trump

6.1 Introduction: Separated by a common semiotic language

The importance of constructing and projecting an image of authority is a commonplace of statecraft. In many ways, the techniques by which this is achieved have changed little from ancient to modern times. Monumentalizing a leader in portraits, hagiographies or statues is a practice that held good for Kublai Khan in the thirteenth century in much the same way as for Kim Jong-un in the twenty-first. With each new advance in communications technology, however, new possibilities present themselves to aspiring leaders, along with new challenges. And those who are most successful in exploiting the media available to them, as well as manipulating the ideological currents within society, are arguably those who will be best at leveraging power. This chapter looks at case studies of two very different leaders, from two different eras, who discursively created distinct and influential political personae which were key to their harnessing of popular power within their respective contexts. The contrast between these two is then used as a means of exploring commonalities in political communications strategies across time, while also looking at the distinctiveness of the modern media environment as a tool for political "self-fashioning". In doing this, the chapter considers the extent to which the medium is a fundamental element of the message when it comes to political persuasion, and if and how modern forms of online social media are having a significant effect on the practice of contemporary leadership.

The two case studies are taken from Early Modern England and the twenty-first century United States, and represent high-profile examples (in terms of the scholarly and media coverage they have both attracted) of the way that media construction of the image of the political leader played a central role in their success. The chapter begins by revisiting well-known contemporary accounts and scholarly analysis of Elizabeth I's self-presentation as queen, and her

---

Philip Seargeant, The Open University, School of Languages and Applied Linguistics, Milton Keynes, UK, e-mail: philip.seargeant@open.ac.uk

status as one of the most successful monarchs of the late Renaissance at constructing and managing an image which facilitated the process of governance. This is contrasted, in the second half of the chapter, with the case of the presidential campaign and early presidency of Donald Trump in the USA, whose communication style and contrarian image purposefully placed itself in conflict with established channels of media, and yet, in creating what often appears to be a chaotic and divisive self-image, successfully connected with a large proportion of the electorate. A great deal has been made of the role played by social media, and particularly Twitter, in the way Trump presented himself to the electorate. His use of Twitter, and the distinctive personality he has been able to express via it, became a major element of his public persona, and an emblematic factor of what he has called his "modern day presidential" style (Wootson 2017). In contrasting these two cases, therefore, the chapter will consider how politically-focused (social) media use in the early twenty-first century differs from the way in which leaders in the past have managed and projected their image as part of the business of statecraft. Drawing on theories of self-fashioning (Greenblatt 1980) via textual and visual artefacts, and the construction and performance of identity online, the chapter examines the continuities and differences in practice between the media resources available in two eras which are separated by almost half a millennium, but which both, in their way, were dealing with the implications of an information-communication revolution in English-speaking society, as well as a dramatic shift in ideological landscape.

6.2 Elizabeth I: A composite of texts

6.2.1 Spectacle and self-fashioning

In a letter to Philip II, Don Diego Guzman de Silva, Spain's ambassador to England during the 1560s, writes of the scenes that accompanied Elizabeth's progress into London in September 1568 on her accession to the throne:

> She came by the river as far as Reading, and thence through the country in a carriage, open on all sides, that she might be seen by the people who flocked all along the roads ... She ordered her carriage to be taken sometimes where the crowd seemed thickest and stood up and thanked the people.   (Quoted in Smith 1980: 4)

This picture of the queen placing herself on display before her subjects, in an open carriage, seeking out the most populated areas of the crowd, accords with a tenet of Renaissance politics described by Tennenhouse (1986: 155), whereby the "monarch understood himself or herself as deriving power from being the object of the public gaze". According to the historian John Hayward, writing seven years after Elizabeth's death, this was an idea she herself purposefully pursued. On the eve of her coronation, for example, a procession was organised through the city, where she

> passed from the Tower through the City of London to Westminster, most royally furnished, both for her person and for her train, knowing right well that in pompous ceremonies a secret of government doth much consist, for that the people are naturally both taken and held with exterior shows. (Quoted in Smith 1980: 1)

Hayward's suggestion that Elizabeth knew from the very earliest stages of her reign of the importance to good government of theatrical presentation – including that of her own self – is borne out by the proliferation of images of her in the literature and art of the time. This notion of self-fashioning is one which, according to Greenblatt (1980: 2), defines this period in many ways. In the sixteenth century, he writes, "there appears to be an increased self-consciousness about the fashioning of human identity as a manipulable, artful process". This awareness coincides with a shift in the way the word "fashion" began to be used. Its meaning started to encompass not only the shaping and design of the appearance of things, but also of the person. It was applied to the practices of parents and teachers, and became associated with manners and comportment, as well as the ways in which one spoke and acted. Self-fashioning, Greenblatt (1980: 3) suggests, derives its interest in this period "from the fact that it functions without regard for a sharp distinction between literature and social life". It was, in other words, to do with the persona as both a text itself – one which could be inscribed with meaning – and a concept constructed out of other texts. As Frye (1993: 7) writes, the "historical subject we call Elizabeth I exists as a composite of texts – speeches, letters, recorded actions, rumors, pictures, spectacles, and literature". And we could add to this non-verbal texts such as fashion and visual art. The understanding we have of this subject comes from looking at the way in which these texts cultivate particular images in order to produce particular effects – and crucial to Greenblatt's thesis is that these images are purposefully cultivated as a form of political exercise by those wielding power.

For Elizabeth, then – at least according to contemporary commentators such as Hayward – the construction and control of her own image was an essential element of the way she manipulated power. But likewise, those around her also used the way she was represented to further their own interests. As Strong (1984: 21) writes, "the creation of an 'image' of a monarch to draw people's allegiance was the task of humanists, poets, writers and artists". Issues ranging from personal hopes of patronage (see below) to overt religious propaganda were all raised and conducted through her image. In this way, the persona of the queen acted as a contested text, with different factions aiming to make political advantage by pushing their own interpretations through the cultivation of competing discourses.

6.2.2 Writing history, shaping ideology

As well as possessing an understanding of the way in which the theatrics of self-presentation could work, as in the examples of the ceremonial processions, Elizabeth also appears to have been explicitly aware of the importance of verbal texts in the shaping of her persona and legacy. For example, sending a copy of one of her speeches to her godson John Harington, she included a brief note suggesting that he "Ponder them in the howres of leysure, and plaie wythe them tyll they enter thyne vnderstanging; so shallt thou hereafter, perchance, fynde some good frutes hereof when thy godmother is oute of remembraunce" (Harington 1930). Although she claims a teaching purpose for this action, and couches her words in a language of modesty (suggesting that during his lifetime she will already be forgotten), she is, at the same time, engaging in a specific form of myth-management. In the absence of biological heirs (an issue which was a defining element in her persona, as is discussed below), Elizabeth instead takes steps to ensure that the cult of her personality is preserved in written texts such as these. And although a private letter, the implication of what she writes is that she does not see this as an ephemeral communication, but rather as something which will be preserved by her godson, and thus has a relative permanence (on the common practice of authorially controlled epistolary circulation – royal or otherwise – see Daybell 2016).

A reflective awareness of the way her own person can be inscribed with meaning – and the importance this will have for her role as queen – can be found in the very first speech of her reign, where she stated that "at this daie I stand free from anie other meaning that either I have had in tymes paste, or have at this present" (quoted in Frye 1993). The suggestion here is that by being placed within the new context of queen, the meaning of her identity is necessarily changed, and that all that has gone before is of little or no bearing for her present situation. This was not, of course, the actual case by any means. From her birth, Elizabeth's person was encoded with very specific meanings, and it was the way these were then discursively moulded and manipulated which played a significant part in the construction of her image – both by herself and others. As the daughter of Anne Boleyn, for whom Henry

VIII had divorced his first wife because she had failed to produce a male heir, Elizabeth's gender was of great embarrassment to her father. In addition, the fact that the divorce necessitated the break with Rome and the establishment of the independent Church of England meant she was inexorably linked to the Reformation. The cultural and political meaning of this early part of her biography depended, however, on the context in which it was being interpreted. A decade after her death the scene of her birth could be portrayed as an epiphanic moment in the development of English history, as it was in Shakespeare and Fletcher's 1613 play *Henry VIII*. At the end of this play the Protestant martyr Cranmer delivers a prophetic speech at the new princess's christening:

> This royal infant – heaven still move about her! –
> Though in her cradle, yet now promises
> Upon this land a thousand thousand blessings,
> Which time shall bring to ripeness (5.4.17)

Just out of view in such a revisionist reading of the history of the previous generation is the memory of what happened to Anne Boleyn soon after the birth of her daughter (she was beheaded for treason), as well as, presumably, what happened to Mary Queen of Scots, the mother of Elizabeth's successor, James I. The fate suffered by Mary Queen of Scots, executed as a victim of the sectarian politics of religion (Goodare 2004), was something which may easily have befallen Elizabeth during her sister Mary Tudor's reign. During her time as a princess, Elizabeth not only feared for her life as the Protestant heir of a Catholic queen, but was also constantly being used as a symbolic resource in the politicking of others. Throughout her childhood therefore, the "promises" that time would bring to "ripeness" were more in the nature of threats to the ruling (Catholic) authority, or vehicles for various politically expedient measures, rather than the triumphal portents they could be portrayed as by the time that Shakespeare and Fletcher wrote their play.

6.2.3 Gender and power

With her accession to the throne, however, the balance of authority shifted, and Elizabeth, along with those around her, could attempt to inscribe a new meaning on her person – yet one that was still founded on ideologies related to her gender and religion. Unsurprisingly, the gender of the queen was the focus of much attention in what was an overtly patriarchal society. As Montrose (1983: 64) writes, "With one vital exception, all forms of public and domestic authority in Elizabethan England were vested in men: in fathers, husbands, masters, teachers, magistrates and lords". In this context, much of the attention generated by her gender had a specifically misogynistic slant. The Spanish ambassador sent by Philip II – Mary Tudor's husband and therefore king regent during her reign – to help handle the transition from Mary to Elizabeth wrote home that "It gives me great trouble every time I write to your Majesty not to be able to send more pleasing intelligence, but what can one expect from a country governed by a Queen" (quoted in Smith 1980: 3). Elizabeth's own subjects too, while remaining loyal, would speak detrimentally on the issue of her gender: "First of all you must consider with whom you have to deale", writes the poet Edward Dyer, "& what wee be towards her, who though she does descend uery much in her Sex as a woman, yet wee may not forget her Place, & the nature of it as our Soveraigne" (quoted in Frye 1993: 12). In this equation, the determining factors of the queen's meaning are due to both biology and place within the hierarchy, and yet, importantly for her efficacy as monarch, the latter is seen as taking precedence over the former for this particular subject.

However, her "Place, & the nature of it as our Soveraigne" was by no means sufficient to keep all her subjects loyal. Some disputed her right to the throne, considering her parents' marriage to have been illegal (which thus meant that she herself was illegitimate). Having disposed of the determining fact of her status within the societal hierarchy, they seized hold of this other key constituent of her identity – her gender. Cardinal William Allen, for example, who fled England for the continent in 1561, wrote an open letter back to his countrymen on the eve of the Armada's attack and what was expected would be its easy victory. Focusing his own personal attack on the figure of Elizabeth, he writes

> She hath abused her body, against God's laws, to the disgrace of princely majesty, and with the whole nation's reproach. By unspeakable and incredibly variety of lust, which modesty suffreth not to be remembered ... she hath defiled and inflamed her person and country, and made her court as a trap ... The whole world derides our effeminate darstady that has suffered such a creature almost thirty years to reign over our bodes and souls, and to have the chief regiment of all our affairs as well spiritual as temporal, to the extinguishing not only of religion but of all chaste living and honesty.
>
> (Quoted in Frye 1993: 10–11)

This attack on the monstrous female let loose on the nation, where the gender of the monarch is transferred onto the country as a whole, making it by implication effeminate, concentrates its assault on Elizabeth's sexuality which, unchecked, marks her out as a whore, thus suggesting that she was after all her mother's daughter, "being indeed taken and known for an incestuous bastard, begotten and born in sin, of an infamous courtesan Anne Boleyn, afterwards executed for adultery, heresy and incest, amongst others with her natural brother" (quoted in Frye 1993: 8). In invoking this sort of imagery, however, the diatribe constructs its concept of the queen using the very same ingredients that Elizabeth herself was using – and in particular the key notion of chastity. The success of Elizabeth's self-fashioning, in other words, was to co-opt concepts which were staples of the discourse around a female monarch (and were being used as a weapon in attempts to undermine her authority), and instead turn them into positive attributes.

Mary Tudor's reign had provided a number of useful exempla for Elizabeth about the problems facing a female monarch. Mary's marriage to Philip II of Spain, and her desperate desire for an heir to ensure that the succession would not go to the Protestant Elizabeth, diluted her position of authority, making the queen herself visibly subject to those two forces which highlighted the traditional weakness of the role of women in the patriarchal structure. Mary in fact used, in her speeches, a number of the same metaphors of self-presentation which were later to become associated with Elizabeth. When, for example, she spoke to the aldermen at the Guildhall at the time of Thomas Wyatt's rebellion in 1554, she drew upon the metaphor of being married to the nation, as well as that of her subjects being her children. Wyatt's rebellion had been provoked by Mary's decision to marry the Spanish king, which prompted her response that: "I am already married to this Common Weal and the faithful members of the same", and "I cannot tell how naturally a mother loueth her children, for I was never the mother of anie; but certeinlie a prince and governor may as naturalie and as earnestly love subjects, as the mother dothe her child" (quoted in Frye 1993: 28). Elizabeth was later to use almost identical phrasing in her response to the Commons' petition that she marry: "I am bound unto an Husband, which is the Kingdome of England, and that may suffice you ... And reproach mee no more ... that I haue no children: for euery one of you, and as many as are English, are my Children, and Kinsfolkes" (quoted in Axton 1977: 38–9). That the words have come to be associated with Elizabeth more than with her sister has much to do with the effect they had within their respective contexts. That Mary was married, and trying desperately to produce an heir, undermined the potency of the metaphor, as the sense seems to be in conflict with her actions. For Elizabeth, who made a great deal of her belief in the bond between the words and deeds of a monarch (Smith 1980), the metaphor was complemented by the way she conducted her life, thus creating a coherent discourse. It was in her very first speech to Parliament in 1559, in fact, when she suggested she would remain unmarried, and that "it shall be sufficient that a marble stone shall declare that a Queen, having lived and reigned so many years, died a virgin" (quoted in Smith 1980: 27).

Constructing this image of the Virgin Queen (which still resonates as part of her identity even today) thus allowed Elizabeth to avoid many of the difficulties of perception that Mary had had to deal with. It meant that, with her brother and father both dead, she would not have to render up any authority to male influence, as her gender might otherwise have dictated. In the famous speech attributed to her at Tilbury, on the eve of the battle with the Armada, she alludes to precisely this idea when she declares to her soldiers that no "prince of Europe should dare invade the borders of my realm" (quoted in Smith 1980: 38). Given that it was common in artistic representations of the time for the queen's body and the country to be bracketed together – Tennenhouse (1991: 29) gives the example of the Ditchley portrait that shows Elizabeth standing on the map of England – it is possible to read this phrase in terms of her status as Virgin Queen, so that it becomes both a political and sexual assertion. She thus positions herself as a symbolic example of inviolability for the country as a whole, communicating this meaning both in her rhetoric and her (public) actions.

The image of chastity that Elizabeth cultivated also proved to be very fertile ground for artists and writers wishing to mythologise the era. Not only did it invoke the iconography of the Virgin Mother (thus giving spiritual authority to Elizabeth's position), it also gave itself over readily to analogies from Classical literature. At a time when English literature was rediscovering cultures of the past, and constructing an indigenous literature around such models, the image of the Virgin Queen provided an ideal literary subject. It worked as a native complement to the tradition of the goddesses of the ancient world, with Elizabeth being variously portrayed as everyone from "Cynthia, Phoebe, Flora, Diana and Aurora" to "Astrea, Zabeta, Deborah, Laura, Oriana, and, of course, Belphoebe and Gloriana" (Greenblatt 1980: 168). In addition, the image could function as the object of chaste desire in love poetry, as, for example, in Edmund Spenser's *Shepheardes Calender* (Spenser 1995). In these ways, then, Elizabeth's image was assimilated into the literary imagination of the age, which resulted in a considerable body of work that informed the popular idea of her as leader of the nation.

Both the contemporary commentary and subsequent academic analysis thus suggest that Elizabeth had a reflective awareness of the importance of shaping a public persona, and of the ways in which this could be achieved both discursively and through performance and spectacle. Central to this awareness was the subtle manipulation of the symbolic resources available to her – particularly those relating to her gender – as a means of creating a narrative which lent itself to poetic and artistic adoption, thus ensuring it would be shared and spread throughout the literary and artistic culture of the time. And while the media may be vastly different from those used today, a number of these same fundamental principles remain central to the way that modern political personae attempt to leverage power, as we can see in the case of Donald Trump.

6.3 Donald Trump: Antagonistic nonconformity

6.3.1 The power of numbers

Donald Trump's 2016 presidential campaign can, if we simplify matters a little, be reduced to two elemental parts. It consisted firstly of his various inflammatory views on social issues: immigration, gun control, climate change and so on. Then there was the way he communicated these views – both the rhetoric and the choice and manipulation of media. These two elements were both instrumental in attracting a frenzy of attention to his campaign, and in shaping the political persona that was constructed around him in the news media. But while both have been important, it is the means by which he communicated his message which was, perhaps, the most influential aspect of his self-fashioning – and which marked his campaign, and subsequent presidency, apart from the many rivals who shared much of his agenda.

We looked above at the way that the progress of the newly acceded monarch through the country and into the capital was an important symbolic act in the exercising of power in Renaissance England. Elizabeth, as we have seen from the reports from the Spanish ambassador, was successfully able to exploit this tradition as a way of positioning herself as the object of the public gaze. Her successor, James I, was far less successful with his experience of the practice. His procession coincided with a severe outbreak of plague in the capital and thus became a muted affair, associated in the superstitious imagination with divine discontent (Seargeant 2007).

Despite the many other ways in which a leader can present their image to the population in modern-day culture, ceremonial practices such as this continue, and often have similar symbolic meanings associated with them. A modern equivalent of the monarch's progress is the inauguration ceremony of the sort which still happens for the office of US president. And the continuing symbolic value of this as an expression of power was clearly apparent in the dispute that followed the circumstances of Trump's inauguration before the United States Capitol Building in Washington, D.C. in January 2017. When compared to the two inaugurations of former President Obama – and particularly the first in 2009 – the size of the crowd which turned out in person to watch Trump was markedly smaller. Video footage of the two events from precisely the same vantage point indicated that the crowd for Trump was much thinner than that for Obama, and estimates published by *The New York Times* suggested that Trump attracted only around a third of the 1.8 million who came to see Obama in 2009 (Wallace, Yourish & Griggs 2017).

Of note in the way this incident reflects self-presentation strategies, however, is not merely the circumstances of the 2017 event itself, but the mediatisation of it, and the discourse that then developed around this mediatisation. Mediatisation (Flew 2017) – i.e. the ways in which the media frames political discourse, and how the political system is influenced by non-state controlled mass media – is an important part of modern-day politics in ways that cannot in any straightforward sense be compared to the Elizabethan era. The way that Trump disputed the statistics and visual evidence presented by the news media, and instead had his press secretary insist that his was actually the bigger crowd ("This was the largest audience to ever witness an inauguration – period – both in person and around the globe" [Politico 2017]), points to the way that this type of show of power still has symbolic relevance, in Trump's mind at least. But it also points to a central element of Trump's communications strategy: to attempt to control the way in which his persona is presented by means of public proclamations which preach a subjective narrative that is often at odds with reports from other traditional sources of news. Just as with Elizabeth, Trump's is an image constructed through texts – those created by himself, and by others based on his provocations. Yet as we'll see, his is also a persona in which media itself (the means by which he and others attempt to control the narrative) is very much *part* of the message, and often acts as a flashpoint around which he can promote the key characteristics that constitute the persona he is projecting.

6.3.2 Flaunting expectations

As with Elizabeth, Trump also had a high-profile public image prior to his transition to political candidate. But unlike Elizabeth he did not attempt to draw a decisive line between the earlier, pre-politics persona, and the (candidate for) leader. However, the symbolic distinction between layperson and political leader arguably played as much a part in the defining of his persona as the pre-/post-accession distinction did for Elizabeth – albeit in a contrary way. Expectations in media discourse throughout the presidential campaign and into the presidency were that he would purposefully alter his behaviour so as to conform to a more traditional template of presidential candidate (e.g. *New York Times* 2017). By constantly confounding these expectations he was able not only to continually attract media attention, but also to build a persona around the idea of an anti-establishment character, unwilling to conform to Washington norms (Seargeant forthcoming).

The means Trump used to explicitly challenge expectations about the persona of a leader included his communication practices themselves. His choice of media, his rhetorical style, the dialogic relationship he had with the news media and other forms of institutional authority – all these became focal points around which his strategy of self-fashioning was based. As Sclafani (2017: 1) writes, Trump "became famous, and infamous, not so much for his political stances, which were rarely expressed in any detail during his political campaign. It was rather *how* he expressed his stances linguistically that fascinated pundits and the public alike". This involved employing a register which was often evaluated in press reports and other media commentary as inappropriate for political exchanges (e.g. Cohen 2017; Judd 2018). But it wasn't simply the shock of the unexpected; it was also the way his ability to attract attention to his pronouncements often also had the effect of skewing the media narrative about his opponents by introducing issues or ideas which then came to frame the debate.

One salient example of this was his use of tapinosis – a rhetorical form of name calling, aimed at debasing one's opponent – which he used extensively, both in speeches and on Twitter, to denigrate his rivals. His use of derogatory and highly informal nicknames for his opponents usually involved blatantly appropriating the criticisms that others were making of him. Thus, for instance, he somehow managed to characterise his rivals as being intrinsically untruthful, while portraying himself as simply a plain speaker (Seargeant 2017a). His Republican challenger Ted Cruz and Democratic opponent Hillary Clinton thus became "Lyin' Ted" and "Crooked Hillary" whenever he referred to them, despite the fact that statistics were showing that Trump himself was more untruthful in what he said than almost any previous presidential candidate in history (Politifact 2018).

6.3.3 Appropriation and voice

A related rhetorical strategy is his appropriation of the language of others: a good example being his use of the term "voice". Throughout the election campaign a central pledge was that he would be the one to give a voice to the voiceless: the "forgotten men and women of our country", the communities affected by economic decline, the laid-off factory workers. For all of these he suggested, "I am your voice!" (Rowland 2016). It had resonance as a mantra for his campaign specifically because he portrayed himself, both in what he said and how he said it (and specifically in his use of Twitter as a direct and unfiltered channel of communication), as someone beyond the control of traditional institutional concerns and frameworks. The refrain was so central to his campaign that his website even sold "I am your voice" bumper stickers.[1] On becoming president he continued using this conceit by announcing the creation of a new agency for dealing with what he referred to as "immigrant crime", which would specifically target unlawful behaviour conducted by those illegally residing in the country. This agency, he said, would be a way of "providing a voice to those who have been ignored by our media, and silenced by special interests" (Campoy 2017). The initiative was named "Victims of Immigration Crime Engagement", or VOICE.

Creating a context in which the "voices" of those disaffected by history and politics can be heard has been a key aim for development and postcolonial studies over the years (Spivak 1999). It is a central strategy for challenging societal inequalities, and for countering the way that these are often institutionally reproduced within social structures such as the law and education. The word is also used by advocate organisations such as America's Voice, who work for the civil and political rights of the immigrant population. Trump's "VOICE" initiative on the other hand had the effect of specifically stigmatising migrant communities by associating the immigrant experience with a discourse of criminality (despite clear evidence showing that immigrants are in fact less likely to commit a crime than people native born in the USA (Gurman & Caldwell 2017)). As such his use of the word would seem to be an attempt to undermine the vocabulary that is conventionally associated with movements which offer support to precisely those communities which this new policy maligns.

Trump's argument would likely be that he too was providing a voice for groups which have been disenfranchised (i.e. white-working class communities), and is taking a stand for them against a political tradition which has marginalised them over the years. Yet the issue is *how* he goes about doing this. The rhetoric used is typically divisive and stigmatising rather than inclusive, pitting one marginalised group against another. Take, for instance, his remarks made at a California Sanctuary State Roundtable in May 2016, where he

---

[1] https://shop.donaldjtrump.com/products/i-am-your-voice-bumper-stickers-set-of-3

justified his immigration policy plans by saying that "We have people coming into the country, or trying to come in – and we're stopping a lot of them – but we're taking people out of the country. You wouldn't believe how bad these people are. These aren't people. These are animals" (White House 2018). Thus, by appropriating the concept of "voice" for his own agenda (and thus for his own political persona), he simultaneously silences the legitimate concerns of numerous others.

6.3.4 Media battles

Rhetorical strategies such as these are not only a way of drawing attention to Trump's own discourse, but also of muting or dulling the discourse of opponents. Possibly the most overt way in which he has done this though is by condemning the whole of the (mainstream) news media itself, and in this way attempting to undermine the entire context in which critical opinions can be voiced. In essence, the presidential campaign itself came down to a tale of two media practices. Hillary Clinton was undone by allegations that she had mishandled diplomatic communication by using an unofficial email server. Donald Trump made a virtue out of being bluntly undiplomatic (e.g. his use of insulting nicknames), and for embracing the stylistic affordances of social media (e.g. his staccato assertions on Twitter). Clinton was pilloried not for what she had actually said – there were a few socially embarrassing revelations in the emails released by WikiLeaks, but nothing truly scandalous – but for the protocol. The story was all about the medium; and the message was mostly irrelevant. For Trump, as was discussed above with relation to his rhetorical style, protocol was very different.

Yet we also know that Trump connects to an audience. According to certain polls, a large number of people during his Presidency felt he was in fact more trustworthy than the media (Concha 2017). Part of this is no doubt due to his strategy of demonising the media, and his sustained attempts to undermine their legitimacy and impugn their professional objectivity with his constant cries of "fake news" (Seargeant 2017b) and his branding of them as the "opposition party" (Kludt 2017). In this respect, Trump's campaign and presidency was, from one perspective, all about media. In other words, not only was his image discursively constructed in the media (in what he wrote himself, as well as what others wrote about him), but it was founded on symbolic ideas about the form and role of media in modern-day politics. Key to his strategy of self-fashioning then was foregrounding a metadiscourse about mediatisation as a means of promoting the idea that his persona is based on authenticity and plain speaking.

6.4 Contrasts and conclusions

The media used in the discursive construction of Elizabeth's persona range from theatrical spectacle through private and public letters to speeches and works of literature and art. Although there are suggestions that she did have a reflective awareness of the importance of harnessing contemporary communicative resources as a means of managing her image, the extent to or explicitness with which she purposefully embraced this is negligible in comparison with the twenty-first century culture of public relations. What then can we say about similarities between Elizabeth and Trump, and the ways in which their strategies of self-fashioning have played a part in their political careers?

One notable dynamic that the two of them have in common is their ability to attract media attention, and in this way have others reproduce, extend and spread their image and message. As we have seen, by providing the symbolic ingredients which allowed writers and artists of the day to reimagine her as one of a string of characters from Classical mythology, Elizabeth ensured that her persona spread far beyond any audience that she herself could have physically addressed. A similar process occurred with – and was arguably a key ingredient in the success of – Donald Trump. Throughout the 2016 presidential campaign he regularly boasted of the way in which he was able to dominate news media cycles, and of how the exposure he was achieving was managed without having to pay for advertising space on the TV networks (Geier 2016). As Hope Hicks, one of his directors of communications, remarked, he was able to "own the news cycle with one tweet" (Associated Press 2017).

In both cases, the construction of a fairly simple but culturally-relevant and subversive "character" – the Virgin Queen, the anti-establishment celebrity businessman – resulted in a process whereby other people publicised and spread the message the respective leaders wished to put forward. The profile of both leaders, in other words, is a product of their ability to have those involved in cultural production magnify and project forward the persona they initially instigated.

Another similarity between the two is that in both cases they were able to link their message directly to the medium of communication, so that any time their persona was cited or reproduced, so too was the political agenda associated with it. In the case of Elizabeth, her self-fashioning as Virgin Queen complements perfectly the way that English Renaissance sentiments were primed to produce a native body of literature. The synergy between the two – the constructed persona of the queen and contemporary artistic trends – resulted, again, in the queen's political agenda being furthered with each representation that was made of her. For Trump this was achieved by taking a combative stance against what he derogatorily characterises as the "mainstream media", and in doing so, being able to portray himself as an anti-establishment figure, a straight-talker, and someone aligned with the populace at large rather than the elite institutions which traditionally govern politics. Any coverage which mentioned the way in which he communicated (be it his use of Twitter, his ad hominem attacks, his rhetorical style) further highlights this aspect of his persona, and the ideological values it has come to represent.

What does all this say about the use of media in the building, wielding and maintaining of power? In these two cases, political success has been built around attracting publicity through their use of the media of the day, and finding a way to make that media itself part of the ideology – which in turn resonates with a background set of norms which can be used as a foil for this "new" message. While Trump did this with a mixture of online and traditional media, drawing on the affordances of social media as a way of disseminating his message, while also provoking traditional media (newspapers and television) to further broadcast that message, Elizabeth's image was similarly constructed and circulated in the media of her day. In both these cases, the media has been a fundamental element of the message, either explicitly or implicitly, for fashioning the apparatus of political persuasion.

References

Associated Press. 2017. Fourth time lucky? Former model Hope Hicks is Trump's new spin doctor in chief, *The Guardian*, 19 August, https://www.theguardian.com/us-news/2017/aug/19/fourth-time-lucky-former-model-hope-hicks-is-trumps-new-spin-doctor-in-chief (accessed 13 March 2018).

Axton, Marie. 1977. *The queen's two bodies*. London: Royal Historical Society.

Campoy, Ana. 2017. Trump is creating a government office to serve US victims of crimes perpetrated by immigrants, *Quartz*, 28 February, https://qz.com/921712/trump-speech-to-congress-a-new-government-office-called-voice-will-support-us-victims-of-crimes-perpetrated-by-immigrants/ (accessed 13 March 2018).

Cohen, Claire. 2017. Donald Trump sexism tracker: Every offensive comment in one place, *Daily Telegraph*, 14 July, https://www.telegraph.co.uk/women/politics/donald-trump-sexism-tracker-every-offensive-comment-in-one-place/ (accessed 19 March 2019).

Concha, Joe. 2017. Trump administration seen as more truthful than news media: poll, *The Hill*, 8 February, http://thehill.com/homenews/media/318514-trump-admin-seen-as-more-truthful-than-news-media-poll (accessed 13 March 2018).

Daybell, James. 2016. Scribal circulation of Early Modern letters. *Huntingdon Library Quarterly* 79 (3). 365–85.

Flew, Terry. 2017. The "theory" in media theory. *Media Theory* 1 (1). 43–56.

Frye, Susan. 1993. *Elizabeth I: The competition for representation*. Oxford: Oxford University Press.

Geier, Ben. 2016. Donald Trump has spent $0 on TV advertising, *Fortune* 9 August, http://fortune.com/2016/08/09/donald-trump-tv-ads-clinton/ (accessed 13 March 2018).

Goodare, Julian. 2004. Mary [Mary Stewart] (1542–1587), Queen of Scotland. In H. Colin G. Matthew & Brian Harrison (eds.), *The Oxford dictionary of national biography*. Online edition. Oxford: Oxford University Press, www.oxforddnb.com (accessed 10 December 2019).

Greenblatt, Stephen. 1980. *Renaissance self-fahioning*. Chicago: University of Chicago Press.

Gurman, Sadie. & Alicia. A. Caldwell. 2017. Trump's office on immigrant crime is dramatic overhaul, Associated Press, 1 March, https://uk.news.yahoo.com/trumps-office-immigrant-crime-dramatic-overhaul-190652046.html (accessed 13 March 2018).

Harington, John. 1930. *Letters and epigrams of Sir John Harington, together with the prayse of private life*. Philadelphia: University of Pennsylvania Press, https://archive.org/details/lettersepigramso00hari (accessed 13 March 2018).

Judd, Donald. 2018. DeVos calls on Trump to not use foul language, CNN, https://edition.cnn.com/2018/03/12/politics/betsy-devos-donald-trump-chuck-todd/index.html (accessed 19 March 2019).

Kludt, Tom. 2017. Trump echoes Bannon: Media is 'opposition party', *CNN*, 27 January, http://money.cnn.com/2017/01/27/media/opposition-party-media-donald-trump/ (accessed 13 March 2018).

Montrose, Louis A. 1983. A midsummer night's dream and the shaping fantasies of Elizabethan culture: Gender, power, form. In Richard Wilson & Richard Dutton (eds.), *New historicism and Renaissance drama*, 65–87. Abingdon: Routledge.

New York Times. 2017. Are we seeing the Trump 'pivot' at last? If so, why? 11 September, https://www.nytimes.com/2017/09/11/opinion/president-trump-congress.html (accessed 11 May 2018).

Politico. 2017. Transcript of White House press secretary statement to the media, 21 January, https://www.politico.com/story/2017/01/transcript-press-secretary-sean-spicer-media-233979 (accessed 19 March 2019).

Politifact. 2018. Donald Trump's file, http://www.politifact.com/personalities/donald-trump/ (accessed 13 March 2018).

Rowland, Darrel. 2016. Donald Trump accepts nomination, says he's voice for the voiceless. *The Columbus Dispatch*, 21 July, http://www.dispatch.com/content/stories/local/2016/07/21/0721-GOP-main-story.html (accessed 13 March 2018).

Sclafani, Jennifer. 2017. *Talking Donald Trump: A sociolinguistic study of style, metadiscourse, and political identity*. Abingdon: Routledge.

Shakespeare, William. 1990. *Henry VIII*, ed. John Margeson. Cambridge, UK: Cambridge University Press.

Seargeant, Philip. 2007. Discursive diversity in the textual articulation of epidemic disease in Early Modern England. *Language and Literature* 16 (4). 339–360.

Seargeant, Philip. 2017a. Lies, damned lies, and executive orders, *Diggit Magazine*, 13 February, https://www.diggitmagazine.com/articles/lies-damned-lies-and-executive-orders (accessed 13 March 2018).

Seargeant, Philip. 2017b. How 'Fake News' became Trump's favourite insult, *The Huffington Post*, 1 March, http://www.huffingtonpost.co.uk/philip-seargeant/donald-trump-fake-news_b_15082756.html (accessed 13 March 2018).

Seargeant, Philip. Forthcoming. *Disrupting the narrative: The power of storytelling in post-truth politics*. London: Bloomsbury.
Smith, L. B. 1980. *Elizabeth I*. Orange County: Forum Press.
Spenser, Edmund. 1995. *Selected shorter poems*, ed. Douglas Brooke-Davis. London: Longman.
Spivak, Gayatri C. 1999. *A critique of postcolonial reason*. Cambridge, MA: Harvard University Press.
Strong, Roy. 1984. *Art and power: Renaissance festivals, 1450–1650*. Berkeley: University of California Press.
Tennenhouse, Leonard. 1986. *Power on display*. London: Methuen.
Tennenhouse, Leonard. 1991. Playing and power. In David S. Kastan & Peter Stallybrass (eds.), *Staging the Renaissance*, 27–39. Abingdon: Routledge.
Wallace, Tim, Karen Yourish & Troy Griggs. 2017. Trump's inauguration vs. Obama's: Comparing the crowds, *The New York Times*, 20 January, https://www.nytimes.com/interactive/2017/01/20/us/politics/trump-inauguration-crowd.html (accessed 13 March 2018).
White House. 2018. Remarks by President Trump at a California Sanctuary State Roundtable, Transcript, 16 May, https://www.whitehouse.gov/briefings-statements/remarks-president-trump-california-sanctuary-state-roundtable/ (accessed 19 March 2019).
Wootson, Cleve R. 2017. Trump says his tweets are "modern day presidential." We checked with other modern-day leaders, *The Washington Post*, 2 July, https://www.washingtonpost.com/news/worldviews/wp/2017/07/02/trump-says-his-tweets-are-modern-day-presidential-we-checked-with-other-modern-day-presidents/ (accessed 13 March 2018).

Korina Giaxoglou
7 From *Rest in Peace* to *#RIP*: Tracing shifts in the language of mourning

7.1 Introduction

Registers of mourning have been changing as a result of increasing secularization and globalization in large parts of contemporary societies. These processes are attested, for example, in the gradual de-ritualization of the traditional Christian funeral ceremony, where high and formal registers have been giving way to everyday and informal registers (Cook & Walter 2005). In networked societies where mourning expands temporally, spatially and socially to online "technospiritual spaces" (Brubaker, Hayes & Dourish 2013), informal registers for sharing grief are also found to be prevalent (Giaxoglou 2014). This is part of a broader move away from formal and institutionalized rituals to more informal and personalized practices of mourning and memorialization online (Gibbs et al. 2015).

Online mourning encompasses a wide range of activities, which attest to the extension of online life sharing to the sharing of death-related moments and events. It includes posting reactions to highly mediatized death, i.e. death which has attracted increased media attention, such as the death of a celebrity or a public figure, the sudden death of a young adult, or death in attacks and natural disasters. This form of sharing has been described as *ecstatic sharing*, which is focused on the instant proximity of the here-and-now (Giaxoglou 2018) and echoes modes of ecstatic news common in the live-reporting of disaster news (Chouliaraki 2006). There are also cases of more intimate sharing of affect in reaction to a personal loss relating to the loss of a friend, a family member or even a pet. Such reactions can be shared as one-off messages or they can involve more or less sustained interactions with the dead and other mourners on the dead person's memorialized profile page, in memorial pages or in group chats across different platforms. Despite their differences, all these activities attest to the remediation of death and mourning online, which is shaped by, with, and for networked publics, i.e. the imagined communities that emerge out of the interconnection between users, technologies, and practices (boyd 2010).

Sharing death and mourning online has implications for the styles and registers of the language of mourning. Users' language practices online can

---
Korina Giaxoglou, The Open University, School of Languages and Applied Linguistics, Milton Keynes, UK, e-mail: korina.giaxoglou@open.ac.uk

https://doi.org/10.1515/9783110670837-010

affirm social and linguistic conventions, but also extend, rework and creatively contest them, resulting in shifts in features, styles and registers of language which can become widespread. Despite the considerable scholarly attention paid to online mourning in terms of its impact on how we mourn and how we remember our dead (e.g. Christensen & Sandvik 2014; Giaxoglou, Döveling & Pitsillides 2017; Pitsillides, Walker & Fairfax 2013; Walter 2017), little attention has been paid so far to the study of language use in these practices.

This chapter draws attention to shifts in the language of mourning and memorialization in line with Cook and Walter's (2005) call for the study of "small" changes in the language of transition rituals in relation to "big" social changes. Tracing shifts in registers of mourning online requires a historicizing angle, which builds on Herring's (2012) call for studying all the different types of digital discourse phenomena, be they *familiar, reconfigured* or *emergent*. It is also suggested that a combination of sources from different contexts can prove useful to developing a transmedia approach as part of a historicizing angle – that is, one which looks at how discourse phenomena are articulated across different contexts and media platforms, involving individuals' "meaningful selection of platforms, the combining of different media and a great deal of movement between them" (Tagg & Jankowicz-Pytel 2016: n.p.). This approach makes it possible to contextualize "small" shifts in language and registers as well as users' attitudes to them.

The focus in this chapter is on the changing uses and meanings of the expression *R.I.P* and the attitudes related to these. The expression is often described as an initialism of the expression *Rest in Peace*, which is pronounced by saying each letter individually. Its increasing use on social media has attracted media and social media attention and raised concerns in some circles about the appropriateness of its use. As will be argued, public views and debates about the expression *R.I.P.* are grounded either in the acknowledgment or the erasure of the linguistic and discourse antecedents that connect it to ritual practices and religious beliefs, while its online use points to the extension of its meaning to suit different communicative purposes in users' here-and-now.

The selection of this particular expression for analysis is motivated by its pervasiveness across ritual and secular contexts, offline and online, personal and public as well as commodified affective domains of language practice, as evident for instance in sympathy cards and custom images.[1] The study will address the following questions:

---

[1] For example, as of 10 December 2019, Getty Images lists 2174 *Rest in Peace* stock images and photos on their website.

1. What are the key aspects of the public discourse on the meaning and appropriateness of contemporary uses of the expression R.I.P.?
2. What are the key forms, meanings and functions of the expression R.I.P. as it is used in online contexts?

The chapter is organised as follows: section 7.2 presents the data and methods for the study. Section 7.3 contextualizes the public discourse around the meaning and appropriateness of the expression by tracing its language and discourse antecedents in ritual language. Section 4 discusses a debate in a specific religious circle, which has also attracted media attention. It also discusses public questions and answers relating to the meaning of the expression R.I.P. in crowd-sourced sites, such as Quora, and media commentary on the social behaviours associated with its use. Section 7.5 presents the findings of the linguistic and discursive analysis of current uses of the expression R.I.P. online, focusing on the micro-blogging platform Twitter, and provides empirical evidence about the key forms, meanings and functions of the expression in real contexts online. The chapter concludes by underlining the broader importance of drawing on a range of sources to trace shifts in language use and attitudes to these changes, which index bigger sociocultural changes. It contributes, thus, to the sketching of a transmedia approach to historicizing language and communication practices.

7.2 Data and methods

The present study has adopted a partial ethnographic perspective, which is a common angle adopted in virtual ethnographies (Hine 2000), i.e. ethnographies that are adaptive to the conditions in which they are employed (see also Androutsopoulos 2008). This perspective has made it possible to browse online and locate public views and opinions about the expression under focus, thus addressing the first research question above. In addressing this question on the public discourses surrounding R.I.P., the study also draws on citizen sociolinguistic methods. Citizen sociolinguistic methods are motivated by new perspectives in the sociolinguistics of mobility (Blommaert 2010), which seek to enhance understandings of contemporary language practices in web-based contexts. To this end, the internet counts as an important source of data and also as a generator of social value: the accretion of comments, shares and responses to a particular post contributes to the increase of its social value, meaning and relevance (Rymes and Leone 2014: 31). Citizen sociolinguistic methods prioritize the second order descriptions of language users, i.e. metacomments on language use and meanings shared in affinity groups and often found in Facebook comments and discussion forum contributions, as primary data sources positioning lay individuals as shapers of emergent language expertise (Rymes and Leone 2014: 29; Rymes 2014). In this study such public insights have been drawn from the crowd-sourced site Quora, based on a search for questions and answers relating to the expression under focus. The search yielded a user's question "What's the meaning of RIP" and eleven answers in response to it posted between April 25, 2015 and March 25, 2017.

In addition, following a Google-based search for media commentary devoted to the discussion of uses of the expression *R.I.P.*, ten media articles published between 2014 and 2017 were selected for discussion (see Media Articles). The preliminary consideration of these articles pointed to a debate among Protestants in Northern Ireland about the use of *R.I.P.* – that sparked mainstream media attention and social media commentary on a religious commentator's Facebook page – as a key event that deserved further attention as a source of citizen sociolinguistic insights shared among a specific religious group. This debate has been captured in two Facebook wall events extracted from the page of the religious commentator whose comments sparked the debate in the first place. A wall event refers to any individual update and all the comments that accumulate underneath it in a sequence of posts and which appear in reverse temporal order (Androutsopoulos 2014) – in this case seventy-four comments in total. The two wall events are related to each other and have been selected given that they include explicit references and public comments on using the expression *R.I.P.* within Protestant circles. These are further explicated below.

The first Facebook wall event involved the following update posted on 24th July 2017 by Wallace Thompson, the Secretary of the Evangelical Protestant Society.[2] The post, which is reproduced below, refers to the user's participation in a public discussion on the use of *R.I.P.* by Protestants, prompting fifteen comments:

> I took part in a studio discussion on BBC Radio Ulster "Talkback" at lunchtime today on the growing use of "RIP" in Protestant circles. The other participants were Fr Martin Magill and Rev Ken Newell. My only regret is that I didn't take the chance to praise the Orange and Black institutions for their excellent doctrinal material on the 500th anniversary of the Reformation.

The second Facebook wall event involved an update posted by Wallace Thompson on the next day, 25th July 2017, noting the heated reaction sparked

---

[2] The Evangelical Protestant Society is a mainstream inter-denominational umbrella organisation for evangelical Protestants in Northern Ireland.

by his comments on the BBC Radio Ulster "Talkback" (see Post 2). The post, which is reproduced below, accumulated a total of sixty comments:

> I have been subjected to some vile abuse in the last few hours, but some folks have stood by me, and I am grateful to Ruth Dudley Edwards for his article in today's Belfast Telegraph.

The comments to these two posts were coded for metalinguistic references to the form or meaning of *R.I.P.*, while comments touching upon broader issues of faith were left out of the analysis.

To address the second question about the different forms, meanings, and functions of the expression *R.I.P.*, a keyword search for the hashtag #RIP was conducted on the micro-blogging platform Twitter, which facilitates the broadcasting of short messages (until recently restricted to 140 characters) with and for networked 'followers'. The choice of Twitter was motivated by the fact that this platform has become the main hub for sharing breaking news and reactions to breaking news, including breaking news of death, thus making it an apt site for the study of generic uses of *R.I.P.* in memorial posts. Given that hashtags constitute resources for sharing and storying significant events, moments and stances (Giaxoglou 2018) and offer networked publics connective affordances enacting ambient affiliation (Zappavigna 2015), their study can point to uses of the expression as part of online participation practices.

In total two hundred and fifteen tweets were compiled for analysis (>400 before sorting and removal of retweets and irrelevant results). The tweets were extracted using Twitter's API which returns a filtered collection of relevant tweets matching a specified query. The results of this search included both popular and real time results.[3] As noted by Twitter developers, this search service is not meant to be an exhaustive source of tweets, as not all tweets are indexed or made available via the search interface (Twitter Developer 2019).

The linguistic and discourse analysis of the tweets is based on the coding of data for particular aspects of form, grammar and discourse (see table 7.1 in the appendix). Discourse analysis is used in this study as an open-ended heuristic (Johnstone 2017: 8), which can be used to answer different questions and shed light into the production of meaning in context or the use of language as meaningful symbolic behaviour (Blommaert 2005).

Even though the sample is relatively small and random, given that results are subject to Twitter's filtering algorithms, it arguably captures a sufficiently

---

[3] The extraction method did not allow the recovery of the specific emoji used, although it was possible to note which tweets had included one.

representative sample of mainstream uses of the expression on this social media platform, given that the filtering brings up the most popular tweets from official Twitter and influencers' accounts' posts. The analysis offers an insight into the changing norms and meanings of the expression *R.I.P.* and points to more specific directions for further empirical research. First, however, the chapter seeks to historicize our understanding of the contemporary uses and attitudes to the expression *R.I.P.*, by considering its antecedents, which relate to ritual language and religious discourse.

7.3 Antecedents to *R.I.P.*: *Rest in Peace* in ritual language

The brief overview in this section draws on the *Book of Common Prayer*, which sets forth the services and rites by authority of the Church of England, focusing on tracing the antecedents of the expression *R.I.P.* in ritual language. The expression is often glossed as an initialism of the expression *(May his/her soul) Rest in Peace* and linked to the Latin expression *Requiescat in pace* (singular) or *Requiescant in pace* (plural). Within the *Book of Common Prayer*, the expression *Rest in peace* forms part of a longer versicle at the end of the brief ritual part of the funeral service, known as *Committal*, which takes place at the graveside, in a crematorium chapel or in the church. The prayer, reproduced below, accompanies the lowering of the coffin in to the grave or the transportation of the body to the crematorium (emphasis mine):

> *Rest eternal grant unto him/her, O Lord;*
> *And let light perpetual shine upon him/her.*
> ***May his/her soul, and the souls of all the faithful departed,***
> ***through the mercy of God, rest in peace.***
> ***Amen.***
>   (The Book of Common Prayer, Burial II 1979: 501)

The versicle is addressed to God and expresses a wish about the soul of the departed as well as the souls of all the "faithful departed", contributing to the creation of a sense of a community of the dead among the congregation. The use of these expressions in the ritual sets up mediated positions between celebrants, mourners, God, and the dead. Mourners are receivers of what is said as is conventional in religious ceremonies, more generally, where even when they are invited to actively participate, their participation takes the form of a response.

When inscribed on headstones, however, uses of the expression *Rest in Peace* construct a different configuration of participants to the one just described. Instead of embodying the word of God via the words of worship, mourners appropriate fragments of these conventional words and personalize them to address the dead directly, as in the case of the address *Rest in Peace Mom* inscribed on a headstone. Such uses indicate the disjoining of the expression from its ritual context in an attempt to establish an unmediated relationship between the mourner and the deceased.

At the discourse level, prayers and petitions to God project a wish for the dead to "rest in peace". These are often associated with a widespread belief about the need to purify the dead's soul of their sins. This belief echoes medieval Christian beliefs in the West about the Purgatory, a place imagined somewhere between Heaven and Hell, where the souls of the departed were thought to be subjected to the final judgment – unless they were saints and would go straight to Heaven, or unrepentant sinners who were destined to Hell. In light of this belief, believers were expected to hold masses and pray to God on behalf of the dead not only as part of the grieving process, but also for helping to alleviate the cleansing process in the purgatory and hasten the successful transition of the soul to "the country of peace and light". Although the notion of the purgatory has in some ways been central to Western attitudes towards time (see Fenn 1995), it has also divided Christians, leading to theological debates about the place of prayers for the dead in different denominations. For those who believe in the existence of the in-between space of the purgatory, prayers for the dead are necessary and constitute a mourner's duty. For those who don't believe in the purgatory, prayers for the dead are unnecessary given that in their belief system there's nothing to be done to save the dead's soul after the death has transpired – having conducted one's life morally is the only assurance of "peace" and redemption after death. Although the details of theological debates surrounding the purgatory are beyond the scope of this chapter, this brief mention of them points to how the use of the expression *Rest in Peace* as a prayer for the dead invokes particular religious beliefs underlying views of the afterlife.

As the next section will show, it is often the case that uses of *R.I.P.* are straightforwardly linked to the ritual expression *Rest in peace*, a prayer addressed to God for blessing the soul of the departed, and taken to index religious beliefs about the afterlife. This link has motivated, for instance, the condemnation of the widespread use of *R.I.P.* among evangelical Protestants in Northern Ireland, which will be discussed in the next section.

7.4 Citizen sociolinguistic insights into the meaning of *R.I.P.*

One occasion during which concerns about the use of *R.I.P.* among Protestants became public was in 2017, when Wallace Thompson, secretary of the Evangelical Protestant Society, shared a Facebook post noting that the use of *R.I.P.* was against Protestant custom. This attracted media attention and social media reactions on Thompson's Facebook wall. Talking to BBC Talkback (Kentish 2017), Thompson explained that there is no use praying for the dead, given that there is no interim place of judgment and the only secure way to heaven is to lead one's life in line with God's word:

> The issue is obviously a sensitive one because people are expressing their grief. Just observing social media we have noticed the letters RIP are used a lot by Protestants, and some are evangelical Protestants. From a Protestant point of view we believe when death comes a person either goes to be with Christ for all eternity or into hell. [...].

Comments to Thompson's Facebook post offer important citizen sociolinguistic insights about perceptions of what the expression means and what beliefs it is associated with in this particular religious group. Most of the comments examined provided support for Thompson's view, showing their alignment to him – and to each other – through references to the scripture (1). Some were also quick to affirm that they have never used the expression before and would never use it[i] (2) (emphases mine).

(1) I must agree with Wallace on this one. If we do not know Christ as Saviour, we will not rest in peace. Sadly, to think otherwise **is unscriptural and gives false hope**.

(2) **Wallace I have never used the term RIP** even when I didn't know the Lord. As a Christian and a brother orange man I stand shoulder to shoulder with you. And if anyone is reading this and thinks I am a bigot and Roman Catholic hater, I certainly am not. I love every romantic Catholic for Christ what I am against is the error they are being taught. I stand for the truth of Scripture.

Others sought to contextualize the increased use of *R.I.P.*, attributing it to the importance of the memory of war dead within particular groups in the Protestant Orange Order (3) or its use of as a term of affection (4) (emphases mine):

(3) The orange order forsook their Biblical roots a long time ago ... loyal to the obsessive memorys [sic] of war dead ... **no wonder the term RIP is used so much, because sadly orangemen/protestants are more obsessed with dead people today than the Papist are.**

(4) I think you're correct from a scriptural point of view Wallace, but I don't think there's any harm using it. **These days it's simply used as a term of affection**, especially if the person who's died has suffered over a long period of time. When my dad died last year I'd have had no objection to people using the term.

Others, still, explicitly disaligned themselves from Wallace's condemnation of the use of *R.I.P.* (5) or sought to bridge the different views shared and lighten up the discussion by suggesting a reworked meaning to the expression more in line with this religious group's beliefs about the afterlife (6) (emphases mine).

(5) Indeed the dead are gone and beyond help but the Rest in Peace endearment helps those still living and suffering grief. **Let's not be petty denying those in grief comfort because of misplaced superiority.**

(6) **Maybe it means rejoice in peace** if you are lucky enough to die and repented [sic] in Peace Rejoice in Peace (thumbs up emoji)

This debate attests to differences between evangelical Protestantism and more traditional strains but also reflects long-held differences of faith between Protestants and Catholics. Overall there seems to be no consensus about the meaning of *R.I.P.* among members of this Protestant group. Members are divided about whether *R.I.P.* is false hope and unscriptural, whether it's used as a term of endearment for the bereaved or an expression of love for the departed and whether it should be used, adapted, or not used at all. Users' views diverge on the matter, depending on whether they recognize and foreground the ritual antecedents of the expression which connect it with religious beliefs about life and death, or whether they by-pass such links to foreground instead the personalization – or even adaptation – of the expression by users for their own purposes.

More broadly, the debate attests to broader trends of secularization in society. As acknowledged in the *Catholic Herald* by Lucie-Smith (2017 n.p.): "uses of R.I.P. as a tag on social media points less to a mass conversion to Catholicism and more a turn to a handy expression" [...] "the term has been divorced for most people from its living roots; it does not indicate any faith in the afterlife, or belief in Purgatory, nor is it, usually, in any sense a prayer made on behalf of the deceased." This de-coupling of the expression from the ritual contexts with which it used to be associated is exactly what turns it into a potent prompt and site for debates about faith and religious affinity among some religious groups.

Such debates show the important role that language and discourse antecedents play in shaping largely decontextualized interpretations and assessments of digital language practices. In cases when antecedents are assumed to be straightforwardly connected to current uses, they can be offered as prescriptive guides to language use in connection to appropriate religious custom. Yet, linguistic meaning is contextualized and dynamic: so even though there is no doubt that the expression *R.I.P.* is associated with ritual language and (different) religious beliefs about life and death, these associations can be – and often are – overridden (largely unconsciously) by users – even when they are expressly religious – and in the process, new meanings and new associations are created.

Interestingly, religious connotations are also prevalent in contexts outside religious group discussions as the examination of additional citizen sociolinguistic insights has shown. On Quora, a platform where people ask questions and crowdsource answers, many users have been seeking crowdsourced definitions of the meaning of *Rest in Peace* and *R.I.P.* Similarly to the debate among the members of the Protestant group discussed above, Quora users are also divided among those who trace its antecedents to Latin language and liturgy, associating it with prayers to God for the dead (7–8).

(7) "Rest in peace" (Latin: Requiescat in pace) is an expression wishing eternal rest and peace to someone who has died [...] This blessing is given so that the person's soul may find peace AT LEAST AFTER THEIR DEATH.

(8) RIP has its origin in Latin language where it's called "Requiescat in pace" which meant prayer to God for someone who has died.

Others suggest their own interpretation of the expression, referring to popular uses on gravestones (9) or other uses they've come across (10).

(9) The acronym R.I.P., meaning "rest in peace", continues to be engraved on the gravestones of Christians from several denominations, especially the Catholic Church, the Lutheran Church and the Anglican Church.

(10) R.I.P. is just a saying that people made to comfort themselves after the death of a loved one (or whoever).

Still others consider it to be a spiritual expression which serves as an incantation to spirits:

(11) "Rest in peace" refers to ones supposed "eternal rest", i.e. death. Those who rest in peace do not walk the earth after death, as do "restless spirits" (again, supposedly). If one is "resting in peace", one is not haunting ones [sic] earthly friends and/or relatives.

While commentators with explicit religious affiliations oscillate between judging it as "un-Protestant" or as "consoling" and are concerned about whether it is appropriate to use it or not, internet users express curiosity about what the expression means and offer a wider range of glosses to the expression, depending on their focus on the religious, spiritual or secular aspects of the expression. Internet users do not seem to be concerned about its appropriateness. The next section will turn to the consideration of mainstream media commentary on uses of *R.I.P.* which provides an additional angle to the use of the expression in relation to norms for mourning.

7.5 *R.I.P.* in the media: Debating social media communication norms

Media commentators seem to be less concerned with the linguistic and discourse antecedents of the expression or its different meanings. They instead draw attention to aspects of communication norms in social media and express their stance about whether the use of the phrase conforms to social norms of mourning or not. In other words, their comments revolve around the use of the expression as an index of social behaviours.

Some see its use as "trite", "uncreative" or even "lazy" in comparison, for example, to wishes and commodified words in the case of other life events (e.g. birth, engagement, wedding). For instance, Julie Gray in the *Huffington Post* (2015) gives four reasons to stop using it: "1) It's lazy. 2) It's reductive. 3) It's unimaginative. 4) It's not really what we mean". The expression *R.I.P.* is seen here as another of those social media neologisms, analogous to *LOL* or *HAH!*, which express an emotion and more specifically, a three-letter shorthand for "aw, I'm sad this person died!" (Gray 2015). Such criticisms reflect popular concerns about social media language and communication, which are also often about young people. Such media accounts, in fact, say more about adults' ideas about digital communication than about anyone's actual language use online, especially given that abbreviations are common in online interaction but their meaning and function emerges out of sustained interactions among communicators (Tagg 2012).

More recently, others, as for instance Rachel Moss, have drawn on their personal experiences of mourning and loss to revisit their negative views about writing *R.I.P.* on Facebook. Moss (2015) explains that *R.I.P.* is a way of saying "someone I knew and cared about died and I'm not coping very well, so please can you help me?", thus linking the expression with a cry for help and support.

Unlike Moss, Taya Johnson's personal experience (Johnson 2016), brings to the fore a darker side of *R.I.P.* posts: when *R.I.P.* posts started appearing on her Facebook timeline about an hour after her husband's death without her having announced his death online, seemingly well-intended expressions of sadness became the cause of serious upset for the bereaved. Johnson is not alone in this negative experience, which points to *posting-first* hierarchy norms reflecting existing social hierarchies of grief. This highlights the expectation that members of the family will be the ones who set the tone and ground rules for the public displays of mourning, before friends, colleagues or acquaintances of the deceased start sharing their grief publicly. Cases like this one connect debates on the use of *R.I.P.* to debates about digital mourning norms and etiquette, which revolve around perceptions of mourning either as a valid expression of emotion and the creation of a community of mourners or an indication of over-sharing and unnecessary affective competition (Giaxoglou & Döveling 2018).

In these and related public discussions connecting uses of *R.I.P.* to behaviors and social norms, people are often judged on their use of the expression without consideration as to why they use it or in what context they are using it in; instead, it is assumed that, for instance, using any abbreviation online serves as a quick way of communicating or that using *R.I.P.* can serve a single function, irrespective of who says it where, when, and why.

This public interest in the origins and meaning of this expression makes empirical insights into its uses and functions necessary. As Tagg (2012: 26) notes, mainstream media tend to amplify – or in some cases create – the fears surrounding digital communication, often focusing on sensational or alarmist cases of digital language use. The last section of this chapter presents the findings of the empirical study of uses of #RIP on Twitter and provides insights into the new forms, meanings and functions that the expression seems to be taking on in digital communication contexts.

7.6 Uses of #RIP on Twitter

Most commonly in the corpus of tweets the hashtag #RIP occurs in capital letters (in 94% of instances). A small number of instances (12.5%) feature the expression in small letters: #rip. All of these occurrences of #rip with one exception are associated with figurative meanings, expressing sadness as something comes to an end (12) or with jocular meanings making reference, for example, to the "loss" of hair after a haircut (see 13).

(12)   Not to be sappy but I love my team and I cried like a baby when we got done dancing and I'm just gonna miss dance and my girls so much #rip [hyperlink to image]

(13)   im cutting my hair #rip

The use of #rip for humorous purposes is a case of use that is not directly connected to death and one that wasn't mentioned at all in any of the public comments discussed above. This type of use attests to the extension of the expression's meaning, whereby the association of *R.I.P.* with mourning the loss of a loved one extends to things, and also mundane and even trivial life moments, often marked by the use of small letters, rather than capitals. This seems to suggest in these cases an iconic connection between letter size and degree of seriousness or triviality.

An even smaller number of the full expression *Rest in Peace* or *May her soul rest in peace* (2.3% of instances) was attested in co-occurrence with the abbreviated version #RIP in the same message (14) (emphasis mine).

(14)   Senior film and television actress #Shammi ji is no more with us. **May her soul rest in peace.** #ShammiAunty #actor **#RIP**.

Co-occurrences of the full expression with the tag #RIP point to the fact that these serve different functions. The full expression serves as a prayer for the dead remediated in the context of Twitter, whereas the abbreviated expression preceded by the hashtag functions as a meta-comment to the message. This use highlights the de-linking of *R.I.P.* from ritual language and religious discourse antecedents.

There was also a single instance of adaptation of the linguistic form, in which the same three letters were used to create a new acronym; again this co-occurred with the use of the keyword #RIP (15).

(15) R"esponsibility_"I"ntensity_"P"erseverance 3/07/18: A new era begins. #RIP [hyperlink to image].

In this case, the new acronym is not related to the expression Rest in Peace; rather, it is used as an advertising hatch to promote a swim and dive team. Such reworkings may benefit the commercial aspirations of the swim and dive team and attest to an additional way of extending the function of the expression for commercial purposes.

In terms of the grammar of the expression *R.I.P.*, if taken as a direct antecedent of *Rest in Peace*, then the verb "rest" would be in the subjunctive, expressing various states of unreality such as wish, emotion, possibility, judgment, opinion, obligation, or action that have not yet occurred. It would also be followed – or in some cases directly preceded – by the name of the departed. In the corpus, however, uses of *R.I.P.* in the subjunctive followed by the name of the departed (e.g. RIP Christy) were not common (19% of instances). There is only one instance in the corpus of "rip" (in small letters) used in the subjunctive as a shorthand for "Rest in Peace" (16). The lack of instances of uses of the subjunctive is not surprising, given the broader decline of the subjunctive in English more generally, which is considered slightly old-fashioned and excessively formal.

(16) Top right was a caricature of #BudLuckey for the janitor in #toystory 3. He passed on February 24th. He was one of the most influential designers on Toy Story but most of all he was an amazing person. God bless you Bud. **May he #rip** [hyperlink to picture]

Most commonly, the tag *RIP* was used as an interjection at the end of a tweet (66.5%), not directly preceded or followed by the name of the departed (17).

(17) Not sure why the good ones are always taken so early! Rest easy brother!! **#RIP**

There were also some cases – though few in this corpus – in which *R.I.P.* functioned as a noun (5.1% of instances), e.g. "RIP to my cousin" and very few instances of *R.I.P.* used as an epithet, e.g. "David Owen, RIP" (2.4% of instances).

The grammatical function of uses of *R.I.P.* is further clarified when the discourse position of the hashtag is taken into consideration. In the majority of the tweets, the hashtag #RIP appears at the end of the message on its own (46.9%) or among other hashtags (32.5%). In these positions, the tag marks the closing of the message and at the same time flags its content as a particular type of message, a

R.I.P. post, i.e. a message expressing sorrow about the loss of someone adding to – and increasing visibility of – the accumulating messages on the event, moment or feeling. In these cases, *R.I.P.* connects to a wider discourse of mourning and remembrance. This use seems to suggest more generic uses of *R.I.P.* by people who are not necessarily making a claim to personal loss, but rather engaging in public memorializing online. In Facebook RIP posts shared on a Facebook group mourning the loss of a young adult, uses of RIP followed by the name, nickname of the departed or an endearment term were very common, e.g. "RIP bro"; "RIP Davey", making a claim to personal loss (Giaxoglou 2014). In the corpus of tweets, however, this type of discourse patterning is noted only in the few cases which involve similar expressions of personal loss (18).

(18) I lost my dad today. This feeling I don't wish on anyone. I will miss u so much dad. I only wish that I could have spoken to u, seen u & even hugged u one last time before u left. Your baby girl remembers all our special moments we shared together daddy. **#RIP #POPS**

The use of *R.I.P.* as an interjection points to a shift in its grammatical, syntactic and pragmatic use. *R.I.P.* is currently used as a stand-alone expression that is not directly preceded or followed by the name of the departed. In such uses, *R.I.P* is not a ritual expression, a prayer to God for the soul of the departed, or even a way of marking of the last words of the living to the dead as in the case of gravestone inscriptions. Its main addressee is not God or the dead but rather networked publics. As a tag, it adds a meta-comment to the message and marks it off as a special type of tweet, part of an accumulating number of hashtag mourning tributes. In its hashtag use it serves as a resource for banding and bonding networked publics together, while increasing the visibility of the event as well as that of the user beyond local groups and communities of mourners.

7.7 Concluding remarks

The above discussion shows how the meaning of the expression *R.I.P.* is being reconfigured as a result of its increased use on social media, prompting public debates about its meaning and appropriateness. Citizen sociolinguistic insights on the meaning of the expression depend on which uses are taken as its antecedents, indexing different kinds of religious or social symbolic order.

Three general types of use and meanings were identified in users' meta-comments:

1. Uses linked to the ritual expression "Rest in peace" (Latin: *Requiescat in pace*) and serving as a prayer addressed to God for blessing the soul of the departed; these uses index religious beliefs about the afterlife and norms of communication with the dead mediated by God. Such uses were only rarely attested in the corpus.
2. Uses de-linked from ritual uses and serving, instead, as incantations aimed at protecting the living from the haunting spirits of the dead. These are addressed directly to the dead and index supernatural or paranormal beliefs about the after-life; notably, this meaning was suggested by citizen linguists, but it was not found in the corpus of tweets.
3. Everyday uses that are associated with digital language practices and practices of mourning online. In these cases, as shown in the analysis of the corpus of tweets, *R.I.P.* is used as a tag and meta-comment creating a frame that allows the message to be interpreted as a memorial message even if the reader does not know the user, the deceased or the death event referred to. These uses are mainly oriented to networked audiences, calling for support or seeking to enhance the visibility of the death event – as well as that of the user.

Finally, there are also commodified uses of *R.I.P.* (e.g. greeting cards, custom images), which further attest to securalization trends in Western society and foreground functions of the expression as a consolation addressed to the bereaved. These were outside the scope of this chapter.

Based on the above, the expression *R.I.P.* can be best described as an indexical and as situated in the here and now, similarly to every utterance and action. It is embedded in a range of social and cultural practices and its meaning needs to be seen in the context of these practices rather than as straightforwardly emerging out of its language and discourse antecedents. On social media *R.I.P.* follows the norms of online interaction, participation and sharing and can serve as a resource for positioning oneself as mourner and as participant in public acts of mourning. Its meaning can also extend to refer to a sense of loss on account of a seemingly mundane life moment (e.g. "i'm having my hair cut **#rip**"; "Its [sic] 17 degrees and I'm wearing 3 layers. I don't know how I'm going to cope in England next week. **#RIP #Me**" [hyperlink to image]).

Looking beyond the parameters of this study, it is worth noting that on Twitter, the expression *R.I.P.* is often accompanied by the use of emoji, e.g. folded hands emoji, heart emoji or a combination of these, where emoji further intensifies the specific affective undertone of the message; or that on Instagram the abbreviation is often found in co-occurrence with a range of related hashtags bringing together different possibilities for reacting to the news of a death;

for example, the account #rip on Instagram counting 20,733,560 posts describes the account using the following sequence of hashtags: #restinpeace #gonebutneverforgotten #restinparadise #wemissyou #inmemory #neverforget #youwillbemissed #resteasy #tragic #gonetoosoon. These co-occurrences would be worth of further empirical study as a way of investigating the multimodal extension of the expression's meaning.

Undoubtedly, the meanings and forms of *R.I.P.* will continue to change as the practices around mourning and remembering change, too; it might even be replaced by other popular expressions and forms, sparking new public debates and fuelling more moral panics. To further our understanding of registers of mourning and memorialization online, but also of language practices online more broadly, it is important to examine them as part of broader sociocultural practices that cross-cut online and offline realms. To do this, a historicizing and empirical angle, which considers evidence across media is necessary. This can provide a contextualizing lens to discourse phenomena – be they familiar, reconfigured, or emergent – that can complicate public views on the impact of social media use on language and communication.

References

Androutsopoulos, Jannis. 2014. Moments of sharing: Entextualization and linguistic repertoires in social networking. *Pragmatics* 73. 4–18.
Androutsopoulos, Jannis. 2008. Potentials and limitations of discourse-centred online ethnography. *Language@Internet* 5 (9). 1–20.
Blommaert, Jan. 2010. *The sociolinguistics of globalization*. Cambridge, UK: Cambridge University Press.
Blommaert, Jan. 2005. *Discourse: A critical introduction*. Cambridge, UK: Cambridge University Press.
boyd, danah. 2010. Social network sites as networked publics: Affordances, dynamics, and implications. In Zizi Papacharissi (ed.), *Networked self: Identity, community, and culture on social network sites*, 39–58. Abingdon: Routledge.
Brubaker, Jed R., Gillian R. Hayes & Paul Dourish. 2013. Beyond the grave: Facebook as a site for the expansion of death and mourning. *The Information Society* 29: 152–163.
Chouliaraki, Lillie. 2006. *The spectatorship of suffering*. Thousand Oaks: Sage.
Christensen, Dorthe Reflsund & Kjetil Sandvik (eds.). 2014. *Mediating and remediating death: Studies in death, materiality and the origin of time* (Vol. 2). Farnham: Ashgate.
Cook, Guy & Tony Walter. 2005. Rewritten rites: language and social relations in traditional and contemporary funerals. *Discourse & Society* 16 (3). 365–393.
Episcopal Church. 1979. *The book of common prayer and administration of the sacraments and other rites and ceremonies of the Church: Together with the psalter or psalms of David according to the use of the Episcopal Church*. New York: Seabury Press.

Fenn, Richard. 1995. *The persistence of the purgatory*. Cambridge, UK: Cambridge University Press.
Gibbs, Martin, James Meese, Michael Arnold, Bjorn Nansen & Marcus Carter. 2015. #Funeral and Instagram: Death, social media, and platform vernacular. *Information, Communication & Society* 18 (3). 255–268.
Giaxoglou, Korina. 2018. #JeSuisCharlie? Hashtags as narrative resources in contexts of ecstatic sharing. *Discourse, Context, and Media* 22. 13–20.
Giaxoglou, Korina & Katrin Döveling. 2018. Mediatization of emotion on social media: Forms and norms in digital mourning practices. *Social Media + Society* 4 (1). 1–4.
Giaxoglou, Korina, Katrin Döveling & Stacey Pitsillides. 2017. Networked emotions: Interdisciplinary perspectives on sharing loss online. *Journal of Broadcasting & Electronic Media* 61 (1). 1–10.
Giaxoglou, Korina. 2014. "R.I.P. man ... u are missed and loved by many": Entextualising moments of mourning on a Facebook Rest in Peace group site. *Thanatos* 3 (1). 10–28.
Herring, Susan. 2012. Discourse in web 2.0: Familiar, reconfigured, and emergent. In Deborah Tannen & Anne Marie Trester (eds.), *Georgetown University Round Table on Languages and Linguistics 2011: Discourse 2.0: Language and new media*. Washington, D.C.: Georgetown University Press.
Hine, Christine. 2000. *Virtual ethnography*. Thousand Oaks: Sage.
Johnstone, Barbara. 2017. *Discourse analysis*. 3rd edn. Hoboken, NJ: Wiley-Blackwell.
Pitsillides, Stacey, Mike Waller & Duncan Fairfax. 2013. Digital death. What role does digital information play in the way we are (re)membered? In Steve Warburton & Stylianos Hatzipanagos (eds.), *Digital identity and social media*, 75–90. Hershey: IGI Global.
Rymes, Betsy. 2017. The Ghost emoji: A riddle wrapped in a mystery inside an enigma. *Citizen Sociolinguistics Blog*. Available at: https://citizensociolinguistics.com/category/emoji/ (accessed 10 July 2018).
Rymes, Betsy & Andrea R. Leone. 2014. Citizen sociolinguistics: A new media methodology for understanding language and social life. *Working Papers in Educational* Linguistics *(WPEL) 29* (2). https://repository.upenn.edu/wpel/vol29/iss2/4 (accessed 31 May 2019).
Tagg, Caroline. 2012. *Exploring digital communication. Language in action*. Abingdon: Routledge.
Tagg, Caroline & Daria Jankowicz-Pytel. 2016. From translanguaging to transmedia meaning-making. *TLANG blog*. Available online at: https://tlangblog.wordpress.com/2016/06/23/from-translanguaging-to-transmedia-meaning-making/ (accessed May 20, 2019).
Twitter Developer (2019) Search Tweets. Available at: https://developer.twitter.com/en/docs/tweets/search/api-reference/get-search-tweets.html (accessed 20 May 2019).
Walter, Tony. 2017. *What death means now. Thinking critically about dying and grieving*. London: Polity Press.
Zappavigna, Michelle. 2015. Searchable talk: The linguistic functions of hashtags. *Social Semiotics* 25 (3). 274–279.

Media articles

Collins, Pádraig. 2017. Orange Order: Protestants told not to use "RIP" as it is Catholic superstition, *The Guardian* [online]. https://www.theguardian.com/world/2017/jul/29/orange-order-protestants-told-not-to-use-rip-as-it-is-catholic-superstition?CMP=share_btn_tw (accessed: 8 March 2018).

Gray, Julie. 2015. 4 reasons to stop saying RIP, *Huffington Post*. https://www.huffingtonpost.com/julie-gray/4-reasons-to-stop-saying-_b_7774708.html (accessed 8 March 2018).

Johnson, Taya D. 2016. STOP! Read this before you post another RIP on social media, *MEDIUM*. https://medium.com/@MrsTDJ/stop-read-this-before-you-post-another-rip-on-social-media-4c879cf69c5b (accessed 27 February, 2018).

Kentish, Benjamin. 2017. Orange Order tells members to stop saying "RIP" because it is "unbiblical" and "un-Protestant", *The Independent* [online]. http://www.independent.co.uk/news/uk/home-news/orange-order-rip-stop-say-un-prostestant-northern-ireland-loyalists-unbiblical-dup-unionists-a7859766.html (accessed 20 April 2018).

Lucie-Smith, Alexander. 2017. The Orange Order are right: RIP is a Catholic phrase, *The Catholic Herald*. http://www.catholicherald.co.uk/commentandblogs/2017/08/01/the-orange-order-are-right-rip-is-a-catholic-phrase/ (accessed 20 April 2018).

Mackie, Bella. 2014. RIP "RIP": We need to be more creative with mourning in the digital age, *The Guardian* [online]. https://www.theguardian.com/commentisfree/2014/oct/20/rip-hashtag-lynda-bellingham (accessed 27 February 2018).

Malle, Chloe. 2014. RIP to #RIP: Why we should give up public mourning on social media, *VOGUE*. https://www.vogue.com/article/public-mourning-social-media (accessed 22 April 2018).

Montgomery, Sarah J. 2017. Women's March catches heat for tribute to Barbara Bush, *COMPLEX*. http://www.complex.com/life/2018/04/womens-march-tweet-about-barbara-bush-is-catching-some-heat/ (accessed 20 April 2018).

Moss, Rachel. 2016. Why I changed my mind about "attention seeking" RIP Facebook updates, *Huffington Post*. http://www.huffingtonpost.co.uk/rachel-moss/dying-matters-writing-rip-on-facebook_b_7354604.html (accessed 27 February 2018).

Thompson, Rachel. 2017. A guide to Facebook etiquette after someone has died, *Mashable*. https://mashable.com/2017/04/08/facebook-etiquette-grief/ (accessed 8 March 2018).

Appendix

Table 7.1: Coding categories of corpus of tweets.

Form	Abbreviated form in capital letters (RIP)
	Abbreviated form in small letters (rip)
	RIP followed by name (e.g. RIPStormin or RIP Charles Emerson)
	Full form *Rest in Peace*
	Other forms *May her soul rest in peace, Rest in Power*
Grammar	Verb (e.g. RIP Christy, may her soul rest in peace)
	Noun (e.g. RIP to my cousin)
	Interjection (e.g. RIP)
	Epithet (e.g. David Owen, RIP)
Discourse	Initial
	Body of text
	Final
	Hashtag space
Pragmatics (addressivity)	Addressing:
	The dead (e.g. RIP Katie)
	God (e.g. I pray to god that the dead is with you/reunited with Christ/that her soul rests in peace)
	The bereaved (e.g. remember you who are in mourning that your loved one is resting in peace)
	Not specified or vague (e.g. #RIP)
	Other (e.g. #RIP NME)

David Barton
8 Digital literacies and the long history of the academic article

8.1 Introduction

In this chapter I outline the 300-year history of the development of the genre of the academic article as revealed by textual analysis. This is then juxtaposed with the historical development of academic writing practices around the turn of the twenty-first century, as captured in interviews with academics about their contemporary writing practices. Data for the history of the academic article is taken largely from the work of John Swales (1990), where he draws together the literature on the development of academic articles in Europe and North America from their origin as letters between scientists in the seventeenth century, through to the academic article of the 1980s with its standard structure and distinct sections. The data on recent decades, which have led to the development of the digital scholar within the lifetimes of contemporary academics, comes from observations and interviews with academics collected as part of a UK ESRC research project on knowledge creation and changes in academic writing practices. The project has been examining contemporary changes in academics' writing practices, viewing the contemporary university in England as a work place where the production of knowledge is central, and much of this is through writing.

A 300-year historical development and a 30-year life time development are two different scales of time and the aim is to see how the longer historical development can illuminate contemporary change. These two different time periods fit in well with Lev Vygotsky's ([1930–1934] 1978) socio-cultural framework and notions of different time frames. They can be adapted here to contrast long term cultural history with individuals' life histories (see Marginson & Dang 2017 for more recent discussion). According to Vygotsky, there are four time scales of value in understanding human development, and in particular what are

---

Note: I am pleased to acknowledge the support of the other members of the Academics Writing research team, Ibrar Bhatt, Mary Hamilton, Sharon McCulloch and Karin Tusting and their contributions to the ideas in this chapter. This work was supported by the ESRC grant number ES/L01159X/1.

David Barton, Lancaster University, Department of Linguistics and English Language, County South, Lancaster University, Lancaster, UK, e-mail: d.barton@lancaster.ac.uk

https://doi.org/10.1515/9783110670837-011

referred to as higher cognitive processes, such as the development of writing. The first time scale can be loosely described as phylogenetic or evolutionary development. In terms of writing and literacy, examples would be the development of the human hand-eye co-ordination, brain power and spoken language. Secondly, there is broad socio-cultural development such as the historical development of writing systems, the coming of printing and the development of institutions of literacy practices such as publishers. Thirdly, there is the shorter development within individuals' life span, referred to as ontogenetic development. This often focusses on children's development of language and literacy but can be used to cover many sorts of development in adulthood, including learning the practices of academic literacies. Finally, there is the microgenetic context of social interaction and the dynamics of immediate events. These four time frames are embedded in each other and overlap. Vygotsky's work was the basis for the later development of socio-cultural notions of language and literacy as social practice, as in Scribner and Cole (1981). This current chapter focuses on two of the time periods, firstly, that of the historical socio-cultural development of academic writing and, secondly, the shorter term development of academic articles in the age of the "digital scholar" (Weller 2011).

8.2 The long history of the academic article

Data to be discussed here for the history of the academic article are taken largely from the work of John Swales who traced the development of academic articles from handwritten letters which scientists sent to each other in the seventeenth century, through to the published academic article of the twentieth century with its distinct sections and specific structure. I draw particularly on Swales (1990), especially the section "Episodes in the history of the research article" (pp. 110–117) where he draws together the literature on the development of the academic article up until the 1980s, including detailed studies on the development of specific journals carried out by Charles Bazerman.

There is a great deal of data available to study the textual genre of the academic article historically as many examples of texts exist from the eighteenth century to the twenty-first century (see, for example, the extensive work by Ken Hyland and colleagues, including Hyland 2004). However it is less easy to examine the practices of that historical period. There is some reference to practices and conventions in the early discussions held during the development of Royal Societies in Britain. This was the time of Johnson's dictionaries, the development of the Encyclopaedia Britannica and other early Encyclopaedias, as well as the creation of scientific societies, their journals and associated artefacts in the development of academic literacies.

The associated practices of how knowledge was recorded, stored and made accessible as reported by Swales (1990) are interesting. In the experimental sciences, early on other researchers would be invited to watch experiments being carried out. There was an important role of witnessing experiments, with stands built for observation. People would attend these experiments and would be asked to sign a register that they had witnessed the results. Then came virtual witnessing where observers wrote explicit reports about experiments. This led to a genre where all the information had to be in the text so that it could then be read and evaluated by someone who had not been present at the experiment. Individual handwritten letters to known readers made way for published letters to less known publics. This was a shift from communicating with people you know to people you don't know. These published letters also provided a common public written record. In the eighteenth century came royal societies which effectively reviewed articles and oversaw their publication and circulation in their newly created journals.

Specialist forms of writing were developed to reflect the changing practices including the distinct genre of the academic article. For example, there was a shift from the reputation of the experimenter being paramount to experiments which could be carried out by any skilled researcher. There were developing norms of what had to be included in these reports and what sections and subsections they had to be divided into. In short: there is a long history of the development of the academic article going back to the 1600s and even earlier. More recently in the twentieth century we can see the shift from the results normally being the last section of a scientific paper, with the idea that the "facts speak for themselves", towards longer discussion sections and more interpretation of data and explicit conclusions. Different disciplines have developed their own formats for journal articles, including conventions for different methodologies. The work of Swales and others went up to the 1980s and, thus, was effectively pre-digital. Examining other work from that period, there was uncertainty in the 1980s about the likely impact, if any, of the digital world on formal genres of writing, as in Yates (1990), for example. In fact there has been a remarkable amount of change.

8.3 The rapid development of the digital scholar

The development of the digital scholar since the 1980s has been explored in our research project where we interviewed scholars about their changing practices and their memories throughout their lifetimes. This has included techno-biographical interviews of individuals' practices across their life span up to their contemporary practices which can also be observed and recorded (as described in more detail below). The research reported here is located in the current literature on digital scholarship and accepts that all aspects of academic life are transformed in the digital world. Looking specifically at technology in academic life, Weller (2011), referred to "the digital scholar" when comparing the process of writing a book in 2004 with writing one 6 years later. Every step of the process had changed. For the later book, he made use of electronic books and journals, set up alerts to track online conversations about his topic, and bookmarked sources, while few of these platforms were available in 2004. We have found that this experience of change applies to every aspect of academic life, and the current project has explored how technological shifts influence academics' writing practices.

The research project was entitled *The dynamics of knowledge creation: Academics writing in the contemporary university workplace* (2015–2017). In the broader project we approach academic writing as a workplace practice and explore what professional academics do in their work of academic writing. We investigate academics' work as knowledge production with writing being central. We adopt a social practice view of language and literacy which is informed by literacy studies and linguistic ethnography. This assumes that practices differ across contexts and are always situated. In the research we aim to make sense of individual people's lives. Analysis then consists of weaving common themes across individual cases (see Barton & Lee 2013 for more on this approach). The data in this chapter are drawn from interviews conducted with academics at different levels of seniority in three different disciplines. They worked in three English universities which differed in their mix of teaching and research. The three disciplines studied, mathematics, history and marketing, were chosen to include what can broadly be described as a science discipline, a humanities discipline and a professional discipline. We also carried out preparatory work with academics in social science departments and their data were included in the analysis. Data were collected from January 2015 to December 2016.

The study has been undertaken within the backdrop of broad changes in the university workplace. It has examined how academics' writing practices are shaped by the sociomaterial aspects of their situation and how managerial practices are shaping writing work. Further overall details of the study, including extensive data analysis and direct quotations from our informants, can be found in Tusting et al (2019). For other project findings, see also: McCulloch (2017) on how research evaluation frameworks shape academics writing; Tusting and Barton (2016) on disciplinary changes in academic writing; and Barton and McCulloch (2018) on stress in academics' writing lives.

This chapter focusses primarily on academic articles and does not pursue in any detail differences across disciplines or institutions. The data drawn upon here come from interviews. Three sorts of interviews examined different time frames within the overall life span. Firstly, as mentioned above, there were techno-biographic interviews held in informants' offices. Techno-biography potentially covers their whole life times, but in fact informants tended to report on their work careers since becoming academics. The techno-biographic interview covers working in different places, and identifies work done at home, in cafes, on public transport, and so on (see Page et al. 2014, chapters 6 and 7, for more details of these methodologies). The second sort of interviews, walk-around interviews, cover the here and now and regular routine activities such as using the photocopier or chatting to colleagues. The walk around was usually located in a department, often on one floor of a building. It reflected a network of colleagues and other interactions, academic discussions but also administrative and teaching. (Incidentally, Swales [1998] 2018 provides an insightful study of literacy practices in contrasting disciplines in one university building.) Thirdly, day-in-the-life interviews took place in one location, usually the office but they could refer to other locations and like the earlier interviews these were also to some extent attending to routine activities and typicality. Informants would report chronologically on their practices on a recent work day. Other methods in this project included recording live working sessions with academics at their computer often with a speak-aloud component in which they reflected on their current real time activities whilst writing in their offices.

Overall, 56 participants were interviewed in the main study, in addition to pilot work, giving a total of 116 interview transcripts. Interviews were audio recorded and transcribed. They were then imported into the ATLAS.ti qualitative data analysis software, and coded following a provisional coding scheme based on the research questions of the project. This coding scheme was then refined as further ideas and concepts emerged through working with the data.

8.4 The digital scholar: Findings

8.4.1 General findings

To begin with we located people in the places where they worked and we identified physical changes in their surroundings. Usually they had individual or shared offices in a department where they worked with colleagues. Many had moved office in the past few years often to more cramped spaces. Related to this we found that most academics write in more than one place. In particular people find places for academic writing such as research articles that are often away from their offices. They create boundaries in their lives, so that a specific sort of writing might be associated with a particular place, or computer, or time of the day. Many reported increasing work pressure, and it was dedicated time for academic writing which got squeezed out. Administration, record keeping and answering emails have to take priority as other people depend on them. The participants complain that email is invasive and draws time away from research writing, often referred to as "real" work. This leads to stress and developing strategies for coping with their work. Contemporary changes in university life are sources of additional pressures on them. People deal with the possibilities and constraints in different ways and in the example of email they work out for themselves how to sort out their time and how to make room for research writing. Older informants remembered literally cutting and pasting pieces of paper to change the ordering of sentences or paragraphs of an article and getting their research papers typed out by a professional typist before submitting a hard copy to journal editors. Meanwhile, younger early-career researchers we interviewed had used computers and new technologies all their professional lives.

These are general findings from the study which can contextualise the closer focus on the academic article. With the inspiration of the past, the long history of academic writing, we can have insight into contemporary change in academics' article writing, both in the genre and in the practices surrounding the texts. The remaining part of the chapter provides some pointers about change taken from this perspective. This works in both directions: history raises questions for contemporary digital research and current changes provide topics for further historical investigation. These should be seen as speculative and as going beyond the data of the *Academics Writing* project. They point in directions for further research and analysis. Topics from the analysis of the interview data which are covered here are: innovations in the genre of academic articles; text type, audience and purposes; the multimodal basis of genres of writing; forms of collaboration; how written articles act as a measure of academic value; and conflicting demands and stress in the academic workplace.

8.4.2 The academic article: New practices around a familiar genre

We counted the different types of text our participants talked about in their interviews, and found that they mentioned what can be regarded as 100 different genres. Most of the genres involved some sort of digital technology in their production. Journal articles were the most commonly mentioned genre with 67 instances. This was followed by student feedback with 40 mentions, lecture slides with 30, conference papers with 27 and monographs 25 (for further discussion of genres and the relation to disciplines, see Barton & McCulloch 2018). Within the academic research sphere of writing there was a cluster of research-related genres which were mentioned including articles, abstracts, monographs, conference presentations and research proposals.

In our study people talked about changes in the ways these texts were produced. This was partly as a consequence of technological changes and partly as a consequence of some of the changes in higher education mentioned earlier. Genres associated with academic writing are changing, in general ways, with greater informality, while new sorts of texts get referenced, there are new visualisations, and articles in many cases becoming shorter. These are ongoing changes which our informants were in the middle of. Properties which continue to make an academic article a distinct genre include broad phenomena such as length, the existence of references, indications of an existing written literature, the use of graphics, as well as syntactic and lexical features. Within experimental studies there is an overall structure such as opening with a problem, discussion of earlier studies, a plan of what is to be done in relation to this earlier work and ending with further work. Within a discipline there can also be differences related to research methodologies. These observations fit in well with the work done by Hyland (2004) on textual aspects of genres and disciplinary differences in research articles.

Returning to the links with history we can still see the influences of the origin of academic articles in the genre of letters, with similar concerns recurring today such as layout, or how to show the intended level of formality. Our interviews suggested that particular forms of argumentation and discoursal features such as the use of "I" are still being disputed. The use of the first-person singular was originally part of the conventions of letter writing (Swales 1990). It was initially a component of scientific writing as it was accepted that the researcher played a central role and that individual skill was needed to deal with any apparatus. In addition, scientists were consciously developing a style of writing which encouraged personal honesty and modesty. These demands for the first-person pronoun were relaxed as apparatus became more reliable alongside acceptance that anyone could operate the equipment and replicate the experiment. This is still contentious and as Swales (1990: 114) points out "the issue of impersonality in scientific writing, despite its apparent innocent simplicity, turns out to be complex and vexatious, and is yet to be fully understood".

A related contemporary issue which has grown in importance is whether it is appropriate to cite blog posts or draft versions of papers and how to cite them. In our data we found strongly held notions of which new media forms could be cited in articles and how they should be cited. Similarly, people did not necessarily agree on whether pre-final versions of articles were acceptable for citation. These examples all relate to the broader topic of the history of authorship. This will not be pursued here (but see Lunsford & Ede 1990).

8.4.3 New text types with new audiences driven by new purposes

There are constant new text types being developed in academic life for new purposes with new audiences. In our list of 84 genres reported by our informants, it was clear that some were completely new, for example new text types associated with blogging, tweeting and Facebook. They are new in that the software supporting the practices of blogging and tweeting did not exist 30 years ago. With more longstanding genres such as research proposals, conference papers and journal articles there were ways in which they were also changed by being digital.

Our informants referred to many online platforms which they might contribute to. These included ones addressed to specialist audiences, or to novices wanting simple information, such as online health sites, and explanations of how things work or how to mend them. Amongst these existing and new genres, research articles have to fit in with this wider mediascape of academic life. These are all seen to be influencing the shape of academic articles. For example, with the existence of academic research tweets and research blogs, work in progress reports, preprints, succinct summaries, and constant updating, academics no longer perceive there to be one definitive version of an article. Online publication may be ahead of hard copy publication with slightly different versions circulating. Overall this seems to be a practice in transition. With changing time scales and the speeding up of academic life we suggest that there are likely to be more, shorter papers which are published more quickly. There will probably be no hard copy publication of journals and maybe no definitive versions of articles. According to our interviewees, pre-publication versions already get cited. There seems to be a rise in the proportion of special issues of journals, and edited books perhaps becoming more similar to special issues of journals, with individual chapters being available separately from the overall book.

New forms of writing are leading to different audiences, including ones for impact. For instance, in our data we have the example of an academic realising that he could easily find out through online citation indexes who was citing his work. He noticed that it was getting cited beyond his discipline and his work had an audience he had not intended nor expected but nevertheless welcomed. Earlier there would have been no simple possibility of finding out patterns of citation except by trawling through paper-based indexes. Now there was another new audience and he took account of it in his writing. However, unknown audiences may be unwanted: another academic, an historian, was annoyed to receive emails from amateurs who had come across his papers online and wanted to comment on them.

These examples provide a good link to history. It is useful to keep in mind the idea of the origin of the academic article in letter writing and to see how contemporary research articles are, along with tweets and blogs, different forms of letter writing. Crucially they have different audiences and they are located within a range of related practices which shift over time. For the academics studied, article writing could vie for time with the use of blogs and other social media. Some of our interviewees were concerned with professional identity and the purpose and value of such writing. Some held the view that the availability of short pieces of writing, pre-publication drafts and other provisional texts provided a space to try things out and learn to write, albeit in a rather public space where others can be watching. Others, who tweet regularly, were balancing this kind of writing with other kinds of writing, such as journal articles, which have historically been more highly valued in the academy (see Barton & McCulloch 2018).

8.4.4 Cross modal differences: Visuals in writing an academic article

Academic articles have always been multimodal, with changing possibilities over time as to what modes to employ alongside written language. As Swales (1990) documents, the earliest articles had tables and drawings of equipment. Later there were also photos, graphs and equations. The development of statistics led to more complex tables. Jumping to the time of writing, the twenty-first century has seen an explosion of computer-aided data visualisations. Each development has led to additional visual possibilities alongside written language.

Examining cross-modal as well as transmedia practices is important in showing how different academic genres are brought together to create an academic article and how they rely upon each other. It also shows the affordances of different modes and media and what possibilities people take up.

The historically old practice of lecturing by standing at a lectern in a lecture theatre and reading a script is in many ways unchanged since medieval times. However, the lectern may now be regarded as a digital lectern with the possibility of live streaming, massive open online courses (MOOCs) and TED talks, as well as use of the ubiquitous presentation software, PowerPoint. In our study most people saw PowerPoint as the default software for a research paper presented at a conference. In terms of writing an academic article we found interesting differences and developments in the role of PowerPoint presentations. It was common for academics to report that they were starting from written notes or a written paper and turning it into a PowerPoint by adding visual material. However, others worked in the opposite direction of starting from a PowerPoint presentation with images and later developing it into a written paper. An historian explained how he wrote papers from scratch in Word, how conference papers were written-to-be-read-aloud and how he used PowerPoint images to illustrate his paper as he spoke. However, other people reported different practices around using PowerPoint.

People provided insights into their practices of creating texts for presentation and publication and these seemed to be individual routes of creation. For example, when making a research presentation most academics used some sort of notes as support. These could be the actual words on the PowerPoints or they could be separate notes. Several people said they had a script which they read or had partly memorized. This was especially true for conference papers. The historian mentioned above prepared a complete written paper for any conference presentation. He would have roughly 12 slides for a 40-minute paper. For him PowerPoints were used for images, not text. As this suggests, digital technologies often facilitated new multimodal practices. One informant from a marketing department explained how she made videos as research data and had embedded them in an online article. She explained "writing doesn't have to be words on a paper now, writing can be through the medium of the lens". Some contemporary journals, such as Kairos, deliberately explore and encourage re-evaluating multimodal boundaries (e.g. Lambke 2019 on podcasting).

8.4.5 Different forms of collaboration

Most of our participants were working on some form of collaborative writing at the time of the study and they often expressed extremely positive affective stance towards this. By chance two of the three disciplines we studied, history and mathematics, are ones where the ideas of individual work and the "lone scholar" are common. Despite this characteristic in both disciplines there seemed from the interviews to be an increasing recognition of collaborative work. In history, which is often viewed as an individual endeavour, scholars reported working with other academics, often across international borders. Some of our participants working in maths departments also provided examples where co-authorship was becoming more common. Technologies enabled oral and written modes of communicating to be combined, yet sometimes this brought its own problems. The video conferencing software, Skype, was cited as a useful but sometimes frustrating means of discussing writing in progress and thrashing out the conceptual aspects of an article before or during the writing process. Likewise, traditional, hard copies of materials were often combined with virtual file sharing when working together on projects (cf. Thompson & Collins, this volume).

Collaboration with colleagues on writing was often the stimulus for learning about new tools or changing practices. For example, many academics described using cloud-based file-sharing platforms such as Dropbox or Google Docs for the first time because scholars with whom they were collaborating wanted to use them. In this way, technology can facilitate the social side of collaborative writing, but it was often combined with face-to-face meetings rather than being seen as a substitute for actually meeting face-to-face. Email was often important when organising the exchange of drafts, but social contact in person remained important and could play a role in securing commitment from co-authors.

Research collaborations between people were often international, aided by software and new sources of funding supporting international collaborations. There were different forms of collaboration. Some was within disciplines, where people worked well with colleagues they had much in common with. There were also collaborations across disciplines where people complemented each other. Another form of collaboration, which is often not recognised as such, is where administrators who are experienced in writing ethics forms, impact statements, or justification of resources sections of grant proposals make specific contributions to sections of a bid. These could be drawn upon later when writing an academic paper. When people reflected on their working lives they seemed to have experienced a growth in these specialist contributions to academic research. We also saw examples of technical support from people who extract online data for a corpus, for example, or process data, or do the statistics. Again these areas appears to be growing. Translators of data have always contributed to social research. These too are hidden collaborations and these participants are not normally attributed as authors. Grant givers, such as funding councils, and journal editors may resist recognising collaboration and their associated software packages may demand a single "corresponding author" or "principal investigator". This broadening of ideas about collaboration complements the work of Lillis and Curry (2010) on international contexts and issues around getting research articles published in English.

8.4.6 Evaluating the academic article

The academic article has been around for more than 300 years, developing all the time, and being adapted for different disciplines and research methodologies. It is embedded in a wide range of different forms and looser genres such as pre-prints, summaries, highlights and keywords. There are many possible ways of evaluating academic success. One way, which is growing in importance as a measure of academic value, is to draw upon digital aspects of the academic article. The academic article is becoming the key measure of academic productivity as it is easy to have as a measure, for example with Google Scholar citations and the H index which are easy to understand and implement – even if there are concerns about their validity as measures of value. As one informant in our study put it: "Our currency is really journal articles".

We found that history academics prioritised single authored monographs but were increasingly accepting the importance of articles. Journal articles had a priority over book chapters. There also appears to be a growth in special issues of journals across several disciplines. At the same time, whilst edited books have a lower status some publishers will sell chapters individually, making them more like journal special issues. Academics in the discipline of management were under pressure to publish in specific journals with a list of permitted journals, and articles were rated primarily on the basis of which journal they were published in.

Citation levels are taken as a measure of support or significance of the work and can be counted by viewing activities, or measuring the amount of downloading, or liking, or retweeting. Measures such as number of citations or the prestige of the journal or a publisher are extensively used as proxies for quality. There is an ongoing battle over the research article and citations. Academic networking and sharing sites like ResearchGate, LinkedIn and Academia.edu, along with international publishers, are involved in competition over getting the attention of academics. As well as knowing who has downloaded a paper or searched an ebook, technology can now easily measure how much time is spent on reading a paper or what parts of a book have been opened or read. Learning analytics can be put to new purposes. Whilst designed for monitoring students, these measures can easily be turned onto academics and used for measuring their activity and outputs.

Returning to historical change, we cannot really predict what will happen to the academic article as different stakeholders are pushing in different directions. So far we have concentrated on individuals and their practices. Nevertheless, our interviews pointed to the many institutions which have an interest in the development of the academic article. Academics are caught between their professional self-interest and that of their institutions, as well as publishers. It is broader than this. Individual academics can be caught between the demands of professional associations, their own institutions, research councils (representing the government), software companies and publishers all having different interests. Bloggers and tweeters and job search websites are all jostling to offer help to students learning the genres of academic writing. We believe that a relative online freedom will, as it did with the coming of printing, become more regulated. The stakeholders in the collaborative activity of writing a research proposal are many and support for learning how to write a research proposal can come from many directions including courses provided by a union or university library staff, dedicated blogs, job websites and more. Formal courses seemed relatively unimportant to our informants, except for learning about technical equipment or software. They talked about informal learning academic literacy practices such as working it out oneself, following examples and learning from each other (Tusting & Barton 2003).

8.5 Conclusion: Conflicting demands

Whilst there has been a focus on technological change in this chapter, this needs to be discussed in the context of other social changes affecting the university system, such as massification, internationalisation, and increased managerial control, as discussed in Tusting et al. (2019, chapter 1). For example, the expectation that academics demonstrate the impact of their research on non-academic audiences is closely linked to the role that new media can play in achieving this. The project uncovered evidence about the increasing range of writing academics are participating in across teaching, administration and service work as well as in research. People are dealing with constant change. In our data we found examples of what can be seen as more general characteristics of the changing internet: such as greater informality, shifts in imagined audiences and context collapse. Audiences and purposes are changing and work is speeding up. Academics from the disciplines studied reported experiencing stress in their work lives. This was true, for instance, in their dealings with email and feeling they always had to be online. It was also apparent with article writing which has become a key proxy measure for academic value. As we have seen there are new audiences making different demands. The perceived acceleration of academic life (Vostal 2016) is not simply an artefact of new technologies, but also reflects longer-term reductions in governmental support for universities.

Academics in the early twenty-first century face conflicting demands in several ways. For instance, the call for increased individual accountability goes against the demands for collaboration. Also, interdisciplinary work is being pulled in two contradictory directions where funding may only be available for collaborative work whereas research frameworks may reward individual achievement. Social media offer possibilities for greater surveillance alongside more openness in a world of self-promotion and developing online identities. These examples all show how academics have greater possibilities alongside greater compulsion.

In these ways this study represents a snapshot of a particular point in history. It has highlighted the pervasiveness of digital technology and its relationship with wider issues shaping the research article. We have a long history of academic writing to help understand contemporary change. At the same time insights about contemporary changes can provide new ways of looking at history. It is salutary to realise that contemporary themes like shifting audiences have in fact been around for a long time. Other areas where greater understanding of the long history may illuminate the present and where greater understanding of the present can be of value when looking at history include: issues of authorship and collaboration; multimodal influences on academic writing; and the over-arching power of the genres of letter writing.

References

Barton, David & Carmen Lee. 2013. *Language online: Investigating digital texts and practices*. Abingdon: Routledge.
Barton, David & Sharon McCulloch. 2018. Negotiating tensions around new forms of academic writing. *Discourse, Context & Media* 24. 8–15.

Hyland, Ken. 2004. *Disciplinary discourses: Social interactions in academic writing*. Ann Arbor: University of Michigan Press.
Lambke, Abigail. 2019. Arranging delivery, delivering arrangement: An ecological sonic rhetoric of podcasting. *Kairos* 23 (2). http://kairos.technorhetoric.net/23.2/topoi/lambke/index.html (accessed 28 May 2019).
Lillis, Theresa & Mary Jane Curry. 2010. *Academic writing in a global context*. Abingdon: Routledge.
Lunsford, Andrea & Lisa Ede. 1990. *Singular texts/plural authors: Perspectives on collaborative writing*. Carbondale: Southern Illinois University Press.
McCulloch, Sharon. 2017. Hobson's choice: The effects of research evaluation on academics' writing practices in England. *Aslib Journal of Information Management* 69 (5). 503–515.
Marginson, Simon & Thi Kim Anh Dang, 2017. Vygotsky's sociocultural theory in the context of globalisation. *Asia Pacific Journal of Education* 37 (1). 116–129.
Page, Ruth, David Barton, Johannes Unger & Michele Zappavigna. 2014. *Researching language and social media*. Abingdon: Routledge.
Scribner, Sylvia & Michael Cole. 1981. *The psychology of literacy*. Cambridge, MA: Harvard University Press.
Swales, John M. 1990. *Genre analysis: English in academic and research settings*. Cambridge, UK: Cambridge University Press.
Swales, John. [1998] 2018. *Other floors, other voices: A textography of a small university building*. Mahwah: Lawrence Erlbaum.
Tusting, Karin & David Barton. 2003. *Models of adult learning: A literature review*. Leicester: NIACE.
Tusting, Karin & David Barton. 2016. Writing disciplines: Producing disciplinary knowledge in the context of contemporary higher education. *Ibérica (Journal of the European Association of Languages for Specific Purposes)* 32. 15–34.
Tusting, Karin, Sharon McCulloch, Ibrar Bhatt, Mary Hamilton & David Barton. 2019. *Academics writing: The dynamics of knowledge creation*. Abingdon: Routledge.
Vostal, Filip. 2016. *Accelerating academia: The changing structure of academic time*. Dordrecht: Springer.
Vygotsky, Lev. [1930–1934] 1978. *Mind in society: The development of higher psychological processes*. Cambridge, MA: Harvard University Press.
Weller, Martin. 2011. *The digital scholar: How technology is transforming scholarly practice*. London: Bloomsbury.
Yates, Simeon J. 2000. Computer mediated communication: The future of the letter. In David Barton & Nigel Hall (eds.), *Letter writing as a social practice*, 233–52. Amsterdam: John Benjamins.

Alison Sealey
9 Reflections on historicizing discourses: Connections, linkages, continuities

The chapters in this section all provide evidence, though in diverse ways, of connections, linkages, continuities – pointing to the relevance of the concept of "assemblages"[1] – that is, a rejection of an ontology comprising discrete and fixed entities, in favour of a recognition that matter (both organic and inorganic), as well as social phenomena, are characterised by entanglements and relational processes. We are used to thinking of human beings as singular entities and individual producers of discourse, and of discourse as comprising components (phonemes, morphemes, lexis, syntactic structures) that are analytically discrete. Discourse analysis, of course, recognises diverse combinations of these notional ingredients in any specific interaction. Speakers and writers may be theorised as performing multiple identities, for example, and in the chapters to be found here, Seargeant (citing Greenblatt 1980: 2) draws attention to "the fashioning of human identity" becoming "a manipulable, artful process" as long ago as the sixteenth century, while other authors describe the "professional", "online" and "digital" identities associated with the people they studied. Another theme in discourse analysis is the bi-directional influence of discourses and social norms and practices. As Lyons and Ounoughi express it, "[t]exts are both shaped by the contexts in which they occur and ... [affect] interactants' relationships to each other and the environment". These chapters also illustrate developments in discourse analysis theories and methods that take increasing account of "contexts", as well as the growing recognition of the significance of both time and place in the production of discourse.

In their different ways, all of the chapters in this section also provide evidence of continuities and transformations relating to developments in the affordances and effects of technology on human communication. For example, Seargeant draws attention to the role of material artefacts such as portraits and

---

[1] Space does not allow thorough discussion of assemblage theory, which derives from the philosophy of Deleuze and Guattari (e.g. 1988), and has been developed and debated by scholars in various disciplines, each of whom has added to the definitions, interpretations and nuances. My (relatively loose) use of the concept here draws on assemblages' characteristics of heterogeneity, relationality and transience, and its opposition to anthropocentrism.

Alison Sealey, Lancaster University, Department of Linguistics and English Language, County South, Lancaster, UK, e-mail: a.sealey@lancaster.ac.uk

https://doi.org/10.1515/9783110670837-012

statues in the projection of an image of authority by political leaders. The controversies about the meaning and appropriateness of the expression *R.I.P.*, discussed by Giaxoglou, are facilitated by contemporary technologies, but reach back to material artefacts such as sacred texts and carved headstones. Barton reminds us how structured labour relations are modified by the surveillance that is facilitated by digital monitoring of interactions between readers and texts. And Lyons and Ounoughi provide particularly clear examples of the way communications are embedded in specific locations, so that landscapes, weather and non-human entities such as "traffic" and so on, affect both what is said and written and how interactions may be accomplished.

Thus all these chapters include extensive references to many facets of the non-human. And yet, as Lyons and Ounoughi explicitly acknowledge, "the human stands in the centre of discourse in motion and about motion", and "spatial representation across centuries" has been consistently anthropocentric. So even as we explore the exponential growth of virtual communities, we inevitably do so from the perspective of our own species. At the same time, in the contemporary political climate, we are routinely exhorted to see ourselves as individuals in competition with each other, so that technology is deployed to measure proxies for "output" and "success" – as Barton illustrates, for example, with reference to the academic domain. In the broader political context, economic "growth" and "productivity" trump concerns for the preservation of clean air, safe habitats and biodiversity.

Returning to my earlier observation, conventional approaches posit human beings not only as the "anchor" (Lyons & Ounoughi), or vantage point around which reality is perceived and discourse is shaped, but they also encourage the perception that human individuals are singular, bounded physical entities. Notwithstanding the burgeoning field of multimodal analysis, discourse is still routinely understood to be the preserve of humans, since humans are taken to be the only "truly" linguistic animals (e.g. Anderson 2006). This is despite increasing evidence of myriad modes of communication via diverse channels of semiosis throughout the non-human world (e.g. Dillard-Wright 2009; Hoffmeyer 2010; Wolfe 2003), and the increasing difficulty of defining "language" in human exceptionalist terms, other than with reference to circular arguments (e.g. Despret 2016; Tudge 2013). So in what remains of this short reflective piece, I offer some thoughts on the interconnectedness of people, discourse and the more-than-human.

My first observation relates to the nature of the human body. As anyone familiar with introductory courses on the anatomy and physiology of speech knows, the interaction of lungs, larynx, pharynx, velum, tongue and nasal cavity enables the production of meaningful sounds, so that these components *in combination with air from outside the body* may be thought of as a speech-producing "assemblage". Yet each of these components of human anatomy is an assemblage in itself, dependant for survival not only on myriad microorganisms but also on the ingestion of external substances, so that, rather than "a self-contained, unified organic whole, distinct from its environment", the body may be understood "as a fragmented assemblage made up of transferable and translatable parts that depends much more on interactions with its surroundings" (Sharon 2014: 113; see also Gilbert, Sapp & Tauber 2012).

Secondly, as already indicated, these studies all provide evidence of the assemblages constituted by discourse-producing agents in combinations – not only with other, co-present people, but also with distant others (some long dead, some in other spaces and time zones), and, importantly, with organic and inorganic matter, including artefacts, both material and virtual.

Finally, there are traces in these chapters of potential alternatives to the default anthropocentric stance in the human and social sciences. Barton contrasts "long term cultural history with individuals' life histories", which brings to my mind the much greater contrasts between the lifespans of other species, such as trees (up to thousands of years), and insects (sometimes a few days). What might be the implications of incorporating alternative timescales, with reference to these contrasting life-spans, into our analyses?

As we reflect on continuities and connections in relation to human-produced discourse, technologies and material products, I'd like to think that there is room too to imagine our impact, discursive and material, on the other living beings who, with us, both constitute and are constituted by assemblages.

References

Anderson, Stephen R. 2006. *Doctor Dolittle's delusion: Animals and the uniqueness of human language*. New Haven: Yale University Press.
Deleuze, Gilles & Félix Guattari. 1988. *A thousand plateaus: Capitalism and schizophrenia*. London: Bloomsbury.
Despret, Vinciane. 2016. *What would animals say if we asked the right questions?* Translated by Brett Buchanan. Minneapolis: University of Minnesota Press.
Dillard-Wright, David B. 2009. Thinking across species boundaries: General sociality and embodied meaning. *Society & Animals* 17 (1). 53–71.
Gilbert, Scott F., Jan Sapp & Alfred I Tauber. 2012. A symbiotic view of life: We have never been individuals. *The Quarterly Review of Biology* 87 (4). 325–341.
Greenblatt, Stephen. 1980. *Renaissance self-fashioning*. Chicago: University of Chicago Press.
Hoffmeyer, Jesper. 2010. A biosemiotic approach to the question of meaning. *Zygon®* 45 (2). 367–390.

Sharon, Tamar. 2014. From molar to molecular bodies: Posthumanist frameworks in contemporary biology. In Tamar Sharon (ed.), *Human nature in an age of biotechnology*, 113–134. London: Springer.
Tudge, Colin. 2013. *Why genes are not selfish and people are nice: A challenge to the dangerous ideas that dominate our lives*. Edinburgh: Floris Books.
Wolfe, Cary. 2003. In the shadow of Wittgenstein's lion: Language, ethics, and the question of the animal. In Cary Wolfe (ed.), *Zoontologies: The question of the animal*, 1–58. Minneapolis: University of Minnesota Press.

Section 3: **Media Trajectories**

Introduction to media trajectories

In light of the multimodal and material "turns" that have shaped humanities research in the early years of the twenty-first century, sociolinguistic and pragmatic scholarship has re-evaluated the relationship between their traditional focus – language, typically spoken – and the other semiotic resources used for human communication. Within the digital domain, the emergence of supposedly innovative and domain-specific features, such as emoji (Parkwell 2019), GIFs (Bourlai & Herring 2014) and the internet meme (Lugea forthcoming) enrich and augment the still predominantly written medium of digital interactions. In parallel with the increasing reappraisal of the primacy of language in present-day communication, there has been a similar "turn" in historical studies of language and texts. The three chapters in this section build on the landmark work of Carroll et al. (2013), Machan (2011) and Peikola et al. (2017), among others, to explore how the trajectory of technological developments in the past similarly shape and change communicative practices at the level of the visual, as well as the verbal, perhaps allowing us to step a little closer to how historical readers would have engaged with their texts (in the case of the three case studies, specifically early and late modern readers), and understood their properties as material objects as well as linguistic texts. In this section, the transhistorical perspective relates primarily to the researchers' awareness of the dominant ideologies surrounding written communication, recognising how this has shaped our traditional approaches to and understanding of the textual practices of digital and pre-digital genres. In pursuing readings which attend to language as part of a wider set of semiotic resources, new lines of comparison and consistency can be investigated, enriching our understanding of the history of English before and after the establishment of print culture.

In her chapter, Joanna Kopaczyk explores the stability of content and its presentation in the transmission of Scottish burgh laws, the *Leges Quatuor Burgorum*, focussing in particular on evidence of the transformative impact of printing. Her focus on language and the visual dimensions of the written page finds little evidence that printing wrought transformation in practice, but instead built on those innovations already underway in the manuscript tradition, which provided an important vehicle for the Scots vernacular in the early modern period.

Hanna Rutkowska's chapter considers the diachronic trajectory of the paratextual properties of the early modern English conduct book, *The School of Vertue* (1557–1687). Rutkowska develops the "pragmatics on the page" framework, initiated by Carroll et al. (2013), to provide a comprehensive and granular exploration of the 12 editions published over the course of the sixteenth and seventeenth centuries. The analysis exploits the advantages of digital databases, such as EEBO, to examine the visual properties of the text, identifying practices coherent with the recognised narrative of book history, such as the increasing use of typeface switching to guide the reader (see Kaislaniemi 2017), as well as more culturally-embedded developments, such as the late sixteenth-century omission of the thirteenth chapter. Rutkowska's study testifies to the complex meanings arising from the interplay of verbal and visual elements in early modern texts, and the importance of reading these in their historical (commercial, political, technological) contexts.

The chapter by Varila et al. undertakes a similar diachronic pragmatic exploration of a single early modern text; their focus being the legal textbook of Christopher St German's *Doctor and Student* (1528–1886). Their interest is, in particular, in the ways in which paratextual features may have had promotional effects, and the extent to which a transhistorical perspective can reveal continuities or disunities in practice within the changing market place; providing a framework for investigating textual trajectories, as proposed by Blommaert (2005: 62–4). Their detailed study indicates how the longevity of *Doctor and Student* arises, in part, from its consistent re-framing through paratextual features to appeal to successive audiences, and the specific and cumulative effect of components such as contents pages, prologues, authorial biographies and footnotes, in contrast with the stability of the main text.

Collectively, the chapters in this section illustrate the potential for pragmatic frameworks to capture the complex interactions between visual and verbal resources at synchronic and diachronic levels, reading across the iterations of the "same" text in their varying media and contextual environments. As Claudia Claridge notes, when reflecting on the resonance of the approach for our understanding of historical textual practices, we need increasingly to attend to, and account for, the visual dimensions of a text, including their relation to genre conventions, the technological affordances of the medium, and their temporal context of use. Her proposal of the "efficiency/effectiveness" ratio – as with van Driel's (this volume) present-day assessment of reader response – foregrounds the relationship between text and consumer; a relationship that surely has many continuities (as much as there are inevitable differences) across time.

References

Blommaert, Jan. 2005. *Discourse: A critical introduction*. Cambridge, UK: Cambridge University Press.

Carroll, Ruth, Matti Peikola, Hanna Salmi, Mari-Liisa Varila, Janne Skaffari & Risto Hiltunen. 2013. Pragmatics on the page: Visual text in Late Medieval English books. *European Journal of English Studies* 17 (1): 54–71.

Bourlai, Elli E. & Susan. C. Herring. 2014. Multimodal communication on Tumblr: "I have so many feels!" Proceedings of WebSci 2014, ACM, New York. Available: http://info.ils.indiana.edu/~herring/tumblr.pdf (accessed 20th May 2019).

Kaislaniemi, Samuli. 2017. Code switching, script shifting and typeface switching in Early Modern English manuscript letters and printed tracts. In Matti Peikola, Aleksi Mäkilähde, Hanna Salmi, Mari-Liisa Varila & Janne Skaffari (eds.), *Verbal and visual communication in Early English texts*, 165–200. Turnhout: Brepols.

Lugea, Jane. Forthcoming. The pragma-stylistics of "image macro" internet memes. In Helen Ringrow & Stephen Pihlaja (eds.), *Contemporary media stylistics*. London: Bloomsbury.

Machan, Tim. 2011. The visual pragmatics of code-switching in Late Middle English literature. In Herbert Schendl & Laura Wright (eds.), *Code-switching in Early English*, 303–33. Berlin: De Gruyter Mouton.

Parkwell, Corina. 2019. Emoji as social semiotic resources for meaning-making in discourse: Mapping the functions of the toilet emoji in Cher's tweets about Donald Trump. *Discourse, Context & Media* 30: article 100307.

Peikola, Matti, Aleksi Mäkilähde, Hanna Salmi, Mari-Liisa Varila & Janne Skaffari (eds.). 2017. *Verbal and visual communication in Early English texts*. Turnhout: Brepols.

Joanna Kopaczyk
10 Unstable content, remediated layout: Urban laws in Scotland through manuscript and print

10.1 Dissemination of law through old and new media

One may argue that the possibility to disseminate textual content to billions of people via digital media follows in the footsteps of the first such revolutionary turn in dissemination, enabled by the printing press. The quick progress of printing across the late fifteenth- and early sixteenth-century Europe was linked to the realisation that faster, less laborious and less costly text production could disseminate the contents of these texts much more widely and quickly (Eisenstein 1979). But it was not just about reaching a wider audience. An additional asset was the ability to reproduce content without changes (or with minimal changes) in multiple copies.[1] It is easy to imagine that such stability would be welcome in the legal context – a faithful transmission of legal regulations could enhance the authority of the law, and provide the administrators and rulers with a stable point of reference.

This study looks at manuscripts and the earliest printed version of Scottish burgh laws, written in chapter format in Latin and then in the vernacular, Scots, and asks about the stability of legal content as it gets transmitted through

---

[1] The ideas of repeatability and uniformity were not new. McLuhan (1962: 77–79) has already pointed out that they lay at the very core of inventing a phonetic alphabet as a means of capturing speech but print took this to a new level of larger replicable units on a replicable page – "the first uniform and repeatable 'commodity'" (McLuhan 1962: 125).

Note: I would like to thank my colleagues at the University of Glasgow, Jeremy J. Smith and Alison Wiggins for their advice on this chapter, as well as Alpo Honkapohja (University of Edinburgh) for providing me with images of the Cambridge MS Kk.1.5., and historians Alice Taylor (King's College London) and Dauvit Broun (University of Glasgow) for helping me decipher a particularly challenging Latin entry.

Joanna Kopaczyk, University of Glasgow, English Language & Linguistics, Glasgow, UK, e-mail: joanna.kopaczyk@glasgow.ac.uk

https://doi.org/10.1515/9783110670837-014

different copies and different media.[2] An important and unique collection of rules regulating life in Scottish medieval towns, the *Leges Quatuor Burgorum*, henceforth *Leges*, were consistently copied into manuscripts containing the canon of Scottish medieval laws, including early legal treatises (typically *Regiam Maiestatem* and *Quoniam Attachiamenta*), royal statutes, acts of parliament and other collections of laws, e.g. *Leges Forestarum*, the laws of the forests (Innes 1844; Dolezalek 2010). The order of the legal chapters, their specific linguistic form as well as their layout on the page, was never the same from one manuscript copy to another. With the arrival of printing, the content and format of the laws could be fixed. The question is whether the leap towards the new medium affected the *Leges* in a different way than the textual transmission which had been ongoing via the traditional medium, i.e. handwriting.

As the meaning of a text is derived from its form (Street 1984: 90), this study brings together two perspectives: the visual aspects of discourse management, and the actual contents making up this particular instance of legal discourse. This approach goes hand in hand with the study of the communicative aspects of layout and *ordinatio*, important for manuscript studies (Parkes 1976, 1991) but also increasingly popular and fruitful for historical linguistics in general, and historical pragmatics in particular (Pahta & Jucker 2011; Horobin 2016: 126). Using the concept of remediation (Bolter & Grusin 2000), and in congruence with the broad transhistorical approach explored in this volume, I argue that access to the printing press did not bring about any radical change in the visual shape of the laws. I show what major innovations in visual discourse occurred before the printing revolution, and what additions to the already existing practices were developed for the printed text.

In terms of the linguistic shape of the laws, this chapter looks at how the vernacular – Scots – was employed to carry complex legal meanings from the fifteenth to the seventeenth century. This was a period of vernacularisation of legal discourse but the underlying point of reference for the Scots versions was still the Latin text. I used an automatic collation engine, Juxta Commons (Wheeles & Jensen 2013), to pinpoint differences between the extant vernacular manuscript versions of the burgh laws and juxtapose them with the printed text. In this manner, I discovered a radical change in the linguistic formulation of the laws, which, admittedly, did fluctuate between manuscript copies, but became much more altered in the new medium (for an examination of consistencies

---

[2] As the transition from manuscript to print was genre-specific, a wider perspective on this process can be gleaned from studies of literary texts (e.g. Caie 2011), plays (e.g. Culpeper & Demmen 2011) or medical texts (Pahta et al. 2011).

across print, see Rutkowska, this volume). This suggests new technology had enabled a fresh approach to reproduction and dissemination of legal ideas, but its users chose to do it in a familiar visual format.

10.2 Urban laws and their transmission in Scotland

Lowland Scotland was the scene of a concerted effort to regulate and promote urbanisation within the feudal framework in the twelfth century (Lynch, Spellman & Stell 1988: 3; Cairns 2000: 24). Both consolidating settlements and newly established urban centres started to be referred to as *burghs* and were granted royal charters which secured their legal status and trading privileges. Life in royal burghs was regulated by customary laws, whose "more sophisticated version" emerged as the *Leges* – still "a jumble of substantive rules and procedural technicalities with a smattering of economic legislation" (Duncan 1975: 482). There is evidence that these laws were consulted across the country. Frankot (2012: 157) suggested that towns pursued uniformity in legal practice as they would exchange correspondence about the *Leges* (cf. Robinson et al. 1985: 268 on the *Leges* providing a model "for the particular customs of individual burghs"; Walker 1990: 425).

The oldest manuscript version of the *Leges* is the Berne MS from c.1270 (MacQueen & Windram 1988: 209), showing glimpses of the pre-existing vernacular legal culture through Scots borrowings in the Latin text (Kopaczyk 2011: 10–13). The earliest Scots version of the laws is found among Latin legal texts in the Bute manuscript from the late fourteenth century (Innes 1844: 181, National Library of Scotland MS 21246), and starts with a Latin rubric. The first dated Scots version (National Library of Scotland MS 25.4.15) was complied in 1455 and starts with the title *Hir begynis ye lawis of burrowys* (henceforth *Lawis*). An edition of parallel Latin and Scots versions was prepared in the nineteenth century by Thomas Thomson and included by Cosmo Innes in his comprehensive edition of the *Acts of the Parliaments of Scotland* (henceforth *APS*, Innes 1844). Table 10.1 presents all manuscripts identified by the APS and Dolezalek (2010) which contain Scots versions of the laws with various ordering and quantity of individual laws, or *chapters*. The alphabetical labels will be used in the discussion below. The APS text was later antiquated (see Kopaczyk 2018) and printed in 1868 as *Ancient laws and customs of the burghs of Scotland* (Innes 1868). In the preface to his edition, Innes gives an account of how the transmission of the laws was handled in the past: "In the

Table 10.1: Catalogue details and dates and of all known Scots versions of the burgh laws, including the first printed version.

	Bookshelf mark	Date
A	NLS MS 25.4.15 (Adv. Lib. W.4.ult)	1455
B	NLS MS 25.4.14 (Adv. Lib. W.4.28, Cokburn)**	la15c
C	Cambridge MS Kk.1.5	la15c
D	NLS MS 25.5.7 (Adv. Lib. A.1.32)**	1470s
E	NLS Acc 11218/5 (Adv. Lib. Fort Augustus A.1)	la15c
F	NLS MS 7.1.9 (Adv. Lib. A.3.22, Malcolm)*	1560
G	NLS MS 7.1.10 (Adv. Lib. A.3.16, Lumisden)	1602
H	Printed version by John Skene	1609
	NLS MS 21246 (Bute)** – unavailable to photograph	la14c
	Marchmont MS** – missing or privately owned	1548

*the manuscript not listed as Scots in Dolezalek (2010)
**manuscripts missing from Dolezalek's list

course of the fifteenth, sixteenth, and seventeenth centuries, there may be traced a very interesting series of attempts ... to restore [the more ancient laws of the Realm] to a state of purity and authenticity; and ultimately to reduce the whole into a more systematic form" (Innes 1844: 21).

It took a while in Scotland to employ the new technology, printing, to record the current legislation (from 1541 onwards)[3] and it was not until 1590s that a printed version of older acts within the existing record was commissioned. John Skene, as the Clerk Register, was allocated the task of consolidating the ancient statutes and laws of the kingdom (Walker 1995: 364–365; Mann 2000: 155). He presented the fruits of his labour to the Scottish Parliament in 1607, and the resulting volumes were printed in Latin and Scots in 1609 in Edinburgh by Thomas Finlason.[4] In the "Epistle to the Reader", Skene made some self-conscious comments about the translation from Latin into what he called "Englifh":[5] "I am the firft that ever travelled in this mater, and

---

[3] The printing of legal texts in England has a much longer history (Harvey 2015).
[4] It is significant that work on consolidating ancient Scots laws was going on during James VI's ascent to the English throne and published not long after the Union of the Crowns (1604). The same Latin text – but not the Scots version – was printed in London in 1613 by John Bill (see Early English Books Online). On English laws being consolidated during James VI's reign in a semiotically important printed format, see Callister (2014) and Harvey (2015).
[5] In earlier times, the term *Inglis* was used for the continuum of Germanic dialects spoken in the Lowlands while *Scottis* referred to the Celtic language of Scotland (McClure 1981). Skene is

therefore am fubject to the reprehenfion of many quha fall ['who shall'] follow after me" (Innes 1844: 27). Indeed, he was subject to criticism from later generations of lawyers. Innes (1844: 28) quotes Lord Haies, saying in 1769 that "to all appearance, Skene was a careless, if not an unfaithful publisher". In this chapter, I will not question the quality of Skene's work but rather signal some of the choices he made in his printed version in comparison to the extant manuscripts. My intention is to showcase how different the printed text was in terms of phrasing and displaying the contents of the *Lawis* in particular, and relate these differences to the change in the medium, as part of the more general changes in the early modern legal culture in Scotland.

10.3 (Re)mediating content: From manuscript to print, and back

A new medium may pretend it is not new. It may try to create an illusion that the old medium is still the main conduit for the message, as in online texts where one "turns the pages" in a book-like fashion. Such practices have been conceptualised as *remediation* (Bolter & Grusin 2000). In the case of the transition from manuscript to print, not only was the adoption of the new medium slow and gradual (Jucker & Pahta 2011: 4), but also the new format of the textual content continued the earlier practices in many respects. Eisenstein (1979: 52–53) lists some design features that early printers experimented with before 1500: graduated type, running heads, footnotes, cross references, tables of contents, title pages, and woodcuts. It is fair to say that these visual tools had been developed in manuscript culture, and the technology of print simply made them more robust. In his *Five hundred years of printing*, Steinberg ([1955] 2017: 25) pointed out that "printed books were at first hardly distinguishable from manuscripts", especially when they were produced as copies of existing manuscripts – "a seeming continuity without a radical change" (Eisenstein 1979: 51). At the same time, manuscript versions of early prints were also produced (Bühler 1960: 16). To paraphrase McLuhan's (1964) famous statement, the medium was trying *not* to be the message, to stay transparent and not draw

---

using "English" with reference to his vernacular at the start of the seventeenth century, by which time written Scots had started undergoing Anglicisation (Devitt 1989; Agutter 1990; McClure 2010). Indeed, Skene's text is anglicised (which is a topic for a different study), but still clearly written in Scots, showing diagnostic spelling variants such as <quh> for /hw/ and typically Scots vocabulary and syntax.

attention to itself. Harvey (2015: 9) points out that in the context of communicating the law, this "co-existence" of handwritten and printed texts has not yet been analysed; however, printing definitely had a pronounced impact on communicating and sharing legal information, especially in terms of consistency. This distinguishing feature of print goes hand-in-hand with Eisenstein's "standardization" and "fixity" (although see the criticism of Eisenstein's interpretations in Johns 1998 and McKitterick 2003). If we shift the focus from mediated form to mediated content, however, new questions about repurposing the older content in a new medium can be asked. In this study, I will show how the new medium opened an opportunity to remodel the content of burgh laws linguistically, while holding on to earlier visual discourse strategies.

10.4 Visual discourse of legal texts

Parkes established a relationship between the "structure of reasoning" and the "physical appearance of books" (Parkes 1991: 35–70) in the context of scholastic engagement with the text. He drew attention to the role of rubrication, titles, *litterae notabiliores* (enlarged letters), paraph marks, colour, and other features in the design of the *mise-en-page*, or page layout (see also Varila et al. 2017: 5–10), which fed into the text's *ordinatio*, roughly understood as the ordering of textual information in a meaningful way (Parkes 1976, 1991). In textual transmission, the segments of information may fluctuate, depending on the changing cultural and social environment; such a dynamic approach to text was certainly characteristic of legal scribes and clerks – a community of practice operating in early administrative centres in Scotland (Kopaczyk 2013a: 226–229). The laws swapped order, changed wording, dropped out, and were presented differently in each manuscript witness. The body of legislation was being shaped and transmitted across time in view of the changing needs of the audience and wider interactions with other producers of manuscripts (see Snijders 2015: 183, 209–222 on a similar approach to saints' lives by monastic scribes; cf. Mackay 2017 on the transmission of the earliest Scottish prose chronicle).

The communicative possibilities of layout (Snijders 2015: 37–78) depended on the genre and purpose of the text and its socio-cultural ramifications, including the cost of production. What follows is that the visually salient aspects – size, style, colour and position of elements on the page, as identified by Carroll et al. (2013: 57) – were also in flux. For Scottish burgh laws, the visual choices regarding titles are the most important to analyse. Not only did they encapsulate chapter contents linguistically, but they also marked out the chapters visually, and differed across the manuscripts. The introduction of print is claimed to have introduced new possibilities for *mise-en-page* and *ordinatio*: "Innovations such as tables, catalogues and indices, and cross-referencing material within the text, were characteristics of print. Indexing, cross-referencing and ordering of material was seized upon by jurists and law printers" (Harvey 2015: 6). We should not forget, however, that many of these visual organisational strategies featured in manuscripts already; what was seized upon was the replicability of text after it had been worded and set out on the page.

10.5 Tracing differences in the visual discourse and textual content

10.5.1 Selecting chapters for analysis

Even though the Scots language started to be employed as a vehicle for urban laws in the fifteenth century, Latin versions were still being produced alongside them. The relationship between the two versions and their parallel transmissions is a ripe field for future investigation (cf. Kopaczyk 2020). Earlier research has already identified Scots legal terms in the Latin text and Latin syntactic calques in Scots (Kopaczyk 2011), so for the present study, I decided to focus on laws which displayed an interesting interplay of Latin and Scots. It was important to find chapters which were included in each extant Scots manuscript and in Skene's printed edition, to enable a comparative outlook. Missing chapters and differences in numbering between witnesses can be gleaned from a collation table in the *APS* (Innes 1844). Out of 120 chapters comprising the canonical text of the burgh laws, about forty are present across all witnesses. I selected four for a qualitative discussion and located them in the seven extant Scots manuscript witnesses of Scottish burgh laws for which I could obtain photographs (A-G in table 10.1) and their printed version from 1609 (H).[6] The manuscript coeval with Skene's printed version (G, Lumisden, NLS MS 7.1.10, 1602) opens a crucial question: if the versions compiled roughly at the same time differ, can these differences be attributed to the change of the medium, or do they reflect the changing discourse practices within the legal culture which do not have to be attributed to the introduction of print? In

---

6 NLS MS 25.4.15 (A) lacks Chapter 23, so for the quantitative comparison of difference between witnesses only three chapters were used; see section 10.5.3.

the remainder of the chapter, I unpack the visual structuring of the content, and the linguistic choices made by the compiler in relation to the Scots language tradition of the same body of legal regulations.

10.5.2 Visual differences between the witnesses

The visual practices are consistent within each manuscript, so it suffices to choose a single example to compare how the same information – the same legal chapter – is presented across the material. I have selected Chapter 17 as it is quite short and attested in all witnesses. It is also a good example of the text of one law being incorporated into another law with and without visual cues. The presence of such cues indicates that the scribe must have engaged with a version of the laws where that chapter was explicitly separated from the rest. It is hard to postulate, however, that the surviving Scots versions of the *Lawis* form a continuous copying tradition. The differences in the actual wording and content of the chapters point to a more fluid transmission of the text, which I explore in section 10.5.4.

In terms of visual discourse, the snippets of the manuscripts and the printed text presented below are illustrative of the hand, the ink colour, presentation conventions, layout and other visual aspects employed in each witness of the *Lawis* also for other chapters. In terms of organising information visually, two main approaches can be noticed: the use of rubricated titles i.e. those in red ink (A and B, figure 10.1)[7] and self-standing titles; i.e. those separated from the surrounding text (C, D, E, F, G and H, figure 10.2). Interestingly, the gradual abandonment of coloured ink correlates with a growing preference for space management. Other discourse-structuring devices, such as numbers, are also employed.

Figures 10.1 and 10.2 clearly show that the replication of content across the witnesses came in various formats. In addition to textual cues – in this case, rubrics and self-standing titles – the scribe aimed to support the processing of information with visual cues: the use of different ink colour, spacing, enhanced initials, and letter size in general.

(a) Block text and colour

Only two of the consulted Scots versions of the *Lawis* use red ink rubrics in the black block text: (A) (figure 10.1, top) and (B) (figure 10.1, bottom) both from the

---

7 The Bute MS (late fourteenth century) which contains the oldest known version of the Scots text could not be photographed, but it also organises the text by means of red rubrics.

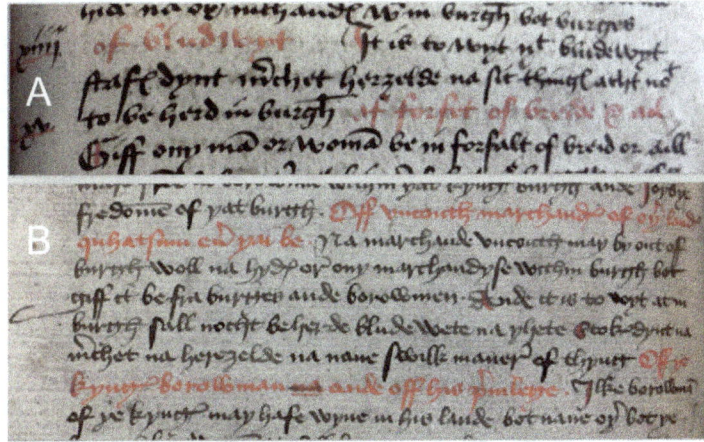

Figure 10.1: Visual discourse structured by rubrics in fragments containing the text of Chapter 17, NLS MS 25.5.15 f.134r (A) and NLS MS 25.4.14 f.109v (B).

second half of the fifteenth century. Both also use colour for emphasising first letters of selected words. It is possible that the scribe in (B) chose to highlight the *littera notabilior* in <Ande> not only because it started a new clause, but because it coincided with the start of Chapter 17 within the text of the preceding law. The correlation between the red ink, *litterae notabiliores* and the significance of the marked lexical item could be investigated in a separate paper (for other discussions of rubrication, see Thompson & Collins; Rutkowska; Moore, all this volume).

(b) Space and colour

Manuscript (C) (figure 10.2) exemplifies a late fifteenth-century transition between red rubrics and one-colour text, where information management is carried out by means of space. Here, the chapters are clearly separated by titles, whose visibility is enhanced by the red ink. Colour is sparsely used for other purposes in this version, with some inconsistent emphasis on initials. Chapter 17 is embedded in the preceding law, as in (B), but the only visual cue is a virgule.

(c) Space with no added colour

The remaining witnesses, as well as the early modern printed version, fall into the category of managing information by means of space alone, typically through line breaks and indenting. Red is used in the late fifteenth-century manuscript (D) (figure 10.2, second from top) for some decorative emphasis

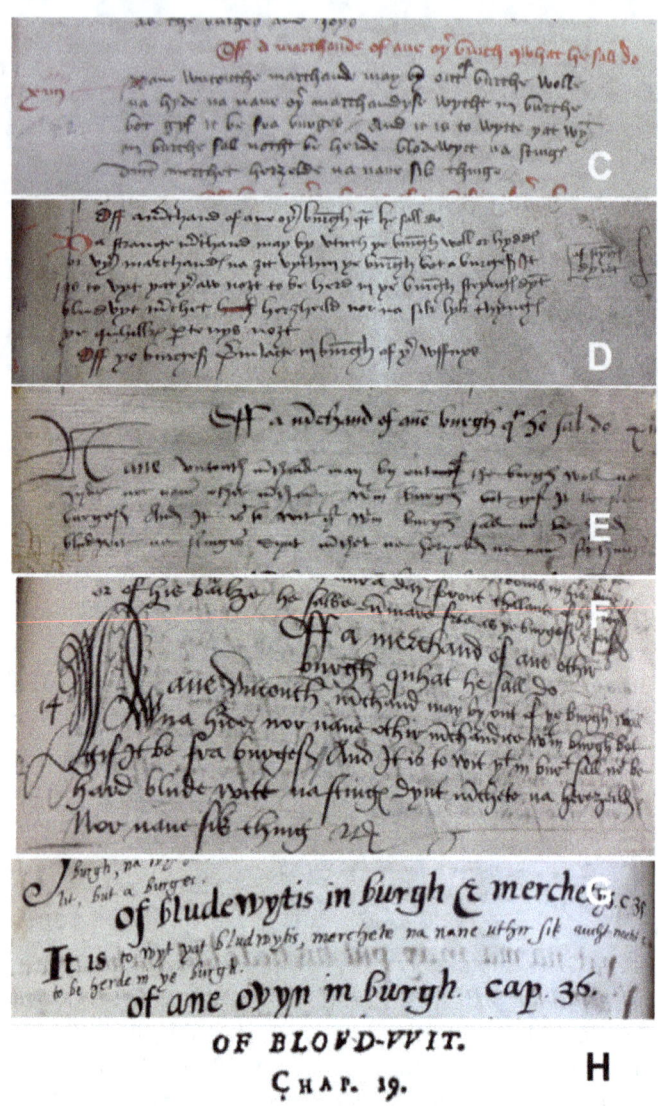

Figure 10.2: Visual discourse structured by space in fragments containing the text of Chapter 17, Cambridge MS Kk.1.5 (C), NLS MS 25.5.7 f.101r (D), NLS MS Acc 11218/5 f.91r (E), NLS MS 7.1.9 f.52r (F), NLS MS 7.1.10 f.249v (G) and Skene (1609) (H).

on the first word in the chapter titles and for the initial letter opening a chapter, but not for structuring discourse. Admittedly, there is a dot of red ink (line 3 in the image) where the text of Chapter 17 has been incorporated into the previous chapter, but this can be seen as another place where red is used for corrections.

On single-colour pages, titles could be enhanced through the letter size and saturation and a more careful execution in a separate line. They could be aligned to the right to create space for decorated and enlarged initials at the start of the paragraph. In the early seventeenth-century witness (G), the scribe shows familiarity with visual strategies employed in earlier manuscripts, for example more prominent titles and other navigation devices, but their treatment resembles what is already happening in printed texts – the titles are surrounded by more free space while the font in the title and in the contents section is radically different in size. This manuscript provides a link between the chirographic written culture and the culture of print; it is a record of the laws created in the old medium, even though the new technology was already well advanced and available (Kamm 2008). There is also a visible change from cursive hand to Elizabethan hand. Even though the start of the chapter is marked with more pronounced initials, as used to be the case in the medieval manuscripts, the overall visual arrangement tends towards space management.

(d) Other discourse-structuring devices

Two early witnesses use Roman numerals in the margin to identify chapters (A, C) and two later manuscripts (F, G) use Arabic numerals. The printed version (H) picks up on this later practice. The margins may also contain lexical prompts making reference to the content of the signposted chapter, as in (D) – *sty(n)g(is)dynt* is one of the concepts covered by Chapter 17. It is interesting to see that this scribe selected a different legal concept than the scribe of (A) to serve as a title.

(e) Visual discourse in the printed *Lawis*

John Skene included the burgh laws in his edition of *Regiam maiestatem*, the collection of the Auld Scots laws and statutes (see section 10.2). He published the Latin and the Scots version in 1609, and both were printed by Thomas Finlason in Edinburgh. It is probably impossible to ascertain who was responsible for the arrangement of the text on the page: the author, the printer, or other craftsmen at the press. From the perspective of visual discourse, the approach was that of remediation to a large degree. The print did not revolutionize the way in which the laws were presented on the page, as the use of titles, enlarged initials and Arabic chapter numbers had already been present in earlier manuscripts. Working with black font on a white page, the typesetter preferred to outline textual units by means of more blank space. A few innovations are notable: dedicated sets of type – capital letters, small caps, as well as italic font – were easily distinguishable on the page and could now carry indexical meaning. There is one crucial thing to remember, though. While each manuscript has unique properties in terms of hand, letter size, arrangement of information on the page, ink colour, the extent of decoration, etc., copies of Skene's printed version would not differ in these respects if I were to add more versions of it to the discussion. The digitally accessible Historical Texts facsimile from the Huntington Library, used in this study, displays the same visual qualities as the six copies available for consultation on site at the University of Glasgow Library, and all the fifty three copies of this printed edition scattered around the world (according to the *English Short Title Catalogue*).

10.5.3 Collating the versions

A similar point can be made about the language in the manuscript versions and in the multiple copies of the same print. The wording of the laws changes from one manuscript to the next, while remaining constant and replicable in the printed text. In order to identify the core contents and the variable parts across all versions of the *Lawis*, I used the free online platform Juxta Commons (Wheeles & Jensen 2013) to collate selected chapters. The Scots versions of the *Lawis* vary in terms of spelling, so any automatic collation of the text cannot rely on diplomatic transcriptions.[8] Thanks to the small size of the sample, it was possible to perform lemmatisation of the text by hand, using the headwords of the *Dictionary of the Scots Language* as lemma labels. Thus spellings such as <gif> (A, E, G), <giff> (B), <gyf(f)> (C, F), <geyff> (D), and <gyfe> (G) became merged under the lemma GIF (DSL *gif* conj. "if, whether"), and all inflections have been eliminated. Skene's printed version (H) exhibited some traits of Anglicisation on the level of spelling, e.g. the past tense suffix was spelled predominantly with the English convention *–ed*, instead of the Scots *–it*, and grammar, e.g. *there is* instead of the Scots *thir ar*. These anglicised forms nothwithstanding, Skene's text was lemmatised by means of a Scots lemma set

---

8 First the texts were transcribed diplomatically by the author, followed by lemmatisation for automatic sample comparisons. In the qualitative discussion of similarities and differences in 10.5.5, the quoted text comes from the diplomatic transcript (line division, capitalisation and punctuation as in the original, abbreviations and raised characters in brackets).

in order to be compatible with the other versions. Also, underlyingly, the language of the laws was Scots, so a few anglicised spellings should not suggest a different target language for lemmatisation. The lemmatised texts were then uploaded in Juxta Commons, and a comparison set was prepared.

In the Juxta Commons visualisation panel it is possible to dynamically change the vantage point of comparison between all witnesses by clicking on a given witness. The change index for every witness adapts automatically and gauges how many points of difference there are when the base version is paired individually with another, one by one. There are three types of difference: missing text, added text, and different text (see 10.5.4 below for further interrogation of these differences). Table 10.2 sets out the difference ratio between the versions in comparison to the selected base text. For instance, if version A is selected as the base text, the least discrepancy appears in comparison with the seventeenth-century manuscript (G).[9]

Table 10.2: Versions of Lawis compared by the degree of change from the base text (Juxta Commons change index).

	A (base)	B (base)	C (base)	D (base)	E (base)	F (base)	G (base)	H (base)
A	0.00	0.73	0.75	0.68	0.76	0.69	0.58	0.79
B	0.88	0.00	0.47	0.62	0.46	0.41	0.90	0.96
C	0.77	0.40	0.00	0.46	0.19	0.19	0.74	0.85
D	0.83	0.63	0.56	0.00	0.56	0.51	0.89	0.80
E	0.83	0.41	0.20	0.49	0.00	0.08	0.78	0.87
F	0.77	0.38	0.21	0.46	0.09	0.00	0.77	0.87
G	0.58	0.75	0.72	0.73	0.72	0.70	0.00	0.78
H	1.03	1.05	1.08	0.86	1.06	1.03	1.02	0.00

---

9 Innes notes that this version of the *Lawis* comes from "the copy in Bute manuscript" (1844: 209). The author of (G) may have well used the 1455 version as his exemplar as well, not to copy verbatim but rather to recreate the tenor of the oldest surviving manuscript of the laws. It will require a larger sample to establish the correlation between Bute (A) and (G) with greater certainty.

All the medieval versions differ substantially from (A). However, there are similarities between them. If (D) is selected as the base for comparison, it becomes apparent that (C), (E) and (F) differ least from it in terms of lemmatised content, while (H) – Skene's print – differs the most. In fact, the print differs even more from all the other manuscripts, including the coeval one (G). (E) and (F) are highly similar in content (although not in spelling practices, which have been eliminated in the lemmatisation). In terms of how other versions compare to the manuscript coeval with Skene's print, (G), it is the print that differs most from its contemporary manuscript counterpart. This finding is surprising, since the manuscript's compilation was apparently performed by Carolus Lumisden under Skene's supervision and was used to prepare the printed version. According to Innes (1844: 208) in relation to (G), "[t]here are frequent corrections and marginal notes in Skene's own hand, as well as directions to his amanuensis, and numerous dates, showing that the work was in progress during the years 1601 and 1602". Conscious of the importance and consequence of the task at hand, Skene may have approached the preparation for the printing with an innovative streak; rather than copying the contents of the laws directly from earlier witnesses, he may have amended the textual content to suit the contemporary trends in recording the law. Legal practitioners would have known the ancient manuscripts of burgh laws, but their relevance was limited since the establishment of the Convention of the Four Burghs in 1564 as a form of centralised administration. Perhaps Skene wanted to distill the most important aspects of the contents for reference, and use contemporary phrasing for a better understanding, rather than obsolete language for the sake of keeping the authority at the cost of comprehension.

10.5.4 Tracing differences in wording between the versions

The Scots *Lawis* were not compiled in a void; they followed the earlier Latin versions of the *Leges Burgorum* and attempted to render the same legal content in the vernacular. Latin calques and borrowings were undoubtedly present in the Scots text (Kopaczyk 2011, 2020).[10] Still, the scribes were able to communicate complex legal matters in the local language, the tenor of the laws was preserved (to a large degree), and the contents were captured in a similar chapter format (setting aside the differences in numbering and missing chapters). The visual discourse responded to the available tools (e.g. ink colour) and comprehension needs but the

---

10 The Latin laws drew on local legal discourse, as evidenced by vernacular legal terminology in the Latin text, for instance *wrang and unlaw* 'wrongdoing' (see Kopaczyk 2011: 10–13).

changes were gradual. Importantly, printing did not bring about drastic innovations (see section 10.5.2). The aim is to explore to what extent the linguistic fabric of the *Lawis*, indebted to Latin as it was, also flowed seamlessly from the traditional medium to the new one, or whether Skene seized the opportunity afforded by printing to change the language of the laws and disseminate them in a revised, modern formulation.

The manuscript and printed *Lawis* were lemmatised and collated in Juxta Commons, as explained in 10.5.3. The resulting comparison sets can be interrogated for the points of difference, which are of three types: (1) the text at a given location in the base and the selected witness is not the same (alteration), (2) there is more text at a given location in the base than in the selected witness (deletion), and (3) there is less text at a given location in the base than in the selected witness (addition). The heat map view in the collation window (figure 10.3) visualises the degree of difference from the selected base across the remaining witnesses – the darker the blue, the more witnesses exhibit difference – of any of the three types – at that location.

The sheer amount of the darkest blue shading indicates how substantial the differences are across the witnesses, if the printed version (H) is taken as the base for comparison. By clicking on highlighted items, one can access a list of witnesses which display a difference at this location. Highlighted in this illustration with an arrow (see figure 10.3) is the lemma STING (DSL *sting* n1c. "a wooden pole used as a weapon"), part of the compound *styngisdint*, that is assaulting someone with a wooden weapon (*dint* n. "a severe blow or heavy stroke"). The differences across witnesses are collated in the margin: versions (G) and (D) are missing this lemma in this location,[11] version (A) has a different term in this location – STAF (DSL *staf(f* n.2. "a stick or pole used as a weapon"), and version (B) has an extended negative phrase and a different lemma – STOK (DSL *stok* n.1e "a stick or cudgel used as a weapon"). Since versions (C), (E) and (F) are not listed in this view, one can assume they have the same wording as the base text (H) at this location. There are over 170 locations which are shaded in the heat map in figure 10.3, which means that there are up to around 1,300 individual differences across the eight versions of these four chapters of the *Lawis*. It will not be possible to discuss them all qualitatively, but one way to narrow down the focus is to pay attention to the areas in the text where earlier research noted interaction between the Latin text of the *Leges* and the vernacular text of the *Lawis*. What is added or amended in relation

---

11 (D) has <stryng(is) dy(n)t> but the <r> seems to be a scribal error, especially that the same scribe wrote the title for this chapter in the margin as <of sty(n)g(is) dynt>. The analysis of spelling differences between the manuscripts falls outside the scope of this paper.

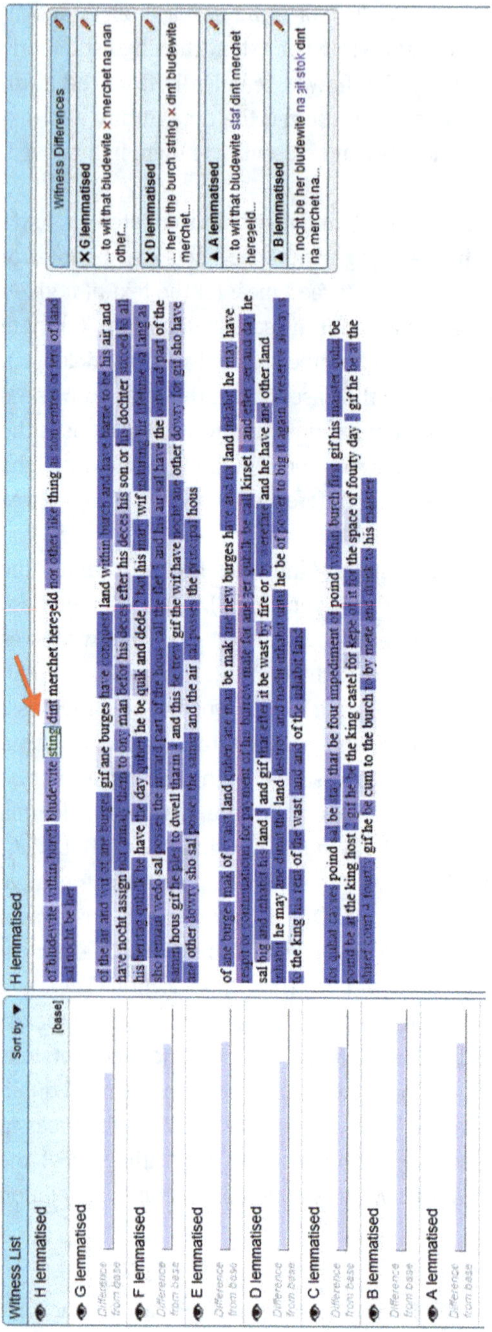

Figure 10.3: Juxta Commons heat map of the degree of difference between the early modern print of the Lawis (H) and the manuscript witnesses.

to Latin may be unique to a particular witness, and it may be possible to trace the patterns characteristic of the manuscripts and juxtapose them with the choices made by Skene in his print (especially since he was preparing the Latin printed version side by side).

10.5.5 Selected laws in focus

(a) Chapter 17: *Of bludewyt and fiklyk thyngis*

This chapter was used as an illustration of visual discourse in the extant manuscripts in section 10.5.2.[12] The title adopted in the *APS* does not correspond directly to any of the manuscript witnesses but it captures the tenor of the chapter. This law regulated what fines and taxes could not be imposed by burgh jurisdiction. The Latin version of the law, as quoted in the *APS* (Innes 1844: 336), incorporated four borrowings from Scots: *blodewit, styngisdynt, merchet* and *herieth*, all of which signify a type of payment in relation to a crime or other activity. The burghs could not impose these. In the vernacular versions, the inventory of fines varies in terms of specific terms and their ordering. The fine for bloodshed (DSL *bludewite* n.) is found in all witnesses and mentioned first in all but (D), which foregrounds *stingisdint*, an armed assault, discussed above. The terms for the weapon are very close in sound and meaning, so it seems that the scribes simply tried to capture the concept of a violent attack with a wooden weapon but did not converge on a single term for that weapon. The third payment that lay outside burgh jurisdiction was *merchet*, which was due for marrying off a daughter of a tenant (DSL *merchet* n., Welsh *merch, merched* pl. "woman, young woman"). This concept appears in all witnesses, and enters the title of Chapter 17 alongside *bludewite* in (G). The final concept which the Latin *Lawis* borrowed from Scots was linked to the claim of "the best living animal" or its monetary value after the death of a husbandman tenant (DSL *hereʒeld(e)* n.). This term appears across the vernacular versions in a variety of spellings but is missing from (G). All versions also contain a potential extension of the list, signalled by the phrase "and suchlike things", or equivalent. Interestingly, Skene's printed version expands the inventory by specifying *other like things (as none entres, or terce of lands)* (DSL *non-entré*, n.1, a type of feudal

---

12 For ease of reference, the subsection titles correspond to the Scots titles and chapter numbers in the *APS* edition (Innes 1844) but one should bear in mind that the manuscripts vary in terms of the actual wording of the titles and the contents, and in the ordering of individual chapters.

property dues; DSL *terc(e)*, n.1, a widow's liferent); these additional specifics are unique to the printed laws. Another place where the print differs from the manuscript witnesses is the opening line, which in Latin reads *et sciendum est*, and the scribes rendered unanimously as *(and) it is to wit* in Scots (DSL *wit* v.1, "to know") (Kopaczyk 2020). Skene's printed version has no introductory formula at all.

(b) Chapter 23: *Of burges ayre in lande til na man affignyt*

This is a law regulating property inheritance, specifically of a house, if a burgess had children and a wife. An interesting discrepancy in terminology is a reference to *child* in all vernacular manuscripts, while Skene prefers a more typically Scots *bairnes* (DSL *barne* n). The children, be it a son or a daughter, inherited everything, but the widow, as long as she remained unmarried, was allowed to occupy the part of the house called the *flet* (DSL *flet* n.1, "the inner part of the house"), unless she had other inheritances. The term *flet* is flagged in the Latin version: *que dicitur le flet*, and in the printed vernacular version: *called, the flett*, but in the manuscripts it only appears in (B) and (D). The (G) manuscript, which Skene seems to have used in preparation for the printed version, has no specific term for this concept. The Latin binomial *vivus et mortuus*, picked up by Skene and (B), (C), (E) and (F) as *quik and dede*, is rendered in (D) as *leyffand and ded* and in (G) as *qwhil he was in lyfe and qwhen|he deid* "while he was alive and when he died". The Latin text uses a rather rare first person singular performative *Et hoc dico* to introduce the condition for the widow, which all manuscripts retain as *and yis/yat I say* "and this/that I say", while Skene has *And this is trew* "and this is true", taking an impersonal stance. The Latin *gaudebit*, in reference to the widow enjoying her part of the house, is rendered in all manuscripts (except (C) and (E) where the whole clause is missing) as *scho sal joys*, while Skene prefers semanticaly more neutral *she sal possess*. The Latin *capitali domo* is typically *ye hede hows* "the head house" in the manuscripts (or *ye cheyff hed houβ* in (D)), while Skene has *the principall house*. In Latin, the wife is described as *uxor eius desponsata*, which is picked up by (B) and (G) as *his spousyt wife*, while the other manuscripts simply talk of *his wife*; Skene changes this to *his married wife*. The Latin modal *voluerit* in reference to the heir (or the widow) wanting to live in the house is rendered in the manuscripts either as *will* (in (D) and (G)) or *lykkis* "likes" (in (B), (C), (E) and (F)), while Skene has *gif he please to dwell therein*.

(c) Chapter 27: *Of a burges hafand kyrſet*
This law granted a new burgess a one-year exemption from payment of the burgh rent, the so-called *kirset* (DSL *kirset(h), kyrset* n.)[13] – another borrowing from Scots in the Latin *Leges* – and required him to build on the allocated plot after the first year. Apart from (C), all vernacular versions, including the print, use this term (although Skene spells it with an unetymological *h-* as <hyrsett>, which may be a typesetting error). Talking about the expectation for the burgess to inhabit his land, the Latin version has *hospitabit terram suam* 'inhabited his property', which in the oldest vernacular texts (A) and (D), as well as in the seventeenth-century manuscript (G), is rendered as *big y(t) lande* (DSL *big* v.1. "to build"). Other manuscripts expand *big* into a binomial *herberyt lande and byggyd* 'to lodge and build on the land' (DSL *herbery* v.1. "to provide with shelter or lod-ging"). Skene also constructs a binomial but adds a different coordinated verb: *big and inhabit*. Although the treatment of pronouns and adverbials from the Latin text varies across manuscripts, there are strong similarities; in contrast, the printed version always chooses a different reading. For instance, the opening *Quicunque* 'whoever' appears as *Quha yat eu(ir)* (D), *Qwhasu(m)eu(ir)* (B), *Quhasa eu(ir)* (C), (E) and (F) and *Quhaevyr* (G). In the print there is a clause instead: *Qvhen ane man*; interestingly, a similar syntactic strategy – *Gif ony man* – is present in (A), the oldest consulted manuscript witness.[14] Then in the body of the chapter there is a time clause introduced by *postea* in Latin, which is rendered as *eft(ir) yat* in (A) and (G), *eft(ir) uart(is)* in (D), and *syne* in (B), (C), (E) and (F), while Skene's version uses *thereafter*. Another time clause, *donec fuerit aysiatus* in Latin,[15] has a few readings in the Scots versions. It seems that the oldest text *quhil y(e) tym he be of eyβ* (A) is closest to the seventeenth-century manuscript's *qwhyl he be of ese* (G), while the concept of *ese* (DSL *ese(e)* n.1d, "able in respect of means"), or *esement*, is also present in (D) with a different time adverbial: *alβ lang as he haβ eyβme(n)t*. The other four manuscripts present a different reading altogether with the verb *avise* (DSL *avise* v.2. "in passive... to take counsel"), which could be interpreted as "until he is advised", but it seems more likely that *avisit* is close enough phonetically to *of ese* to be a potential misinterpretation or mishearing. Skene does something very different here – *vntill he be of power* – so he shifts the meaning from the lack of constraint to having the capacity to act, and the adverbial is also

---

13 The DSL mentions "erroneous forms" such as *kirkset(t), kyrkset, carset, hyr(e)set(t)* in "many MSS. of the *Leges Burgorum*".
14 But not in the Bute MS, the oldest known version, which has *Qwha evir*.
15 The DSL takes *aysiatus* to be the Latin counterpart of *ese* "able in respect of means" but this word seems to be a version of Anglo-Norman *aisement* with the senses "convenience, ease, opportunity, relief" developing in Britain (OED *easement* n.).

unique to this version. The final condition in that chapter is introduced in the Latin text by *salva tamen*, which most of the manuscripts render as *(bot) neu(ir)yeles* "but nevertheless" (C), (D), (F) and (G), or *bot non(e)theleß* (E). Version (B) has *saufande* 'saving', which is a more literal counterpart of the Latin construction, but Skene again does his own thing and uses *Reservand*.

(d) Chapter 33: *Of þe poyntis þat lettis punding in burgh*

This law listed mitigating circumstances against the seizure of goods belonging to someone who was in debt for an overdue payment (DSL *pund* v, 1.).[16] It seems to have been important to stress that there were four such cases, following the Latin version which specifies *quatuor impedimenta*. Most manuscripts, except (C) which surprisingly talks of three impediments, spell out that number or use a Roman numeral in the preamble. The oldest Scots text identifies each impediment with a mixture of strategies: for the first two it has *ane* and *ane oy (ir)* 'another', and then switches to lower case Roman numerals. Other manuscripts simply list the impediments in a paratactically coordinated sequence, as is the case in the Latin version, while Skene lists them in separate lines numbered with Arabic numerals. The prohibition of seizing the goods is expressed in various ways across the witnesses: as "the poinds ought not to be taken" (*aw not to be tane* (pp., DSL *ta(k)* v.I.1, "to capture or seize by force", in (A) and (G)), or as "there are circumstances that prohibit poinding" (*impedimentis / poynt(is) yat lett(is) puynding / pund(is) taky(n)g / to be tayn / to be maid*, DSL *lat* v.2.1, "to hinder, prevent", in (C), (D), (B), (E), and (F)), while the print has simply *impedimentis of poynding* (H).

One of the conditions has to do with the person managing the king's castle for forty days. The versions differ with the choice of the verb: L *custodiendum* > (A) *to ȝem* (DSL *ȝem* v.1, to take care of), (D) and (G) *(for) to kepe* – in the print (H) *for keiping of it*, (B) *for to luke*, and (C), (E) and (F) *for to wake/walk(e)* (DSL *walk* v.6), and the choice of the noun: L *pro spatio* > (A) *to y(e) stag of*, (C), (D), (B), (E), (F) and (H) *(be)/(for) the space of*, while (G) simply lists the number of days. Another condition has to do with the person arriving *ad comitatum*, which has various readings in the vernacular versions: *to y(e) counte* (A), (E) and (G), *to ye cuntre* (B) and (F), *to the comute* (C), *at ye erldom(m)e* (D), but a completely different wording in Skene's print – *Gif he be at the Schiref Court*. He

---

[16] Thorns were not used in any of the manuscripts and were introduced by Innes (1844). I interpret this alteration as a case of ideological antiquarianism (Kopaczyk 2018).

is the only source that makes an explicit link between the involvement of juridical proceedings as a mitigating circumstance, while the manuscript versions all leave this reading between the lines as does the Latin text.

In contrast to the Latin text, all Scots versions (except (A) and (G)), including Skene's print, specify the relevance of this law to the town by adding *in burgh* or *within (the king's) burgh*. Earlier research has shown that such additions to the Latin text were common and testify to a more precise and localised character of the laws (Kopaczyk 2011: 13–14). Similarly, versions (B), (C), (D), (E) and (F) specify the relation to the person's lord (*with quham he duellis* 'with whom he lives'), while the Latin text lacks this reference (and so does the earliest consulted version (A) and the two seventeenth-century ones (G) and (H)). The mention of food (L *cibo*) is rendered in all Scots versions as *mete*, while Skene's print adds in parenthesis *and drinke*, which is not present in any of the other texts in either language.

10.6 Discussion and conclusion

There is no single vernacular text of the *Lawis* and none of the consulted witnesses are an exact copy of another. More than that, the scribes do not seem to have been using the other existing versions as exemplars – the discrepancies in content are simply too great to suggest a copying practice.[17] In his categorisation of medieval scribes working with exemplars, Angus McIntosh (1989 [1973]) saw some of them as "translators", however this meant using spellings and grammar characteristic of one's dialect instead of penning down an exact copy of the exemplar's dialect. In this chapter, the differences in spellings and grammar have only been mentioned as part of an overall assessment of the differences between the texts of the *Lawis* which went beyond a representation of a scribe's dialect. One may speculate that the Scots scribes of the burgh laws relied on the Latin text, perhaps translating it *ad hoc* (from one of the many existing manuscripts, which could also differ from each other), perhaps supporting the translation with another vernacular version, perhaps recovering the vernacular wording of a particular chapter from memory. The most striking and the most extensive differences, however, can be seen between the manuscripts collectively – even when seen as linguistically fluctuating carriers of the laws – and the printed version.

In spite of the differences in contents, the manuscript sources are quite similar in terms of their approach to *ordinatio*. There are two main strategies for

---

[17] Carolus Lumisden, the scribe of (G), probably used (A) and the Bute MS to compose his version, but his was by no means a direct transcription.

information management on the page: by means of rubrics in red ink and *litterae notabiliores*, and by means of titles in separate lines and enlarged initials at the start of paragraphs. Skene fits into the second strategy, and enhances it with the use of capitals and more extensive blank space.[18] His other organisational strategies, such as the use of Arabic numerals, also originated in the pre-print culture, cf. (F). It seems that changes in the visual discourse of the laws proceeded gradually and were not medium-specific to a large degree. The laws in Skene's print are remediated but not transformed.

The transformation of the language is much more obvious. Following Eisenstein (1979), Harvey (2015: 6) asserts that "[s]tandardised content allowed for standardised discourse", which is of particular importance in the context of transmitting the law. Admittedly, handwritten administrative and legal records did exhibit traits of discourse standardisation in Scots (Kopaczyk 2013b), converging on particular formulaic patterns, but in the case of the burgh laws, where one could expect a direct copying tradition, the content was never standardised in the manuscripts, even in terms of the canonical ordering of the chapters, or their inventory. It seems that Skene made an attempt at standardising the content of the *Lawis*, conscious of the replicability and dissemination opportunities afforded by the new medium. The temptation to formalise, fix and adapt to the external pressure, especially when one was given this task by the Scottish Parliament, was greater in the case of print than in the case of a manuscript. Skene's terminology is often different than that found in any of the manuscripts, including the coeval MS Lumisden (G), e.g. *barne* and not *child*, or *married* and not *spousyt*. He preferred innovative syntactic constructions, e.g. *thereafter* instead of *eftir yat*. He adjusted subtleties of meaning to achieve a more detached reading of the laws, e.g. by rephrasing first-person declaratives, and to make the laws more precise through various parenthetical additions and writing out implicit meanings. On the other hand, he strove for simplification of convoluted syntax and dropped superfluous formulae inherited from Latin legal discourse. These decisions were absent from the contemporary manuscript (G), which was still very "medieval" in its linguistic choices, perhaps even using the oldest Scots versions of the *Lawis* as its sources and following them in places where the print chose to diverge.

One may expect that excited users of new, digital media should promote novel and creative ways of presenting information. Historical investigations,

---

18 This chapter did not systematically consider punctuation; however, it would be incorrect to assume that the print used it differently than manuscripts, since the coeval MS Lumisden (F) employs commas and stops in a similar manner (see figure 10.2). It is the fifteenth-century manuscripts that use different punctuation conventions, so it seems that the new developments were independent of the medium.

such as the ones in this volume, indicate that the availability of a revolutionary communication technology does not always cause a revolution on all communicative plains. This focussed analysis suggests that burgh laws in Scotland took a new shape when being committed to print – a new linguistic shape, rather than a radical visual re-design. From the point of view of standardisation, an ideology underpinning legal practices and legal discourse, it is clear that scribes had already standardised the visual format to a large extent. These longer-term patterns were preferred by printers, who undertook innovations in other areas. The real opportunity seized by the printed text was to reformulate the laws linguistically, and release this newly crafted wording in multiple identical copies. The new medium was thus looking back visually, but looking forward linguistically, which offers important background to the apparent novelty of present-day digital practices.

References

Primary sources

Cambridge University Library MS Kk.1.5
National Library of Scotland Adv. MS 25.4.14
National Library of Scotland Adv. MS 25.4.15
National Library of Scotland Adv. MS 25.5.7
National Library of Scotland Adv. MS 7.1.9
National Library of Scotland Adv. MS 7.1.10
National Library of Scotland Adv. MS Acc 11218/5
National Library of Scotland MS 21246
Skene, John. 1609. *Regiam Majestatem. The Avld Lavves and constitvtions of Scotland, faithfvllie collected fvrth of the register, and other avld authentick bukes* ... Printed in Edinburgh by Thomas Finlason (accessed Historical Texts, 19 August 2018).

Secondary Sources

Agutter, Alex. 1990. Restandardisation in Middle Scots. In Sylvia Adamson, Vivien Law & Susan Wright (eds.), *Papers from the 5th international conference on English historical linguistics*, 1–11. Amsterdam: John Benjamins.
Bolter, Jay David & Richard Grusin. 2000. *Remediation. Understanding new media*. Cambridge, MA: MIT Press.
Bühler, Curt. 1960. *The fifteenth century book, the scribes, the printers, the decorators*. Oxford: Oxford University Press.
Caie, Graham. 2011. The relationship between MS Hunter 409 and the 1532 edition of Chaucer's works edited by William Thynne. In Päivi Pahta & Andreas H. Jucker (eds.),

Communicating early English manuscripts, 149–161. Cambridge, UK: Cambridge University Press.

Cairns, John W. 2000. Historical introduction. In Kenneth Reid & Reinhard Zimmerman (eds.), *A history of private law in Scotland*. Vol. 1. *Introduction and property*, 14–184. Oxford: Oxford University Press.

Callister, Paul D. 2014. The book as authoritative sign in seventeenth-century England: A review through the lens of Holistic Media Theory. In Anne Wagner & Richard K. Sherwin (eds.), *Law, culture and visual studies*, 49–77. Dordrecht: Springer.

Carroll, Ruth, Matti Peikola, Hanna Salmi, Mari-Liisa Varila, Janne Skaffari & Risto Hiltunen. 2013. Pragmatics on the page. *European Journal of English Studies* 17 (1). 54–71.

Culpeper, Jonathan & Jane Demmen. 2011. The development of play-texts. From manuscript to print. In Päivi Pahta & Andreas H. Jucker (eds.), *Communicating early English manuscripts*, 162–177. Cambridge, UK: Cambridge University Press.

Devitt, Amy. 1989. *Standardizing written English. Diffusion in the case of Scotland 1520–1659*. Cambridge, UK: Cambridge University Press.

Dolezalek, Gero. 2010. *Scotland under Jus commune. Census of legal literature in Scotland, mainly between 1500 and 1660*. Vols. 1–3. Edinburgh: Stair Society.

Dictionary of the Scots Language (DSL) dsl.ac.uk (accessed 20 March 2019).

Duncan, A. A. M. 1975. *Scotland. The making of the kingdom*. Vol. 1. Edinburgh: Mercat Press.

Eisenstein, Elizabeth L. 1979. *The printing press as an agent of change. Communications and cultural transformations in early-modern Europe*. 2 vols. Cambridge, UK: Cambridge University Press.

English Short Title Catalogue. British Library, estc.bl.uk (accessed 27 March 2019).

Frankot, Edda. 2012. *"Of laws of ships and shipmen": Medieval maritime law and its practice in urban northern Europe*. Edinburgh: Edinburgh University Press.

Harvey, David J. 2015. *The Law emprynted and Englysshed. The Printing press as an agent of change in law and legal culture 1475–1642*. Oxford: Hart Publishing.

Horobin, Simon. 2016. Manuscripts and early printed books. In Merja Kytö & Päivi Pahta (eds.), *The Cambridge handbook of English historical linguistics*, 111–126. Cambridge, UK: Cambridge University Press.

Innes, Cosmo (ed.). 1844. *Acts of the Parliaments of Scotland*. Vol. 1. Edinburgh.

Innes, Cosmo (ed.). 1868. "Leges et consuetudines quatuor burgorum [Laws and customs of the four burghs]", in *Ancient laws and customs of the burghs of Scotland*. Vol.I. A.D. 1124–1424, 3–58. Edinburgh: Scottish Burgh Records Society.

Johns, Adrian. 1998. *The nature of the book*. Chicago: The University of Chicago Press.

Jucker, Andreas H. & Päivi Pahta. 2011. Communicating manuscripts. Authors, scribes, readers, listeners and communicating characters. In Päivi Pahta & Andreas H. Jucker (eds.), *Communicating early English manuscripts*, 3–10. Cambridge, UK: Cambridge University Press.

Kamm, Antony. 2008. *Scottish printed books, 1508–2008*. Edinburgh: National Library of Scotland.

Kopaczyk, Joanna. 2011. Latin and Scots versions of Scottish medieval burgh laws (*Leges Quatuor Burgorum*). *Scottish Language* 30. 1–17.

Kopaczyk, Joanna. 2013a. How a community of practice creates a text community. Middle Scots legal and administrative discourse. In Joanna Kopaczyk & Andreas H. Jucker (eds.), *Communities of practice in the history of English*, 225–250. Amsterdam: John Benjamins.

Kopaczyk, Joanna. 2013b. *The legal language of Scottish burghs. Standardisation and lexical bundles 1380–1560*. Oxford: Oxford University Press.

Kopaczyk, Joanna. 2018. Scottish burgh laws in transmission from a diachronic pragmaphilological perspective. Paper presented at the 20th International Conference on English Historical Linguistics, University of Edinburgh, 27–31 August.

Kopaczyk, Joanna. 2020. Textual standardisation of legal Scots vis a vis Latin. In Laura Wright (ed.) *The multilingual origins of Standard English*. Berlin: Mouton de Gruyter.

Lynch, Michael, Michael Spearman & Geoffrey Stell (eds.). 1988. *The Scottish medieval town*. Edinburgh: John Donald.

Mackay, Francesca L. 2017. How the page functions: Reading Pitscottie's *Cronicles* in manuscript and print. In Matti Peikola, Aleksi Mäkilähde, Hanna Salmi, Mari-Liisa Varila & Janne Skaffari (eds.), *Verbal and visual communication in early English texts*, 41–65. Turnhout: Brepols.

MacQueen, Hector L. & William J. Windram. 1988. Laws and courts in the burghs. In Michael Lynch, Michael Spearman & Geoffrey Stell (eds.), *The Scottish medieval town*, 207–227. Edinburgh: John Donald.

Mann, Alastair J. 2000. *The Scottish book trade 1500–1720*. East Linton: Tuckwell Press.

McClure, J. Derrick. 1981. Scottis, Inglis, Suddroun: Language labels and language attitudes. In Roderick J. Lyall & Felicity Riddy (eds.), *Proceedings of the Third International Conference on Scottish Language and Literature (Medieval and Renaissance)*, 52–69. University of Glasgow.

McClure, J. Derrick. 2010. The distinctiveness of Scots. Perceptions and reality. In Raymond Hickey (ed.), *Varieties of English in writing. The written word as linguistic evidence*, 99–120. Amsterdam: John Benjamins.

McIntosh, Angus. 1989 [1973]. Word geography in the lexicography of Middle English. *Annals of the New York Academy of Sciences* 211: 55–66. [Reprinted in Margaret Laing (ed.), *Middle English dialectology: Essays on some principles and problems* by Angus McIntosh, M.L. Samuels & Margaret Laing, 86–97. Aberdeen: Aberdeen University Press].

McKitterick, David. 2003. *Print, manuscript and the search for order 1450–1830*. Cambridge, UK: Cambridge University Press.

McLuhan, Marshall. 1962. *The Gutenberg galaxy. The making of typographic man*. Abingdon: Routledge & Kegan Paul.

McLuhan, Marshall. 1964. *Understanding media*. New York: Mentor.

Oxford English Dictionary Online. 2019. http://www.oed.com (accessed 29 March 2019)

Pahta, Päivi & Andreas H. Jucker (eds.). 2011. *Communicating early English manuscripts*. Cambridge, UK: Cambridge University Press.

Pahta, Päivi, Turo Hiltunen, Ville Marttila, Maura Ratia, Carla Suhr & Jukka Tyrkkö. 2011. Communicating Galen's *Methodus medendi* in Middle and Early Modern English. In Päivi Pahta & Andreas H. Jucker (eds.), *Communicating early English manuscripts*, 178–196. Cambridge, UK: Cambridge University Press.

Parkes, Malcolm. 1976. The influence of the concepts of *ordinatio* and *compilatio* on the development of the book. In Jonathan G. Alexander & Margaret T. Gibson (eds.), *Medieval learning and literature: Essays presented to Richard William Hunt*, 115–141. Oxford: Clarendon.

Parkes, Malcolm. 1991. *Scribes, scripts and readers. Studies in the communication, presentation and dissemination of medieval texts*. London: Hambledon.

Robinson, O. F., T. D. Fergus & W.M. Gordon. 1985. *An introduction to European legal history*. Oxon: Professional Books Ltd.

Snijders, Tjamke. 2015. *Manuscript communication. Visual and textual mechanics of communication in hagiographical texts from the southern Low Countries, 900–1200*. Utrecht: Brepols.

Steinberg, S. H. 1955 [2017]. *Five hundred years of printing*. Baltimore: Penguin [Mineola, NY: Dover Publications].

Street, Brian. 1984, *Literacy in theory and practice*. Cambridge, UK: Cambridge University Press.

Varila, Mari-Liisa, Hanna Salmi, Aleksi Mäkilähde, Janne Skaffari & Matti Peikola. 2017. Disciplinary decoding: Towards understanding the language of visual and material features. In Matti Peikola, Aleksi Mäkilähde, Hanna Salmi, Mari-Liisa Varila & Janne Skaffari (eds.), *Verbal and visual communication in early English texts*, 1–20. Turnhout: Brepols.

Walker, David M. 1990. *A legal history of Scotland*. Vol. II. *The later Middle Ages*. Edinburgh: W. Green.

Walker, David M. 1995. *A legal history of Scotland*. Vol. III. *The sixteenth century*. Edinburgh: T. & T. Clark.

Wheeles, D. & K. Jensen. 2013. Juxta Commons. In *Proceedings of the Digital Humanities 2013*. University of Nebraska-Lincoln, 17 July 2013. http://dh2013.unl.edu/abstracts/ab-142.html (accessed 1 August 2017).

Hanna Rutkowska
11 Visual pragmatics of an early modern book: Printers' paratextual choices in the editions of *The School of Vertue*

11.1 Introduction: Aim and methodology

Contemporary texts, or "units of language in use" (Halliday & Hasan 1976: 1–2) are commonly of multimodal nature, especially in electronic media, combining different semiotic modes, such as writing, images and sounds. With regard to written texts, their visual aspects are recognised as particularly important for effective communication by linguists pursuing a variety of scholarly interests, for example language acquisition, new media, pop culture and multimodality (e.g. Barthes 1977; Kress 2003; Yannicopoulou 2004; Kress & van Leeuwen 2001, 2006; van Leeuwen 2006, 2015; Cohn 2013; Tagg et al. 2016). The present recognition of the indispensable multimodality of text and discourse contrasts with the attitudes current from the eighteenth to the first half of the twentieth century, which prioritised "the strictly verbal over the pictorial" (Goodman 2005: 36), considering the latter undeserving of respect and irrelevant to conveying noteworthy information. However, the presence of visual aspects in written documents is not a new phenomenon. The visuality and non-linearity of historical texts, especially medieval manuscripts and early printed books, have been recently appreciated as essential for understanding the meanings communicated by them (e.g. Jucker & Pahta 2011; Machan 2011; Carroll et al. 2013; McConchie 2013; Rogos-Hebda 2016; Kopaczyk; Moore; and Thompson & Collins; all this volume).

The present contribution, likewise, investigates pictorial aspects of a historical text. It fits into the research areas of both *pragmaphilology* and *visual pragmatics*. The former studies the context, including the physical and social circumstances in which a historical text was produced, people involved in the process of its production as well as its recipients (Jacobs & Jucker 1995: 11–12), whereas the latter, also referred to as "pragmatics on the page", is a recent development in historical pragmatics, defined by Carroll et al. (2013: 56) as "anything on the page that adds meaning to the linguistic message" (see also Machan 2011). As subfields of pragmatics, both focus on *utterances*. For historical pragmatics, an *utterance* is an individual instance of handwritten or printed

Hanna Rutkowska, Adam Mickiewicz University in Poznań, Faculty of English,
e-mail: rhanna@wa.amu.edu.pl

text produced in a particular communicative context and for a specific user in the past (Carroll et al. 2003: 4; Carroll et al. 2013: 54, 66–67). Thus, particular versions (or witnesses) of a given book (whether handwritten or printed) can be considered *utterances*.

Considering the importance of the visual side of a historical written document for communicating meaning, one can refer to the set of its pictorial features as a visual text (see Rogos-Hebda 2016). Such text, understood as an utterance, is bound to contain visual pragmatic markers. In the case of early printed books, they can include the format of the book, the size, the placement, and number of illustrations (woodcuts), the style and size of typefaces, the page layout, the characteristics of the title page, as well as the spelling, capitalisation and punctuation (in a broader definition, punctuation can also include the division into pages, lines and paragraphs; see Lennard 1995). These elements are, to a large extent, interrelated and interdependent. They can also be associated with particular levels of discourse, also called spheres of meaning or pragmatic domains (Carroll et al. 2013: 58). These levels have been referred to with different labels. In this study, the terms adopted by Carroll et al. (2013: 58–59; after Erman 2001: 1339–1341) are followed, including the *textual level* (making part of the text and oriented towards it), the *interactional level* ("oriented towards the addressee") and the *stance level* ("oriented towards the speaker and her/his attitude to the content and value of the message"). In their study, Carroll et al. (2013) examine individual pages from ten different witnesses (nine manuscripts and one printed version) of John Trevisa's English translation of the *Polychronicon*, comparing the visual pragmatic markers employed by the scribes (and the printer) at different levels of discourse, and how these contribute to the meanings expressed. They find that markers such as initial letters, decorative borders, and paraphs operate at the textual level, as visual structuring devices. Paraphs function also at the interactional level, guiding potential readers through the text and helping avoid interpretational ambiguity (e.g. syntactic). Other markers, i.e. the double-column layout (resembling biblical texts) and the use of red ink to highlight the names of external authorities referred to, work at the stance level, communicating the high prestige of the book.

The visual elements of a book can also be interpreted as the components of its *paratext*, that is "those liminal devices and conventions, both within the book (*peritext*) and outside it (*epitext*), that mediate the book to the reader: titles and subtitles, pseudonyms, forewords, dedications, epigraphs, prefaces, intertitles, notes, epilogues, and afterwards" (Macksey 1997: xviii). The aim of my study has been chiefly to identify what paratextual, and more specifically visual, elements early printers employed; to explore in what way these elements functioned as pragmatic markers – that is, considering the meanings the printers communicated through these devices at particular levels of discourse – and finally to trace the evolution of these printers' pragmatic strategies, including the inventory and use of visual pragmatic markers in consecutive editions of the title selected for investigation.

Following the methodology proposed by Carroll et al. (2013), I have organised my study into four stages. First, I have identified several utterances of the same text, in this case twelve printed editions of an early modern book of good conduct for children, entitled *The School of Vertue*, issued between 1557 and 1687. The general information on the purpose, content and publication history of this book is presented in section 11.2. Second, I have prepared a detailed *etic* microanalytic description of the textual and visual aspects of the earliest available edition of the book, reported in section 11.3. Third, I have compared the other eleven editions of the same book with the first one with regard to visual differences. Fourth, I have interpreted the meaning of, and motivation behind, diachronic variation which I have traced in the series of utterances under consideration, taking an *emic* and pragmaphilological approach to the material analysed. Stages three and four are discussed jointly in section 11.4, offering a combination of a comprehensive microanalysis of the variation across the editions with a comparative macroanalysis of the pragmatic functions. Section 11.5 is an attempt at identifying these elements of the Renaissance printed tradition which have survived, albeit transformed, in today's new media. Finally, section 11.6 contains a summary of the findings and conclusions.

11.2 Material and context

11.2.1 *The School of Vertue* editions, authors and printers

The material under analysis comprises three sixteenth-century and nine seventeenth-century editions of *The School of Vertue* (the title of the last edition, published in 1687, is adopted here to refer generally to all the editions). The book is a manual of good manners for children, a genre which gained popularity in the early modern period (Leece 2011), accompanied with a few prayers. The steadily increasing interest in handbooks of good conduct as well as in manuals teaching "correct" grammar must have been related to the emergence and gradual rise in economic and political importance of the English middle class, who strove to match what they perceived as the cultural and linguistic standards which would legitimise their social standing (see Nurmi 2017 and Raumolin-Brunberg 2017 on the changes in the early modern English society).

Table 11.1: The analysed editions of *The School of Vertue*.

Publication year	(Printer's and) Publisher's name	Catalogue no.
1557	William Seares (Seres)	STC 22135
1582	H[enry] Denham	STC 22136
1593	[John Charlewood for] Richard Jones	STC 22137
1621	G[eorge]. E[lde] for T. P. and I.[John] W[right].	STC 22137.7
[1626]	M[iles]. Flesher for Robert Bird	STC 22138
[c. 1630]	M[iles]. Flesher for Robert Bird	STC 22138.3
[c. 1635]	M[iles]. Flesher for Robert Bird	STC 22138.5
[c. 1640]	[Miles Flesher for Robert Bird]	STC 22138.7
[c. 1660]	M[iles]. Flesher for John Wright [junior]	*Wing* S2171
[1670]	E[dward]. Crowch, for J[ohn]. Wright [junior]	*Wing* S2412C
1677	Anonym for J[ohn]. Wright [junior]	*Wing* S2412D
1687	Anonym for M[atthew]. W[otton]. and George Conyers	*Wing* S2412E

The publication history of *The School of Vertue* (henceforth *The School*) is briefly presented in table 11.1 (the information enclosed in square brackets is reconstructed; it is absent or obliterated in the original text). Several editions were issued by the same printing house, which helps us to understand some similarities between them, described in section 11.4. The term *printer* employed here is a generalisation (book printing was a joint effort of a group of several workers) and refers to the owner of the printing house. Early printers were also the editors, publishers and booksellers, selecting books for printing and introducing them into public circulation (de Hamel 1983: 29). By the 1580s, many publishers had abandoned printing, switching entirely to book trade (Raven 2007: 37). This change is reflected in the frequent omission of the name of the printer in the colophon (see section 11.2.2) of the book (alternatively, only name initials are provided). Unfortunately, little is known about the division of responsibilities concerning page design and other typographic policies within early modern printing houses.

The School was written originally by Francis Seager (*aka* Segar, active 1549–1563), an English translator and poet (Bayne 1897: 196–197). Its first available edition was printed and published in 1557 by William Seares (*aka* Seres) senior (active 1546–77, see Duff 2011: 145–146).[1] The records in *ESTC* show that Seares also printed some earlier publications authored by Seager (1549, 1553). Likewise, Crowley, the editor of the 1582 version of *The School*, which was expanded with several poems and prayers, cooperated with Seares from at least 1548. Robert Crowley (1518?-88) was a prolific author, printer, and theologian (Tedder 1888: 241; *ESTC*). Henry Denham (active until 1591?), the printer of the 1582 edition, was Seares's assignee. Earlier, he printed two books for Crowley (1566, 1569) (Duff 2011: 145–146; McKerrow 1910: 88–89; *ESTC*).

Another edition of *The School* appeared in 1593, five years after Crowley's death, meaning that he could not influence the publishing process in any way. The copyright of the book was probably among Henry Denham's rights to the fifteen works, which were transferred to John Charlewood (active until 1593) and Richard Jones (active 1564–1602), who jointly printed and published this edition (they had worked together several times between 1576 and 1593), and the former had earlier printed and/or published Crowley's books (1566, 1581) (*ESTC*). Denham also cooperated with Charlewood, at least between 1563 and 1575 (*ESTC*). After a break of nearly thirty years, Edward Allde printed a new edition of *The School* for Edward White, a publisher, in 1620 (*ESTC*), and then another was printed again in 1621 by (probably) George Elde (active 1604–24) for John Wright (active until 1658), a bookseller (Plomer 1907: 197–198; *ESTC*). When George Elde died in 1624, Miles Flesher (active 1611–1664), who had been Elde's associate between 1617–24, took over his printing business (Plomer 1907: 76; McKerrow 1910: 98), presumably including the copyrights. Flesher printed five editions of *The School* (1626, 1630, 1635, 1640, and 1660, *ESTC*), which testifies to the revived popularity of the book, undoubtedly owing to, among other factors, the ever-increasing level of literacy and, consequently, a wider audience than available in the sixteenth century. The first four were printed for Robert Bird (active 1621-38), a bookseller (*ESTC*; McKerrow 1910: 34), and the last one for John Wright junior (active 1634–67), who took over Bird's copyrights. He must have got hold of the right to publish *The School*, because the editions of 1670 and 1677 were also printed for him (*ESTC*), the former by Edward Crowch (active 1649–64; see Plomer 1907: 58) and the latter by an anonymous printer. The last edition of the book was issued in 1687

---

1 According to the information in the title of this edition, it was "[n]ewely perused, corrected, and augmented". The original edition was probably *The Scoole of Vertue* published c. 1550 (*STC* 22134.5). Unfortunately, this document is not available on *EEBO*, so this could not be verified.

by M. W. (probably Matthew Wotton) and George Conyers (active until 1739/40), a publisher and bookseller (Wiles 2012: 91; *ESTC*).

All *The School* editions examined in the present study were consulted as facsimiles available at *Early English Books Online* (henceforth *EEBO*). *English Short Title Catalogue* (*ESTC*) reports the existence of other editions, printed in 1620, 1642 and 1698, but these are unavailable at *EEBO*. However, on the basis of twelve editions, it is possible to determine in considerable detail the formal transformation and functional evolution of the visual devices employed by the printers (and publishers) of the selected text.

11.2.2 Visual aspects of an early modern printed book

In order to analyse and compare the visual aspects of the relevant *utterances* (as defined above), one needs first to realise what features are typical of an early modern printed book. These comprise the format, the foliation (or pagination), and the *mise-en-page* (from French 'putting-on-the-page', see Beal 2008: 255), including, among others, the typefaces, the layout, the illustrations (and other decorative elements), the running heads, the chapter and section headings and the margins. These typical components of an early modern book can also be viewed as a set of conventions (functioning at textual, interactional and stance levels) recognised by two discourse communities: book producers (including authors, publishers and printers) and book buyers/readers.

The most frequent formats of the Renaissance English (and other European) books include the *folio*, *quarto*, *octavo*, *duodecimo* and *sextodecimo*. All these formats were inherited from the manuscript tradition. In the *folio* format the sheet of paper used by the printer is folded in two (giving two leaves), in the *quarto* format in four (with four leaves), in the *octavo* in eight etc. These names are used to refer to formats or sizes of books, but the latter varied depending on the original size of the sheet of paper. Although formats and sizes of early modern books are a complex issue, in general, the smaller the format and size of the book, the less learned the contents and the book, the lower its price, and the more general the target audience (see, e.g., Jensen 1999: 354–356; Lyons 2009: 68–70; Beal 2008: 158). Thus, small formats were associated with schoolbooks, almanacs and pocketbooks of moral and spiritual edification, whereas big ones were employed for bibles used in church, law books, classical literature and scholarly treatises (Bland 1998: 117). The *octavo* format became the commonest one in the seventeenth century (Beal 2008: 270).

The leaves in an early book are grouped in quires, so a quire can be defined as a gathering of leaves in the form of folded sheets (see Beal 2008: 329–31 for more information). Early modern printers rarely used continuous pagination; instead, the first three to five leaves in a quire were marked with the so called signatures (on the recto side only), each of which contained a letter and a numeral, the former referring to the quire (A, B, C etc.), and the latter to the number of the leaf within the quire, e.g. A.i., B.iiij.[2] Signatures were used mainly to guide the binder of the book with regard to the order in which he should arrange the leaves before binding them together. The origins of the Renaissance foliation system (including signatures), like book formats, go back to the scribal times.

As regards the *mise-en-page*, it evolved over time. One of its most conspicuous features was the style of the *typeface* (also called *type* or *face*) employed. In the first half of the sixteenth century, the default type in vernacular publications in England was a *textura blackletter* type (Tschichold 1966: 24; Hellinga 1999: 76; see Bringhurst 2008: 266 for detailed characteristics of particular blackletter types). Blackletter remained one of two main typefaces also in the second half of the sixteenth century, especially for primers (Bland 1998: 92). Roman typeface was the other of the two main types (or groups of types) used by sixteenth-century English printers. It had mostly replaced blackletter in new publications by the end of the sixteenth century. However, blackletter (and other typographic features) tended to be preserved in consecutive editions of books first published in this type, even if they extended well into the seventeenth century, possibly in order to preserve the original style of the book and to meet the reader's expectations (see Rutkowska 2013: 81–88). Likewise, it remained printers' primary choice in several genres, e.g., romances, ballads, plays, jest books, the Bible and legal documents until the 1590s (Bland 1998: 93–94). The early blackletter types were originally modelled on the Gothic script, in particular the handwriting of highly valued calligraphers, e.g. Colard Mansion and David Aubert (Hellinga 1999: 73–74), because the first printed books imitated the existing manuscript ones which were familiar to readers (the interactional level of meaning). As regards *roman type*, its upper case originated in Roman imperial inscriptions, whereas the lower case was based on the script elaborated in France and Germany in the late Middle Ages (Bringhurst 2008: 124). Roman type was first used in England by Richard Pynson in 1509 (Hellinga 1999: 76; Bland 1998: 93), but it is rarely employed in English books in the first half of the sixteenth century. In the second half of that century, both typefaces generally alternate in the same publications, with functional differentiation at the textual level of meaning (e.g. Bland 1998: 100–101; Kaislaniemi

---

[2] The examples in the font imitating blackletter are not enclosed in quotation marks in this chapter, as they seem sufficiently distinctive on their own.

2017). For example, the main body of the text could be typed in blackletter whereas the title page, the running heads, the chapter initials, proper names and passages in foreign languages (especially Latin) were in roman face (e.g. Rutkowska 2013: 81–84; Kaislaniemi 2017: 171–172, 176), presumably in association with the conventions developed on the Continent with regard to Latin humanist texts (e.g., Hellinga 1999: 72). In late-sixteenth-century England, *italic* types (originating in early-sixteenth-century Italy) started to be regularly employed (as subsidiary ones) for a variety of purposes, e.g., emphasis, contrast, exemplification (Bringhurst 2008: 57, 124), code-switching (Kaislaniemi 2017: 169, 172, 176, 189), text structuring (Kaislaniemi 2017: 188, 195) direct representation of speech (Bland 1998: 98–100), or for their "lightening effects" (Hellinga 1999: 77), the last feature presumably referring to the aesthetic appeal of italics.

The typical layout depends on the function of a given page and, as many other aspects of an early modern book, underwent modifications in the course of time. The title page is obviously the most prominent page in most early modern books. The earliest title pages (in the 1480s) contained only the title of the work and the name of its author. The *imprint* (also called the *colophon*), which provides information specifying the name(s) of the printer and the publisher, the place and the year of publication appeared at the end of the book. In the course of the sixteenth century, the imprint was gradually moved to the foot of the title page, so that in the seventeenth century book-final colophons would be an exception. Other optional elements include illustrations and, occasionally, a quotation, a catchphrase or a motto. The latter can also make part of a printer's mark (*aka* a printer's device). Until the mid-sixteenth century, title pages of books in English were mostly printed in blackletter, but by the late sixteenth century, alternating roman type and italics had become the rule. The title wording and the name of the author of late-sixteenth and seventeenth-century books take a considerable part of the page, between a half and three-quarters. Particular components of an average early modern title page form conic or funnel shapes, narrowing downwards. This arrangement, also called double-tapered indentation (McConchie 2013), is evident in figures 11.1, 11.3, 11.4, 11.5 and 11.6. Additionally, figures 11.3, 11.4 and 11.5 show another characteristic of a late sixteenth-century title page, i.e. the alternation of types in neighbouring lines, accompanied by varying sizes of the typeface (see also the examples of title pages provided in McConchie 2013). The prominence of the title page corresponds to several important pragmatic functions at different levels of meaning. For example, at the textual level, the title page refers to the contents of the book. The aim of the title page is likewise to attract a potential buyer/reader, e.g. by specifying the target audience and, optionally, highlighting the topic by

> ✠ **The ſchoole**
> of Vertue, and booke of
> good Nourture for chyldren, and
> youth to learne theyr dutie by.
> Newely peruſed, corrected,
> and augmented by the
> fyrſt Auctour.
> F. S.
>
> With a briefe declaration of the
> dutie of eche degree.
>
> Anno. 1557.
>
> Diſpiſe not councel, rebuking foly
> Deme it as, needfull and holy.
>
>
>
> ¶ Imprinted at London in Paules
> Churchyarde at the ſigne of
> the Hedgehogge by
> Wyllyam Seares.
>
>

Figure 11.1: The title page of *The School* edition printed in 1557.
This and the remaining figures in this chapter are not facsimiles, but imitations, approximating, but not copying the original documents.

illustrations. An illustration can be simultaneously a printer's device, whose role can be considered at the stance level as a guarantee of authenticity and quality (for detailed discussions concerning early modern title pages, their development and functions, see Smith 2000; McConchie 2013; Rautenberg 2016).

The remaining pages in a Renaissance book, likewise, follow certain conventions. The body of the text is usually presented in one column per page (especially in the case of smaller size), whereas two columns indicate a higher prestige and authority of the book (the stance level of meaning). The beginnings of chapters (and sections) are indicated with initials of varied size and degree of elaboration. Their function is primarily structural (textual), marking the division of the text into units, but large initials of intricate design can also operate at the stance level, adding prestige to the book. Other textual devices include running heads, headings of chapters and sections, often starting with paraphs (in the early sixteenth century, these were also used at the beginning of sentences in the body of the text). Similarly to the title pages, headings of chapters and sections normally have double-tapered indentation.

Illustrations were not obligatory elements of an early modern book, but they were often used to enhance the attractiveness of the book for the potential buyer and reader (Barnard 2002: 21; Hellinga 1999: 104; Rautenberg 2016: 167), thus functioning at the interactional level. Their sizes, placement and quality depended on the format and type of the book as well as the price offered for it (Hellinga 1999: 98). The earliest books contained only woodcut illustrations, but in the seventeenth century, engraving techniques became increasingly used (Barnard 2002: 3; Bell 2002: 633).

11.3 The 1557 edition of *The School*: A microanalysis of visual devices

As announced in the introduction, this section provides a detailed description of the first available edition of *The School*, as a stage in the "pragmatics on the page" methodology adopted following Carroll et al. (2013). This description starts with the most general (or external) features, i.e. the format of the book and the foliation system, then moving to the typographic details, including the layout of the page (with particular attention paid to the title page) and the typefaces employed. All these elements have their specific functions in relation to the three levels of meaning (textual, interactional and stance) listed in the introduction and touched upon in section 11.2.2, which will be discussed in detail in the next, comparative section. In the present section, an *etic*, or external and physical, account of visual features is offered, which will form the basis for the later *emic*, functional and internal (with reference to the potential user) analysis and comparisons between the editions.

The earliest edition of *The School* examined here is a relatively small book, in an *octavo* format, corresponding to roughly 4 x 6 inches. The size of the book suggests that it is supposed to be portable and is designed for everyday use. The fifty-eight pages are not numbered one by one. Instead, three to five first leaves in each quire bear signatures on the recto side. The manual is preceded with the title page (A1r),[3] an acrostic featuring the author's surname, Seager (A1v), eight prefatory (half-)lines (A2r) and 𝕮𝖍𝖊 𝖒𝖔𝖗𝖓𝖞𝖓𝖌𝖊 # 𝖕𝖗𝖆𝖞𝖊𝖗 (A2r-A3r), and

---

3 Abbreviations are used here to refer to particular pages (to acknowledge their exact location within the book); the capital letter corresponds to the specific quire, the Arabic numeral to the number of the relevant leaf, "r" to the *recto* side of the relevant leaf, and "v" to its *verso*.
4 The symbol # indicates the beginning of a new line. This chapter uses the font designed by Maciej Ulatowski, imitating and approximating the blackletter type used in the original documents. It is used here as a means of exemplification. It has been inspired by the blackletter types described and illustrated in Stribley (1987: 60–63) and Bringhurst (2008: 266–68), as

followed by 𝔄 prater to be faide when thou # goest to bedde. (D2v-D3r), and the dutie of eche degred. [sic] # brefely declared. (D3v-D5v).

The title page of the 1557 edition (see figure 11.1) is printed almost entirely in blackletter. The first line, containing 𝕿he fchoole and starting with a fleuron-like paraph, is printed in a much bigger type than the rest of the text, pointing to the didactic content of the book. The size of the type in the second line is two-thirds of that of the first one, and still (slightly) smaller in the following five lines. Lines 4–8 have double-tapered indentation (see section 11.2.2). The initials "F. S.", corresponding to the name of the author, are the only element of this sequence printed in roman type. The words 𝔙ertue, 𝔑ourture and 𝔄uctour are headed by capitals. The two lines following the initials and a blank line can be interpreted as the subtitle, announcing an addition to the main book. The year of publication, "Anno. 1557.", in roman type, is placed in the centre of the page. The next element of the title page is a maxim "Difpife …", also in roman type. The last textual element, starting with a paraph,[2] ℭ 𝔍mp𝔷inted… specifies the place of publication and the name of the printer: all in blackletter, with double-tapered indentation throughout. It is separated from the maxim by a single hedera (❦). The funnel shape of the imprint is complemented with a sequence of three hederas, forming its apex, pointing to the bottom of the page. The colophon, in the last page (D4v), offers a shorter version of the information from the foot of the title page: ℭ 𝔍mp𝔷inted at 𝔏ondon in 𝔓aules # ℭhurchyarde. 𝔅y 𝔚illiam # 𝔖eares.

The handbook is divided into thirteen chapters, three to eight pages long, each headed by a title, for example: ℭ 𝔋owe to o𝔷der thy felfe when # thou rpfeft, and in appa= # relynge thy body, # ℭapitulo.i. (A3r-A5r), ℭ 𝔄gainfte the vice of filthy # talkynge. ℭap.𝔯ii. (C7v-C8v). Owing to double-tapered indentation, the lines of chapter headings form funnel shapes (similar to those in the title page). Each chapter title (except chapter two) follows a paraph, a symbol which developed from <C> for Latin *Capitulum* ('chapter'). Additionally, all the headings are followed by ℭapitulo or ℭap, and the suitable Roman numeral set off with a pair of points, one on each side. The paraph is also used in front of the title of the acrostic, the morning prayer, the prayer when going to bed, the poem on the duties of different social ranks, before a section of chapter three starting with the words 𝔖o treatablie fpeakyng as well as in front of the colophon.

Nearly the whole book is printed in blackletter. Other types are used sparsely in the body of the book. Apart from the title page, roman typeface is

---

well as the types used in *The School* editions, but it does not contain a direct copy of the images from these sources.

employed in the running head, featuring the title of the book (spread over two facing pages, with "The ſchoole" on the verso side and "of vertue." on the following recto side). It can also be found in the initials opening most chapters and, occasionally, sections smaller than chapters (A2r, B1r, D3v). Chapters five, nine and eleven start with blackletter initials. Roman typeface is also used for the three maxims, the first one in English (in the title page) and two in Latin, "Face aut Tace" ('compose or be silent'), below the acrostic (A1v) and "Famam virtutis meis # Abolire nequit" ('my reputation for virtue cannot be abolished', D4v), followed by the author's initials, again in roman type.

The School is composed in verse. The text is organised into sets of half-lines with the second half-line in each set indented and ended with a rhyme (see Rutkowska 2016b: 103–105 for an analysis of prosodic devices in *The School*). Nearly all the first half-lines start with a capital, but the second half-lines are capitalised less often and inconsistently (e.g. 34% of the second half-lines start with a capital in the longest, i.e. second, chapter), without any particular pattern emerging in this respect; but with some pages containing more capitalisation (e.g. A7r-A8v) than others. Only the poem on the duties is divided into twenty-one stanzas, each four-half-line-long and accompanied with an Arabic numeral in the margin. The margins are also used for adding over thirty references to Greek philosophers and rhetoricians, e.g. 𝕮𝖆𝖙𝖔., 𝕮𝖎𝖈𝖊𝖗𝖔., 𝕻𝖑𝖆𝖙𝖔., as well as the Bible, e.g. 𝕻ſ𝖆𝖑.𝖑., 𝕸𝖆𝖙𝖍.𝖗. All these references are in blackletter. There is also a one-off reference, 𝕲𝖗𝖆𝖈𝖊 # 𝖇𝖊𝖋𝖔𝖗𝖊 # 𝖒𝖊𝖆𝖙𝖊, next to the author's comment in the margin of B1r. The comment is additionally followed by a horizontal line (in B1v), dividing it from the following part of chapter three.

11.4 Variation and pragmatic functions of visual cues in *The School* editions

The present section offers a description of the modifications concerning the visual aspects, introduced in the eleven editions of *The School* issued over a hundred years, between 1582 and 1687, as well as an analysis of pragmatic functions of particular visual cues at three levels: textual, interactional and stance. It combines microanalytic and macroanalytic features. This detailed analysis places emphasis on bringing out the continuation of visual devices and the ways in which these have been modified and transformed over time, adapting to the changes required by the external context.

The *octavo* format as well as the manuscript tradition of foliation are retained throughout the publication history of *The School*. Likewise, blackletter remains the predominant typeface in the body text of the book even in the seventeenth-century editions, although the running heads are in roman type from Seares's 1557 edition and remain so throughout. Another "old" feature is the preservation of the manual's division into thirteen chapters. Interestingly, chapter thirteen itself nominally disappears in the editions issued in 1582 and 1593, as its heading signals chapter fourteen (following chapter twelve). This could have been due to the printers' errors, but considering Denham's accuracy regarding other features, it may reflect contemporary superstition. Considering the didactic nature of the book, chapters devoted to different topics connected with appropriate behaviour could be used by teachers as consecutive individual lessons read out aloud in the classroom. As suggested earlier (section 11.2.2), such visual conservatism can be associated with the printers' and publishers' intention to preserve the original character of the book, that is the form in which it has been known and appreciated by the readers (see Kopaczyk, this volume). It implies the intent of retaining the recognisability of the book as well as the authority which it has previously gained as a manual of good conduct. Both could likewise be considered as a means to achieve satisfactory sales. With regard to the levels of discourse or pragmatic functional domains, such practice can be interpreted as a combination of all the three levels, the textual one (ensuring consistent structural division and organisation of the text), the interactional one (responding to the reader's needs and expectations), and the stance one (preserving the original authority of the book).

Nevertheless, not all the visual and structural aspects are preserved unmodified in all the editions of *The School*. The most conspicuous change in the 1582 edition of *The School* is the addition of a new part of the book, with several pages of new prayers, which Crowley entitled "Certain Praiers and Graces" (1582, C7v-D7v). Most prayers in this part are composed in verse, except six short graces to be said before and after a meal, and the prayer for Queen Elizabeth and the Realm, covering the last two pages of the text. The content of the prayers themselves remains constant, with the exception of details concerning the references to royalty. Thus, in 1582, three stanzas are added to the poem on the duties, to refer to Queen Elizabeth and her entourage (1582, D2r). These are preserved in 1593 (B8r), but in 1621 the name of the monarch changes to King James, in 1626 to King Charles (retained between 1630 and 1677), and King James in 1687. Similar changes appear elsewhere in the prayers. They indicate that each edition of *The School* was embedded and functioned in a particular wider, external (historical and political) context, to which it had to adjust. Starting from the edition printed in 1582, proper names of monarchs and other authorities are printed in roman type (with few exceptions, e.g., 𝔈𝔩𝔦𝔷𝔞𝔟𝔢𝔱𝔥 in 1582, C7r), which makes them stand out against the background of the regular text in blackletter. By comparison to royalty, references to Greek philosophers and to the Bible remain unchanged across editions, but they are maintained in the margins (in addition to the regular text) only in 1557 and 1582. In 1582, they are, in fact "double-marked", highlighted in roman typeface both in the margins and in the text of the manual. This switch to roman type as well as the use of margins play the role of visual pragmatic markers at different levels. At the textual and interactional levels combined, they signpost the important places in the text, thus guiding the reader. At the stance level, these pragmatic markers point to external authorities, which, being readily recognised by the author, printer and publisher, impart some of their importance and power to the book in the eyes of the reader.

Both Latin maxims from Seares's edition fail to appear in the later versions of *The School*. In 1557, they could have functioned as markers of the authority of the book (the stance level). This impression is strengthened by the use of roman type, signalling code-switching from English to Latin. Yet, considering the fact that the book was designed for teaching small children, perhaps Crowley, in his effort to prepare an enhanced edition of the book, deemed the maxims to be unnecessarily sophisticated at this level of education. Instead, he complemented the edition issued in 1582 with two extra acrostics on the *verso* of the title page (see figure 11.2).[5] The original acrostic with Seager's name was moved to the left bottom corner of the page, and accompanied with another short acrostic, containing the name of the printer (Henrie Denham), in the right bottom corner, both compartmentalised on all sides with the use of straight lines. In contrast, the acrostic indicating the name of the compiler (Robert Crowley), comprises thirteen full lines and covers nearly two thirds of the page. Additionally, it is surrounded with decorative woodcut borders at the top and on both sides. These changes in the layout signal a specific hierarchy and a shift in authority from the original author to the compiler. The author of the manual is relegated to a lower position and equated with the printer. This modification could have been caused by the fact that Crowley's name would presumably be more familiar to a potential reader (and buyer) than that of Seager, who produced fewer books and had died decades earlier (on other promotional kinds of paratext in early modern print, see Varila et al., this volume). In the following editions, only the acrostics with the author's and the compiler's names are recorded, with Crowley preserving his dominant position. Whereas the layout communicates modifications at the stance level in the edition of 1582, the use of roman typeface for the line-initial

---

[5] Here and in the figures below, the decorative elements were drawn by hand by Elżbieta Jędrasiak and then scanned.

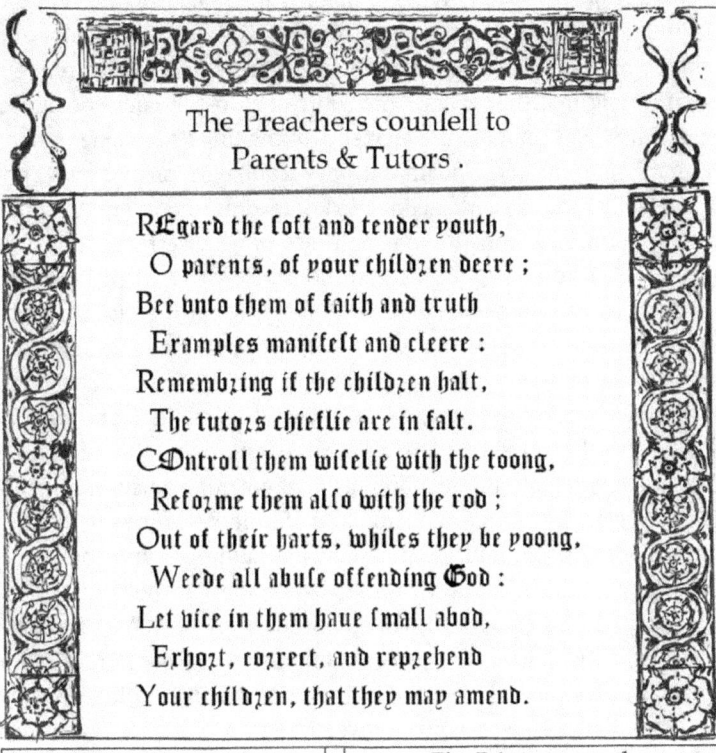

The Preachers counsell to Parents & Tutors.

REgard the soft and tender youth,
 O parents, of your children deere ;
Bee vnto them of faith and truth
 Examples manifest and cleere :
Remembring if the children halt,
 The tutors chieflie are in falt.
COntroll them wiselie with the toong,
 Reforme them also with the rod ;
Out of their harts, whiles they be yoong,
 Weede all abuse offending God :
Let vice in them haue small abod,
 Exhort, correct, and reprehend
Your children, that they may amend.

The Authors name *in verdict* .	The Printer to youth *in generall* .
SAie well some will,	HAnd smooth this booke,
by this my labour,	Deer child learne at large :
Euerie man yet	Expressing plainlie
will not saie the same :	Ech point of thy charge :
Among the good,	Neglect not instruction,
I shall find fauour,	No sie ❧ that is naught :
God them forgiue	Remember, I praie thee,
that doo me blame.	Herein what is taught :
Ech man I wish,	In youth to be ruled,
whom I shall offend,	And schooled vp well :
Rightlie to read me,	Experience declareth ,
& their faults t'amend.	Most things doth excell .

Figure 11.2: Acrostics in the edition of *The School* printed in 1582.

letters has an interactional role to play here, helping the reader understand the acrostics. This guidance stays in force for Crowley's acrostic throughout the remaining editions, but from the 1593 edition Seager's acrostic is printed entirely in roman type, meaning that the typographic contrast is lost. It could be added that acrostics in *The School* combine the elements of the linguistic mode (proper names) with the orthographic and typographic ones (capitalisation and initial position in the line), facilitating the vertical direction of reading and interpretation.

Apart from proper names, roman type continues to be used for section and chapter initials in 1582 and the following editions. However, their size and appearance undergoes variation, presumably depending on the current fashion, the printers' own preferences, as well as the means available to them. Denham introduces decorative woodcut initials, mostly four-lines tall, to open the chapters of the manual, but prayers following the manual are usually opened by smaller, two-line typed initials. This rather consistent differentiation operates both at the textual and interactional level of meaning, ensuring hierarchical structural division of the text into two parts of different genres (a manual as the main genre of the book, and the prayers as an addition) and communicating this hierarchy to the reader. A similar distinction can be observed in 1593, but Charlewood is less consistent, using various sizes of woodcut initials (4–7 lines of height) as well as small, two-line initials (A7r, B4v, B5r, B5v) for opening chapters. George Elde and Miles Flesher retain decorated initials only to open the preface before the morning prayer (A3r) and chapter one (A4r). Crowch abandons them entirely, whereas in each of the last two editions, only one decorative initial is preserved, opening the preface (A3r). This apparent degradation of woodcut initialisations may reflect a gradually lowering prestige of the manual over time, the lack of ornamentation appropriate for the text's perceived mundanity among seventeenth-century audiences. Alternatively, it is possible that the expectations of school masters (the potential target audience for this product) with regard to the layout of a manual to be used in class changed in the direction of simplicity and avoidance of unnatural ostentation.

(1) Forgeue the offences
       this daye we haue wroughte
    Againſte thee and our neighbour
       in worde dede and thoughte
    (1557, D1v)

(2) Remit the offences this daie we haue wrought,
    To thee & our neighbor in word, deed, & thought.
    (1582, C5r)

As regards the layout of the page, the division of the text of the manual into half-lines is preserved in 1582, but the passage referring to the grace before the meal in chapter three (A8v-B1r), as well as the remaining part of this chapter (B1r-B1v), and the prayer said when going to bed (C5r) are presented in full lines (compare examples 1 and 2). Typically, the second half-line in each set is indented, possibly in order to facilitate reading aloud with appropriate diction, including rhythm and rhyme. Thus, the linguistic and typographic elements complement each other, helping the reader's engagement and thus performing together the interactional pragmatic function. In 1593 and all the later versions of *The School*, full lines are regularly used in the manual, except before chapter two, next to chapter initials and in the poem on the duties. Given the limitations of the format, the general shift to full lines necessitated the use of a smaller size of typeface, and contributed to the overall impression of conciseness of the book. The capitalisation of the initial letter in a full line and in each first half-line is an increasingly consistent rule in all the editions, comprising a typographic norm from the 1582 edition and later.

The parts of the book where half-lines remain, as well as the poems in verse, receive extra decoration in the form of woodcut side borders in the margins in all the editions following Denham (1582). Denham himself, apart from Crowley's acrostic (described above), employs a bottom border as a dividing line at the end of the manual (C5r) and before the graces (D3r), as well as a top border in the final pages containing the graces (D3v-D7r). No bottom decorative borders are used in the subsequent editions, whereas top borders are used only in two places: before the preface (A3r; this one is absent in the 1593 edition) and before the prayer when going to bed (B6r). The placement of the latter signals the reinterpretation of the structural (or textual) division between the two main parts of *The School*, as the "bedtime" prayer, originally rounding off the manual, is reanalysed as the first text in the "prayer part" in Charlewood's edition, and retains this classification in all remaining editions. This reanalysis may be due to the need (perceived by the printer or publisher) to differentiate between the genres: the good conduct manual and the collection of prayers and poems (the textual level). Also, the top border may have been used to help the reader find the beginning of the second part of the book (the interactional level).

Concerning the development of the other visual structural devices, the chapter headings follow the first edition in being printed in blackletter. Denham's 1582 edition combines the blackletter headings with paraphs, but employs roman type for the Latin abbreviation following the heading, for instance, "Cap. 2..", "Cap. 5.", as well as for the headings of the acrostics, and a selection of prayers (the prayer said when going to bed, the poem on the duties, the prose graces, and in "Certaine Praiers and Graces # *newlie added, to be ufed of Scholers both* #

afore-noone and after-noone : # *Compiled by R. C.*" C7v). In this last case, roman type alternates with italics, as it also does in Seager's and Denham's acrostics (see figure 11.2). Moreover, the headings of the prayers to be said before and after meals are in italics, e.g. "*Grace before meate.*" (D5v); the headings of graces in prose are opened with fleurons, e.g. "❋ Grace before meate." (D6v); and most prayers in this edition end with "Amen." or "*Amen.*". Thus, Denham introduces more complexity to the system of structural markers, compartmentalising the text and differentiating between particular parts of the book. At the same time, this makes particular sections easier for the reader to find (the interactional level). The system is gradually simplified in the later editions. For example, paraphs are reduced in number in the chapter headings in Charlewood's edition (1593), used to introduce the imprint and six minor sections, mostly in the prayer part. The number of paraphs drops to three in Elde's version, and two in Flesher. Crowch (1670) replaces the paraph with a cross and a double vertical line. In the last two editions only a cross is used. The decreasing use of paraphs from 1593 is accompanied by a shift to roman type in all the headings of the chapters, which was apparently considered as a sufficient highlighting textual device or "episode boundary marker" in this and the following editions (see Brinton 1996: 43; the term is used there with reference to the changes in the narrative rather than visual devices).

The title page is an element which merits a separate treatment due to its visual and functional complexity as well as variation across the editions. Nearly all the editions of *The School* have title pages (the title page of the 1640 edition, assuming it had one, has not been preserved) and those issued in 1557, 1582 and 1593 end with colophons, continuing an earlier tradition. In the seventeenth-century editions, book-final colophons are not evident. In Denham's edition, roman type is used for most of the text on the title page, and – confirming the general tendency in early modern printing (see section 11.2.2) – all the editions, apart from 1557 and 1593, used italics in alternation with roman type, mixing various sizes. This alternation can be interpreted as interactional, drawing the reader's attention to the new or most important information.

Another characteristic feature of the title pages of *The School* before 1670 is the presence of woodcuts. In 1582, the title page is an example of factotum printing (see figure 11.3). In this type of printing, a passage of text (or a single letter in the case of an initial) is integrated into a woodcut illustration element (see Driver 2004: 13–16, 49, for more information and early modern examples). Here, the title of the book and the other verbal components of the title page are framed within a wide, elaborate border, containing the royal arms at the top, and the Stationers' below, with two females in the low corners, and with partly floral, partly architectural, embossed-like ornamentation at the sides. The women hold implements

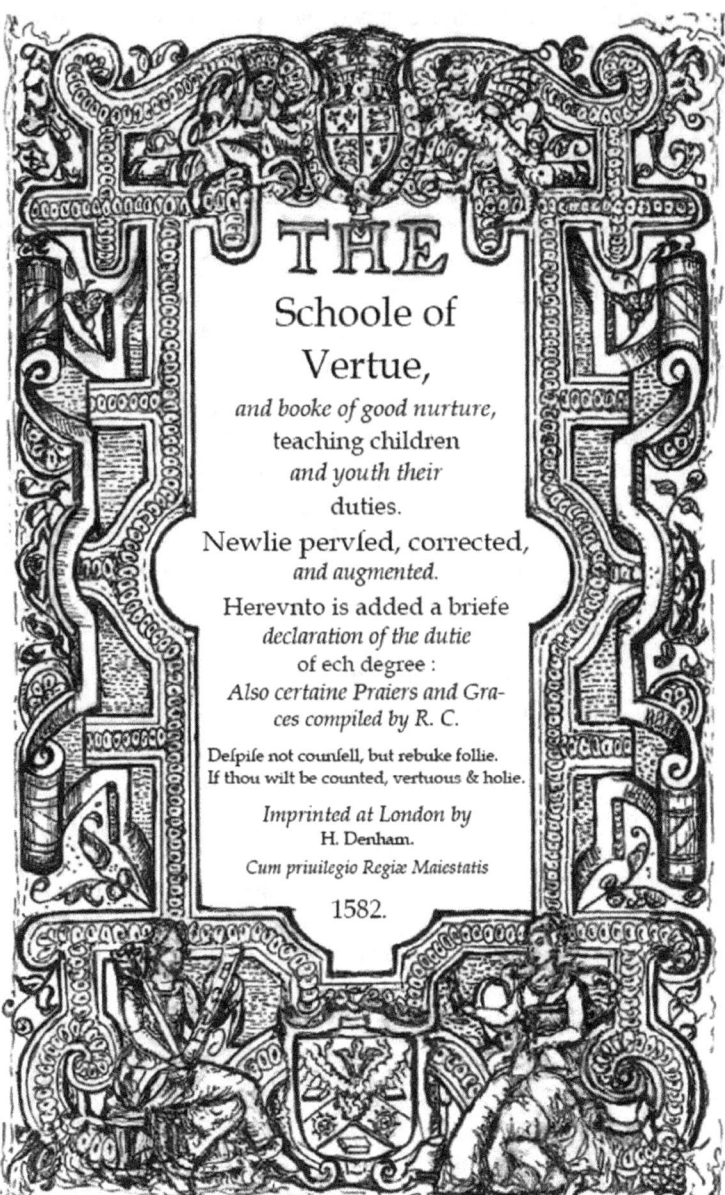

Figure 11.3: The title page in the edition of *The School* printed in 1582.

connected with education and knowledge, including a key, a book, an elongated display page with the letters of the alphabet and (possibly) compasses (the image is obliterated and does not allow a clear interpretation). The architectural and embossement-like motifs are particularly common in the early decades of the seventeenth century, presumably imitating the title-page designs inspired by antique motifs common on the Continent, especially in Italy (e.g. Rice 2010). The text is enclosed within a single compartment with no clear division into segments apart from double-tapered indentation, though the latter can be considered a structuring device operating at the textual level. The title covers three-quarters of the text compartment, the rest being taken by the maxim: "Deſpiſe not...", and the imprint. The capitalisation, size, and the additional convex-like effect of "THE" may be interpreted as suggesting uniqueness at the level of linguistic meaning, but, primarily, it can be described as loaded with graphic semantics, relating the textual content of the compartment to the pictorial frame in which it is enclosed, thus promoting a harmonious aesthetic of the page as a whole. Together with the whole frame, with its embossing and shading effects, it also contributes to the impression of the three-dimensionality of the title page, imitating a real embossed cover of a book. The size of the type in the text compartment gradually decreases, but in the passages "Newlie pervſed, corrected,", "Herevnto is added a briefe" and "1582." it is bigger than in the immediately neighbouring ones, apparently to draw the reader's attention (the interactional function), and encouraging him or her to buy the book.

The book-final colophon (see figure 11.4) in this edition contains an elaborate device of Henry Denham, which covers three quarters of the last page. The device features a large star surrounded by an oval frame with a motto ("OS HOMINI SVBLIME DEDIT", i.e. '[He] gave an upright countenance to man'), the arms of the City of London at the top, with two putti on its sides, as well as the arms of the Stationers' company at the foot, with a woman in each bottom corner, and the initials "H" and "D" at the mid-level, one on each side of the oval frame. The colophon starts with the year of publication at the top of the page, followed by the device, and the remaining information "Newlie imprinted...". The shading effects in the woodcut suggest it is three-dimensional, as if carved in wood or stone.

Although Henry Denham did not hold the post of a Queen's Printer, he obtained the royal privilege for the exclusive printing of several books, including histories (see Clegg 2010: 167) and, apparently, also *The School*. His use of the printer's device together with the elaborate woodcuts as well as references to the city arms, the royal arms and the royal permission (in the title and colophon pages) have at least two functions. On the one hand, they attract attention (the interactional level), and on the other, they give authority to

Newlie imprinted by H. Denham,
dwelling in Pater noster Rowe, at the
ſigne of the Starre, being the
aſſigne of W. Seres.

Cum priuilegio Regiæ Maieſtatis.

*Forbidding all other to print
this booke.*

Figure 11.4: The colophon page in the edition of *The School* printed in 1582.

the book, raising its perceived quality and trustworthiness (the stance level). Both functions could influence a potential reader's decision to purchase the text (see also Varila et al., this volume).

Notably, Denham's edition contains a woodcut image not recorded in any other editions. This depicts a sequence of six staves with neumes (symbols representing musical notes), accompanying the *Our Father* prayer (D2v): a visually arresting image which may also have increased the book's saleability. The visual mode element (staves with neumes) and a linguistic one (rhymes, used throughout the book) both foreground the oral/aural dimension of the text and contribute to its multimodal nature.

The title page of the edition printed in 1593 (see figure 11.5) contains only roman type, without italics, but with variation of the type size. The lines comprising the main part of the title, "THE … augmented." are arranged into the conventional funnel shape, with the type decreasing in size in combination with a double-tapered indentation, starting from the third line. The initial "THE" is smaller than the second line, but its central placement and capitalisation implies the printer's familiarity with the previous edition of the book, where this

Figure 11.5: The title page in the edition of *The School* printed in 1593.

word was visually conspicuous and had a compositionally prominent role. A new element in this edition, covering the lower half of the title page, is a woodcut constituting the printer's device, and representing a man plucking a flower (believed to be the printer himself; see Tedder 1892: 153). The woodcut operates at both the interactional level of meaning (attraction of attention, visual entertainment) and the stance level (the printers' authority and guarantee of quality). The maxim, divided in two halves, appears on the sides of the woodcut, visually forming a kind of frame around it, together with the title (above), and the imprint (below).

The textual components of the seventeenth-century title pages take proportionally more room on the page than the sixteenth-century ones, but variation in size and double-tapered indentation are still employed as structural devices (textual level). The title-page maxim is in italics and set apart from the rest of the text by horizontal lines. In the editions printed between 1621 and 1660, it is followed by a woodcut illustration covering approximately 20 per cent of the title page. In the imprint, appearing at the bottom, the place of publication (London) is highlighted using italics (1670–1687), uppercase roman (1660), or uppercase italics (1621–1635). In the editions printed between 1626 and 1660 the year is not indicated, and in the last two the printer's name is omitted, leaving only the publisher's or bookseller's name. This suggests a shift in responsibility for the published book from the printer to the publisher, and the corresponding shift of authority communicated at the stance level of meaning. As regards the woodcuts employed in the seventeenth-century title pages, in 1621 the illustration presents the royal arms, accompanied with floral and fructal elements as well as three-dimensional embossing effects. The reference to royalty, again, imparts more authority to the book and is likely to make it look trustworthy and worth buying. In 1626, the illustration changes to one presenting a winged putto's (or angel's) head accompanied with some floral motifs. The same image is reused in 1630 and 1635. In 1660, another picture is used, featuring a winged putto against a floral background, with a laurel wreath in his left hand and a spear in the right one. The angel or winged putto epitomises innocence and the presence of God, and is a common classically-derived motif in Renaissance art. The flowers, fruit, laurel and spear also draw on antique models; the latter two symbolise victory (or success) and power, respectively. These symbols could be seen to signify the book's ability to provide the knowledge for success, all in harmony with God, thus working to attract and engage the reader (the interactional level of meaning) and represent its authority as a means of spiritual and intellectual advancement (the stance level). Given the contents of *The School* (frequent references to lessons at school), the target audience must have been mainly school masters, so the symbolic resonance of woodcuts is likely to have been recognised. The woodcuts also operate at the textual or structural level of meaning, sub-dividing the text. The woodcut with the winged putto can be first found in Elde's edition printed in 1621, heralding the beginning of the manual (at the top of A3r), and the beginning of the prayer part of *The School* (at the top of B6r). It is then reused in 1630 and 1635 in the same positions, but in 1626 and 1660, the introductory woodcut (A3r) is supplanted with a winged angel's head. In 1640, in turn, the angel's head is placed both in A3r and in B6r. Additionally, in the editions of 1621 and 1626, there is a frontispiece (i.e. an illustration facing the title page, placed on page A1v) with a domestic scene, featuring, in the foreground, an woman ironing and a small child extending its hands to her as if asking for something, and, in the background, another woman serving a meal to a male member of the family. This picture suggests that *The School* is designed for teaching children who, instead of wasting time on disturbing family members in domestic chores, should rather spend their days in a useful way, either attending school or learning under the supervision of a tutor; this indicates that the group of envisaged purchasers also includes parents. The illustrations in the seventeenth-century editions of *The School* can be divided into symbolic (the woodcuts with angels and putti) and literal (the woodcut with the domestic scene). Both kinds of pictures can operate at the stance level, building up motivation for teaching and learning, and at the interactional level, encouraging the purchase of the book.

The three final editions have no illustration placed centrally in the title page (see figure 11.6), but the text is surrounded with decorative borders, neatly demarcating the linguistic content (the textual level). These editions also use a new woodcut, repeated in different sizes across the text: A2rv and C8rv in 1670, C8rv only in 1677, and in A1rv and C8v in 1687. The woodcut depicts a classroom (the larger version with a door and windows), with a teacher in the foreground, sitting on a chair, and a pupil standing next to him (presumably) reading a book aloud; more children can be seen in the background. The teacher is holding a rod in his left hand and the index finger of his right hand is slightly raised, as if cautioning the child. The image depicts the authority of the teacher over his pupils, and as such operates at the stance level of discourse, as well as the interactional level, as the teacher may also represent a user of the book. In these last editions, the symbolic woodcuts are abandoned. Perhaps the authority of the teacher communicated by the pictures was considered a sufficient incentive for buying the book or, more practically, the printers had no other woodcuts at their disposal. It is also possible that the simplification of the message expressed by the illustrations reflects the changing target audience of the book in connection with the increasingly commonplace character of primary education (for which the book is designed).

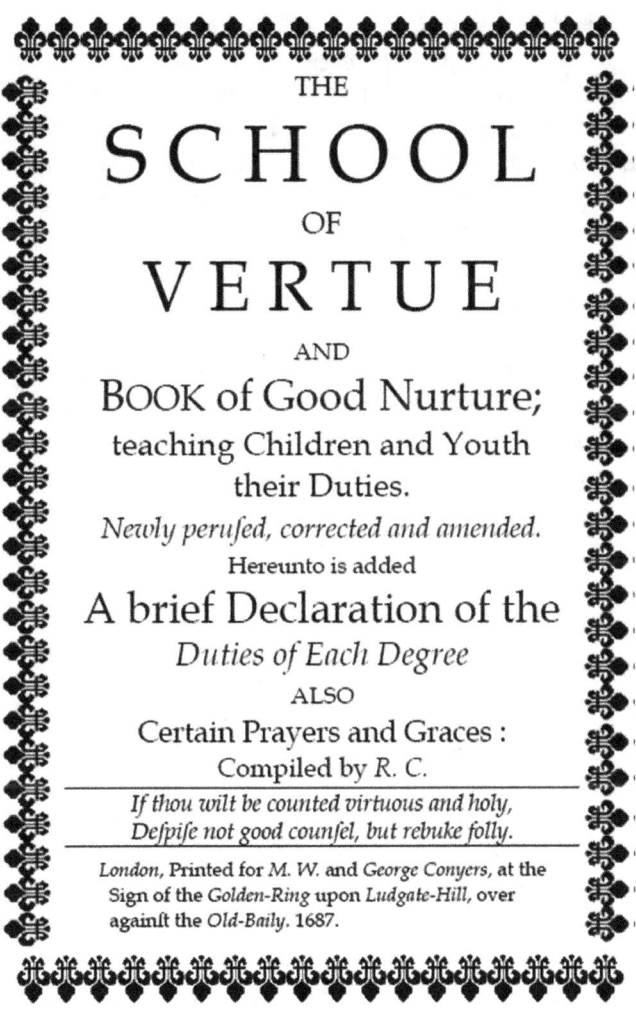

Figure 11.6: The title page in the edition of *The School* printed in 1687.

One final noteworthy structural device employed in the title page is the mid-sentence capitalisation of initial letters in common nouns and other parts of speech. The evolution of this practice suggests an increasing tendency to capitalise over time. In 1557, the only non-proper-name words starting with a capital are 𝔘ertue, 𝔑ourture and 𝔍uctour. In 1582, also "Schoole", "Praiers" and "*Graces*" receive initial capitals. "Booke", "Nurture", and "Counſell" follow suit in 1593, and so do "Children", "Youth", and "Declaration" between 1621 and 1660 (but "counſell" is not capitalised there). In 1670, "Duties" (twice) and "Degree" are likewise capitalised, joined by "Good" and "Each" in 1677 and 1687 (though "brief" does not get a capital). One can interpret these modifications as textual and interactional in nature, emphasising the (perceived) importance of particular words in the text, and also forming part of a general trend in English printed books (see Osselton 1985; Salmon 1999: 50–51).[6] In this device, once again, one can trace the coordination of linguistic elements (semantically prominent words) with typographic and orthographic (i.e. visual) ones (capitalisation).

To sum up the visual practices in *The School* editions, certain elements remain constant, preserving the original character of the book, including: the *octavo* format, foliation, blackletter as the typeface of the body of the text, the primary role of the title page, the division of the manual into chapters. Other components, however, undergo evolution over time: blackletter disappears from the title page; the use of roman typeface increases over time, from highlighting the running head, initials, maxims, the author's initials and the date of publication to marking the headings of chapters (coinciding with the loss of paraphs in this context); italic typeface starts to alternate with roman type in the title page and occasionally with blackletter elsewhere in the book; the role of capitalisation and the size variation grows. These typographical modifications operate at the textual and interactional levels of discourse, enhancing the clarity of text structuring, thus guiding the reader through the book more effectively. The stance level of discourse is expressed in most editions by typeface-switching and capitalisation (e.g. highlighting the names of authorities), page layout (e.g. the importance of Crowley indicated by the proportion of his acrostic, see figure 11.2), and illustrations, whose content develops from highly symbolic to literal, presumably reflecting the changing social circumstances. Nevertheless, the changes are not always unidirectional. For instance, the amount of typographic complexity seems to be, to some extent, a matter of idiosyncratic preferences of book producers, as illustrated by the intricate design of the title and colophon pages (unique in the series of editions under consideration), and the extensive use of italic typeface, identified in Denham's edition (1582).

---

[6] Other orthographic and typographic characteristics of *The School* editions are discussed in Rutkowska (2016a).

11.5 Reflexes of early modern visual devices in digital media

The previous section described the visual changes in the evolution of *The School*, taken as a representative example of early modern English books more broadly. The evolution of these features did not, however, cease with the publication of the last edition of *The School*. Many of these elements discussed have survived, albeit transformed and enhanced, until our times, and can be identified in new media (a perspective accordant with a transhistorical approach to visual communicative practices). With the switch from traditional to electronic media, the format of the book has been replaced by the display size of the device used for reading the text. But although foliation was abandoned long before electronic media came into being, different forms of pagination are often preserved in websites as textual and interactional devices (helping the reader locate the relevant information and return to it when required), even though infinite scrolling has ousted it in social media, in particular on mobile devices.

The early modern title page, in turn, finds its postmodern equivalent in online home or landing pages. Like the title page, the home page has the textual role of signalling the contents of the website, the interactional one to attract the viewer and encourage him or her to proceed to the remaining pages, as well as, optionally, the stance role to ensure the quality of the information (e.g. in the case of news websites) or of the products (in the case of internet shops) it offers. The stance function can be fulfilled by a visual element, typically the logo of the company. Like in the early modern title page, that spatial organisation of a digital page, especially the start page, is of utmost importance (see Thompson & Collins, this volume). For example, marking the division of the information by headings as well as its compartmentalisation into modules containing both text and illustration (reminiscent of factotum printing) is a common convention in online and print media. The roles played by these components are usually both textual (structuring the text into chunks) and interactional (attracting the viewer's attention). One of the greatest developments in electronic media is the variety of fonts (with their origins in early modern typefaces). Their semiotic potential, often in conjunction with other typographic elements, e.g. the layout and illustrations, has been recognised by researchers of both traditional and new media (e.g. McKenzie 1981; Bland 1998; van Leeuwen 2006, 2015; Bringhurst 2008). This brief and incomplete survey of features shared by early modern printed books and current digital media shows that the centuries-old visual devices of printers have a long continuity, extending beyond the early modern period into present-day digital practices.

11.6 Summary and conclusions

This chapter has reported the results of a comparative, longitudinal, qualitative case study, which aimed at determining the pragmatic functions of the visual elements present in the pages of the twelve editions of *The School*, a handbook of good conduct for children, published between 1557 and 1687. It has offered a synergistic approach, including elements of visual pragmatics, pragmaphilology, book history and diachronic pragmatics, drawing on the "pragmatics on the page" methodology recommended by Carroll et al. (2013). The study revealed that producers of early modern printed books had a wide variety of visual means at their disposal for communicating diverse meanings, using a complex hierarchical system of structural elements or punctuation marks (Lennard 1995). The analysis has shown that individual visual markers often function at different levels simultaneously. Printers' devices are a good example: they signal the beginning (and sometimes end) of the publication at the structural level, seek to attract the reader through their symbolism and aesthetic values at the interactional level, and ensure the recognisability of a given publication and its good quality, at the stance level. Such findings confirm that visual pragmatic markers, similarly to linguistic markers (Brinton 1996: 64), tend to be multifunctional.

In the present analysis, the emphasis has been placed on the visual features and their co-existence with the linear written text. The visual and verbal semiotic modes are intertwined and used simultaneously, emphasising that multimodality is by no means a feature specific to digital media. It is also noteworthy that this perspective could be expanded further, as the visual devices described here are likewise interconnected with purely linguistic aspects as well as ones pointing to the oral/aural dimension, such as rhymes and rhythm,[7] and together constitute a text as a unified meaningful whole. The analysis of *The School* editions also highlights the diachronic relations between components. A detailed diachronic form-to-function mapping (Jacobs & Jucker 1995: 13) shows that the creators of each new utterance (the compiler, the editors and publishers) engage in a specific intertextual dialogue with the previous ones through the gradual introduction of new elements. This concerns, for instance, the functional evolution of roman type first employed in the running head, initials, selected elements of the title page and for code-switching from English to Latin (1557), then adopted as the dominant type in the title page, introduced in minor headings of sections and for highlighting the names of authorities (1582), and later used in all the chapter headings (1593). This development did not preclude observing the convention to

---

[7] See Rutkowska (2016b) for more details about prosodic and other stylistic devices in this book.

use blackletter as the default typeface in the body text, established for the first edition. Indeed, no text functions in a vacuum, but rather builds upon and modifies its predecessors. The interaction of the old components with the new ones and the gradual introduction of changes ensures visual continuity, harmoniously combining innovation with continuation.

References

Primary sources: *The School of Vertue* editions

Seager (Segar) [Francis]

1557 *The schoole of Uertue, and booke of good Nourture for chyldren, and youth to learne theyr dutie by. Newely perused, corrected, and augmented by the fyrst Auctour. F. S With a briefe declaration of the dutie of eche degree.* London: Wyllyam Seares. (*STC* 22135)

Seager (Segar) [Francis] & Robert Crowley

1582 *The Schoole of Vertue and booke of good nurture, teaching children and youth their duties. Newlie pervsed, corrected, and augmented. Herevnto is added a briefe declaration of the dutie of ech degree: Also certaine Praiers and Graces compiled by R. C.* London: H. Denham. (*STC* 22136)

1593 *The Schoole of Vertue, & Booke of good Nurture, teaching children & youth their duties. Newly perused, corrected and augmented* ... London: [John Charlewood for] Richard Iones. (*STC* 22137)

1621 *The Schoole of Vertue, and Booke of good Nurture teaching Children and Youth their duties* ... London: G. E. for T. P. and I. W. (*STC* 22137.7)

[1626] *The Schoole of Vertue, and Booke of good Nurture, teaching Children and Youth their duties* ... London: M. Flesher for Robert Bird. (*STC* 22138)

[c. 1630] *The Schoole of Vertue, and Booke of good Nurture, teaching Children and Youth their duties* ... London: M. Flesher for Robert Bird. (*STC* 22138.3)

[c. 1635] *The Schoole of Vertue, and Booke of good Nurture, teaching Children and Youth their duties* ... London: M. Flesher for Robert Bird. (*STC* 22138.5)

[c. 1640] [*The Schoole of Vertue.* London: M. Flesher for Robert Bird]. (*STC* 22138.7)

[c. 1660] *The Schoole of Vertue, and Booke of good Nurture, teaching Children and Youth their duties* ... London: M. Flesher for Iohn Wright. (*Wing* S2171)

[1670] *The School of Vertue, and Book of good Nurture* ... London: E. Crowch for J. Wright. (*Wing* S2412C)

1677 *The School of Vertue. And Book of Good Nurture; teaching Children and Youth their Duties* ... London: for J. Wright. (*Wing* S2412D)

1687 *The School of Vertue. And Book of Good Nurture* ... London: for M. W. and George Conyers. (*Wing* S2412E)

Secondary Sources

Barnard, John. 2002. Introduction. In John Barnard & Donald F. McKenzie (eds.), *The Cambridge history of the book in Britain. Vol IV: 1557–1695*, 1–25. Cambridge, UK: Cambridge University Press.

Barthes, Roland. 1977. *Image, music, text*. London: Fontana Press.

Bayne, Ronald. 1897. Segar, Francis. In Sidney Lee (ed.), *Dictionary of national biography: Scoffin-sheares*, vol 51. 196–7. London: Smith, Elder & Co.

Beal, Peter. 2008. *A dictionary of English manuscript terminology: 1450–2000*. Oxford: Oxford University Press.

Bell, Maureen. 2002. *Mise-en-page*, illustration, expressive form. In John Barnard & Donald F. McKenzie (eds.), *The Cambridge history of the book in Britain. Vol IV: 1557–1695*, 632–35. Cambridge, UK: Cambridge University Press.

Bland, Mark. 1998. The appearance of the text in early modern England. *Text* 11. 91–154.

Bringhurst, Robert. 2008. *The elements of typographic style*. Vancouver: Hartley and Marks.

Brinton, Laurel. 1996. *Pragmatic markers in English: Grammaticalization and discourse functions*. Berlin: De Gruyter Mouton.

Carroll, Ruth, Risto Hiltunen, Matti Peikola, Janne Skaffari, Sanna-Kaisa Tanskanen, Ellen Valle & Brita Wårvik. 2003. Introduction. In Risto Hiltunen & Janne Skaffari (eds.), *Discourse perspectives on English: Medieval to modern*, 1–12. Amsterdam: John Benjamins.

Carroll, Ruth, Matti Peikola, Hanna Salmi, Mari-Lisa Varila, Janne Skaffari & Risto Hiltunen. 2013. Pragmatics on the page: Visual text in late medieval English books. *European Journal of English Studies* 17 (1). 54–71.

Clegg, Cyndia Susan. 2010. Censorship and propaganda. In Susan Doran & Norman Jones (eds.), *The Elizabethan world*, 165–81. Abingdon: Routledge.

Cohn, Neil. 2013. *The visual language of comics: Introduction to the structure and cognition of sequential images*. London: Bloomsbury.

de Hamel, Christopher. 1983. Reflexions on the trade in books of hours at Ghent and Bruges. In Joseph Burney Trapp (ed.), *Manuscripts in the fifty years after the invention of printing: Some papers read at a colloquium at the Warburg Institute on 12–13 March 1982*, 29–33. London: The Warburg Institute, University of London.

Driver, Martha W. 2004. *The image in print: Book illustration in late medieval England and its sources*. London: British Library.

Duff, Edward Gordon. [1905] 2011. *A century of the English book trade*. London: The Bibliographical Society.

Erman, Britt. 2001. Pragmatic markers revisited with a focus on "you know" in adult and adolescent talk. *Journal of Pragmatics* 33 (9). 1337–1359.

Early English Books Online (EEBO). https://search.proquest.com/eebo/ (accessed 17 July 2019).

English Short Title Catalogue (ESTC). http://estc.bl.uk/F/?func=file&file_name=login-bl-estc (accessed 17 July 2019).

Goodman, Sharon. 2005. Visual English. In Sharon Goodman & David Graddol (eds.), *Redesigning English: New texts, new identities*, 35–105. Abingdon: Routledge.

Halliday, M.A.K. & Ruqaiya Hasan. 1976. *Cohesion in English*. London: Longman.

Hellinga, Lotte. 1999. Printing. In Lotte Hellinga & Joseph B. Trapp (eds.), *The Cambridge history of the book in Britain. Vol III: 1400–1557*, 65–108. Cambridge, UK: Cambridge University Press.

Jackson, William Alexander, Frederic Sutherland Ferguson & Katharine F. Pantzer (eds.), Alfred William Pollard & Gilbert Richard Redgrave (compilers). 1976. *A Short-title catalogue of books printed in England, Scotland and Ireland and of English books printed abroad, 1475–1640, Vol 2: I–Z*, 2nd edn. London: Bibliographical Society.

Jacobs, Andreas & Andreas H. Jucker. 1995. Introduction. In Andreas H. Jucker (ed.), *Historical pragmatics: Pragmatic developments in the history of English*, 3–33. Amsterdam: John Benjamins.

Jensen, Kristian. 1999. Text-books in the universities: The evidence from the books. In Lotte Hellinga & Joseph B. Trapp (eds.), *The Cambridge history of the book in Britain. Vol III: 1400–1557*, 354–79. Cambridge, UK: Cambridge University Press.

Jucker, Andreas H. & Päivi Pahta. 2011. Communicating manuscripts: Authors, scribes, readers, listeners and communicating characters. In Päivi Pahta & Andreas H. Jucker (eds.), *Communicating early English manuscripts*, 3–10. Cambridge, UK: Cambridge University Press.

Kaislaniemi, Samuli. 2017. Code-switching, script-switching and typeface-switching in Early Modern English manuscript letters and printed tracts. In Matti Peikola, Aleksi Mäkilähde, Hanna Salmi, Mari-Liisa Varila & Janne Skaffari (eds.), *Verbal and visual communication in early English texts*, 165–200. Turnhout: Brepols.

Kress, Gunther. 2003. *Literacy in the new media age*. Abingdon: Routledge.

Kress, Gunther & Theo van Leeuwen. 2001. *Multimodal discourse: The modes and media of contemporary communication*. London: Arnold.

Kress, Gunther & Theo van Leeuwen. 2006. *Reading images: The grammar of visual design*, 2nd edn. Abingdon: Routledge.

Leece, Jonathan. 2011. An unexpected audience: Manner manuals in Renaissance Europe, *The Forum: Cal Poly's journal of history* 3 (1). Article 11. http://digitalcommons.calpoly.edu/forum/vol3/iss1/11 (accessed 30 March 2018).

Lennard, John. 1995. Punctuation: And – "Pragmatics". In Andreas H. Jucker (ed.), *Historical pragmatics: Pragmatic developments in the history of English*, 65–98. Amsterdam: John Benjamins.

Lyons, Martyn. 2009. *A history of reading and writing in the western world*. Basingstoke: Palgrave Macmillan.

Machan, Tim W. 2011. The visual pragmatics of code-switching in Late Middle English literature. In Herbert Schendl & Laura Wright (eds.), *Code-switching in early English*, 303–333. Berlin: De Gruyter Mouton.

Macksey, Richard. 1997. Foreword. *Paratexts: Thresholds of interpretation*, xi-xxii. Cambridge, UK: Cambridge University Press.

McConchie, Roderick W. 2013. Some reflections on early modern printed title-pages. In Anneli Meurman-Solin & Jukka Tyrkkö (eds.), *Studies in variation, contacts and change in English 14: Principles and practices for the digital editing and annotation of diachronic data*. Helsinki: VARIENG. http://www.helsinki.fi/varieng/series/volumes/14/mcconchie/ (accessed 17 July 2019).

McKenzie, Donald F. 1981. Typography and meaning: The case of William Congreve. In Giles Barber & Bernhard Fabian (eds.), *Wolfenbütteler Schriften zur Geschichte des Buchwesens 4*, 81–125. Hamburg: Hauswedell.

McKerrow, Ronald B. 1910. *A dictionary of printers and booksellers in England, Scotland and Ireland, and of foreign printers of English books 1557–1640*. London: Blades, East & Blades.

Nichols, Stephen G. & Siegfried Wenzel. 1996. *The whole book: Cultural perspectives on the medieval miscellany*. Ann Arbor: University of Michigan Press.

Nurmi, Arja. 2017. Early Modern English: Overview. In Alexander Bergs & Laurel J. Brinton (eds.), *The history of English. Volume 4: Early Modern English*, 8–26. Berlin: De Gruyter Mouton.

Osselton, Noel. 1985. Spelling-book rules and the capitalization of nouns in the seventeenth and eighteenth centuries. In Mary-Jo Arn, Hanneke Wirtjes & Hans Jansen (eds.), *Historical and editorial studies in medieval and early modern English*, 49–61. Groningen: Wolters-Noordhoff.

Plomer, Henry R. 1907. *A dictionary of the booksellers and printers who were at work in England, Scotland and Ireland from 1641 to 1667*. London: Blades, East & Blades.

Raumolin-Brunberg, Helena. 2017. Sociolinguistics. In Alexander Bergs & Laurel J. Brinton (eds.), *The history of English. Volume 4: Early Modern English*, 188–208. Berlin: De Gruyter Mouton.

Rautenberg, Ursula. 2016. The title-pages from the printing shop of Aldus Manutius (1495–1515). In Mario Infelise (ed.), *Aldo Manuzio: La construzione del mito*, 163–81. Venezia: Marsilio.

Raven, James. 2007. *The Business of books: Booksellers and the English book trade 1450–1850*. New Haven: Yale University Press.

Rice, Louise. 2010. Prints for Pentecost. The title plates and frontispieces to an annual sermon in seicento Rome. In Peter Fuhring, Barbara Brejon de Lavergnée, Marianne Grivel, Séverine Lepape & Véronique Meyer (eds.), *L'estampe au Grand Siècle: Études offertes à Maxime Préaud*, 235–75. Paris: École Nationale des Chartes.

Rogos-Hebda, Justyna. 2016. The visual text: Bibliographic codes as pragmatic markers on a manuscript page. *Studia Anglica Posnaniensia* 51 (3). 37–44.

Rutkowska, Hanna. 2013. *Orthographic systems in thirteen editions of the* Kalender of Shepherdes *(1506–1656)*. Frankfurt am Main: Peter Lang.

Rutkowska, Hanna. 2016a. Orthographic regularization in Early Modern English printed books: Grapheme distribution and vowel length indication". In Cinzia Russi (ed.), *Current trends in historical sociolinguistics*, 165–193. Berlin: De Gruyter Mouton.

Rutkowska, Hanna. 2016b. Stylistic devices in *The Schoole of Vertue*, an early modern manual of good conduct for children. *Studia Anglica Posnaniensia* 51 (3). 95–124.

Salmon, Vivian. 1999. Orthography and punctuation. In Roger Lass (ed.), *Cambridge history of the English language. Vol III: 1476–1776*, 13–55. Cambridge, UK: Cambridge University Press.

Smith, Margaret. 2000. *The title-page: Its early development 1460–1510*. London: The British Library.

Stribley, Miriam. 1987. *The calligraphy source book: The essential reference for all calligraphers*. London: Quarto Publishing.

Tagg, Caroline, Rachel Hu, Agnieszka Lyons & James Simpson. 2016. Heritage and social media in superdiverse cities: Personalised, networked and multimodal. *Working papers in translanguaging and translation* (WP17). http://www.birmingham.ac.uk/generic/tlang/index.aspx (accessed 18 May 2018).

Tschichold, Jan. 1966. *Treasury of alphabets and lettering*. New York: Reinhold.

Tedder, Henry R. 1888. Crowley, Robert. In Leslie Stephen (ed.), *Dictionary of national biography: Craik-Damer*. Vol 13, 241–43. New York: Macmillan and Co.
Tedder, Henry R. 1892. Jones, Richard. In Sidney Lee (ed.), *Dictionary of national biography: Johnes-Kenneth*. Vol 30, 153–54. New York: Macmillan and Co.
van Leeuwen, Theo. 2006. Towards a semiotics of typography. *Information Design Journal + Document Design* 14 (2). 139–55.
van Leeuwen, Theo. 2015. Multimodality. In Deborah Tannen, Heidi E. Hamilton & Deborah Schiffrin (eds.), *The handbook of discourse analysis*, Vol. 1, 447–465. Chichester: Wiley-Blackwell.
Wiles, Roy M. [1957] 2012. *Serial publication in England before 1750*. Cambridge, UK: Cambridge University Press.
Wing, Donald Goddard. 1982–1998. *Short-title catalogue of books printed in England, Scotland, Ireland, Wales and British America and of English books printed in other countries*, 2nd edn. New York: The Modern Language Association of America.
Yannicopulou, Angela. 2004. Visual aspects of written texts: Preschoolers view comics. *L1 – Educational Studies in Language and Literature* 4 (2–3). 169–181.

Mari-Liisa Varila, Sirkku Ruokkeinen, Aino Liira
and Matti Peikola

12 Paratextual presentation of Christopher St German's *Doctor and Student* 1528–1886

12.1 Presenting text through paratext

The concept of *paratext* (Genette 1997) refers to the elements that present, explain, and promote the book or text. Paratextual elements can be divided into two categories based on their location: *peritextual* elements are found within the book itself (e.g. prefaces, tables of contents); *epitextual* material is related to the book but outside it (e.g. reviews, advertisements). The verbal and visual forms of paratext are re-shaped historically vis-à-vis the changing cultural, medial and technological processes by which texts are made available to readers in a given period or community (e.g. Genette 1997: 3; Chartier 2014: 135–149; Ruokkeinen & Liira 2017 [2019]). Hence, the functions of paratext may be characterised in various ways depending on the period and medium.

Building on Genette's foundational conceptualisation of paratext, Birke and Christ (2013) propose three major functions for how paratextual items mediate the reader's contact with the text: *navigational* (assisting the reader in "operating" the text in its material context), *interpretive* (guiding the reader's interpretation of the text), and *commercial* (inviting the reader to purchase the text or some other product related to it). In Ciotti and Lin's (2016: vii) threefold model, the *structuring* and *commenting* functions roughly correspond to Birke and Christ's navigational and interpretive functions. Instead of the commercial dimension, however, Ciotti and Lin (2016: vii–viii) – who focus on manuscript paratexts – highlight the *documenting* function: providing information about the text and book and the circumstances of their production. Despite the differences in emphasis, the functions named above all relate to making the text more accessible and desirable to the prospective reader.

Most paratextual elements can be employed in the promotion of the text – either in the narrow sense of influencing the customer's decision to buy a book, or in the wider sense of convincing the reader of the quality and reliability of the contents (see Silva 2016: 609). This promotional orientation,

---

Mari-Liisa Varila (e-mail: mljvar@utu.fi), Sirkku Ruokkeinen, Aino Liira, Matti Peikola,
University of Turku, Department of English, FI-20014 University of Turku, Turku, Finland

https://doi.org/10.1515/9783110670837-016

we suggest, is a transhistorical feature of paratextual communication (see Tether 2017: 27–30, who argues for the relevance of the notion of "blurbing" for the classical and medieval contexts of text production; Varila & Peikola 2019). We argue that paratext theory offers a useful framework for examining textual trajectories (e.g. Blommaert 2005: 62–64, 255) or travels (Rock, Heffer & Conley 2013) and analysing how texts are reappropriated or recontextualised over time and marketed to new audiences (e.g. Birke & Christ 2013). As Maybin (2017: 419) observes, "text artifacts ... are historically constituted traces of particular moments in trajectories which can be traced backwards and forwards across social practice". In this chapter, we aim to show how paratext can play a significant role in extending a text's life-span, and how such longevity depends on the success of culturally context-specific features of paratextual communication.

Our analysis focuses on *Doctor and Student* by Christopher St German (d. 1541). This popular legal work with a long printing history serves well to illustrate the strategies of early and late modern book producers in employing paratext to promote and sustain the success of a single work. Although the scope of the present chapter does not allow for an equally extensive discussion of other works, we draw comparisons to other contemporary legal books where feasible. Paratext played an important role in the early phases of the textual trajectory during St German's lifetime when *Doctor and Student* was still taking shape (see section 12.3). The continuing popularity of the work is manifest not only in its frequent reprints but also in its epitexts; *Doctor and Student* is advertised for both professional and lay readers until the latter half of the nineteenth century (Williams 2017: 75; *Cincinnati Daily Times*, Dec 20th, 1876: 2). Yet, no major changes to the text of the work were made after the author's death, and book producers even displayed a strong reluctance to modernise its language (see section 12.4). Such marked stability of the text itself highlights the importance of paratext in making the work appeal to new generations of readers (see section 12.5).

In what follows, we explore how the paratextual apparatus of *Doctor and Student* was designed and redesigned in the multiple editions that were published from the early sixteenth to the late nineteenth century. In these artifacts, the text of the work was wrapped in layers of interpretive, commercial and navigational framing that evolved throughout the printing history of the work. We examine these paratextual layers to determine how they may have contributed to the long-lasting interest in this sixteenth-century treatise and how they reflect some potentially transhistorical concerns of textual promotion (see also Rutkowska; Thompson & Collins, both this volume). As Genette (1997: 1) argues, the purpose of paratext in presenting the text of a work ultimately entails "ensur[ing] the text's presence in the world, its 'reception' and 'consumption' in the form ... of a book". In this sense, the redesigns of paratext may be viewed as a process of what Bauman and Briggs (1990) call *entextualisation*: successive instances of (more or less subtle) de- and recontextualisation, in which the text of *Doctor and Student* was placed within new metadiscursive contexts and metapragmatic frames (see Blommaert 2005: 47–48, 251–252, 255). In our analysis of the paratextual apparatus as an entextualising device, we focus on both verbal and visual features of promotion that book producers used to construct such contexts and frames.

12.2 Doctor and Student

Christopher St German's *Doctor and Student* consists of dialogues between a barrister and a theologian on the relationship between law and conscience. Central to the work is the concept of *equity* – the understanding that legislators cannot foresee all particular circumstances when creating the letter of the law, and hence, reasonable exceptions are in accordance with the spirit of the law (Behrens 1998: 156–157). In the complex legal system of sixteenth-century England, the Chancellor, and the Court of Chancery, could remedy common law verdicts on the basis of equity in order to avoid injustice resulting from following rigid legal rules (e.g. Endicott 1989: 549–555). However, chancellors were criticised for undermining the common law by establishing their own rules and disrupting the proceedings of common law courts (Behrens 1998: 144). The publishing history of St German's *Doctor and Student* began during this era of heightened tension when the relationship between law and conscience became a central question for both the theory and practice of law.

The exact rationale behind St German's treatise, however, has proved somewhat elusive. Building on previous scholarship, Helmholz (2003: 130–131) provides four possible motivations for the treatise: 1) providing legal information, 2) contrasting common law with that of the church, 3) examining conscience and equity, and 4) applying continental legal thought on the English law of custom. The ambiguity of the work may be related to the politically and religiously tumultuous times during which it was produced. Indeed, a fifth interpretation has been offered by Williams (2017), who argues that large parts of *Doctor and Student* are better understood as a religious argument. He suggests that although *Doctor and Student* was widely received as a legal work, its main focus is the conscience of individuals and the "professional ethics" of lawyers (Williams 2017: 86–87). We revisit this question of genre in section 12.3. Whatever St German's original incentive may have been, this openness to different interpretations perhaps partly explains the continued interest in the work during the following centuries.

The early publication history of *Doctor and Student* was characterised by active reshaping of the work by St German himself. During this period, competing editions of *Doctor and Student* were issued by several printers. This was characteristic of English publishing until the 1550s when the licencing practices became increasingly regulated through the Stationers' Company and the printing of common-law books became a monopoly based on letters patent (see Feather 1991: 36–37; Baker 1999: 426, 2002: 478–481).

The first known edition of St German's *Doctor and Student* is in Latin (*Dialogus de fundamentis legum Anglie et de conscientia*, STC 21559). It was printed in 1528 by the law printer, barrister, and St German's fellow Middle Templar John Rastell (d. 1536). The first English edition, by Robert Wyer, was not a direct translation of the Latin edition but rather a reworking of the text (1530, STC 21561). The first dialogue ends in a promise to continue the discussion between the Doctor and Student, and indeed, the second dialogue was printed in English by Peter Treveris later that year (STC 21565). In 1531, the dialogues were first printed together, by Robert Redman (STC 21567). Both dialogues were also expanded by a series of additional chapters already in the 1530s, and more material was added in *A Lytell Treatise Called the "Newe Addicions"* in 1531 (STC 21563). We refer to the main components of the work as the *First Dialogue*, *Second Dialogue*, and *New Additions*. The additional chapters to the two dialogues became a fixed part of the work, but the *New Additions* treatise was only reunited with the dialogues in 1751. Figure 12.1 presents an overall view of the publication history of the work.

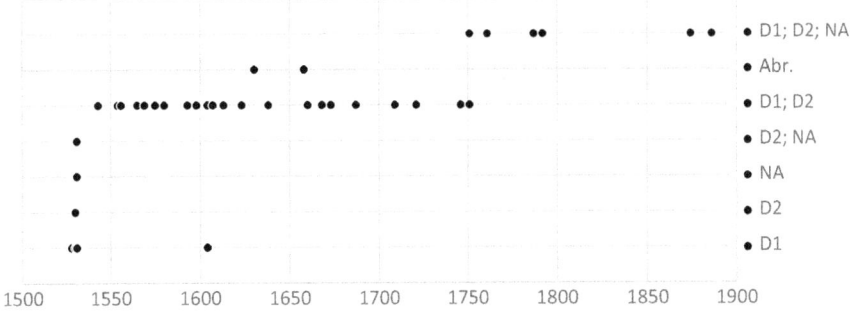

Figure 12.1: Publication history of Doctor and Student.
D1 = *First dialogue*; D2 = *Second dialogue*; NA = *New additions*; Abr. = *Abridgements*. The Latin editions are included within D1. Multiple editions produced during the same year are not represented.

To analyse the evolving paratext of *Doctor and Student*, we listed and consulted all known editions of the work on the basis of the *English Short-Title Catalogue* and secondary literature (leaving out modern scholarly editions). Our focus is on English editions, but we also comment on the Latin editions (1528, 1604). The editions contain different combinations of the components of the work as indicated in table 12.1.[1] We examined all 43 editions of the work from 1528 to 1886 (41 English, 2 Latin) available through digital archives (*Early English Books Online, Eighteenth-Century Collections Online, Google Books* and *Internet Archive*).[2] The peritextual elements analysed include title-pages, illustration,

Table 12.1: The surveyed editions of Doctor and Student sorted by major textual components.

Components	Bibliographic number (publication year)
1) *First Dialogue* only	STC 21559 (1528), 21560 (1604), 21561 [1530], 21562 [1531]
2) *Second Dialogue* only	STC 21565 (1530)
3) *New Additions* only	STC 21563 (1531), 21563.5 (1531), 21564 (1531)
4) *First Dialogue* and *Second Dialogue*	STC 21567 [1531], 21568 [1532], 21570 (1543), 21570.5 (1554), 21571 (1554/56), 21571.5 [1565/54], 21572 (1569), 21573 (1575), 21574.5 (1580), 21575 (1593), 21576 (1598), 21577 (1604), 21578 (1607), 21580 (1613), 21581 (1623), 21582 (1638), 21582.5 (1638); Wing S312 (1660), S316 (1668), S317 (1673), S317A (1673), S318[A] (1687); ESTC T78054 (1709), T108916 (1721), N2156 (1746), T114721 (1751)
5) *Second Dialogue* and *New Additions*	STC 21566 (1531)
6) All three components	ESTC T139490 (1751), T112934 (1761), N7258 (1787), N7521 (1792), two Clarke & Co editions (1874, 1886)
7) Abridgement	STC 21583 (1630); Wing S315 (1658)

---

1 Some early editions were possibly intended to be bound together; the ESTC entry for Berthelet's *New Additions* (STC 21563) notes that the volume was intended to be bound together with Wyer's edition of the *First Dialogue* (STC 21562) and Treveris's *Second Dialogue* (STC 21566).
2 The printer Stephen Sweet's catalogue (1843) records two editions of *Doctor and Student* of which we were unable to locate copies: 1813 (Latin) and 1815 (English).

typography, prologues/prefaces, tables, indexes, and footnotes. Elements with purely navigational functions (e.g. page numbers) were excluded.

The peritextual evidence suggests two main chronological phases for our analysis. We first focus on the early stages of designing *Doctor and Student* (section 12.3) before examining substantial redesigns of the work (section 12.4). While the frames for reading the work constructed through paratext have partly different emphases during these two phases, they both reflect the transhistorical tendency of promoting the text. Finally, we examine evaluative epitextual material such as book reviews to investigate the readership of *Doctor and Student* (section 12.5). The epitextual material was accessed through the *HeinOnline* legal research database and the Gale databases *American Historical Periodicals, British Library Newspapers* and *17th and 18th Century Burney Collection*.

12.3 Designing the work

During its printing history, *Doctor and Student* developed from a modular series of dialogues into a well-known work. In the earliest stages of this trajectory, new textual contents and paratextual elements were introduced as the author St German revised and expanded the work. The present section tracks the development of the paratextual framework during the sixteenth century, showing how paratext was used to construct different ideological frames, authorise new editions and entextualised material, and emphasise the unity of the work.

As mentioned above, Williams (2017) suggests that the intended primary contribution of *Doctor and Student* may have been religious rather than legal (secular). The visual features of the earliest editions show some evidence of this uncertainty or fluctuation regarding the genre. The title-pages of Wyer's *First Dialogue* (STC 21561 [1530], 21562 [1531]) contain a woodcut image of the royal arms. Treveris's title-pages for the *Second Dialogue* (STC 21565 (1530), 21566 (1531)) opt for religious imagery instead. In STC 21566, the name "Jesus" is also inserted on the title-page. The same edition contains an image of John Evangelist on Patmos and, opening the *Second Dialogue*, a woodcut of the Shield of the Trinity. Similarly, Berthelet's title-pages to the *New Additions* (STC 21563, 21563.5, and 21564, all 1531) have a woodblock compartment with religious themes. The title-pages of Redman's editions of the two dialogues (STC 21567 [1531], 21568 [1532]) again employ royal imagery – the Tudor rose and royal arms. Instead of Treveris's Shield of the Trinity, the *Second Dialogue* in STC 21568 begins with a secular cornucopia illustration. Middleton's 1543 edition (STC 21570) contains a woodcut of the English arms. The visual framing provided by Treveris and Berthelet supports Williams's reading of the work as primarily religious, while Wyer, Redman, and Middleton employ royal, secular imagery, potentially encouraging a legal reading instead. These differences may reflect printers' attempts to present the work in a way that makes their product sufficiently different from those of their competitors (cf. Bhatia 2005: 216 on "product differentiation" in advertising discourse).

The early editions contain a number of anonymous prologues, most of them covering contents and themes typical of the period. The Latin prologue (STC 21559), for example, states the topic of the work, gives the motivation for the work's publication, establishes the importance of its subject, and justifies the work's choice of language. The prologue repeats conventional themes expected of prefatory matter (Curtius 1953: 85–89; Minnis 1984: 9–39). By demonstrating familiarity with the prologue tradition, the writer conveys their educational background and establishes their authority. Conversely, the first English prologue to *Doctor and Student* (in STC 21561) differs from the traditional formula. It concentrates on denials of the edition's relationship with the Latin original, demonstrating the work's independence for example by mentioning changes made to the text. This account may simply have been intended to describe the text production process. However, it might also have pre-empted criticism resulting from a comparison of the editions and their mismatch, or encouraged potential buyers to acquire the English edition in addition to the Latin one.

The second English edition of the *First Dialogue* and the first edition of the *Second Dialogue* further develop the prefatory framing of the work. In the former, the corrections and additions to the work are prominently advertised: "Here after foloweth the fyrste Dyaloge in Englysshe [...] newly correctyd: and eft sones Enprynted: with newe addycyons" (STC 21562: a1v; on such promotional claims, see Massai 2011; Olson 2016; Varila & Peikola 2019). Although the additions to the *First Dialogue* were first published in the early 1530s, the headings of the tables of contents continued to advertise them until 1580 (STC 21574.5) by directing attention to the inclusion and visual highlighting of the "newly" added chapters in the table: "Hereafter followeth the table to the first Booke with certaine additions newly added thereto, and ouer all the chapters & questions which bee newly added, yee shall finde entituled this word Addition, both in the table, & also in the booke" (STC 21574.5: Z1r). On title-pages, the new additions were advertised until 1660 – by then, the contents had in fact been fixed for decades.

While the publishing history of *Doctor and Student* was modular in nature throughout the 1530s, Middleton's 1543 edition presents the work in a more cohesive manner. The reworked title, for the first time, accommodates both dialogues:

"The Dialogues in Englysshe/ bytwene a Doctour of dyuynyte & a Studēt in the lawes of Englāde, newly corrected and imprinted with newe addycyons" (STC 21570: A1r). Middleton's edition is also the first one in which the prologue to the *Second Dialogue* refers back to the *First Dialogue*, despite the fact that the dialogues had been printed together since the early 1530s. Finally, this was the first edition in which the tables of contents for the dialogues, which formerly accompanied the text of each dialogue, were no longer physically separated but immediately followed each other. Placing the tables in a single location at the end of the book presumably helped the reader to navigate the text more efficiently. The decisions relating to prologues and tables of contents also helped to frame the two dialogues more emphatically as a unified work. Middleton's edition thus appears to be a conscious effort to present *Doctor and Student* as a whole. This model is followed in later editions.

Richard Tottell (d. 1593) was the first to possess a patent that granted him a monopoly to print common-law books (see Baker 1999: 428–429, 2002: 479). During the forty years in which he operated under this patent Tottell's output consisted largely of reprints (Baker 2002: 480), including seven editions of *Doctor and Student*. Despite the lack of genuine competition from other printers, however, nuances of paratextual design still seem to have mattered to him. The visual design of the title-page changes in 1554 with the first of Tottell's editions (STC 21570.5), and seems to be in constant development throughout his editions of 1554–80. Tottell similarly develops the visual design and paratextual framework of other popular legal texts he reprints, such as *The exposicions of the termes of the lawes of England* (1563–1592, STC 20703.5–20708) and *A profitable booke of Master John Perkins* (1555–1593, STC 19633–19639). Tottell's last edition of *Doctor and Student* (STC 21575, 1593) slightly changes the wording of the title. The plural marker is dropped, the title now beginning "The Dialogue in English" (A1r). This change may represent a conscious effort to emphasise the unity of the work, or simply be a typographical error. This form is nevertheless adopted by the following eight editions (1593–1660). The 1593 title-page is the first to drop blackletter and only employ roman and italic type.[3] It is also the first (and for a long time the only) title-page to inform the reader of the location of the printer's shop.[4] The editions from 1598 to 1623 show further gradual modification of the title-page.

---

3 In comparison, the 1555 title-page of his *Profitable booke of Master John Perkins* (STC 19633) is mostly in blackletter, the next three (1559–1567) use italic only, and the final five (1567–1593) are mostly in roman.
4 Based on the title-page metadata in EEBO, less than 30% of the titles printed in 1593 give the location of the printer's shop.

Although *Doctor and Student* clearly becomes a staple of legal writing, regularly reprinted by successive possessors of the legal patent after Tottell (cf. Baker 2002: 481–489), Christopher St German's name does not appear on the early title-pages apart from Thomas Wight's 1604 Latin edition. This edition also adds a biographical account of St German taken from John Bale's *Scriptorum illustriu[m] maioris Brytanniae* (STC 1296 Variant) and a summary of St German's will. These new elements illustrate the entextualisation of material lifted from two completely different generic contexts (biography, will) to serve a paratextual purpose. In their new context, they lend weight to *Doctor and Student* in praising the author's piety and learning. However, they are not included in the 1604 English edition by the same printer, Wight (STC 21577). In some copies of the English editions, a reader or librarian has added St German's name on the title-page by hand in an effort to connect the work to its author. But it is only later in the printing history of the English text that the author's identity becomes a paratextual selling point.

To sum up, the paratextual strategies of promotion that characterise the first, formative phase of the textual trajectory of *Doctor and Student* laid the foundation for the longevity of the work. This was achieved, on the one hand, by framing the work as a unified whole by giving it a title that accommodated both dialogues, bringing the originally separate tables of contents for the two dialogues together in a single location in the book, and introducing cross-references between their prologues. On the other hand, readers' continuing interest in the work was sustained by drawing attention to the producers' alleged quality control by adding promotional statements on the title-page that mentioned the presence of corrections and new additions. Visual paratext was used to reinforce religious vs. secular interpretations of the work, and the title-page underwent several gradual changes as the work was reprinted.

12.4 Redesigning the work

In the seventeenth and eighteenth centuries, *Doctor and Student* underwent various redesigns. The seventeenth century witnessed a major experiment in the revamping of the work both textually and paratextually through the publication of abridged editions. In the eighteenth century, the paratextual design of *Doctor and Student* was substantively expanded and updated by the inclusion of new prefaces with new bibliographical emphasis, an account of the author, an index and a footnote apparatus.

In contrast to the ongoing paratextual redesign that characterises the trajectory of *Doctor and Student*, there was only one, short-lived experiment that involved substantive reshaping of the text of the work itself. This was the publication of abridged editions in 1630 (STC 21583) and 1658 (Wing S315). The title-page of the 1630 abridged edition names it "An Exact Abridgement of That Excellent Treatise Called Doctor and Student". The title-page contains an epigraph paraphrasing Cicero's oration *Pro Cluentio*: "Legum idcirco servi sumus, ut liberi esse possimus" [We are slaves of the law so that we may be free]. The early history of epigraphs in books has been linked to the armorial motto and inscriptions in printers' devices (Buurma 2019: 167; Fowler 2017: 34). Buurma finds that while epigraphs in early modern books are often concerned with the author rather than the text, the text-oriented epigraph becomes more common in the mid-seventeenth century. Epigraphs are never used on the title-page of the complete *Doctor and Student*. The inclusion of a text-oriented epigraph on the title-page of the 1630 abridgement, a newly designed textual product, perhaps reflects the changing function of the epigraph in guiding the reader's interpretation of the text (cf. Buurma 2019: 168).

The preface to the abridgement differs in both content and style from those discussed above. It uses rhetorical questions and repetition to defend the work in its new form, to describe its contents and to state its usefulness. Defending the project and the merits of the form was common in prefaces to legal abridgements (Rudolph 2013: 54–55). The preface asserts that "[t]he name of the Book proclaims its own esteem" and that "an Epistle to this Book, is of Courtesie, not of Necessity" (STC 21583: A4r-v). In earlier editions the main function of the preface was to state the topic of the text; here, the prologue is considered a formality. This suggests not only that the work's status and popularity were now established, but also that the editor was fully adept in exploiting the marketing value of such information.

The abridged editions contain an alphabetical index designed specifically for the abridgement. Compiling the abridgement and its index must have been a laborious task; the publisher perhaps anticipated good sales for their new product. While the production of abridged editions or adding navigational devices of this kind cannot be viewed as particularly innovative in the early seventeenth-century context, the added promotional value of such textual operations is concretely manifest in statements found on title-pages of early modern books that explicitly mention benefits associated with them. A text could be described for example as "a verie compendious abridgement" (STC 4374, 1596) or it could contain "a table of all the chiefe matters herein handled, and marginall notes very plentifull and profitable; so that it may in manner be counted a new booke in regard of these additions" (STC 6227, 1594).

Another novelty in the abridgement was abandoning the dialogic form of the work and presenting the information in an expository, declarative manner, thus changing the reading experience. Perhaps partly for this reason, the abridgement seems not to have been a commercial success and its trajectory was distinctively short in comparison to the full work. Even the "assignes of John More" themselves, responsible for the 1630 abridgement, produced two editions of the full work in 1638 (for these under-lessees of the patent holder John More, see Baker 2002: 483–484). However, remediated summaries in manuscript form were perhaps created by individual readers. For example, British Library MS Stowe 382 contains such notes on *Doctor and Student*, titled "Observations Taken from the Laws of England" (see Rudolph 2013: 54–74 for the important role of abridgements in legal training and practice in the late seventeenth and early eighteenth centuries).

The abridgement's title-page refers to the full work as "Doctor and Student" already in 1630, highlighting the established status of the work. In comparison, the title-page of the full work itself only adopts this short-title nearly a century later, in the 1721 edition by Nutt and Gosling: "Doctor and Student: Or Dialogues [...]" (ESTC T108916). The 1721 edition also introduced a number of other changes to the paratextual presentation of the work; for example, the tables of contents for the two dialogues were moved from the end of the volume into the preliminaries. The title-page advertises paratextual additions: "To which is now added an Account of the Author, and a General Table of the Principal Matters; never before printed". A new prologue precedes the *First Dialogue*. Unlike the title-page, it identifies the author, St German, and provides biographical information about him. The rest of the preface assumes a distinctly bibliographical approach to the text, comparing the Latin original to the English translation and naming St German as the translator.

The 1721 edition also introduced an alphabetical subject index to the full *Doctor and Student*. This element remained an integral constituent of the work thereafter. Given its usefulness for a reader wishing to locate a specific topic, it is perhaps surprising that this device was not introduced earlier. For example, although Tottell equipped his 1555 edition of the *Profitable booke of Master John Perkins* (STC 19633) with an alphabetical index, he never included one in his *Doctor and Student* editions. The often neglected paratextual framing potential of alphabetical indexes is highlighted by Briggs (1993: 226), who contends that, to a certain degree, indexes "as access media would have influenced and pre-determined what their users might have looked for in the text" (see also Parkes 1976).

Did the inclusion of the index reflect a new more piecemeal way of using *Doctor and Student* in the early eighteenth century, or was the purpose to make an already established mode of consulting the book more transparent and efficient? While the 1721 edition itself does not provide an answer, it may be argued that by this date the alphabetical model for organising knowledge was already deeply rooted among English legal students and lawyers through the legal commonplace book tradition. Legal commonplace books were typically small manuscript notebooks into which their compilers entered notes from their reading of yearbooks and treatises, organised under alphabetised titles (Baker 2002: 476; Rudolph 2013: 40–54). On the basis of the large number of surviving examples of these books from 1590 to 1640, Baker (2002: 476) surmises that "for a time every student must have kept one". The practice continued well into the nineteenth century, and it has been argued to have shaped legal thinking and "the ways in which lawyers defined and accessed information" (Rudolph 2013: 45). Furnishing a work like *Doctor and Student* with an index would have facilitated commonplacing by providing an alphabetised digest of its contents.

The paratextual reshaping of the 1721 edition suggests that the producers felt that the work required updating. Some parts of the visual paratext, however, remain unchanged. The text is in blackletter, a typeface common in the early days of print in England and still used for legal texts in the eighteenth century (e.g. Dane 2011: 88). It is only in the 1746 edition (ESTC N2156) that the font of the text is updated to roman, by then standard in most genres and a predecessor of modern fonts such as Times New Roman. That this typographic change was understood to have promotional value is evident from how the book was advertised as "A new Edition, printed en [sic] a Roman Letter" (*St. James's Evening Post*, Jun 4th–6th, 1747, Issue 5832). Blackletter was still employed on the title-page and for the keywords in the alphabetical index. Blackletter did not disappear from the English editions of *Doctor and Student* until the nineteenth century. Retaining the archaic font in the paratextual elements was possibly intended to evoke a sense of antiquity and, consequently, tenability – as the noun *black letter* came to denote, in law domains, "well-established, time-honoured" (OED Online).

The two 1751 editions introduced further changes in paratextual framing. An edition statement (fifteenth edition) first appears on the title-page of ESTC T114721. Another 1751 title-page (ESTC T139490) advertises the credentials of the printer Henry Lintot, "Law Printer to the King's most Excellent Majesty". The title-page declares: "The Fifteenth Edition, to which are now added. Thirteen Chapters on the Power and Jurisdiction of the Parliament, &c. omitted in all the Editions, since the Year 1531". This is the first edition after 1531 to contain both dialogues and the *New Additions*. Possibly to emphasise the antiquity and originality of the additional questions, Lintot even reproduced Berthelet's

Latin colophon from 1531.⁵ The additions were also promoted in a preface highlighting the venerable age and authority of the text. Despite its brevity, the preface not only addresses the conventional themes such as the contents of the work and its authorisation, but also provides a brief bibliographical note on the text and its previous editions. The preface ends with a recount of the motivation for the work's publication, "to preserve, or restore, any Part of the Works of valuable Writers" (ESTC T139490: A2v). The new developments in the work's paratext continue in the bibliographical vein established in the earlier eighteenth-century editions: all paratextual elements authorise the text through its antiquity, completeness, and originality, but the name of the author is not yet prominent amongst these arguments.

The next major redesign of the paratextual apparatus followed in 1787 (ESTC N7258), in an edition that was "Corrected and improved, by William Muchall, Gent.". Muchall's revised edition contains the last new prologue in our data, presumably written by the editor himself and continuing the bibliographic framing typical of the eighteenth-century editions. The prologue begins by establishing the authority of the text:

> IT is presumed no particular apology is necessary to be made for introducing to the notice of the profession a new edition of the *Doctor and Student*; a book which has been considered of the first authority, not only by the best and most admired of our legal writers, but by the courts of *Westminster-hall*. (ESTC N7258: v)

This endorsement of the work is followed by praise for dialogues as a form of instructional writing. A lengthy apology on the language of the text then follows, highlighting the growing gap between the age of the work and the contemporary audience. Muchall notes:

> Perhaps the language is not so pure as might be expected from a modern author, nor so correct as altogether to adapt itself to the taste of the curious. But this is a defect (if a defect it can be called) which should be overlooked for the intrinsic merits of the book itself. (ESTC N7258: vi)

Muchall suggests that one should "attend more to *things* than words" (ESTC N7258: vi; emphasis in original). The contents are repeatedly and explicitly praised. The preservation of the "defective" language is justified as an editorial decision motivated by respect for the work's status.

---

5 "Thomas Barthelatus regius impressor excudebat, Anno Domini MDXXXI. Cum privilegio a rege indulto." (ESTC T139490: E8r).

The 1787 edition also introduces a new category of paratext to *Doctor and Student*: footnotes. By this time, the footnote had already gained some purchase in scholarly and academic writing (Lipking 1977: 626; Frasca-Spada 2000).[6] The first footnote of the 1787 edition, attached to the start of the preface, names St German as the author, provides a brief biography and praises his legal knowledge, and identifies the first edition of *Doctor and Student* (mistakenly, 1518). The editorial decision to name the author in a footnote perhaps appears slightly curious. However, it is in line with the promotional strategies of the new, bibliographical prologues of 1721–1787: the modern footnote here functions as a space of authority (see Tribble 1993 on marginal notes and the dynamics of authority).

Another major paratextual revision in the 1787 edition was the replacing of the 1721 alphabetical index by a new one, possibly compiled by Muchall himself. All subsequent editions were equipped with this new index. The indexer omitted approximately one half of the headwords in the 1721 index and considerably reworked the contents of most entries under the headwords he retained. Presumably to answer the need to enhance the contemporary relevance of the text, some headwords were furnished with an entry that comments on their obsolescence (e.g. "*Abbots*. Abolished"). These comments do not as a rule refer to the text proper, but to the editorial footnotes that Muchall supplied for this edition. The 1787 indexer also rendered entries more concrete: they often correspond to the text in much more detail than in the 1721 index. In addition to omitting headwords and reshaping entries under the headwords he retained, the 1787 indexer added approximately 80 new headwords to the index. It is difficult to discern any clear agenda behind these additions, apart from the indexer's apparent general aim at clarity and precision to make the text more user-friendly.

The textual statement referring to Muchall as the editor is kept in the last editions in our data (ESTC N7521, 1792, 1874, and 1886). A new statement is present on the title-pages of the last two, however: "To which are added two pieces concerning suits in Chancery by subpœna". These pieces are other texts by St German, now recontextualised by bringing them into the company of the *Doctor and Student*. The last editions thus once more update *Doctor and Student* by adding more related textual content and advertising this on the title-page.

---

[6] There is conceptual overlap between the footnote and other types of notes predating print. The earliest uses of the modern footnote are usually traced to the late seventeenth or early eighteenth century (Lipking 1977; Tribble 1993: 131).

12.5 Reading the work

How might the eighteenth-century paratextual redesigns of *Doctor and Student* be best explained? To answer this question, we must consider the readership and use of the work and possible changes therein. Although *Doctor and Student* "was not a law book at all in the usual sense" (Baker 1999: 412), in the seventeenth century it was viewed as an elementary treatise ("institute") to be read early on by anyone aspiring to a career in the law. In Henry Peacham's 1639 pamphlet *A merry discourse of Meum, and Tuum, or, Mine and Thine tvvo crosse brothers*, one of the two brothers becomes an "under Clerke" for a provincial attorney. To "initiate, and bring him to knowledge", the attorney gives him "*Littleton's Tenures* in English to reade, with Doctor and Student, and such like" (STC 19510: B3v). Sir Matthew Hale's 1668 oft-cited recommendations similarly placed *Doctor and Student* among the basic readings for students of law: "First, it is convenient for a Student to spend about two or three yeares in the diligent reading of Littleton, Perkins, Doctor and Student [etc.]" (cited in Baker 2002: 502).

Legal experts' eagerness to recommend *Doctor and Student* as elementary reading seems to have waned in the course of the eighteenth century. This is suggested for example by an article published in *The Legal Observer* in 1830 that prints a series of reading tips for legal study by Hale and a few subsequent authorities. Of the five experts whose advice is cited in the article, in addition to Hale only Sir Thomas Reeve, writing probably in the 1730s, recommends *Doctor and Student*. Unlike Hale, however, Reeve advises reading it "[d]uring the second stage of study" among those "many books [that] may be brought in for variety, which will be very useful, and not interrupt the main scheme" (*The Legal Observer* 1 (4), Nov 27th, 1830: 54; for advice on legal reading in the eighteenth century, see Lemmings 2000: 136–137).[7] The lengthy reading lists reproduced in the article from three later eighteenth and early nineteenth-century legal authorities (John Dunning, Joseph Chitty and Charles Butler) no longer mention *Doctor and Student* (*The Legal Observer*, 1 (4), Nov 27th, 1830: 54–55).

The shift in emphasis may reflect the arrival in the market of new general treatments of the English law that were considered to offer superior introductory

---

[7] In 1736, the London solicitor Nathaniel Cole wrote a prescription for educating "a young Gentleman of a noble family who was intended for the Law" (cited in Lemmings 2000: 341–345). Assuming the young gentleman to have already completed the basics of the Civil Law "to furnish him with general Notions", Cole recommended reading *Doctor and Student* after Hale's *History of the Common Law* and Fortescue's *De Laudibus Leg: Anglie* (Lemmings 2000: 342). These three works, Cole noted, "are introductory and gradually let the Student into a general view of what he is to meet with afterwards" (Lemmings 2000: 342).

reading for students (for eighteenth-century English law books, see Lobban 1997; Prest 2009). Among such eighteenth-century classics were Thomas Wood's *Institute of the Laws of England* (first published in 1720, 10th ed. in 1772), which was recommended by Reeve as the first work to be read by the student, and especially William Blackstone's *Commentaries on the Laws of England* (first published in 1765–69, 10th ed. in 1787), recommended by both Dunning and Chitty (The Legal Observer, 1(4), Nov 27th, 1830: 54–55).[8] It is not impossible that the two major eighteenth-century paratextual redesigns of the *Doctor and Student* in 1721 and 1787 were to some degree prompted by the publication of these and other new competing legal works in the field.

Newspaper advertisements for Muchall's 1787 edition of the *Doctor and Student* in London and elsewhere in England echo the promotional language of the title-page by mentioning its "improved" text (e.g. *St. James's Chronicle* or the *British Evening Post*, May 26th, 1792 – May 29, 1792, Issue 4871; *Hereford Journal*, Jan 23rd, 1793, Issue 1173). A review in *The Gentleman's Magazine* indicates that the new paratextual features of this edition were also considered to be worth mentioning in a less promotional and potentially more objective context. The anonymous reviewer concludes by noting that "[t]o the present edition are added notes and references to illustrate the subject-matter, and to shew how the law has been altered by acts of parliament and judicial decisions" (*The Gentleman's Magazine*, Feb 1st, 1788, vol. 58: 145).

Despite the eighteenth-century effort invested into updating the *Doctor and Student* paratextually, the practical suitability of the work for elementary legal instruction seems to have become increasingly doubted in the first half of the nineteenth century. This attitude is encapsulated in a letter from a Mancunian reader of *Law Students' Magazine* in 1844, cited by the editors under the heading "Cheap Books for Law Students". According to the letter, legal apprentices (articled clerks) would greatly benefit from the publication of new editions of works like the *Doctor and Student* from which all the "obsolete parts" were omitted – an improvement that would make these works both readable and cheap:

> If you were to publish an edition of "Littleton's Tenures," the "Doctor and Student," and other similar standard works, omitting the obsolete parts, and showing the alterations

---

8 Wood and Blackstone (together with many other eighteenth-century law books) also feature among the titles which the young legal clerk Benjamin Smith Jr. listed as the main sources of his commonplace book compiled in the 1790s when serving as an apprentice in his father's attorney firm in Horbling, Lincolnshire. Smith's list does not mention *Doctor and Student* (see Schmidt 1996: 37, n. 28).

made in the law since the original publication of the work, you would be conferring a great boon on the articled clerk, as now those works and others of a like nature are never read, solely because they contain so much obsolete law, and give so little idea of the present state of things. Besides, the omissions would be so large that we might expect to get the "Tenures" (for example) for 3s. or 4s.

(*Law Students' Magazine* 1844–45 1 (2), Sep 1844: iv; for this and other similar magazines see McKitterick 2009: 514).

Responding to such pleas, the editors of *Law Students' Magazine* announced their plan to launch a new series called *The Law Students' Library* that was to include a new edition of *Doctor and Student* (*Law Students' Magazine* 1844–45 1 (5), Dec 1844: iv). The editors' argument as to why these old legal works still had their place in law students' reading indicates how the old-fashioned style of *Doctor and Student* could now be viewed as a pedagogical virtue that made it an engaging read to supplement the perusal of the often more monotonously written modern core textbooks like Blackstone:

If the student should feel unable to catch the full meaning of Blackstone, let him turn to the pages of the "Doctor and Student" (also in the form of a dialogue), where he is pretty nearly sure to meet with the required explanations, and that, too, clothed in so quaint a language as must needs interest him, or at least form a relief to the flowing and smooth, and sometimes cloying, style of Blackstone.

(*Law Students' Magazine* 1844–45 1 (8), Mar 1845: 206).

The role envisaged for *Doctor and Student* here resembles that suggested for it by Reeve in the 1730s as one of the books that "may be brought in for variety". Despite the announced plan, *The Law Students' Library* never seems to have published *Doctor and Student*.

The book announcements in periodicals for the 1874 Clarke & Co Cincinnati edition show how the perception of *Doctor and Student* had by then firmly moved from required core reading for the law student to a "legal classic" that would appeal to a broad range of readers, also outside the legal profession. The *Legal Gazette* expected the new edition of "their old friend" to be welcomed by "[e]very lover of law literature, every real student in law, every practitioner in our courts" (*The Legal Gazette* 6, Mar 27th, 1874: 100). The writer of the announcement was especially pleased about the packaging of the book "in a nice dress", describing it as "undoubtedly the finest ever published" (*The Legal Gazette* 6, Mar 27th, 1874: 100). Another announcement emphasised the high aesthetic quality of the new edition even more emphatically, stating that "cultured laymen as well as lawyers will be glad of the opportunity to place it in its present attractive form on their book-shelves" (*The American Booksellers Guide* 6 (5), May 1st, 1874: 158). Reading or using the work seems of secondary or no importance.

This brief survey of the (anticipated) readership of *Doctor and Student* from the seventeenth to the nineteenth century suggests that there was a gradual transformation in the perception of the work from a prescribed elementary "textbook" for the law student to a supplementary work of historical interest, and eventually perhaps more an item to be owned by a cultured book owner than a text to be read. Among the changes that took place in paratextual elements of *Doctor and Student* in this period, especially the increased historically oriented bibliographical framing of the work throughout the eighteenth century could be associated with this gradual change in its anticipated readership.

It seems less clear, however, whether the increased paratextual guidance of the reader through indexes and footnotes in the eighteenth century also reflects the gradual widening of the readership of *Doctor and Student*. On the one hand, changes that help the reader to navigate the book and comprehend the work could plausibly indicate that book producers who introduced them were thinking of readers in need of more explicit and detailed paratextual guidance. Publications like *The Gentlemen's Magazine* in which information about the "improved" editions was announced had a wide readership (Feather 1985: 46–47), and law books were also commonly used by "gentlemen–amateurs" in addition to lawyers (Feather 1985: 35). On the other hand, book producers' laborious addition of indexes and footnotes in new editions could also be interpreted as a move to enhance the credibility and usability of the work among professionals. The association of footnotes with scholarly writing and the possible link between indexes and commonplacing discussed in section 12.4 render some support to this interpretation. In either case, the increased paratextual sophistication witnessed in eighteenth-century editions of *Doctor and Student* suggests that the virtually unchanging sixteenth-century text was becoming increasingly demanding for new generations of readers both conceptually and linguistically, and therefore required stronger paratextual measures of promotion.

12.6 Conclusion

Our analysis of the textual trajectories of *Doctor and Student* from the early sixteenth to the late nineteenth century shows how the book producers' regular redesigning of the paratextual apparatus served to present the work for new generations of readers. While the text itself undergoes very few changes after the 1530s, the paratextual apparatus is revised multiple times between 1528 and 1886. Although *Doctor and Student* evidently continues to be used by those in the legal profession throughout the period surveyed, layers of new and revised paratext subtly recontextualise the work by promoting it within new interpretative, commercial, and navigational frames.

In the sixteenth century, verbal and visual paratext is used for example to induce religious vs. secular interpretations of the text, metadiscursively authorise new editions, entextualise material lifted from other genres, and emphasise the unity of the work. The abridged editions of the seventeenth century present the work in an entirely new way. Despite their considerable investment into paratextual promotion, however, this trajectory is notably short in comparison to that of the unabridged version. In the eighteenth and nineteenth centuries, the paratextual apparatus was used to reframe the text and highlight its antiquity and value. In the final editions studied, the language of the work appears dated, but the editors turn this potential flaw into a virtue in their paratextual frame.

Connecting the use of paratextual framing to what we see as a transhistorical umbrella of promotional strategies helped us to better discern the major trends that characterise the textual trajectories and travel of *Doctor and Student*. While our research reported in this chapter has focused on the printed medium, it would be possible, and indeed desirable, to conduct a similar study on works whose trajectories include textual artifacts of manuscript, print, and digital media alike.

References

Baker, John H. 1999. The books of the common law. In Lotte Hellinga & Joseph B. Trapp (eds.), *The Cambridge history of the book in Britain, vol. 3: 1400–1557*, 411–432. Cambridge, UK: Cambridge University Press.

Baker, John H. 2002. English law books and legal publishing. In John Barnard & Donald F. McKenzie (eds.), *The Cambridge history of the book in Britain, vol. 4: 1557–1695*, 474–503. Cambridge, UK: Cambridge University Press.

Bauman, Richard & Charles L. Briggs. 1990. Poetics and performance as critical perspectives on language and social life. *Annual Review of Anthropology* 19. 59–88.

Behrens, Georg. 1998. An early Tudor debate on the relation between law and equity. *Journal of Legal History* 19 (2). 143–161.

Bhatia, Vijay K. 2005. Generic patterns in promotional discourse. In Helena Halmari & Tuija Virtanen (eds.), *Persuasion across genres: A linguistic approach*, 213–225. Amsterdam: John Benjamins.

Birke, Dorothy & Birte Christ. 2013. Paratext and digitized narrative: Mapping the field. *Narrative* 21 (1). 65–87.

Blommaert, Jan. 2005. *Discourse: A critical introduction*. Cambridge, UK: Cambridge University Press.

Briggs, Charles F. 1993. Late medieval texts and *tabulae*: The case of Giles of Rome, *De regimine principum*. *Manuscripta* 37 (3). 253–275.
Buurma, Rachel Sagner. 2019. Epigraphs. In Dennis Duncan & Adam Smyth (eds.), *Book parts*, 165–175. Oxford: Oxford University Press.
Chartier, Roger. 2014. *The author's hand and the printer's mind*. Transl. Lydia G. Cochrane. Cambridge, UK: Polity Press.
Ciotti, Giovanni & Hang Lin. 2016. Preface. In Giovanni Ciotti & Hang Lin (eds.), *Tracing manuscripts in time and space through paratexts*, vii–xii. Berlin: De Gruyter Mouton.
Curtius, Ernst Robert. 1953. *European literature and the Latin middle ages*. Transl. Willard R. Trask. Princeton: Princeton University Press.
Dane, Joseph A. 2011. *Out of sorts: On typography and print culture*. Philadelphia: University of Pennsylvania Press.
Endicott, Timothy A. O. 1989. The conscience of the king: Christopher St. German and Thomas More and the development of English equity. *University of Toronto Faculty of Law Review* 47 (2). 549–570.
Feather, John. 1985. *The provincial book trade in eighteenth-century England*. Cambridge, UK: Cambridge University Press.
Feather, John. 1991. *A history of British publishing*. Abingdon: Routledge.
Fowler, Alastair. 2017. *The mind of the book: Pictorial title-pages*. Oxford: Oxford University Press.
Frasca-Spada, Marina. 2000. Compendious footnotes. In Marina Frasca-Spada & Nick Jardine (eds.), *Books and sciences in history*, 171–189. Cambridge, UK: Cambridge University Press.
Genette, Gérard. 1997. *Paratexts: Thresholds of interpretation*. Transl. by Jane E. Lewin. Cambridge, UK: Cambridge University Press.
Helmholz, Richard H. 2003. Christopher St. German and the law of custom. *The University of Chicago Law Review* 70 (1). 129–139.
Lemmings, David. 2000. *Professors of the law: Barristers and English legal culture in the eighteenth century*. Oxford: Oxford University Press.
Lipking, Lawrence. 1977. The marginal gloss. *Critical Inquiry* 3 (4). 609–655.
Lobban, Michael. 1997. The English legal treatise and English law in the eighteenth century. In Serge Dauchy, Jos Monballyu & Alain Wijffels (eds.), *Auctoritates: Law making and its authors*, 69–88. Brussels: Koninklijke Academie voor Wetenschappen, Letteren en Schone Kunsten van België.
McKitterick, David. 2009. Publishing for trades and professions. In David McKitterick (ed.), *The Cambridge history of the book in Britain, vol. 6: 1830–1914*, 500–530. Cambridge, UK: Cambridge University Press.
Massai, Sonia. 2011. Editorial pledges in Early Modern dramatic paratexts. In Helen Smith & Louise Wilson (eds.), *Renaissance paratexts*, 91–106. Cambridge, UK: Cambridge University Press.
Maybin, Janet. 2017. Textual trajectories: Theoretical roots and institutional consequences. *Text & Talk* 37 (4). 415–435.
Minnis, Alastair J. 1984. *Medieval theory of authorship: Scholastic literary attitudes in the later middle ages*. London: Scolar Press.
OED Online. Oxford: Oxford University Press. http://www.oed.com (accessed 14 March 2019).

Olson, Jonathan R. 2016. "Newly amended and much enlarged": Claims of novelty and enlargement on the title pages of reprints in the Early Modern English book trade. *History of European Ideas* 42 (5). 618–628.

Parkes, Malcolm B. 1976. The influence of the concepts of *ordinatio* and *compilatio* on the development of the book. In Jonathan G. Alexander & Margaret T. Gibson (eds.), *Medieval learning and literature: Essays presented to Richard William Hunt*, 115–141. Oxford: Clarendon Press.

Prest, Wilfrid. 2009. Law books. In Michael F. Suarez and Michael L. Turner (eds.), *The Cambridge history of the book in Britain, vol. 5: 1695–1830*, 791–806. Cambridge, UK: Cambridge University Press.

Rock, Frances, Chris Heffer & John Conley. 2013. Textual travel in legal–lay communication. In Chris Heffer, Frances Rock & John Conley (eds.), *Legal-lay communication: Textual travels in the law*, 3–32. Oxford: Oxford University Press.

Rudolph, Julia. 2013. *Common law and Enlightenment in England, 1689–1750*. Woodbridge: The Boydell Press.

Ruokkeinen, Sirkku & Aino Liira. 2017 [2019]. Material approaches to exploring the borders of paratext. *Textual Cultures* 11 (1–2). 106–129.

Schmidt, Albert J. 1996. A career in the law: Clerkship and the profession in late eighteenth-century Lincolnshire. *Lincolnshire History and Archaeology* 31. 29–41.

Silva, Andie. 2016. Mediated technologies: Locating non-authorial agency in printed and digital texts. *History of European Ideas* 42 (5). 607–617.

Sweet, S. 1843. *A catalogue of modern law books, including the Irish and Scotch, with all the reporters from the earliest period*. London: S. Sweet.

Tether, Leah. 2017. *Publishing the Grail in medieval and renaissance France*. Cambridge, UK: D. S. Brewer.

Tribble, Evelyn. 1993. *Margins and marginality: The printed page in early modern England*. Charlottesville: University Press of Virginia.

Varila, Mari-Liisa & Matti Peikola. 2019. Promotional conventions on English title-pages to 1550: Modifiers of time, scope, and quality. In Birte Bös & Claudia Claridge (eds.), *Norms and conventions in the history of English*, 73–97. Amsterdam: John Benjamins.

Williams, Ian. 2017. Christopher St German: Religion, conscience and law in reformation England. In Mark Hill & R. H. Helmholz (eds.), *Great Christian jurists in English history*, 69–91. Cambridge, UK: Cambridge University Press.

Claudia Claridge
13 Reflections on visuality and textual reception

Once a text is fixed on a page, it looks like a very static object. But this obscures the fact that any given text represents only a kind of still in the ongoing film of textual and genre transformations. Aspects like reader focus and/or reader response, visual and paratextual aspects of written text, as well as types of intertextuality are prone to be involved in or affected by such transformations. All of these have gained increasing importance in recent (historical) linguistics and are also paid attention to in the papers in this section. The adaptation of texts to new contexts and readerships can have various effects, namely as changes in linguistic form and content as shown by Kopaczyk, or as changes in the paratextual embedding in the case of Varila et al.'s data. Intertextuality also appears in different guises, as in versions or adaptations of one and the same text (Kopaczyk, Rutkowska), and through paratext, authors interacting with the same basic text (Varila et al.), thus all supplying multiple voices or perspectives within and on the text. These aspects hang together and may be combined in the question how the intertextuality and, more generally, interactivity of written texts is expressed or enhanced by visual and paratextual features across time.

Holly (2013: 5–6) posed the question whether visuality should be included as a central criterion for textuality and answered it in the affirmative at least as far as genre is concerned. The visual and paratextual features of a text contribute to realising and signalling its generic functions, partly even independently of the linguistic elements (e.g. the shape of a poem makes it recognizable as such without reading it). We may link these aspects with Beaugrande and Dressler's (1981: 11) regulative principles of efficiency, effectiveness, and appropriateness seen from the point of view of the reader. Efficiency arises if a text does not make high demands on processing, i.e. is user-friendly. A text is effective if it is optimally geared towards the achievement of the textual aim(s), i.e. primarily meets authorial intentions. The ratio between efficiency and effectiveness in relation to a specific communicative context results in the degree of appropriateness of a text.

Claudia Claridge, Universität Augsburg, Englische Sprachwissenschaft, Augsburg,
e-mail: claudia.claridge@philhist.uni-augsburg.de

https://doi.org/10.1515/9783110670837-017

Let us use two very different historical examples, published trial proceedings and history writing, to look at things in more detail. Both types of text are highly intertextual, the former with regard to the actual courtroom interaction with its many voices, and the latter with respect to historical documents and scholarly literature. How is this interaction with other texts and authors highlighted and made accessible to the reader, so that they in turn may interact with the immediate *and* the mediated texts? While the trial proceedings work mainly via different linguistic choices, the visual aspects come more to the fore in the history texts.

The Proceedings of the Old Bailey, 1674–1913 (Hitchcock et al. 2012), apart from generally omitting large chunks of especially monologic, speech-like material by lawyers and judges, have essentially three styles of representing the spoken, mostly dialogic interaction of the late Modern English courtroom, namely (i) narrative summary (e.g. trial t16740429-5), (ii) question-answer dialogue produced as direct speech and with speakers usually on alternating lines (e.g. t18500506-922),[1] and (iii) answers only, rephrased for coherence (e.g. t17750531-1). Styles (i) and (iii) help to produce a shorter text, with perhaps some fewer redundancies than in the trial itself, such as linguistic or content repetition. Brevity may help reader comprehension, and thus be efficient (in Beaugrande and Dressler's terms), but at the price of the wholesale transformation of the original discourse. The interactive and in particular antagonistic nature of legal discourse is drastically reduced or removed completely in these two styles; in addition, one of them, (iii), also gives more prominence to lay, everyday speech than to the interplay between professional and lay voices. The text is thus transformed more into a crime narrative, such as found in the press, than a record of the trial itself. The effectiveness of these two styles must be rated low with respect to making the trial interaction accessible, but somewhat higher if simply informativeness was the aim. Style (ii), which in contrast certainly makes the impression of a more faithful reproduction of the antagonistic interaction, brings with it a touch of fictionality: as readers will have been familiar with this style from drama especially and also from novels, generic expectations triggered by form may have carried over. While there is no established way of calculating the efficiency/effectiveness ratio, it may be assumed to be fairly good for this style (ii): it patterns closely like the most familiar discourse form, everyday conversation, and thus is easy to read, while at

---

[1] This style seems to be the default in modern trial transcripts, see for example the Simpson trial (https://simpson.walraven.org/) or the Avery murder trial (http://www.stevenaverycase.org/).

the same time it is more informative about the courtroom interactions and topics than the other two styles. The reader thus gets a more intimate insight into the mediated text and context than in the other two styles. Nevertheless, due to the visual similarity of drama and trial record (and also the omission of more clearly legal segments such as the judge's summing up) the entertainment factor of the text is enhanced, which may not be called fully appropriate to the original text/context. The entertainment aim was in line with the purpose of the early proceedings, however, so that there was also no paratext accompaniment that would counteract this tendency.

My second example, history writing, has always relied on exterior discourse, first of the oral, later also the written kind, and made reference to relevant authors and works in the running text. With the advent of print and the increasing professionalization of historiography, paratextual and visual elements become more important for highlighting this aspect. Marginalia, footnotes, prefaces, and font or size changes now serve to point outside the text, even if often in a fairly imprecise manner. Holinshed's sixteenth-century chronicles, for example, give a list of authors the work is based on before the table of contents and provide author names in marginalia near an otherwise unmarked (linguistically or visually) case of textual import. However, this and the highlighting by font change of (author) names, important/technical terms, and longer quotes makes it possible for the reader to spot intertextual passages quickly (Claridge forthcoming). These practices show change over time. From about 1700 onwards, footnotes become the prime locus for intertextual engagement, letting the reader share in intellectual debates (Claridge & Wagner forthcoming). Footnotes could be numerous and they could also be lengthy. Potential drawbacks of the above practices are pages that could become overloaded by visual features and by the presence of many paratexts on the page. In particular the creation of non-linear text (main text and various annotations) will interrupt the flow of the reader, who needs to constantly switch back and forth between the main running text and subordinated small texts. Therefore, efficiency must be rated as low in these cases, as the text processing is rather demanding. In terms of effectiveness, however, it is exactly these features that contribute to the generic aims. The highlighting of place, time, and persons by font or in the margins singles out precisely the main "ingredients" of historical events. The link to other texts and authors in marginal paratexts makes transparent the way history writing is produced in the first place. It gives insights into the mental world of historians and the discussion among them, and it also allows the readers to access the texts mentioned themselves and thus to partake more fully of the interaction and intertextuality within historiography. Even if readers did not read the paratexts (thus boosting efficiency of the reading process), the page layout would still signal the overall generic appropriateness of the text through its visual setting within the interacting community of historical voices – as also demonstrated by the findings of the other chapters in this section of the volume.

What these two examples show is that visual features – alone or in combination with verbal features – may indeed adequately reflect underlying contexts, namely the to-and-fro interaction in court as well as the virtual discursive community of scholars. The higher the complexity and abstractness of the interaction, the more efficiency may be impeded. The link between efficiency and effectiveness is not direct, however, but mediated by generic considerations. Thus, the trial proceedings seem less effective than the historical chronicles. How such aspects develop in genre evolution across time is clearly in need of further research.

References

Beaugrande, Robert de & Wolfgang Dressler. 1981. *Introduction to text linguistics*. London: Longman.

Claridge, Claudia. Forthcoming. Discourse representation in Early Modern English historiography. In Peter Grund & Terry Walker (eds.), *Speech representation in the history of English*, Oxford: Oxford University Press.

Claridge, Claudia & Sebastian Wagner. Forthcoming. The footnote in historiographical writing. In Birte Bös & Matti Peikola (eds.), *The dynamics of text and framing phenomena in the history of English*, Amsterdam: John Benjamins.

Hitchcock, Tim, Robert Shoemaker, Clive Emsley, Sharon Howard & Jamie McLaughlin, *The Old Bailey Proceedings Online, 1674–1913*. www.oldbaileyonline.org, version 7.0, 24 March 2012 (accessed 17 July 2019).

Holly, Werner. 2013. Textualität-Visualität. *Zeitschrift für Germanistische Linguistik* 41 (1). 1–7.

Section 4: **New to Old**

Introduction to new to old

The final section explores the methodological and analytical applications of a transhistoricizing approach to message and media. The four chapters consider, in different ways, the insights that can be obtained through the contrastive application of the new to the old. They therefore engage with the issues raised in the first section of the volume concerning the novelty of digital language practices and the associated need for new theories. Here, the four case studies illustrate the potential of making connections between the digital and pre-digital datasets, interpretative frameworks and methodologies, as well as indicating some potential directions for transhistorical language research: a way of exploring the degree of continuity in message and medium, and the meanings that derive from, and arise out of, such consistencies as well as disunities.

In the first chapter, Colette Moore considers how present-day frameworks for information design and information structure, as developed within the fields of digital humanities and linguistics respectively, can offer a coherent and relevant approach for the analysis of historical literature. Moore focusses on the Middle English chronicle *Brut* as a case study to show how connections between new and old can be bridged through an analytic approach and, via her choice to combine two conventionally distinct frameworks, to bring out the relationship between sentence structure and the visual organisation of the page as understood within its medieval context. The analysis foregrounds the connections between past and present textual practices, and therefore the potentially ahistorical facets of human communication.

A similar argument is presented in Riki Thompson and Matt Collins' chapter, which undertakes a broader comparative analysis of past and present linguistic and visual practices in expository text types. Drawing on corpora of US digital news-sites and Middle English manuscripts at the British Library, the authors highlight the similar strategies in meaning-making between manuscript and digital texts, raising the possibility that print, rather than being the natural configuration of textual stability, permanence and single-author provenance, is in fact an interruption to the usual state of play of a more fluid, collaborative written communication.

In her chapter, Martine van Driel provides a synchronic snapshot of two twenty-first century adjacent technologies that undertake the same communicative objectives: the communication of news. Her interest in live blogs and older news media lies in how readers engage with different practices of quotation as sources of new information, finding that the tweets embedded into live blogs provoke a more positive reaction than traditional news reporting techniques. The chapter draws on the advantages of working with contemporary data – for which the intended readers are still alive and able to provide empirical evidence – whilst indicating the importance of recognising the transitional impact of technology within a synchronic timeframe.

The final chapter, written by Emma Moreton and Chris Culy, looks at how digital methodologies for data curation and analysis can be applied to historical (pre-digital) texts, helping to diversify the kinds of materials traditionally considered within humanities scholarship. Their focus is nineteenth-century emigrant correspondence sent between Ireland and America. The case study highlights the potential for digitization to provide new perspectives, showing how the linguistic overlaps with the historical and the social in tracing topics and themes of the migrant letter-writers, and their strategies for maintaining familial relationships through a textual object. The authors argue that wider application of the digital, corpus-based approach will allow for a more coherent perspective on migrant experiences, and their communicative practices, over time.

The relationship between the present and the past is foregrounded throughout this book, but particularly so in this section, in which the methodological approach and/or empirical evidence of the present-day is applied to or compared with past artefacts of verbal (and visual) meanings. Elizabetta Adami's reflection highlights the interpretative potential of distant and contrastive datasets, as a means of seeing what is truly new about a practice and the interactions that practice has with its predecessors, in order to develop appropriate analytical frameworks. A transhistorical perspective does not necessarily have to take digital media as its data source; as these chapters show, it can profitably encompass a range of ways of reappraising language practices of one period through a recognition of their connections and continuities with those of another.

Colette Moore
14 Information design and information structure in the Middle English prose *Brut*

14.1 Introduction

The "new media" of the digital era are no longer quite new. We continue to use the term, though, and, indeed, continue to experience digital and electronic texts as new because many long-established registers of written language retain features and conventions derived from print media. Users, therefore, are still continuing to experience the greater flexibility in visual, grammatical, and paratextual features of electronic texts as culturally novel. The sensation of freshness is a relational one, built of familiarity with the genre-specific conventions of print and assumptions based upon those conventions (Lister et al. 2009). New(ish) media, then, draw upon a range of possibilities for their organization and presentation that appear quite flexible and liberating to users who have developed their expectations around print conventions.

Before the development and spread of print in the Early Modern period, however, the linguistic structure of late Middle English and the visual design of the manuscript page in a pre-print era also offered a different range of possibilities and constraints for texts (see Kopaczyk, this volume). Scholars have pointed out many ways in which texts from earlier periods share features with texts from digital media (Brantley 2013; Guillory 2010; see Szpiech 2014; Thompson & Collins, this volume). Some criteria shared by both include fluidity and openness; non-linearity; interaction of text, image, and sound; reception; integrity and scalability of information; and creation of an open text (Kiss et al. 2013). This chapter draws upon the present-day linguistic field of information structure and the digital humanities field of information design to consider the Middle English prose *Brut*, the historical chronicle of England from the late Middle Ages, as an illustrative text of old "new media". Information structure and information design are not typically understood to be related, since they come from different disciplines, but this research posits that the two can be methodologically combined and applied transhistorically to illuminate the organization of the premodern manuscript. The prose *Brut* makes a good case

---

Colette Moore, University of Washington, Department of English, Seattle, WA,
e-mail: cvmoore@uw.edu

study because it appears to have been a popular work by medieval standards — we have more surviving manuscripts of the *Brut* than of any other Middle English text except the Wycliffite Bible — and it exemplifies organizational and textual features that characterize digital media. This chapter will first introduce frameworks of analysis from information studies and then move on to apply these to the prose *Brut*. This provides a new, transhistorical methodology for reading the *Brut*: although many of the insights about manuscript layout are not novel, the coexamination of the layout with new consideration of the sentence structure – as developed for present-day textual organization – advances our thinking about both. Further, the analysis presents a map for how information structure and information design can be fruitfully employed together. Combining these analytic categories from two different fields and using these contemporary terminologies helps us to see the interrelations of organizational structures: the ways that *Brut* and other early works are organized both by the page and by the words themselves.

14.2 Information structure and information design

Information studies (or informatics or information science) is the name for a collection of approaches to and perspectives on how information is analyzed, organized, classified, processed, and disseminated. If *data* is the base level of observation, research, gathering and discovery, then *information* is the next level up: the presentation and organization of these data, according to a schema by Shedroff (1999: 271). In this model, *knowledge* is the next level of integration, being made from constructed discourses of information, and *wisdom* is still another level of understanding: evaluation, interpretation, and contemplation. The field of information studies is a recent designation, though many of its approaches and questions have a long history. Although the boundaries of inquiry for the area are not always clear, the field incorporates methodology and questions from computer science, library science, telecommunications, law, cognitive science, and other disciplines. It also has many areas of overlap with textual studies, the history of reading, linguistics, and digital humanities studies and it is these connections that are the most relevant for this research.

As one kind of information analysis, information structure examines the presentation and organization of information in the sentence. Information structure comes from linguistics; it is part of the study of the interface of syntax and pragmatics in language. It examines several kinds of questions: which information is assumed to be given and which new? What is the central thing being talked about (topic) and what is the comment about that? How does the sentence focus our attention on different aspects? (Lambrecht 1994; Ward, Birner & Huddleston 2002; Ward & Birner 2004; Erteschik-Shir 2007). There have not been many studies of the information structure of historical texts, but there is one principal collection by Meurman-Solin, López-Couso and Los (2012). The volume sets out the challenges of examining material from earlier periods for which development of written styles as opposed to spoken ones might confuse the evidence. It can also be a little more difficult to discern strategies of marking information as given vs. new in historical material, and it can be challenging to disentangle patterns in an adequate way when syntactic variation can present as options rather than absolutes (Meurman-Solin, López-Couso & Los 2012: 10–12). Nevertheless, it is important to be aware that the linguistic constraints of information structure influence scribal and authorial choices in medieval manuscripts, as is also the case in present-day texts.

While information structure examines sentence construction, information design deals with the presentation of information in a visual way. It is part of the study of visual layout, and examines questions about how ideas are represented for ease of understanding, how spatial presentation affects interpretation, how to maximize clarity in arrangement, and how texts are related to one another. The field of information design is founded on the principle that systematic arrangement of communication channels and tokens can increase the understanding of people participating in a given discourse (Jacobson 1999: 4). Scholars of graphics and visual semiology have investigated the graphic principles of visual sign systems (Bertin 1983; Saint-Martin 1990; Horn 1998; Malamed 2009) and proposed rubrics for considering their order. Drucker (2014), for example, offers central principles of graphical analysis, described as follows: *the rationalization of a surface* is how areas and spaces are set apart in order for them to signify meaning; *the distinction between figure and ground* marks the elements of related shared spaces in a graphical field, foregrounding and backgrounding aspects of the visual space; and *the delimitation of the domain of visual elements so that they function as a relational system* indicates how aspects of the layout are framed and understood in relation to a shared reference (Drucker 2014: 71). For Drucker, other graphical elements and variables of spatial organization derive from these. Another central focus of information design is how users experience or move through a space, a topic called *wayfinding* (Katz 2012: 152–187). Wayfinding was coined to talk about built environments (Lynch 1960), but extended to analyze graphical interface ("Information Design"), in, for example, the hierarchies of font sizes and choices, color grading, and image placement (described for sample websites like the Chronicle of Higher Education site in *Wayfinding in Web Design*).

Although tools from information structure and information design have not been used together, nor have they been transhistorically applied as such to premodern works, this research finds that they are useful for analyzing the presentation of information on the medieval page: the way that words and layout work together to organize written language.

14.3 The Middle English *Brut* Chronicle

The *Brut* Chronicle, also known as the Prose *Brut* to distinguish it from Layamon's *Brut* in verse, is the name for the chronicle history of Britain that survives in more than 240 total manuscripts in the three major literary languages of medieval Britain. The work is often untitled in its manuscripts, but has been called the *Brut* because the texts typically begin with a narrative of the founding of Britain by Brutus of Troy (great-grandson of Aeneas). Medieval history writing is unlike modern genres of historical study in being more narrative-based and more teleological (Claridge 2017: 7–8), and examination of the *Brut* manuscripts indicates characteristic tropes of the genre of the chronicle history.

The first versions of the text, written in the thirteenth century, were in Anglo-Norman and were based on Geoffrey of Monmouth's *Historia regum Britanniae*. The Middle English versions start to appear after this; there are nearly 180 surviving manuscripts containing the work, more than any other work in English before 1500 except the Wycliffite Bible (Kennedy 1989: 2598, 2629; Marx & Radulescu 2006: xiii).

The *Brut* manuscripts make a good case study for information structure and design because some of their features seem less analogous to the conventions of print than they do to more recent modes in electronic publication (see Thompson & Collins, this volume, for a discussion of similar properties in medieval manuscript and online publications). These parallels include textual instability, collective authorship, a higher degree of acceptable variation, orthographic creativity, flexibility in punctuation, and unfamiliar practices for negotiating the genre of a historical text. This section will examine the features of textual transmission in order to prepare the way for considering elements of the information structure and design as they shape the features and construction of the page.

14.3.1 Textual instability

The consistency of the process of printing results in what superficially appears to be a stable product: a single mass-produced version of a work. This stability is a facade, of course, as textual scholars have demonstrated, particularly when applied to earlier printed texts: works come in many editions, sometimes contradictory, and the singular text is often a constructed idea rather than an innate feature of literary production (e.g. McGann 1991; McKenzie 2002; Kopaczyk, this volume). And yet, the revelatory findings of these textual scholars were noteworthy precisely because the medium has become so relatively stable; centuries of production of printed materials have resulted in conventions and economies of print consistency. With caveats, and despite the instability of some famous literary examples (e.g. Joyce's *Ulysses*, the poems of Emily Dickinson), most recent printed works do present a relative level of stability: a constancy of identity that is even more apparent when contrasted with the plasticity of web-based texts.

Digital textuality, by contrast, might be better described by the *panta rhei* principle ("everything flows"), since it is fluid, changeable, and under continual revision (e.g. Tyrkkö 2007). And medieval manuscripts are a little more like this. Certainly, not all digital texts are equally plastic; a Wikipedia page might be subject to continuing revision whereas an eBook might be released once and not changed. Similarly, medieval texts are variable: a chronicle or a catalog might invite continuing revision since these are open-ended works whereas a translation of Boethius's *Consolation of Philosophy* might have more obvious closure. Some texts that might seem complete, though, turn out to be less so – manuscripts of saints' lives might add additions or revisions from other manuscripts, for example, and even a poetic work like the *Canterbury Tales* is characterized by variation in manuscripts: some unfinished tales are completed by scribes, and some get included from different sources.

The prose *Brut*, for its part, is not remotely a stable text (Marx 2006: 54). To call it *a* text, in fact, represents the triumph of optimism over reality, given that the versions of the text are so different from one another. This is not unusual for works that survive in multiple medieval manuscripts, of course, as A. Taylor (2002: 16) remarks: "only a few novels or poems of the last two centuries would approach the degree of fluidity … that is the norm for vernacular texts in the Middle Ages". Scholars have carefully mapped out textual connections and stemmata for some medieval literary works with multiple versions: consider the detailed textual rescensions of the A, B, C (and sometimes Z) variations of the manuscripts of *Piers Plowman* or the fact that it was considered reasonable even in the nineteenth century to print an edition of Chaucer's *Canterbury Tales* which contained full versions from six different manuscripts. There are some clusters of manuscripts of the prose *Brut* which may have been created at one time; Mooney and Matheson (2003) propose that the AV:1419B manuscripts were produced by a common workshop. The fullest description of the *Brut*'s textual tradition is provided by Matheson (1998), though, and it is apparent that the network of texts that comprises "the Brut" is quite a tangled web. Copies were made at different times by many different scribes and the variations can be as small as a changed spelling of a single word or as large as added or removed sections. Changes can be intentional (respelling a word to reflect a regional dialect) or inadvertent (miscopying a word, potentially changing its meaning). Even in its disparate traditions of copying and additions the text is not consistently inconsistent. As Wakelin (2014: 51) suggests, within the divisions of particular copied sections, the manuscripts are often fairly faithful to previous copied versions, providing some consistency in particular portions of the text. The result is a collection of manuscripts which share many general perspectives, chunks of content, and some elements of information structure and design, but were under continual revision during their period of production and contain significant differences. There is a sense, therefore, in which every manuscript of the *Brut* presents a unique work through its variations in structure, design, and interpretation.

14.3.2 Collective construction

Print culture has been accompanied by an auctor model of authorship: the iconic image of an author working alone at a writing desk undergirds many of our assumptions about composition. The notion of individual authorship is not a necessary condition of print culture, of course, and certainly does not characterize all printed works. Yet, the emergence of the figure of the author was facilitated by the medium and the publication conventions of print, so the two are not unconnected either. The directions of correlation are perhaps analogous to the question of textual stability: the medium of print does not impose an auctor model for authorship or an expectation of textual stability and for the first period of printed works it does not result in either one. Yet, as the auctor model and the expectation of relative textual stability emerged, they built upon conventions and economies of print culture (e.g. Loewenstein 2002).

By comparison, then, present-day internet texts can feel decentered or depersonalized, since many are written collectively, by several or by many (and sometimes even anonymous in the case of crowd-sourced resources like Wikipedia) contributors. This lack of authorship credit particularly characterizes large crowd-sourced constructions, but it applies to many other internet documents as well. In this respect, also, many medieval texts share features with texts from electronic media.

Some scholarship on medieval authorship has promoted it as centrally collaborative, in view of the collection of authors, scribes, compositors, and book binders that were involved in manuscript book production (see Lunsford & Ede 1990: 76–87; Woodmansee 1997; Bryan 1999). This perspective has been tempered and treated in more nuanced ways more recently (Gillespie 2006: 9); the function of the author as an auctor that organizes and grounds the literary project does seem to characterize the presentation of many medieval works, seen clearly in the marketing of Chaucer and the Chaucerians. As a narrative of national history, the prose *Brut* text is not the same kind of work, however, and the invocation of authority in the work relies more upon the material than upon the creator; in other words, the force of the text seems to draw less upon the authority of an inspired *auctor*/composer than upon the authority of the genealogy of kingship and nationhood.

The *Brut* does not represent the primary work of one person, but rather it presents work that was put together through the combined influence of "many diu*er*se good men", as one manuscript describes (MS Hunter 83, f15r, cited in Wakelin 2014: 51). This group includes writers, translators, and compilers, all of whom exercised creative influence over their texts, but most of whom seemed to assume that their work would be continued by later scribes. A study of Caxton's first print edition of the *Chronicles of England*, for example, shows that his continuation did more than just append more information to the end: it also fortified what he sees as key themes of the narrative history, and ideologically positioned the text to separate the authority of monarchy from the weaknesses of particular monarchs (Weijer 2016: 130). A model of authorship for the *Brut*, then, cannot conform to an idea of composition by one discrete authority, but must reflect its construction over time, involving various sources, linguistic traditions, scribes, and compilers, and must acknowledge the expectation that later scribes may add continuations to the work. In this respect, it shares several aspects with authorship of digital texts.

14.4 Information structure and design in *Brut* manuscripts

The central organizational principle of the *Brut* Chronicle is chronology: the forward progress of time. The chronology of the events is not structured primarily around the Julian/Gregorian year numbers as a present-day text might be, however, but around the progression of kings. In the premodern chronicle, the narrative of the nation is held up by a backbone of monarchical vertebrae. It is this framework of royal succession, we see, that drives and is shaped by the information design and structure of the manuscript.

The information design of the work, therefore, is governed by time (demarcated in this case by monarchs and by year), by theme, by category (Shedroff 1999: 276). In discussing information design, Shedroff sketches out what he calls the "understanding spectrum" which, as mentioned earlier, moves from data to information to knowledge to wisdom (Shedroff 1999: 271). These terms are culturally-dependent, certainly: the "data" of the *Brut* Chronicle is constituted by the collection of accounts of given events — which would not be a usual methodology in modern historical research. The sources for the *Brut* are never explicit in the text either, and the sections of the work range from folk history to political summary. Yet the parallels with Shedroff's schema are instructive: the "data" of the accounts are organized into the "information" of the entries which present narratives that serve as historical "knowledge". Paratext and information design are not precisely equivalent, because paratextual strategies are more expansive than visual elements alone, but paratext in manuscripts certainly draws upon elements of the visual design for marking levels of discourse. This section investigates some aspects of the organization of the information in the *Brut* manuscripts.

14.4.1 Wayfinding

Information design investigates the linear experience of a visual design and the strategies for directing a viewer through it, known as *wayfinding*. In the *Brut*, the reader is primarily able to navigate the accounts of events by means of rubricated headings beginning each section and enlarged initials which flag the onset of new sections. Some manuscripts additionally have tables of contents at the outset. Manuscripts can also employ illuminations for wayfinding; Bryan (2013: 38) describes seven manuscripts which use illuminations for the King Arthur sections, observing that each of these seven constructs different visual *ordinatio* to shape its presentation of history. This notion of *ordinatio* – the visual tools for organizing on the page – is the medievalists' anticipation of the field of information design, as is, likewise, the conception of the *mise-en-page*, the textual layout (Parkes 1991). Modern scholars of information design are often going over the same ground with new words to examine how layout affects the organization of content.

The choice of new terms like wayfinding for old concepts about layout and organization is an issue of scholarly context. Certainly, terms like *ordinatio*, *compilatio*, and *mise-en-page* already have a methodological precedent in manuscript studies, and they employ analytic modes that are derived more responsibly from premodern categories rather than anachronistically from backprojected terms (for a fuller discussion, see Varila et al. 2017: 5–10). I am not suggesting that we should supplant the categories of manuscript studies more generally, but I do suggest that employing the terminology of information design here does allow us to see better the connections with other analytic tools for examining and modeling information presentation. Further, while the Latin and French analytic terms are more conscientious categories for premodern texts, they also underscore the unfamiliarity of early texts – the distance between ourselves and the medieval scribes. Using terms for present-day layout design like wayfinding, on the other hand, encourages contemporary theorists of the electronic page to see the links with the manuscript page, providing greater connection between the contemporary and the premodern (that is, a transhistorical approach). The insights gained by applying information design to medieval manuscripts are not original; the perspectives about layout on the page were there already. What is new is how the terminology invites connections to information presentation and to contemporary analysis.

14.4.2 Rubrication

Bryan (2009: 223) points out that rubrication (the use of red ink) becomes a way that texts with variant passages could share *ordinatio* and therefore be tailored to look alike. As a wayfinding tool, red ink is an aspect of information design used for headings; it also structures the events of the narrative, flagging thematic and chronological anchors in the text (see Thompson & Collins, this volume). The headings are frequently in red ink in *Brut* manuscripts (see MS 225 in figure 14.1).

Even in texts where the lettering of the headings is not rubricated, the letters are usually marked in other ways; see, for example, Hunter 83 (T.3.21) in which these headings are in slightly larger letters that are underlined in red.

The words of the headings combine with the red ink to mark them paratextually. Headings typically read like this:

(1) Of Kyng Donewall, þat was Cloteneȝ sone, and how he hade wonne þe lande (Brie 1906: 23)

[Of King Donewall, that was Cloten's son, and how he had won the land]

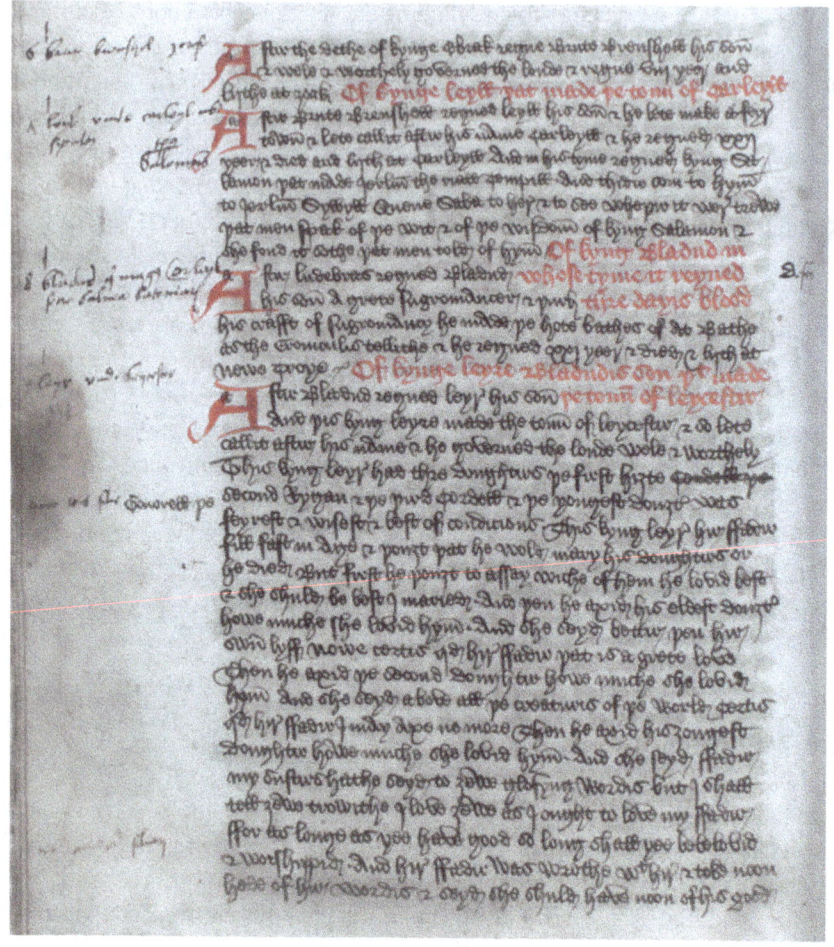

Figure 14.1: University of Michigan Library, MS 225, f5v.

(2) How Donewal was þe ferst kyng þat euere Werede crone of golde in Britaigne (Brie 1906: 23)

[How Donewal was the first king that ever wore a crown of gold in Britain]

(3) How Kyng Morwith deide þrouȝ meschaunce, þrouȝ a beste for his wickednesse. (Brie 1906: 28)

[How King Morwith died through mischance, by a beast, for his wickedness]

Grammatically, these rubricated headings are not sentences but nominal relative clauses and prepositional phrases: most of them are *how*-clauses or *of*-phrases or both. They read, then, discursively as topics rather than as narration; they are syntactically marked, in fact, as being *not* part of the narrative. One could almost see them as resembling truncated sentences: "(This chronicle tells) of King ... " or even continuations of a larger metasentence that is threaded through the volume: "(The chronicle tells) of King ... (and) how ... (and) how ... ". Although these headings are both visually and syntactically separate from the narrative, they are integrated into the discursive topic marking. They occur on nearly every page, often a few times on a page, to flag the introduction of major topics, and their ink color visually organizes them as waypoints for the marking of topics.

14.4.3 Paraph marks

Other kinds of narrative shifts are marked medially in some manuscripts with paraph marks, often in red or blue ink. These paraph marks typically flag shifts in the narrative content or mode, turns of the narrative, and occasionally direct speech. Often, in an organization confluence common to medieval manuscripts, the paraph marks are paired with discursive connectors like *And* or *But* as the first word after the paraph. An impressionistic look at Bodleian Library, MS Rawlinson B.171, the manuscript on which Brie based his edition, suggests that nearly half of paraph marks co-occur with *And*.

Consider a sample page from University of Manchester Library, English MS 102 (figure 14.2). Here are the paraph marks and the words following:

¶So that managles kyng of scotland...
¶And or other half yere...
¶And whan he was come...
¶and hir lorde...
¶Tho made he sorwe...
¶Tho began leir...
¶And now y wote wel...
¶And tho shulde y haue...
¶In this maner... (f4v)

The discourse is often double-marked by design and by structure: (a) in the design, through the red paraph marks that draw the reader's eyes to these flagged points on the page, and (b) in the structure, through the syntactic breaks and discourse connectors like *and* and *tho* that join together the structural and narrative units of the text. The manuscripts of the *Brut* draw upon both kinds of

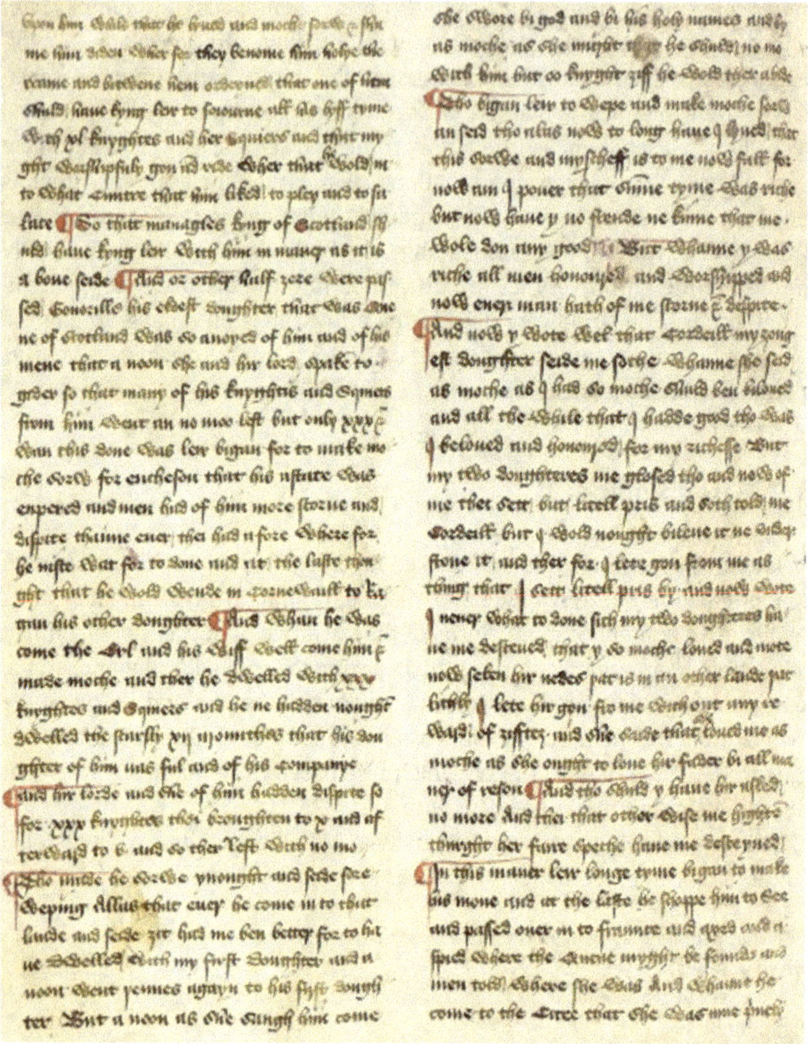

Figure 14.2: University of Manchester Library, English MS 102, f4v.

divisions, and using information structure and design together both heightens the effect and serves to instruct the reader in the functionality of different kinds of markers.

14.4.4 Clause structure marking of given and new information

The information structure of the sentences themselves can also aid in the chronological marking of royal succession. Consider these clause structures, from three sentences that occur directly after headings and thus begin new sections within the text:

(4) After þis Kyng Bladud, regnede Leir his sone; and þis Leir made þe toune of Leycestre,... (Brie 1906: 16)

[After this King Bladud, reigned Lear his son; and this Lear made the town of Leicester...]

(5) And after þis Conenedag, regnede Rynallo his sone, an Wise kny3t, and an hardy and curteise,... (Brie 1906: 21)

[And after this Conenedag, reigned Rivallo his son, a wise knight, and a hardy and courteous one...]

(6) After þis Ryuallo, regnede Gorbodyan his sone xv 3ere, and deide and lith at 3ork. (Brie 1906: 21)

[After this Rivallo, reigned Gorbodyan his son for 15 years, and died and lies at York.]

These sentences all begin with an initial adverbial followed by the main verb in verb second (V2) position, a constituent order that was common in Old English, fading in Middle English, and uncommon in present-day English (Stockwell 1984; Los 2009). Both the V2 order and the clause-initial adverbial have been discussed as aspects of information structure, particularly as strategies for putting given information first (van Kemenade & Westergaard 2012; Los 2015: 15–16). Each of these clauses, too, contains the deictic demonstrative adjective *þis*, referring back to the last section. In these sentences above, therefore, the clause-initial adverbial with deictic marker points backward to the previous monarch – the given information – and is followed by the main verb in second position, which creates a separation before the subject in third position. The subject of each of these is the successor king, in the third position – the new information.

The order of constituents in the main clause, therefore, is an aspect of historical English syntax that can be shaped by factors of information structure. In this case, the order of constituents assists the features of information design in laying out the chronological bonds of royal succession.

14.4.5 Ruling

The ruling of the manuscript page – the lines inscribed on each side of the leaf to create blocks of text and straight horizontal guides for writing – also organizes the reader's path through it. Some manuscripts of the *Brut* (e.g. University of Michigan MS 225 or Dartmouth College, Rauner Special Collections Library, MS 003183) are laid out in a single column, such that the reader's route across a page tracks from left to right across each line and from top to bottom. Others (e.g. University of Manchester University Library, English MS 102) are written in two columns, creating a sightline which progresses from left to right across each column, so that the eye moves from top to bottom twice per page (compare figures 14.1 and 14.2). Narrower columns can make it easier for the eye to track through more compressed text; the eye must linger longer over denser concentrations of characters and must move more slowly from left to right (e.g. Beymer et al. 2005). This is not to say that choices in column layout were directly motivated by imagined comprehension, of course: ruling of the manuscript page was influenced by a combination of conventions in scribal tradition and production (e.g. Peikola 2013: 31).

Further, it is interesting to consider the ruling of the manuscript page as it organizes the figure and ground: the written text and the margins. The first part of ruling is to inscribe the lines that demarcate the division between the words and the margins. Did a scribe who was ruling a blank vellum page imagine that he was marking out the writing space or the margins? de Hamel suggests the latter, given the process of construction and the defining of the margins (de Hamel 2001: 42). de Hamel describes the well-proportioned manuscript page as containing a lower margin that is approximately twice as wide as the inner margin, leaving the center of an opening with two inner margins that would be fairly close to the measure of the lower margin. The outer margin is two-thirds the width of the lower margin, and the width of the upper margin is half. Marking the margins produces a writing frame on this well-proportioned page that is roughly the height that the page is wide (de Hamel 2001: 43). For the reader, the question of which of the writing area or the margins is the figure and which the ground, though, is perhaps not straightforward, in fact, and the answer may vary depending on textual circumstances. A book may seem to have the written word at its central element, and as such the letters aligned in ruled blocks would seem to be the figure and the margins and empty spaces the ground. Margins are partly for placing fingers, resting pens, and creating a material and visual frame which emphasizes the words; they often serve as a background to the words' foreground. Yet this assessment can be complicated by other functions for margins. If the manuscript is illuminated, the illustrations are often located in the margins, as are many paratextual structures, scribal notae, and commentary from later readers. One could argue in this manner that the parallel lines of letters in formation become the visual backdrop for the illuminations, or the background to the commentary's foreground. So the distinction of figure and ground is perhaps not fixed for the medieval work, and may shift from page to page given the layering of different aspects of the text, as we will see in the next section.

14.4.6 Interactive reading

Features of the information design both encourage and reflect a reader's active experience with the written page. One form of active reading which contributes to the collective construction of the text can be found in manuscript marginalia. The annotators of the Rauner *Brut*, for example, make a wide range of comments: criticizing the price of grain in the 1315 famine, remarking on a great earthquake, and complaining cryptically: "it is to harde for my lernyng". Marvin, in working with the Rauner *Brut*, describes the annotators of the text (at least 3 of them in different centuries) as participating in an ongoing collaborative creation of the manuscript (Marvin 2014: 308).

Another example of later readers leaving their marks upon the text can be found in the University of Glasgow copy of an early printed edition of the *Brut* Chronicle from St. Albans, based upon William Caxton's first edition (1480) and interpolated with an ecclesiastical history of different popes ("The Chronicles of England"). The book is heavily annotated by later readers (particularly in the seventeenth and eighteenth centuries) in ways that show that the text was being read as history for centuries and that later readers wished to aid in shaping the narratives. A post-reformation reader, for example, appears to have energetically and consistently struck out the word *pope* with heavy ink, and the 9-line passage concerning a female pope ("Pope Joan") is also struck out, though an even later reader has restored it in the margin. This is not unique in Early Modern reception of medieval books; we see similar responses in reader responses to *Piers Plowman*, for instance. The work, in other words, instantiates ways that historical narratives get filtered through the transforming ideologies of later readers; we see the debates between these shifting values inscribed upon the page. Marginal notes characterize print books as well, of course, but these tend to be more in the vein of private notes to self rather than being included in the public-facing book. Such public-facing commentary becomes even more usual in online texts for which readers expect to be able to add comments: responses that then become part of other readers' experience of the text.

The design creates marginal space that admits the possibility of reader interaction. The information structure and design, then, does not foreclose the possibility that information is dynamic, that it will be continually negotiated with future scribes and readers.

14.5 Conclusion

Some of the ways that conventions of information structure and design in digital texts stretch the expectations created by print media point to the kinds of flexibility that texts had before print so effectively codified, conventionalized, and smoothed organizational practices. The reinvention of convention in new media feels fresh and plastic rather than hide-bound, but we can see analogues to some very hide-bound English works.

Looking at the *Brut* with the transhistorical tools of information structure and information design helps us to see parallels to digital texts. Information design allows us to think about how we navigate a page, the directions that our eyes take across it. Information structure examines the ordering of the sentences for organizational purposes. These strategies can often overlap – a discursive break in the narrative might be flagged by a syntactic marker like a discourse connective and be accompanied by a design feature like a paraph mark. Red ink is often used to underscore divisions that are also marked in syntax: headings, for example, are marked in red, but also through structure as nominal relative clauses and prepositional phrases. They are clearly set out as paratext, as topical waypoints for the narrative. The manuscripts of the *Brut* exhibit a greater range in wayfinding strategies in the narrative than many print texts since each version can uniquely combine aspects of the manuscript page such as ink color, illumination, topic marking, marginalia, and so forth. This flexibility can also extend to constructional aspects of the text, such as the potential for variation in orthography, in syntax, in discursive marking, even to the inclusion or omission of sections.

As a novel form of media, electronic forms like websites have not yet fully conventionalized practices of discourse marking. Pages draw upon a range of strategies for information design and structure, such as color, text boxes, toolbars, different sizes and styles of type, topic marking, lists, links, images, and so forth (e.g. Jones & Hafner 2012: 50–65). Although there are shared conventions – e.g. larger print for headings, particular colors for links and visited links – to some extent, each page invents its own system, drawing upon the options in original ways. This less codified style of organization also characterized the written texts of the late Middle English period, in which organizational conventions had multiplied, but the practical constraints of print had not yet emerged to winnow down the options. Although manuscripts were not "new media" in the fifteenth century, the proliferation of English manuscripts in many genres did present a new situation for literacy and textual production. The advent of new forms and channels for written communication comes, perhaps, with an overgrowth of possibilities for information structure and design: a cultural window of flexibility and creativity in strategies of discourse organization.

References

Manuscripts and Editions

Brie, Friedrich, W.D. (ed.). 1906, 1908. *The Brut, or The Chronicles of England*. 2 vols. The Early English Text Society, os 131, 136. London: Oxford University Press.
Brie, Friedrich, W.D. (ed.). *The Brut, or The chronicles of England*. Edited from Ms. Raw. B171, Bodleian Library, &c., by Friedrich W. D. Brie, with introduction, notes, and glossary. Corpus of Middle English Prose and Verse. http://name.umdl.umich.edu/APG1531 (accessed 17 July 2019).
Ann Arbor, University of Michigan, MS 225 https://quod.lib.umich.edu/b/brut?auth=world; q1=brut;rgn1=ic_all;size=20;type=boolean;view=thumbnail;start=1 (accessed 17 July 2019).
Dartmouth, Dartmouth College, *Rauner MS 003183* https://www.dartmouth.edu/~library/digital/collections/manuscripts/ocn312771386/ (accessed 17 July 2019)
Glasgow, University of Glasgow, MS Hunter 83 (T.3.21) http://special.lib.gla.ac.uk/manuscripts/search/detail_c.cfm?ID=34505 (accessed 17 July 2019).
Manchester, University of Manchester Library, English MS 102 http://luna.manchester.ac.uk/luna/servlet/workspace/handleMediaPlayer?lunaMediaId=Man4MedievalVC~4~4~105145~103642 (accessed 17 July 2019).

Secondary Sources

Bertin, Jacques. 1983. *Semiology of graphics: Diagrams, networks, maps*. Madison: University of Wisconsin Press.
Beymer, David, Daniel M. Russell & Peter Z. Orton. 2005. Wide vs. narrow paragraphs: An eye tracking analysis. In Maria F. Costabile & Fabio Paternò (eds.), *Human-Computer Interaction – INTERACT 2005*. Lecture Notes in Computer Science, vol 3585. Berlin: Springer.
Brantley, Jessica. 2013. Medieval remediations. In Katherine Hayles & Jessica Pressman (eds.), *Comparative textual media: Transforming the humanities in the postprint era*, 201–220. Minneapolis: University of Minnesota Press.

Bryan, Elizabeth J. 1999. *Collaborative meaning in medieval scribal culture: The Otho Laȝamon*. Ann Arbor: University of Michigan Press.
Bryan, Elizabeth J. 2009. Rauner Codex MS 003183: The Beeleigh Abbey Brut at Dartmouth College. *The Journal of the Early Book Society* 12.
Bryan, Elizabeth J. 2013. Picturing Arthur in English history: Text and image in the Middle English prose Brut. *Arthuriana* 23 (4). 38–71.
The Chronicles of England. Book of the month: University of Glasgow special collections. http://special.lib.gla.ac.uk/exhibns/month/sep2001.html (accessed 7 January 2018).
Claridge, Claudia. 2017. Voices in medieval history writing. *Nordic Journal of English Studies* 16 (1). 7–40.
de Hamel, Christopher. 2001. *The British Library guide to manuscript illumination: History and techniques*. Toronto: University of Toronto Press.
Drucker, Johanna. 2014. *Graphesis: Visual forms of knowledge production*. Cambridge, MA: Harvard University Press.
Erteschik-Shir, Nomi. 2007. *Information structure: The syntax-discourse interface*. Oxford: Oxford University Press.
Gillespie, Alexandra. 2006. *Print culture and the medieval author: Chaucer, Lydgate and their books*, 1473–1557. Oxford: Oxford University Press.
Guillory, John. 2010. Genesis of the media concept. *Critical Inquiry* 36. 321–362.
Horn, Robert. 1998. *Visual language: Global communication for the 21st century*. Bainbridge Island: MacroVU Press.
Information design: Concepts and theories. https://avitalshapira.wordpress.com/2013/02/21/wayfinding-information-design-theory/ (accessed 1 July 2018).
Jacobson, Robert (ed.). 1999. *Information design*. Cambridge, MA: MIT Press.
Jones, Rodney H. & Christoph A. Hafner. 2012. *Understanding digital literacies*. Abingdon: Routledge.
Katz, Joel. 2012. *Designing information: Human factors and common sense in information design*. Hoboken, NJ: Wiley.
Kennedy, Edward Donald. 1989. Chronicles and other historical writing. In Albert E. Hartung (ed.), *A manual of the writings in Middle English 1050–1500*, vol. 8. New Haven: The Connecticut Academy of Arts and Sciences.
Kiss, Farkas Gábor, Eyal Poleg, Lucie Doležalová & Rafal Wójcik. 2013. Old light on new media: Medieval practices in the digital age. *Digital Philology: A Journal of Medieval Cultures* 2 (1). 16–34.
Lambrecht, Knud. 1994. *Information structure and sentence form: Topic, focus, and the mental representations of discourse referents*. Cambridge, UK: Cambridge University Press.
Lister, Martin, Jon Dovey, Seth Giddings, Iain Grant & Kieran Kelly. 2009. *New media: A critical introduction*. Abingdon: Routledge.
Loewenstein, Joseph. 2002. *The author's due: Printing and the prehistory of copyright*. Chicago: University of Chicago Press.
Los, Bettelou. 2009. The consequences of the loss of verb-second in English: Information structure and syntax in interaction. *English Language and Linguistics* 13 (1). 97–125.
Los, Bettelou. 2015. *A historical syntax of English*. Edinburgh: Edinburgh University Press.
Lynch, Kevin. 1960. *Image of the city*. Cambridge, MA: MIT Press.
Lunsford, Andrea & Lisa Ede. 1990. *Singular texts, plural authors: Perspectives on collaborative writing*. Carbondale: Southern Illinois University.

Malamed, Connie. 2009. *Visual language for designers: Principles for creating graphics that people understand*. Beverly, MA: Rockport Publishers.

Marvin, Julia. 2014. "It is to harde for my lernyng": Making sense of annotations in *Brut* manuscripts. *Digital Philology: A Journal of Medieval Cultures* 3 (2). 304–322.

Marx, William. 2006. Reception and revision in the Middle English prose *Brut. Trivium* 36. 53–69.

Marx, William & Raluca Radulescu. 2006. Introduction: Readers and writers of the prose Brut. *Trivium* 36: xiii-xvi.

Matheson, Lister M. 1998. *The prose Brut: The development of a Middle English chronicle*. Tempe: Medieval & Renaissance Texts & Studies.

McGann, Jerome. 1991. *The textual condition*. Princeton: Princeton University Press.

McKenzie, Donald. F. 2002. *Making meaning: Printers of the mind and other essays*. Amherst: University of Massachusetts Press.

Mooney, Linne R. & Lister M. Matheson. 2003. The Beryn scribe and his texts: Evidence for multiple-copy production of manuscripts in fifteenth-century England. *The Library* 4. 347–370.

Meurman-Solin, Anneli, María José López-Couso & Bettelou Los. 2012. *Information structure and syntactic change in the history of English*. Oxford: Oxford University Press.

Parkes, Malcolm. 1991. The influence of the concepts of *ordinatio* and *compilatio* on the development of the book. *Scribes, scripts and readers: Studies in the communication, presentation and dissemination of medieval texts*. London: Hambledon Press.

Peikola, Matti. 2013. Guidelines for consumption: Scribal ruling patterns and designing the mise-en-page in later medieval England. In Emma Cayley & Susan Powell (eds.), *Manuscripts and printed books in Europe 1350–1500: Packaging, presentation and consumption*, 14–31. Liverpool: Liverpool University Press.

Saint-Martin, Fernande. 1990. *Semiotics of visual language*. Indianapolis: Indiana University Press.

Shedroff, Nathan. 1999. Information interaction design: A unified field theory of design. In Jacobson, Robert (ed.), *Information design*, 267–292. Cambridge, MA: MIT Press.

Stockwell, Robert P. 1984. On the history of the verb-second rule in English. In Jacek Fisiak (ed.), *Historical syntax*, 575–92. Berlin: De Gruyter Mouton.

Szpiech, Ryan. 2014. Cracking the code: Reflections on manuscripts in the age of digital books. *Digital philology: A journal of medieval cultures*, 3 (1). 75–100.

Taylor, Andrew. 2002. *Textual situations: Three medieval manuscripts and their readers*. Philadelphia: University of Pennsylvania Press.

Tyrkkö, Jukka. 2007. Making sense of digital textuality. *European Journal of English Studies* 11 (2). 147–61.

Van Kemenade, Ans & Marit Westergaard. 2012. Syntax and information structure: Verb-second variation in Middle English. In Anneli Meurman-Solin, María José López-Couso & Bettelou Los (eds.), *Information structure and syntactic change in the history of English*, 87–118. Oxford: Oxford University Press.

Varila, Mari-Liisa, Hanna Salmi, Aleksi Mäkilähde, Janne Skaffari and Matti Peikola. 2017. Disciplinary decoding: Towards understanding the language of visual and material features. In Matti Peikola, Aleksi Mäkilähde, Hanna Salmi, Mari-Liisa Varila & Janne Skaffari (eds.), *Verbal and visual communication in early English texts*, 1–20. Turnhout: Brepols.

Wakelin, Daniel. 2014. *Scribal correction and literary craft: English manuscripts 1375–1510*. Cambridge, UK: Cambridge University Press.
Ward, Gregory & Betty Birner. 2004. Information structure and non-canonical syntax. In Laurence R. Horn & Gregory Ward (eds.), *The handbook of pragmatics*, 153–174. Oxford: Blackwell.
Ward, Gregory, Betty Birner & Rodney Huddleston. 2002. Information packaging. In Rodney Huddleston & Geoffrey K. Pullum (eds.), *The Cambridge grammar of the English language*, 1363–1447. Cambridge, UK: Cambridge University Press.
Wayfinding in Web Design. https://www.viget.com/newsletter/wayfinding-in-web-design/. Accessed 1 July 2018.
Weijer, Neil. 2016. Re-printing or remaking? The early printed editions of the *Chronicles of England*. In Jaclyn Rajsic, Erik Kooper & Dominique Hoche (eds.), *The prose Brut and other late medieval chronicles*, 125–146. York: York Medieval Press.
Woodmansee, Martha. 1997. On the author effect: Recovering collectivity. Faculty Publications 283. https://scholarlycommons.law.case.edu/faculty_publications/283 (accessed 17 July 2019).

Riki Thompson and Matthew Collins

15 Disruptive practice: Multimodality, innovation and standardisation from the medieval to the digital text

15.1 Introduction

Superficially, digital technologies that rely on a keyboard with preset icons to translate characters onto a digitized screen look like extreme divergences from earlier, pre-digital writing practices. Yet, in this paper we argue that contemporary digital writing practices, while adaptive to technological architecture, remediate the practices of specifically medieval manuscript production and consumption. To demonstrate this, we historicize writing and reading practices to argue for the importance of multimodality in communicative situations across time. Taking a transhistorical interdisciplinary approach, we consider the importance of visual rhetoric as both aesthetic and functional components that help readers navigate texts (compare also Moore, this volume). Visual rhetoric in this sense can be understood as the use of visual imagery to communicate and the processes by which such imagery influences viewers (Foss 2005), drawing on the affordances – the capabilities – of a given mode. Our focus is on continuities in the visual properties of the text, engaging with Bolter and Grusin's (2000: 14–15) argument that "new media are doing exactly what their predecessors have done: presenting themselves as refashioned and improved versions of other media". We discuss how medieval readers may have interacted with texts, based on their visual arrangement, and examine how the affordances of digital multimodality mirror, and in a sense recover, the same fluid, contingent and participatory textual experience of their medieval predecessors.

15.2 Methodology

Our approach uses a visual rhetorical framework to conduct a review of literature across the fields of historical linguistics and digitally mediated communication,

---

Riki Thompson, University of Washington, Tacoma, USA, e-mail: rikitiki@uw.edu
Matthew Collins, University of Birmingham, Birmingham, UK,
e-mail: mcc315@student.bham.ac.uk

drawing upon illustrative examples of medieval manuscripts and digital texts. In looking transhistorically, our method reflects our argument that writing and reading practices transcend time, an argument which in turn draws on what Labov calls the "Uniformitarian Principle", whereby "linguistic processes taking place around us are the same as those that have operated to produce the historical record" (Labov 1972: 101). We illustrate this approach through a comparative analysis of expository English language texts from two periods, with contingent modal differences: medieval illuminated manuscripts and twenty-first century digital texts.

In exploring the array of digital media texts, we examined online newspapers, digital fiction, and the texts produced in the course of this collaboration. We focused on newspapers to consider issues related to visual mediation and style, colour and rubrication, and imagery. Digital fiction was utilised to discuss narrative linearity and word processing texts – specifically, Microsoft Word and Google Docs with their collaborative writing affordances, such as comments and track changes – allowed for the examination of composing practices in the modern era. Our focus was on news articles and home pages sampled from the most popular daily metropolitan newspapers in the U.S. This sample source provides an indication of the extent of engagement of modern readers in the present day.

With the move to digital journalism, metrics for tracking newspaper readership in recent years have become more complex as the ranking may include attention to modes of online consumption. While Agility PR and WorldAtlas rely upon print circulation numbers to rank top newspapers, Muck Rack uses data about "unique visitors per month" and Cision Media Research has a secondary database that tracks top newspapers on Twitter. Since we are concerned with the historical shifts in the visual rhetoric of news, our dataset pays attention to readership that accounts for both print and digital texts. Seven newspapers ranked within the top ten of popular newspapers across all five of these media tracking databases, specifically: *Chicago Tribune, Los Angeles Times, New York Post, New York Times, Wall Street Journal, Washington Post,* and *USA Today*. Four newspapers, namely *amNewYork, Boston Globe, Newsday,* and *New York Daily News*, were ranked in the top ten for multiple media databases whereas five newspapers, *Atlanta Journal-Constitution, Dallas News, Denver Post, Houston Chronicle, Seattle Times,* and the *StarTribune,* ranked top ten in only one. To account for the disparity in ranking across media databases, we opted to examine the top sixteen newspaper sources that listed a readership of more than 200,000 in at least one of the data sources. From the newspapers listed above, our dataset included all except the *Denver Post* which has a circulation of approximately 177,000 daily readers.

In contrast, the selection of manuscripts based on readership numbers is not possible. We may speculate however that circulation correlates to those texts that survive in a number of different reproductions. The medieval texts were selected from the British Library's online Digitised Manuscripts collection. The texts selected are all in (Middle) English, to again account for broader readership communities, but this has also affected the types of text included. As many manuscripts that deal with legal and religious affairs were composed in Latin or French, this has had the side-effect of focusing this dataset on narrative texts.

Whilst there are other manuscript archives, the texts were selected for their pictorial and verbal qualities, alongside their expository and didactic function. (It is worth considering, also, that this digital archive is an example of how many modern readers now engage with medieval manuscripts, illustrating the impact that digital frameworks have on how the past is perceived and interrogated; see Moreton & Culy, this volume). One final criterion is date. Only manuscripts from the fourteenth and fifteenth centuries were selected. As our exploration discusses the disruptive nature of medieval and digital texts in contrast to print, this date parameter provides a dataset that was contemporary to the introduction of printing. The texts selected for this study were the *Lancelot Grail* (Add. MS 10292), the *Winchester Manuscript* (Add. MS 59678), *The Fall of Princes* (Harley MS 1766), *The Harley Lyrics* (Harley MS 2253), *The Carthusian Miscellany* (Add. MS 37049), a "Miscellany of treatises relating to prognostication, astrology and braiding in verse and prose" (Harley MS 2320), a Middle English Biblical manuscript (Harley MS 6333), and *Pearl, Cleanness, Patience and Sir Gawain and the Green Knight* (Cotton MS Nero A X/2).

We use multimodal discourse analytic methods to focus on visual dimensions of style, specifically orthographic and typographic elements (font, colour, rubrication) as well as composition and navigational features (imagery, links, page structure). Thus, we conceive of visual rhetoric as a defining, transhistorical feature of both medieval and digital texts, both in the forms used and in the rhetorical function. Analysis of digital and printed texts shows how the design serves communicative purposes through semiotic means (e.g. Jewitt, Bezemer & O'Halloran 2016; Ledin & Machin 2018), and this is the case for medieval manuscripts as well (Parkes 1991: 52, 224). Our argument is that although the affordances of digital media can be seen to supplant many of the recent norms of print, it does this not through the "new", but through the revivification of manuscript practice.

Before exploring the connections between the digital news text and its medieval predecessors, it is helpful to illustrate the richness of medieval multimodality by examining some of the key visual features of a medieval manuscript.

John Lydgate's *The Fall of Princes* (figure 15.1) was created in the middle of the fifteenth century. As a moralistic verse translation of considerable length (Mortimer 2005), it employs a wide range of multimodal resources to communicate with readers, many of which are representative of medieval manuscripts (see also Moore, this volume). Lydgate's text is itself a web of antecedent sources, notably de Premierfait's 1409 translation of Boccaccio's *De casibus vivorum illustrium* as well as Ovidian and Biblical stories, providing a collaborative, composite selection of narratives.

The text employs multiple features engaged in visual rhetoric, connected to textual organisation, ideational meaning and indicative of its compositional narrative. The image of Lydgate (pictured kneeling on the right-hand side, alongside another unknown monk) dedicating his work to St Edmund, is large and centralised, signalling its significance for the reader. The inclusion of the translator/author, Lydgate, personalises the manuscript, as does his name emblazoned on the scroll depicted alongside him. The miniature's header position, a feature of many medieval manuscripts (Galvez 2012: 103), establishes a platform for an authorial, authenticating power, providing an iconic representation of a writer presiding over his work. The colour illustration also has an organisational function, integrating with text as a decorated initial foliates into margins and rubricated marginalia, which through their glossing summaries orientate the reader towards the different parts of the text (narrative text, paratext), that creates a multimodal web of voices. The interplay of these elements implies the collaborative nature of manuscript composition, by which images were superimposed on pages of text for which a scribe left accommodating blank spaces. The Gothic cursive script[1] is clear and consistently formed, indicating the literacy of the manuscript's scribes.

To many present-day readers, Lydgate's manuscript may seem exotic, or archaic, and far removed from the texts produced within the digital world. However, in its strategies and functions we wish to argue that there are striking similarities with more recent communicative technologies, particularly digital writing strategies. To support this argument, we focus on these elements: linearity, compositional practices, visual mediation and style, colour, and imagery, exploring the continuities in the visual rhetoric of these features as found in the samples of digital texts and their medieval manuscript predecessors.

---

[1] Script is used in this article to indicate handwritten forms as opposed to font for digitized forms.

Figure 15.1: © The British Library Board. John Lydgate's *The Fall of Princes*, British Library Harley 1766 f.5. (c.1450-c.1460). British Library Catalogue of Illuminated Manuscripts.

15.3 Linearity

The principle of linearity, a "formal discoursal progression" (Monroy-Casas 2008: 176–177), can be understood as a prototypical feature of a narrative reading experience. In traditional print books, the reader is led through the narrative sequence in a linear progression, word by word, page by page. However, this practice is context specific, sensitive to linguistic and cultural norms. For example, whilst English is written and read from left to right, other languages, like Hebrew, follows a right-to-left directionality. From a Western perspective, Japanese Manga comics are read "backwards", navigating from the back cover to the front. Within the print medium, linearity has a claim to being the dominant organising principle, with some exceptions. One "disruptive" twentieth-century example is the "choose your own adventure" franchise, created in the 1980s, which gave readers the choice to pick preferred storylines by jumping between pages rather than following a predetermined route set by progressing by page numbers.

It is well known that digital literacy practices allow writers and readers to participate differently (Page & Thomas 2011). A digital platform entails that the directionality of narrative is not limited by the medium of the printed page. For example, Iain Pears' novel *Arcadia* (2015), presented through the i-pad app, uses a "choose your own adventure" format, giving the reader autonomy to follow particular characters or settings. The nonlinear narrative is presented in two color-coded formats; one option provides a table of contents with a list of tales related to ten characters, and the other is a map of story lines that interweave at junctions, similar to a subway map, with three different endings based on the final destination. The digital non-linear narrative offers a different set of affordances to the print equivalent, with a potentially different reader experience, as demonstrated in research on digital fiction (Bell 2011). The digital technology offers an illusory "linear" or sequential experience because the reader is directed from section to section seamlessly through hyperlinks, rather than in the printed book, which foregrounds to the reader the physical chunks of text, and therefore narrative, they are omitting when moving from section to section in their chosen path (Page & Thomas 2011). Research in literacy and multimodal studies has theorized how images and interactions are taken up to make meaning (Hiippala 2012). Broadly, van Leeuwen (1993: 214–5) proposed that a reading path "proceeds through visually salient images to visually salient text" and more specifically Kress (2003: 4) has suggested that reading paths may be created in three ways: by the designer through the construction of images, by a process of transformation between the designer and the reader, or constructed by the reader independently. In online newspapers, titles and abstracts of top stories are embedded on the front page with links that encourage a reader to follow a different pathway to what we would assume from a print newspaper, which might be read linearly from page to page. Of course, readers can follow a non-linear path through print newspapers, reading stories and pages out of order, but the online experience is quite different in how it is guided through links. For example, readers of the *Washington Post* may follow the link to the story that leads with "At tense meeting with Boeing" to read further and then use the back button on their browser to return to the front page so they may follow another link to a different story, such as the video on Trump's tax cut. This recursive reading process is common for online newspaper reading, as it is unlikely that there will be a link connecting these two stories nor that readers will be led from one story to another regardless of the ordering of contents on the homepage (figure 15.2).

The "seamlessness" of the digital, autonomous reader trajectory, rather than a beginning-to-end, novelistic experience, has antecedents in medieval reading practices. A medieval reader was exposed to much looser formations of narrative assemblage, such as the multiple arrangements of Chaucer's *Canterbury Tales*, or the medieval miscellany (Boffey & Thompson 1989). Clemens and Graham note that "few books in the Middle Ages would have been read from cover to cover. Most books were read discursively — that is, the reader would read some chapters or lines in one part of the book and then skip to another book" (Clemens & Graham 2007: 43). Indeed, these non-linear characteristics reflect several aspects of text production. The first is function. A miscellany like *The Harley Lyrics* illustrates this mix. Its forms include prose and poetry, its content ranges from biography to lyrics and religious thought and even its language is a macaronic mix of English, Anglo-Norman and Latin. For manuscripts like MS Harley 6333, which was used to conduct masses, contents rubric assisted readers in navigating the text (Peikola 2015: 49). Secondly, reception: a text like *The Carthusian Miscellany* was assembled in such a way as to map a reader's private reading experience in terms of public spectacle (Brantley 2007: 3–4). Finally, it is indicative of circulation. The various re-orderings of the *Canterbury Tales* reordered are indicative of how these circulated as distinct tales as much as a story cycle.

In the spirit of medieval and digital practices, as well as academic writing (e.g. Bolter & Grusin 2000: 85), readers of this article are invited to disrupt the norm of linear reading practices: navigate to sections and following your curiosity as you read this chapter (See <u>Linearity</u>, <u>Composition Practices</u>, <u>Visual Mediation and Style</u>, <u>Colour</u>, <u>Imagery</u>).

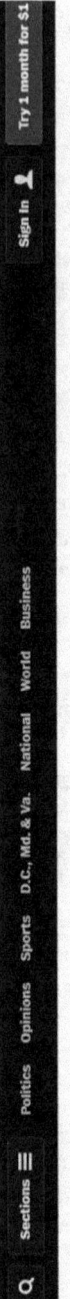

Figure 15.2: Screenshot of The Washington Post online newspaper front page (March 14, 2019).

15.4 Composition practices

In the history of English-(language) literacies, composition practices are understood at different times to be primarily associated with solo-authorship or with collaboration. Indeed, if the digital is viewed as the new norm, then the print age – privileging solo endeavors – can be seen as a disruption of the usual collaborative practices that typify manuscript culture in medieval England and present-day digital media. This reflects the fact that technology, in and of itself, is not the primary driver of composition and reception practices. It is the communicative cultures that surround texts which inform how knowledge is disseminated and engaged with (Jenkins 2006). Thus, iterative and collaborative writing does not rely on technology, but rather how producers and consumers interact with text.

Medieval authorial texts are rare. Most manuscripts represent distant copies of an original "authorial version" and in some instances were compiled from several witnesses, from different areas over a lengthy period. In our sample these practices are evident in both self-referential illustration, for example images depicting the scribe in a scriptorium (e.g. the historiated initial in a fifteenth-century lunar prognostication *Harley 2320*, f.31r) and in the material traces of composition: individuated scribal handwriting, erasure, strikethroughs and subpunction (a series of dots beneath a word to identify corrections).

While some digital writing practices reflect single-authorship and a final fixed version, Web 2.0 technologies made composition increasingly iterative and collaborative in ways reminiscent of the medieval. For example, in our own collaborative practice using Microsoft Word and Google Docs (figure 15.3), our track changes, strikethroughs, and comments, functionally (and in some ways visually in their page placement) resemble medieval manuscript addenda and marginalia. When we composed together with Google Docs, the version history allowed us to see the evolution of a document and revert to earlier versions as needed, as well as continually edit and revise. This fluidity and impermanency with which these digital texts can be collated has similarities with the unbound and open-ended status of the medieval manuscript which generally lack the "terminal" paratextual elements, such as a title page or inner and outer covers which typify printed books. Digital and manuscript authorship processes are therefore distinguishable from the writing norms established in the print age in two ways, in their collaborative authorship, and in the practices of iteration (copying, extension, revision) associated with this. This is not to say that print is not collaborative and the production process of most written texts is not iterative, but such instances depart from the norm. The difference between the

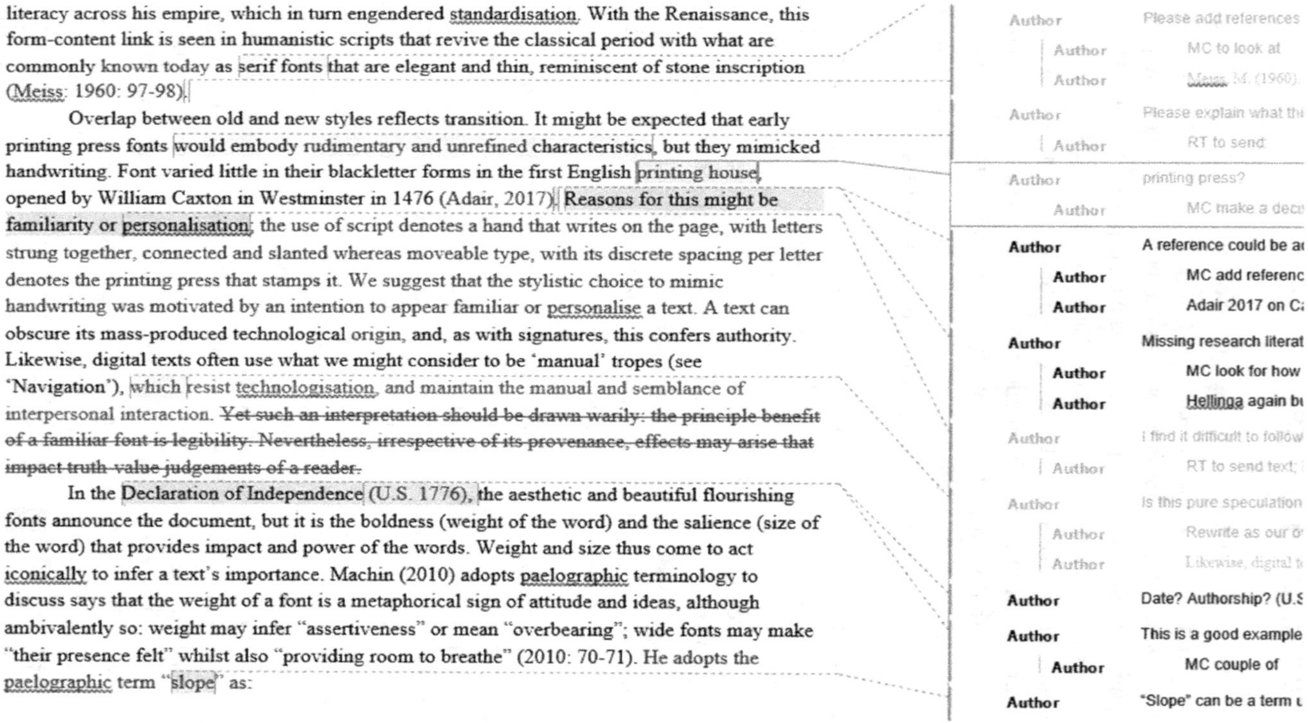

literacy across his empire, which in turn engendered standardisation. With the Renaissance, this form-content link is seen in humanistic scripts that revive the classical period with what are commonly known today as serif fonts that are elegant and thin, reminiscent of stone inscription (Meiss: 1960: 97-98).

Overlap between old and new styles reflects transition. It might be expected that early printing press fonts would embody rudimentary and unrefined characteristics, but they mimicked handwriting. Font varied little in their blackletter forms in the first English printing house, opened by William Caxton in Westminster in 1476 (Adair, 2017). Reasons for this might be familiarity or personalisation; the use of script denotes a hand that writes on the page, with letters strung together, connected and slanted whereas moveable type, with its discrete spacing per letter denotes the printing press that stamps it. We suggest that the stylistic choice to mimic handwriting was motivated by an intention to appear familiar or personalise a text. A text can obscure its mass-produced technological origin, and, as with signatures, this confers authority. Likewise, digital texts often use what we might consider to be 'manual' tropes (see 'Navigation'), which resist technologisation, and maintain the manual and semblance of interpersonal interaction. ~~Yet such an interpretation should be drawn warily: the principle benefit of a familiar font is legibility. Nevertheless, irrespective of its provenance, effects may arise that impact truth-value judgements of a reader.~~

In the Declaration of Independence (U.S. 1776), the aesthetic and beautiful flourishing fonts announce the document, but it is the boldness (weight of the word) and the salience (size of the word) that provides impact and power of the words. Weight and size thus come to act iconically to infer a text's importance. Machin (2010) adopts paelographic terminology to discuss says that the weight of a font is a metaphorical sign of attitude and ideas, although ambivalently so: weight may infer "assertiveness" or mean "overbearing"; wide fonts may make "their presence felt" whilst also "providing room to breathe" (2010: 70-71). He adopts the paelographic term "slope" as:

Author Please add references
Author MC to look at
Author Meiss, M. (1960).
Author Please explain what th
Author RT to send
Author printing press?
Author MC make a deci
Author A reference could be a
Author MC add referenc
Author Adair 2017 on C
Author Missing research literat
Author MC look for how
Author Hellinga again b
Author I find it difficult to follow
Author RT to send text;
Author Is this pure speculation
Author Rewrite as our o
Author Likewise, digital t
Author Date? Authorship? (U.S
Author This is a good example
Author MC couple of
Author "Slope" can be a term u

Figure 15.3: Screenshot of collaborative writing process with Microsoft Word's track changes and comments feature.

ideology of print is that the process of collaboration and production is hierarchical (i.e. editorial) rather than horizontal between peers working together to co-create a shared artifact.

15.5 Visual mediation and style

The relationship between writing technology and embodiment is closely aligned. The handwritten text can be seen as the most embodied kind of writing, with subsequent developments showing a general trajectory away from an embodied process. The printing press introduced a more mechanical, removed means of textual production, and this was expanded further in the twentieth century with the invention of the typewriter which "changed the way people wrote" (Jones, Chik & Hafner 2015: 35). In the twenty-first century, however, the affordances of digital technologies have started to offer ways of recreating a more embodied writing experience, such as the replication of handwriting (i.e. a stylus, or digital ink) or even body-specific identifiers, such as fingerprint and retinal scanners.

One way of tracing this embodied trajectory over time is to consider the form of the written word. In this view, fonts and scripts are modality markers that shape the meanings of a text, through the stylization of visual content. The visual word has two levels of meaning: a "word image", the idea represented by the word itself via a string of letters, and a "typographic image", the "holistic visual impression" (Bellantoni & Woolman 2000: 6); the latter of which include properties such as weight, expansion, slope, curvature, connectivity, orientation, and regularity, all contributing to the font's or script's meaning potential (van Leeuwen 2005).

Scripts in illuminated manuscripts are not static, but show changing conventions linked to technological affordances and cultural fashions. Some are (seemingly) aesthetic: flourishes attached to letters disappear then reappear between the eighth and ninth centuries (Tillotson 2005). In the twelfth century, the Gothic phase sees rounder and weightier letterforms, as there is a move towards legibility, illustrated in figure 15.1's Gothic cursive script. Other meanings arise from the strong association forged between a text, its usual script, and its social function. For example, medieval cursive scripts, such as *chancery* (Fisher, Richardson & Fisher 1984), are associated with governmental offices. Their cursive form (i.e. the pen is not removed from the page) reflects their context of use, but also came to symbolise bureaucracy and professional discourse. Other associations apply to specific scripts and individual scriptoria. Whilst today handwriting is an example of personalization, admissible evidence of authorial identity in forensic linguistics, the medieval hand was, through scriptoria "house-style" (Thomson 2018: 69), standardised and communal to ensure consistency in appearance. In this, the practice of writing mirrored the lack of individuation evident in a text's creation, where originality was not praised as highly as the ability to (re)write an antecedent, authoritative work. Scribes were educated in writing and transcribing the "official word" and their text, albeit by hand, conformed to the strictures of predefined types. That said, the identification of particular scribes is possible. In the Winchester Manuscript (British Library, Add. MS 59678) differing hands have enabled the analysis of the two different scribes' accuracy (Field 2004). Figure 15.4 illustrates the different hands (albeit same script) of the Winchester Manuscript. Any associations between authority and the handwritten must therefore be viewed in the context of communal practices.

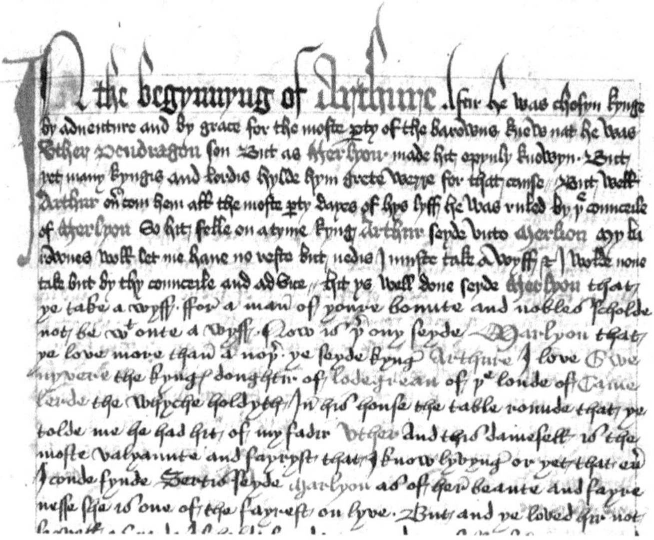

Figure 15.4: © The British Library Board. Thomas Malory's *Morte Darthur*, British Library Add MS 59678 f.35r (1469–70).

Disruptive practices need to be examined in the context of continuous practices. This is critical to understanding the scale and level of disruption in contrast to continuity across time, and it is from this social perspective that we can understand the continuity in the visual representation of the written word across print and digital media. Early printing press fonts mimic contemporary handwriting. William Caxton, who opened his printing press in Westminster in

1476, acquired type from the continent, including some which are noted for their similarity to scribal handwriting (Robinson 2014: 65), providing a continuity with manuscript forms, perhaps to engender familiarity or greater personalisation (i.e. embodiment). Caxton followed Gutenberg in using Gothic typeface (known as blackletter). Ironically, when first introduced as a script in the twelfth century, Renaissance literati disparaged it as "barbaric" (hence "Goths") in comparison to the simplicity and clarity of classical letterforms (Mishra 1994: 47–48). In manuscript and print, however, Gothic script was economic, both compositionally (that is, time required to write it) and spatially. This is an instance where late scribal practices overlap with print practices, in which the composition and presentation practices of the written text give priority to that text over the page (white space). This was ideologically significant, in that both Western medieval manuscripts and early printed books were first and foremost the word of God, enforcing this association between textual space, authority and truth.

Digital media show similar continuities in the representation of the written word. In the early days of the internet, webpage kits included a suite with a limited number of fonts, usually Helvetica, Arial, and Century, that were most commonly available and readable through widely used programs and web browsers.[2] With technological developments, fonts have become increasingly visually rhetorical, including personalised and embodied meanings similar to those evinced by handwritten scripts. This is what Thompson calls visual synthetic personalization (Thompson 2012), and this strategy is used by individuals (i.e. blogs) and also by corporate entities to project a position of friendliness and intimacy, pragmatically interpretable as an act of positive politeness, whereby a speaker wishes to appeal to the desires of the addressee (Brown & Levinson 1987: 62). In other contexts, similar to the cursive functionality of bureaucratic scripts, some fonts have a minimalist function – and are therefore more distinct from their handwritten predecessors – to prioritise navigation of the text, with social connotations of orderliness and consistency, pragmatically adhering to Gricean cooperativeness.

Fonts and their contexts of use, therefore, have complex associated meanings which are evident across manuscript, print and digital media. Machin (2010) suggests that the weight of a font is a metaphorical sign of attitude and ideas, although ambivalently so: weight may infer "assertiveness" or mean

---

[2] Research suggests there is no significant difference between the readability of serif and san serif font of both screen display category and print display category (Rello & Baeza-Yates 2013).

"overbearing"; wide fonts may make "their presence felt" whilst also "providing room to breathe" (Machin 2010: 70–71). In the manuscript Declaration of Independence (U.S. 1776), the aesthetic and beautiful flourishing letterforms announce the document, but it is the boldness (weight of the word) and the salience (size of the word) that provides impact and power of the text's meaning. Weight and size thus come to act iconically to signal a text's importance.

It is useful to work through some specific examples, taken from our sample of online daily metropolitan newspapers, to see the continuities between manuscript and digital writing. In this contemporary material, publishers use fonts for organisational and interactional functions. Online newspapers tend to rely on a mix of fonts to organize information, utilizing Gothic, modern, and print forms such as Blackletter, Helvetica, and Century Old Style. An examination of online newspaper logos in figure 15.5 demonstrates how the largest metropolitan papers employ Gothic typeface to announce the news whereas smaller papers tend towards modern and print forms.

Figure 15.5: Online newspaper logos.

Six of the top online newspapers in our dataset use a Blackletter typeface for their logo; a decision that draws directly on the print and manuscript heritage to signal the expository function and authority of the text. *The Boston Globe, New York Times, The Washington Post, Los Angeles Times, Chicago Tribune*, and

The Seattle Times all rely upon Olde English font, or a customized version of it, for the masthead. Five of the top papers (*USA Today, New York Post, Newsday, amNewYork,* and *Star Tribune*) take a modern approach, utilizing a customized sans-serif font whereas another four (*Atlanta Journal-Constitution, Houston Chronicle, New York Daily News,* and *Wall Street Journal*) use serif-fonts that reflect print forms. The online version of *The Dallas Morning News* is the one publication that employs a hybrid style, with a masthead that combines the modern and old, with "Dallas News" in a stylized modern font and "powered by The Dallas Morning News" underneath in a smaller Olde English font. For newspapers that have opted for a modern look, not only are fonts that are representative of the medieval or print era abandoned, but sans-serif fonts are often stylized and/or combined with iconography that brands the publication.

Below the masthead, online newspapers rely on modern and/or print typefaces (figure 15.5). Among the dataset, it was common to see serif fonts used for article headlines, reminiscent of early type-setting whereas the text for articles does not follow any pattern of specific font usage although the text is organised through other typographic features such as size and boldface. One aspect of online newspapers where the contemporary era is reflected throughout the dataset is the use of modern sans-serif fonts (like Arial and Helvetica) in the navigation menus. The latter is part of the contemporary technology of "the web" through their heritage in early web design, and in their practical suitability to the screen. Another notable feature of the online daily news-page – although not a strategic choice of the newspaper publisher – are the banner advertisements; these use their own product-specific branding typography, which represents an additional category of fonts that provide navigational cues to readers. This remediation of fonts in online newspapers demonstrates how producers of new media borrow from the historical – relying upon the ideological meaning potentials associated with the era – and refashion the old to meet the rhetorical needs and expectations of modern-day readers.

15.6 Colour

Another feature that demonstrates the "disruptive" intervention of print is the use of colour as a semiotic resource in written texts. Manuscripts and digital texts intentionally employ colour for design and meaning potential. Although culturally and locally dependent, and therefore complex for analysis (Machin 2010: 9), "colour is a semiotic resource like others: regular, with signs that are motivated in their constitution by the interests of the makers of the signs, and not at all arbitrary or anarchic" (Kress & van Leeuwen 2002: 345). Kandinsky (1977 [1914]) has distinguished between colour having a direct value, which is a physical effect on the viewer, and an associative value; as when a colour has high symbolic and emotive value on account of an association with a particular phenomenon or culturally recognizable object. The use of colours in medieval manuscripts provides direct value and associative values, to the extent that those texts in which gold leaf was used, are now defined as "illuminated" manuscripts. Gold's expense, and therefore cultural value, ensured that this was reserved for the most revered texts. Other associations were functional. Red lettering foregrounded text, to prompt reader action, or to signal different voices, which is also the case with hyperlinks in digital texts. In early digital writing, hyperlinks were a bright blue, alerting the reader as to where to click. Recently, hyperlinks are part of document design meaning that hyperlink colours are part of the page's colour palette and are often recognizable via hovering over text rather than foregrounded by colour.

As evident across our sample texts, medieval manuscripts draw on the affordances of colour as an organisational and signposting feature (see Kopaczyk; Moore; Rutkowska; all this volume). Rubrication (from the Latin *rubricare*, to colour red) denotes the process of adding red lettering to manuscripts. Such colouring primarily functioned as signals to the reader, directing their attention as to the organisation of the text in terms of how it sequences its content and foregrounding. Palettes differed in terms of availability of inks based on the ingredients required. Other colouring effects were dependent upon scribal skill sets; for example, gold leaf needed specialist limners (Driver & Orr 2000: 109–111). This in turn meant that the creation of a manuscript was a specialist and necessarily highly collaborative activity; the text became a site evidencing numerous skills brought into synthesis. The financial costs of inking also meant that it came to accrue connotations (or "associative values") of contextual luxuriousness. And these connotations grew, depending on the text type employed. For example, the word of God was frequently rubricated due to its importance (Ghosh 2000: 30); the ideological significance of Scripture, as truth, meant that rubrication also became linked with truth. In other words, the value or significance of rubrication was both direct (signalling the salience of particular text items) and associative (carrying various connotations of, for example, luxuriousness or truth).

Yet inking practices are also open to subversion. In the Winchester Manuscript of Malory's *Morte Darthur*, proper names (of characters, places, and objects) are foregrounded through rubrication. Whetter (2017: 1) argues that this rubrication is unprecedented for the period, but performs an important number of functions that link the visual form of the page with the narrative content of the text. He gives the example of folio 484v and states "for what quite literally stands out in Gwenyvere's speech is the rubricated name of her lover: 'Cryste Jesu' and 'God' are never rubricated and so disappear" (Whetter 2017: 155). What Whetter argues is that manuscript affordances, more traditionally associated with God, are transposed to the secular, and this in turn reinforces the thematic concern the narrative has for earthly chivalry and its status as a book of arms. The rubrication also has a navigational function, what Toolan (2009: 53) calls "the guiding function that repeated use of a character's proper name can have". Figure 15.1, depicting the start of Lydgate's *Fall of Princes*, provides an example of how marginalia can summarise a manuscript's content and thus act as a resource for readers by which they can quickly navigate through the text.

The use of coloured letters to steer readers across medieval texts to follow characters can be compared with modern day digital texts; specifically, hyperlinks that take a reader within and between websites. However, whilst rubrication and marginalia assist in the navigation of the text at hand, hyperlinks allow the reader to navigate the text at hand in reference to other texts. This is of course an affordance peculiar to digital texts and indicative of the web-like structure of the internet. For a reader, the intertextual nature of links offers access to further information beyond the text, functioning to give more information, provide evidence, give credit, lead to action, solve a puzzle, or tell something different (Myers 2010). Links may be analysed in terms of truth-value, as often the function of these links is elaborative and corroborative. In figure 15.2, for example, we see how headline links have elaborative quality when leading readers from story openings about Boeing pilots, the search for remains in Ethiopia, and motorcycle gangs in Venezuela to the complete stories on later pages via the click of a mouse (or tap of a finger on the screen). The link to the "Fact Checker" video story about Trump's tax cut can be seen as corroborative in that the goal is to verify the truth of a story and educate readers.

Links are similar to rubrication in the role that they afford the reader: deferring responsibility as to whether to engage, whilst at the same time suggesting a level of authority and corroboration. A similar level of optionality and reader control is afforded by manuscript rubrication, allowing a reader to navigate through a text and select those passages of interest and relevance to "tell us more of what we already know from the linking" (Myers 2010: 38). For example, readers of online newspapers can click on article abstracts posted on the left-hand side of the front page to follow the link to the complete story (figure 15.5).

15.7 Imagery

As with colour, manuscript and digital texts use symbolism and imagery as visual rhetoric strategies. We argue that imagery in both acts as a form of navigation. Some images are explicit in their organisational function, such as manicules: sketches of hands, which point to an important section of a manuscript text (Sherman 2005: 16). Manicules have a modern-day descendant, of sorts, in the cursor hand that hovers over a link. Whilst its function differs, it reminds us of the specifically embodied nature of reader-text interaction, through the symbolic representation of the hand. As digital readers, we are encouraged through manicula and links to read not just discursively (Clemens & Graham 2007: 43) but to read disruptively, rather than linearly, using digital bookmarks, strings and tags to find and mark relevant passages.

An important aspect of the visual rhetoric of images and imagery in written media is their placement in relation to text. In manuscript production each element was created separately, probably by different people (Driver & Orr 2011). This labour-intensive production suggests that such layout choices were calculated and meaningful across a scribal community. Medieval imagery is "illustrative" and can be seen to have low modality, having indistinguishable figures and scenes that lack detail and realism. Having lower modality, the reader faces a greater interpretative burden. In medieval manuscripts, their format allows for the illustrative imagery, such as the depiction of Lydgate in figure 15.1, to closely interact and inform the meaning of the written text. This contrasts with digital media, for example, which can make use of high-resolution images as seen on the front pages of online newspapers (figure 15.2).

One aspect to consider is the social significance of the aesthetic or "craft" of the image and its textual environment: we propose that the more elaborate, ornate and detailed a text, the more skilled the perception of the text producer and thereby, by implication, the more authoritative the text. The aesthetic quality of a work can create the authority, or truth-value, of that work. In medieval manuscripts, aesthetic proficiency, evidenced in illumination, rubrication and even the skilled scribal hand, lends an air of authority to those texts. These connotations are partly a consequence of the fact that illumination was most frequently applied to religious texts (i.e. the Word of God, Truth), rubrication represented verbatim speech, and precise scribal legibility came to distinguish the texts produced by political authorities. In the digital age, the availability and ease of access to professional modes of publishing have complicated this connection: specialist skills are no longer required, with "fake news", and the difficulty of distinguishing this from accredited news sources, demonstrating the powerful implications of the democratization of publishing. On the basis of the association between quality and truth-value, readers tend to trust websites that conform to a clean and professional aesthetic whereas websites that appear to be poorly designed are often perceived as having less credibility (George, Giordano & Tilley 2016; Liu 2004). This helps explain the consistency in shared visual features, such as colour and typeface, seen in the news media websites (see figures 15.2 and 15.5). The Gricean maxim of *quality* (Grice 1975) reminds us that people are persuaded by aesthetics that are appropriate to the medium: in digital media, the print traditions are remediated in part because of their socially-conventionalised authority. In the web 2.0 environment, however, any writer can replicate, reproduce and circulate texts that are believable and plausible to the web user based on their visual rhetoric and appearance.

The depiction of a narrative series-of-events offers an interesting example of the affordances (positive and negative) of the manuscript page in endeavoring to use a static image to portray dynamic, temporal phenomena through a "comic-strip" format (see figure 15.6). Cotton MS Nero AX contains *Pearl, Cleanness, Patience* and *Sir Gawain and the Green Knight*, four anonymous Middle English poems. Each of the poems is prefaced with miniatures reflecting key events from the narrative. In addition, *Sir Gawain and the Green Knight* concludes with three images depicting Bertilak's attempted seduction of Gawain (f. 129r), the meeting at the Green Chapel (f. 129v) and Gawain's reunion with King Arthur and Queen Guinevere (f. 130r).

In medieval manuscripts, such images sometimes adhered to narrative linearity, but as the example above illustrates, this, due to the segmented nature of manuscript illustration, might be divorced from its correlating text. In addition, images would also be used to portray simultaneous events, and not necessarily events segmented by frames of narrative progression as found in present-day graphic novels and comics. The tendency for medieval scribes to integrate text within images (for example, to show speech) further indicates the fluid interaction between word and image that was intended for how a reader engaged with the text.

The modality of digital news websites is high as a result of the integration of high resolution colour photography and, more recently, video content. Social semiotic theory uses the concept of modality to explain the degree to which visuals represent a perceived sense of reality and truth (Kress & van Leeuwen 1996). While print newspapers and online newspapers may use the same photographs within a story to portray real events, online images tend to have higher modality due to the higher degree of articulation, compared to the soft-focus version created on newsprint, that offers a greater sense of realness to viewers. Ravelli and van Leeuwen (2018: 394) suggest that modality is not about what is

Figure 15.6: © The British Library Board Cotton MS Nero AX, Four anonymous poems in Middle English: *Pearl, Cleanness, Patience* and *Sir Gawain and the Green Knight* (1375–1424) f. 94v.

or is not real, but rather is inherently interactional – based on "what is represented as (and what we see as) real". They point to changing perceptions in which images captured with contemporary wide-angle cameras are increasingly considered the norm whereas they would have been viewed as hyper-real compared to those produced with traditional 35 mm cameras. Additionally, Ravelli and van Leeuwen (2018: 385) argue that modality is historically situated and subject to change, such that "the norms for 'standard average naturalism' are evolving as a result of the affordances and constraints of new digital image technologies". In our sample of online newspaper texts, more than half of the top newspapers embed video content for featured stories on the front page (figure 15.2), reflecting an increasing use of movement, as well as depth, as additional modality markers that increase perception of truth based on changing expectations of norms for audiences in the digital age.

Consequently, the words on the page no longer carry the full burden of mimetic imitation, whereas in other media text remains the main or even sole means of communicating the extra-linguistic reality to the reader. With a video "text", mimesis has been replaced by the real, actual, and evidential. This has implications for how readers interact and consume the textual information in a digital environment compared to the paper (print and manuscript) predecessors, and here differences can be detected. This can be conceived of in terms of the top-down and bottom-up effort of processing for the reader. For example, the manuscript comic-strip narrative miniature finds its loose equivalent in the embedded video in a webpage. However, a manuscript story panel requires more top-down processing effort by the reader than a web video, which is bottom-up more manifestly detailed and real. Thus, where the manuscript is mimetic the webpage is realistic. The realism of the presented video, embedded within the web-page text, creates a *dependence* between modal elements, one which can be seen to disrupt the privilege of the word in earlier textual formats, such as manuscript and print. One entailment of this realism of digital media is the expectation that the text's meaning is "true": that it depicts reality to be critiqued directly. This contrasts with medieval texts which necessarily relied on the aesthetic effect of reality, mimesis, constructed through the low modality image and their verbal frames. This is not to say that web reading is more passive but that approaches to interpretation have shifted. Web readers perhaps judge more critically the extra-linguistic reality of what they read whereas medieval readers perhaps judged the verisimilitude of the mimetic efforts of the text. It is a hermeneutic difference perhaps characterised, if not defined by, medieval readers schooled in the exegetical reading practices, whereby text was a revelation of the divine; a belief codified in Article Six of the Thirty-nine Articles of Religion that defined the English Reformation, which stated "Holy Scripture containeth all things necessary to salvation ... In the name of the holy Scripture, we do understand those Canonical books of the Old and New Testament, of whose authority was never any doubt in the Church."

15.8 Conclusion

This paper is a preliminary sketch of how medieval and digital visual rhetoric aligns, and contrasts, in expository texts. Marked by their fluidity in composition, standardisation and navigation, manuscript and digital texts disrupt many of the writing and reading practices of the print age. The printing press was a technological change which made text accessible to a wider readership

(Eisenstein 1979). This resulted in a payoff between reproduction and textual affordances, which digital technologies have been able to redress. As pointed out in Jones, Chik & Hafner (2015: 3) "digital practices are always nestled or nested with other cultural practices, some new and some old". The similarities are evidenced in the text's modality, and it is this modality that gives a text its authority, a power derived from cultural understandings of those features. The transhistorical similarities have also come to inform textual practices, as have the metaphor and metalanguage used that demarcate how we understand and participate in those textual practices.

With each technology shift, there are associated anxieties which follow; an anxiety about authenticity, accuracy, and validity (Baron 2009; Tagg & Evans, this volume). These fears are alleviated by the promise of accuracy as enforced by those individuals and/or institutions that have been legitimized to give sources authority. With print, publishers became the authority that alleviated the anxiety that came when the medium was considered new and controversial. With digital sources, questions of authority are still in flux. Websites with URL domain names such as *.edu* or *.org*, for example, tend to be more readily granted authority on account of the connection to the institutional power of education and nonprofit organisations, understood to be working towards the greater good rather than consumer interests (Kakol, Nielek & Wierzbicki 2017).

We argue, perhaps controversially, that a web user and a medieval reader have more in common than either reader does with their modern print-based equivalent. The way that people interact with medieval manuscripts and digital texts reminds us that print was the disruption in discursive practices, shifting the ways in which people collaboratively participated with texts in fluid ways. The digital is not (only) new, but also a return to the historical.

References

Manuscripts

London, British Library, Add. MS 10292.
London, British Library, Add. MS 37049.
London, British Library, Add. MS 59678.
London, British Library, Cotton MS Nero A X/2.
London, British Library, Harley MS 1766.
London, British Library, Harley MS 2253.
London, British Library, Harley MS 2320.
London, British Library, Harley MS 6333.

Secondary Sources

Baron, Denis. 2009. *A better pencil: Readers, writers, and the digital revolution*. Oxford: Oxford University Press.
Bell, Alice. 2011. Ontological boundaries and conceptual leaps: The significance of possible worlds for hypertext fiction (and beyond). In Ruth Page & Bronwen Thomas (eds.), *New narratives: Stories and storytelling in the digital age*, 63–82. Lincoln, NE: University of Nebraska Press.
Bellantoni, Jeff & Matt Woolman. 2000. *Type in motion: Innovations in digital graphics*. London: Thames and Hudson.
Boffey, Julia & John. J. Thompson. 1989. Anthologies and miscellanies: Production and choice of texts. In Jeremy Griffiths & David Pearsall (eds.), *Book production and publishing in Britain 1375–1475*, 297–315. Cambridge, UK: Cambridge University Press.
Bolter, Jay D. & Richard Grusin. 2000. *Remediation: Understanding new media*. Cambridge, MA: MIT Press.
Brantley, Jessica. 2007. *Reading in the wilderness: Private devotion and public performance in late medieval England*. Chicago: The University of Chicago Press.
Brown, Penelope & Stephen C. Levinson. 1987. *Politeness: Some universals in language usage*. Cambridge, UK: Cambridge University Press.
Clemens, Raymond & Timothy Graham. 2007. *Introduction to manuscript studies*. New York: Cornell University Press.
Driver, Martha & Michael Orr. 2011. Decorating and illustrating the page. In Alexandra Gillespie & Daniel Wakelin (eds.), *The production of books in England 1350–1500*, 104–128. Cambridge, UK: Cambridge University Press.
Eisenstein, Elizabeth. 1979. *The printing press as an agent of change: Communications and cultural transformations in early-modern Europe*. Cambridge, UK: Cambridge University Press.
Field, P. J. C. 2004. Malory and his scribes. *Arthuriana* 14 (1), 31–42.
Fisher, J., Malcolm. Richardson & Jane L. Fisher. 1984. *An anthology of chancery English*. Knoxville: University of Tennessee Press.
Foss, Sonja K. 2005. Theory of visual rhetoric. In Smith, Kenneth L., Sandra Moriarty, Keith Kenney & Gretchen Barbatsis (eds.), *Handbook of visual communication: Theory, methods, and media*, 141–152. Abingdon: Routledge.
Galvez, Marisa. 2012. *Songbook: How lyrics became poetry in medieval Europe*. Chicago: University of Chicago Press.
George, Joey. F., Gabriel Giordano & Patti A. Tilley. 2016. Website credibility and deceiver credibility: Expanding prominence-interpretation theory. *Computers in Human Behavior* 54. 83–93.
Ghosh, Kantik. 2000. Manuscripts of Nicholas Love's The Mirror of the Blessed Life of Jesus Christ and Wycliffite notions of authority. In Felicity Riddy (ed.), *Prestige, authority, and power in late medieval manuscripts and texts*, 17–34. Suffolk: York Medieval Press.
Grice, H. Paul. 1975. Logic and conversation. In Peter Cole & Jerry L. Morgan (eds.), *Syntax and semantics* 3, 41–58. New York: Academic Press.
Hiippala, Tuomo. 2012. Reading paths and visual perception in multimodal research, psychology and brain sciences. *Journal of Pragmatics* 44 (3). 315–327.
Jenkins, Henry. 2006. *Convergence culture: Where old and new media collide*. New York: NYU Press.

Jewitt, Carey, Jeff Bezemer & Kay O'Halloran. 2016. *Introducing multimodality*. Abingdon: Routledge.
Jones, Rodney H., Alice Chik & Christopher A. Hafner. 2015. *Discourse and digital practices*. Abingdon: Routledge.
Kakol, Michal, Radoslaw Nielek & Adam Wierzbicki. 2017. Understanding and predicting Web content credibility using the Content Credibility Corpus. *Information Processing & Management* 53 (5). 1043–1061.
Kandinsky, Wassily. 1977 [1914]. *Concerning the spiritual in art*, revised edn. New York: Dover Publications.
Kress, Gunther. 2003. *Literacy in the new media age*. Abingdon: Routledge.
Kress, Gunther & Theo van Leeuwen. 1996. *Reading images: The grammar of visual design*, 2nd edn. Abingdon: Routledge.
Kress, Gunther & Theo van Leeuwen. 2002. Colour as a semiotic mode. Notes for a grammar of colour. *Visual Communication* 1 (3). 343–368.
Labov, William. 1972. Some principles of linguistic methodology. *Language in Society* 1 (1). 97–120.
Ledin, Per & David Machin. 2018. *Doing visual analysis: From theory to practice*. Thousand Oaks: Sage.
Liu, Ziming. 2004. Perceptions of credibility of scholarly information on the web. *Information Processing & Management* 40 (6). 1027–1038.
Machin, David. 2010. *Analysing popular music: Image, sound and text*. Thousand Oaks: Sage.
Mishra, Vijay. 1994. *The Gothic sublime*. Albany: State University of New York Press.
Monroy-Casas, Rafael. 2008. Linearity in language. Rhetorical-discursive preferences in English and Spanish in the light of Kaplan's model. *IJES* 8 (2). 173–189.
Mortimer, Nigel. 2005. *John Lydgate's "Fall of Princes": Narrative tragedy in its literary and political contexts*. Oxford: Clarendon Press.
Myers, Greg. 2010. *The discourse of blogs and wikis*. London: Continuum.
Page, Ruth & Bronwen Thomas. 2011. *New narratives: Stories and storytelling in the digital age*. Lincoln, NE: University of Nebraska Press.
Parkes, Malcolm B. 1991. *Scribes, scripts, and readers: Studies in the communication, presentation, and dissemination of medieval texts*. London: Hambledon Press.
Pears, Iain. 2015. *Arcadia: A novel*. New York: Knopf.
Peikola, Matti. 2015. Manuscript paratexts in the making: British Library MS Harley 6333 as a liturgical compilation. In Sabrina Corbellini, Margriet Hoogvliet & Bart Ramakers (eds.), *Discovering the riches of the word: Religious reading in late medieval and early modern Europe*, 44–67. Leiden: Brill.
Ravelli, Louise. J. & Theo van Leeuwen. 2018. Modality in the digital age. *Visual Communication* 17 (3). 277–297.
Rello, Luz & Ricardo Baeza-Yates. 2013. Good fonts for dyslexia. In *Proceedings of the 15th International ACM SIGACCESS Conference on Computers and Accessibility – ASSETS '13*, 1–8. Bellevue, Washington: ACM Press.
Robinson, Peter. 2014. Materials, Paper and Type. In Vincent Gillespie & Susan Powell (eds.), *A Companion to the early printed book in Britain 1476–1558*, 61–74. Cambridge, UK: D.S. Brewer.
Sherman, William. H. 2005. Toward a history of the Manicule. In Robin Myers, Michael Harris & Giles Mandelbrote (eds.), *Owners, annotators and the signs of reading*, 19–48. New Castle: Oak Knoll Press.

Thompson, Riki. 2012. Looking healthy: visualizing mental health and illness online. *Visual Communication* 11 (4). 395–420.
Thomson, Rodney. 2018. Scribes and scriptoria. In Eric Kwakkel & Rodney Thomson (eds.), *The European book in the twelfth century*, 68–84. Cambridge, UK: Cambridge University Press.
Tillotson, Dianne. 2005. Caroline Miniscule. http://medievalwriting.50megs.com/scripts/history5.htm (accessed 1 March 2019).
Toolan, Michael J. 2009. *Narrative progression in the short story: A corpus stylistic approach*. Amsterdam: John Benjamins.
van Leeuwen, Theo. 1993. Genre and field in Critical Discourse Analysis: A synopsis. *Discourse & Society* 4 (2). 193–223.
van Leeuwen, Theo. 2005. *Introducing social semiotics*. Abingdon: Routledge.
Whetter, Kevin S. 2017. *The manuscript and meaning of Malory's Morte Darthur: Rubrication, commemoration, memorialization*. Woodbridge: Boydell and Brewer.

Martine van Driel

16 "It makes it more real": A comparative analysis of Twitter use in live blogs and quotations in older news media from a reader response perspective

16.1 Introduction

Many researchers hail the Arab Spring as the spark for the development of citizen journalism (Allagui & Kuebler 2011; Khondker 2011; Russell 2016). As journalists were unable to enter countries in Northern Africa, news institutions relied on information from citizens "on the ground" relayed via social media (Russell 2016). The inclusion of social media sources in news texts has since become increasingly common. Live blogs (or LBs), a type of online news text, are a prime example of this, as their inclusion of social media is considered as one of their defining features. An LB is defined as "a single blog post on a specific topic to which time-stamped content is progressively added for a finite period – anywhere between half an hour and 24 hours" (Thurman & Walters 2013: 2). It has become the default news format for breaking news stories and "outperforms all other online journalism sources" in numbers of webpage visitors (Thurman 2013: 85). They have been held up as "a crucible in digital journalism" (Thurman & Schapals 2016: 1), and Beckett (2010: 4) attributes LBs' popularity to the fact that they meet the audience's "demand for immediacy, reflection, context and diversity", as they mix sources, media, tone and content into one continually updated platform.

This chapter investigates how the use of social media in LBs can be placed in the historical development of digital news reporting, considering how readers respond to LBs as compared to more traditional forms of online news reporting. I compare the LB, an "emergent" form of digital media that is specific to the web (Herring 2012: 8), to the "traditional online news article" or TONA (Bunz 2010; Thurman & Schapals 2016), a "reproduced genre" (Crowston & Williams 2000: 207) that takes print news articles and their structural characteristics and presents them through a webpage. TONAs follow the inverted-pyramid structure as they are based on offline news texts whereas LBs follow a reverse-chronological structure consistent of short updates; this structure is

---

Martine van Driel, University of Birmingham, Birmingham, UK,
e-mail: m.a.vandriel.1@bham.ac.uk

https://doi.org/10.1515/9783110670837-021

new, and therefore "emergent", in online news texts. TONAs show some distinction from offline news texts, in particular their use of hyperlinks and embedded pictures as well as the larger co-text of the webpage. However, both the structure of TONAs and the editorial process of completing writing and editing before publication remains the same as offline news texts. While comparing LBs to offline news texts would certainly be an interesting approach to take, it would also need to consider the different reading experiences that online and offline texts provide as well as the surrounding co-texts of newspapers versus news websites. By comparing two online news genres, I am able to focus my comparison; and, specifically, focus on differing styles of quotations in both news genres, as opposed to the different reading experiences that online and offline texts provide.

Importantly, research (Thurman & Walters 2013; Thurman & Newman 2014) has shown that readers rate LBs as more trustworthy than TONAs due to the frequency of updates and the mixture of information sources included in the respective news reports. I investigate how the presentation of these information sources in LBs differs from the presentation in TONAs, and consider how readers respond to these social media sources through a linguistic analysis of the respondents' use of evaluative language.

16.2 Personalisation and sourcing in news

Interest in information sourcing in news is not new to digital journalism. Discussing emotionality in the pre-digital age, Tuchman (1978: 122–123) argued that journalists use quotations to convey emotional impact while remaining an objective, emotionally uninvolved reporter. Wahl-Jorgenson (2012: 130) named this "the outsourcing of emotional labour". In non-digital contexts and in TONAs, this outsourcing is achieved through quotations, while in digital contexts such as LBs – which have not yet received the same extensive analytic attention – I argue that it is achieved through both quotations and embedded social media.

In digital news texts, emotional outsourcing takes place primarily through citizen witnesses on social media (Allan 2016). Stories containing these emotional narratives are more likely to be shared, causing emotionality to become "a form of news currency" (Myrick & Wojdynski 2016: 2076–2077). In addition, emotional news narratives have been shown to increase monetary donations from audiences (Wahl-Jorgenson 2012). While researchers have investigated the rising response rate associated with affective journalism, there has been a lack of focus on the linguistic responses of readers, therefore discouraging detailed analysis of what readers are responding to, and the impact of affective journalism on their descriptions and evaluations of reported news events. Additionally, digital journalism research often focuses on the "newness" of digital texts (Thurman & Walters 2013; Tereszkiewicz 2014; Thurman & Schapals 2016) rather than investigating how LBs developed from TONAs and thus the similarities in their features and therefore their impact upon readers. This concern has been echoed in other forms of digital research (Crowston & Williams 2000; Herring 2012). By focusing solely on change and on the "newness" of live blogs, digital journalism research runs the risk of negating years of research into offline news reporting, which not only informs our online research but can also provide insights into digital journalism.

Breaking-news LBs are more likely to contain citizen sources – people who do not identify as professional journalists or members of authorities such as governments – than TONAs (Thurman & Rodgers 2014), and often present these sources more directly than how those same source types are presented in TONAs. Use of direct speech has been shown to increase vividness of the speaker and the reported speech (Yao, Belin & Scheepers 2011). This has also been investigated in news texts, as Caldas-Coulthard (1994) argued that even reporting verbs that appear objective have an effect when compared to the use of other reporting verbs. Thurman and Schapals (2016) found that LBs used direct quotes in 68 per cent of included references, while TONAs used direct quotes in 57 per cent. This percentage was only slightly lower at 54 per cent for print articles, showing a comparable use of direct quotes between TONAs and print news (Thurman & Schapals 2016: 289).

While Thurman and Schapals (2016: 8) looked at direct quotes in news texts, they did not provide a clear definition of what a "direct quote" entails; apart from that direct quotes are "opposed to indirect quotes". The assumption I make based on my research of LBs, is that Thurman and Schapals (2016) used the term "direct quotes" to refer to instances of direct speech and direct writing (including tweets) within the news texts. Direct speech can be defined as words that are quoted verbatim (Leech & Short 2007: 255) while direct writing refers to quotes from anterior discourse presented in written form (Semino & Short 2004: 98). Direct speech can be characterised by "inverted commas around the reported speech", first and second person pronouns, present tense, and close deixis (Leech & Short 2007: 256). This has been shown to be applicable to news texts (Caldas-Coulthard 1994). Tweets in LBs, which Thurman and Schapals (2016) appear to count as "direct quotes", do not contain direct speech markers, but are marked by the layout designed by Twitter. Additionally, tweets are hyperlinked to their original context: the profile of the author, creating "posterior discourse accessibility" (Short, Semino & Wynne 2002: 350). This accessibility increases the perceived reliability of the tweet, as readers are able to "check" the anterior discourse for accuracy. Direct quotations as presented through direct speech markers are generally not hyperlinked as the quotation has often been taken from interviews by the reporter with the original author, which causes them to be seen as less trustworthy because the faithfulness of the quotation cannot be authenticated (Short, Semino & Wynne 2002; Ikeo 2009).

While the inclusion of social media in LBs has been positively evaluated for involving "civilian" sources, it should be noted that the sources of tweets in LBs are primarily professional, such as journalists, news agencies or other news publishers (Chouliaraki 2015), or those that are already known to the journalist (Broersma & Graham 2013). This indicates a reliance on known sources reminiscent of pre-digital news, where reporters did not have the extensive access to online eyewitness accounts that Twitter provides.

The increased access to news actors, or perceived news actors, in LBs as compared to TONAs may have effects on the reader. Each of these aspects of digital news texts has the potential to impact reader responses to both the news text and the news event. While consumption habits of LB readers have been studied thoroughly (Thurman & Walters 2013; Thurman & Newman 2014; Thurman & Rodgers 2014), there has yet to be research conducted on consumers' perceptions of LBs and the influence of the inclusion of social media on their perceptions of the news event (Thurman & Schapals 2016: 283). As news texts, and especially live blogs, are often used to report on breaking news, readers may use these texts to learn about news events for the first time. It is therefore crucial to understand if and how these news texts may affect readers' perceptions of the news events. This chapter therefore analyses the presentation of sources, both through quotations and embedded social media, in hard news LBs and its effect on reader evaluations of the news texts and the news events. I compare these results to the use of quotations in TONAs and reader evaluations of TONAs and their respective news events. I show that while sources in LBs are presented through direct speech in a similar way to quotations in TONAs, readers evaluate speech presentations in LBs as more affective than those in TONAs, with implications for how they view the news event being depicted.

16.3 Research design

16.3.1 Methodology approach

The study of "real" reader response is based on the assumption that to understand reading practices, research needs to study actual readers. This has been done through two methodological approaches: naturalistic and experimental empirical. Peplow and Carter (2014: 441–442) use the term "naturalistic study of reading" to encompass qualitative studies of readers who are discussing reading in a natural environment. This approach to the study of reading grew from criticism of an empirical approach to reader response studies, as it was argued that empirical studies provide no insight into naturalistic reading (Allington & Swann 2009; Hall 2009). However, most of this naturalistic research takes place within literary studies (Van Peer 1983; Miall & Kuiken 1994; Miall 2006; Peplow & Carter 2014; Nuttall 2017) and can exploit the existence of informal reading groups. As readers of news do not naturally come together to discuss specific news texts similarly to book groups, and online news comments do not accurately represent the news texts' audiences (Steensen 2014: 1203), there are few natural settings which can be used for a naturalistic reader response study in news media. This research into news media therefore takes an experimental empirical approach to reader response. By pre-selecting news texts for readers, withholding the exact purpose of the study and using semi-structured interview techniques, the effects of different news formats can be studied and compared.

16.3.2 Data: News texts

This research focuses on readers of news within England, specifically native English speakers studying in Birmingham (UK). Therefore, news texts from the news publications with the most page-views in the UK were selected: *The Guardian* and the BBC (Schwartz 2015; Alexa 2017). Two different news events were selected to negate the influence of the news event on the reader responses: a day in the Gaza conflict in 2014 and a college shooting in the United States of America. For each news event, two news texts were selected from the same publication: one TONA and one LB. This resulted in a total of four news texts. The BBC published the news texts about the Gaza conflict on 20 July 2014. The TONA about the Gaza conflict consisted of 853 words (BBC 2014b). The LB about the Gaza conflict consisted of 2902 words and contained 45 updates (BBC 2014a). It started on 20 July 2014 at 16.12 British Standard Time (BST) and finished on

20 July 2014 at 19.06 BST. This news event was used in the first round of data collection. The TONA about the college shooting consisted of 1705 words and was published on the same date as the LB (The Guardian 2015b). The LB about the college shooting consisted of 6799 words and 61 updates (The Guardian 2015a). It started on 1 October 2015 at 2.06am BST and finished on 2 October 2015 at 6.15am BST. There were two rounds of data collection, with each round gathering reader responses to the news events: the first round held interviews to discuss the Gaza news event, and the second round focussed on the college shooting news event. Section 16.3.3 explains the interview process.

16.3.3 Data: Reader response interviews

Earlier research found that LBs are generally consumed while a news event is developing. Readers will return to LBs throughout the day, often while at work, to find new information added about the news event (Thurman & Walters 2013). As LBs present breaking news stories, respondents would have had to be available to read LBs and be interviewed on very short notice, which is why this research takes a more experimental approach with some mitigations to simulate the reading experience of an LB. The interview data for this research was collected through two rounds of data collection between March 2015 and October 2015 with a total of 20 participants. The participants were randomly assigned to read either an LB or a TONA. They were given 15 minutes to do so. The limited time frame forced LB readers to self-select updates to read, while giving the TONA readers enough time to read the whole text. This was done to mimic natural reading experiences of both news texts, given that LBs tend to be read in short bursts over the duration of a day as readers return to the LB to check for updates as the news events develop (Thurman & Walters 2013).

The interviews were semi-structured and lasted between 30 and 60 minutes, following typical interview length (Dörnyei 2007; Richards 2009). Questions included open and probing constructions, e.g.: "can you tell me about the news you just read?", "what do you think of this event?", "does this article represent the event that is being described well?" and "what do you think about the style of the news?". In transcribing interviews, I followed the principle that the transcription procedure should focus on transcribing "the essential elements" based on the research questions (Richards 2009). These choices should be made explicit (Fuoli & Hommerberg 2015). As this research is concerned with evaluative language used by readers and in news texts, its main focus is on lexis (Bednarek 2006). Therefore the transcriptions contained all lexis, including re-starts. While paralinguistic features could add an interesting angle to this research, I focused solely on lexis to limit the scope of the research. The semi-structured approach allowed me to probe respondents about any specific aspects of the news texts that may have caused positive or negative evaluations such as the sourcing and use of social media. Table 16.1 shows the word counts of the interview data set.

Table 16.1: Interview dataset.

	Gaza Conflict	College Shooting	Events Combined
Interviews with the TONA respondents	Total: 11,828 Mean: 2,365 Range: 1,536–3,778	Total: 6,722 Mean: 1,344 Range: 795–1,843	Total: 18,550 Mean: 1,855
Interviews with the LB respondents	Total: 15,543 Mean: 3,108 Range: 2,096–5,659	Total: 8,868 Mean: 1,773 Range: 1,232–2,415	Total: 24,411 Mean: 2,441
Interview groups combined	Total: 27,371 Mean: 2737	Total: 15,590 Mean: 1,559	Total: 42,961 Mean: 2,148

16.3.4 Analytical framework

The analysis of the interviews focuses on the respondents' use of evaluative language. This field of research encompasses many different approaches (e.g. Hunston & Thompson 2000; Martin & White 2005; Englebretson 2007). As I am concerned specifically with lexical evaluations of news texts and news events, this analysis was carried out following the Appraisal framework (Martin & White 2005). This framework is considered to be one of the most thorough approaches to evaluative language (Thompson 2014; Goźdź-Roszkowski & Hunston 2016) as it focuses on both the interpersonal and the ideational evaluative functions of language, combining stance approaches with discourse analysis (Lemke 1998; Bednarek 2006; Englebretson 2007). It accounts for both modality and affect, which Thompson and Hunston (2000: 20) identify as "the two main types of evaluation". Within this framework, I focus my analysis on the sub-category Appreciation which is concerned with the evaluation of objects, as opposed to evaluations of people (Judgement) or expressed emotions (Affect) (Martin & White 2005). Appreciation is most appropriate for current purposes as the focus is primarily on evaluating the text and the news event as entities rather than, for example, the ethics of the journalist. Table 16.2 provides an overview of the categories within Appreciation (Martin & White 2005: 56).

Table 16.2: Overview of appreciation categories (Martin & White 2005: 56).

	Positive	Negative
Reaction: Impact "did it grab me?"	Interesting, exciting, moving	Boring, flat, predictable
Reaction: Quality "did I like it?"	Good, appealing, beautiful	Bad, ugly, plain
Composition: Balance "did it hang together?"	Balanced, considered, logical	Unbalanced, flawed, contradictory
Composition: Complexity "was it hard to follow?"	Simple, precise, intricate	Extravagant, unclear, simplistic
Valuation "was it worthwhile?"	Profound, original, unique	Worthless, shallow, pricey

The transcripts were analysed for evaluative instances, focusing only on explicit evaluative language, so as to limit subjective interpretations of evoked evaluation (Thompson 2014). To aid the rigour of the analysis, I coded each evaluation as one instance regardless of the number of words. As an example, an evaluative statement such as "as bad as the other conflict" is classed as one evaluative instance, as is the one-word evaluative statement "sad". These instances were coded and counted using nVivo and the frequencies were normalised per 100 words to account for the different sizes of the two interview data sets. Before the reader responses are analysed in detail, the next section analyses how sources are presented in both the TONAs and the LBs.

16.4 Overview: Speech presentation in reproduced and emergent news text genres

The news texts were analysed for the number of satellites; that is, sections of the body of the news texts that provide more detail about the information provided in the headline and the abstract (White 1997), to allow for a more direct comparison between the news texts than word count can provide.

Both LBs, containing 82 and 97 satellites respectively, were longer than the TONAs, which contained 32 and 33 satellites respectively. Additionally, the LBs contained more sources than the TONAs as can be seen in table 16.3. The *Guardian*'s news texts were consistently longer than the corresponding *BBC*

Table 16.3: Frequencies of news text characteristics.

	BBC TONA	The Guardian TONA	BBC LB	The Guardian LB
Satellites	32	33	82	97
Sources	16	21	51	64
Quotations (direct speech)	5	14	11	36
Tweets	0	0	34	25
Emails	0	0	5	0
Total instances of direct language (incl. quotations, tweets, and emails)	5	14	50	61

texts and they also contained more sources in both the TONAs and the LBs. All news texts included instances of direct speech presentation through the use of quotations and, at times, reporting clauses. These instances are labelled as "quotations". Within the LBs, there were presentations of direct speech through the inclusions of emails from readers. These were only present in the LB published by the BBC. Finally, and most significantly for this chapter, the LBs included embedded tweets: the BBC LB had 34 tweets and the *Guardian* LB had 25 tweets. It should be noted that TONAs can also include tweets and these may have the same effects on readers as tweets within LBs. However, in the case studies used to collect response data for this chapter, the TONAs did not contain any such examples. Further work on the affective potential of tweets across news media is desirable.

Not only do the LBs contain more direct speech, the instances are also foregrounded, especially when compared to the instances in the TONAs. Quotations in the TONAs, their only instances of direct speech, were presented within the news narrative, an instance of which is shown in figure 16.1.

> The gunman's father, Ian Mercer, said he was "just as shocked as everybody" at his son's actions. Speaking from his home in the US, he told reporters: "I've just been talking to the police and the FBI and all the details I have right now is what you guys [reporters] have already.

Figure 16.1: Quotation in TONA (The Guardian 2015b).

The quotation is identifiable only through the use of quotation marks and, in this instance, two reporting clauses, one per quotation, and the font, type-size

> 2 Oct 2015   Stacey Boylan, father of 18-year-old Anastasia Boylan who was
> 05:04   injured in the attack, has told CNN his daughter survived by "playing
>   dead".
>
>> ❝ *He came in and there was gunfire immediately and he scattered the room. From what I understood what she said was he shot the professor point blank, one shot killed him.*
>>
>> *Others had been injured and then this man had enough time - I don't know how much time elapsed - he was able to stand there and start asking people one by one what their religion was. 'Are you a Christian?' he would ask them, and 'if you are a Christian then stand up' and they would stand up. He'd say 'because you are a Christian you're going to see God in about one second' and then he shot and killed them. And he kept going down the line doing this to people.*
>>
>> *How much time do you need?*
>>
>> *She said he had a handgun. It wasn't a big rifle or an assault rifle. This was a single handgun and he had enough ammunition and enough time to drop the magazine out of it, put another one in and continue his thing. How does he have that much time at a facility?*
>>
>> *I don't understand that. How he could have that much time to kill that many people."*
>
> ⓕ ⓥ ⓖ₊   Updated at 5.50am BST

Figure 16.2: Direct quotation in LB (The Guardian 2015a).

and presentation are consistent with the non-quoted text, meaning that the quotation is not foregrounded through typographical means. The LBs, on the other hand, foreground quotations extensively. Figure 16.2 shows an instance of a quotation within an LB.

The figure depicts one update in the LB. The update contains a lead-in, identifying the speaker and justifying their expertise of the news event (White 1997): "father of [victim]". The main quotation is presented in a different colour from the rest of the text, italicised, indented and has comparatively large opening quotation marks. Each of these features foregrounds the quotation, marking it as different from the other text. This is similar for the presentation of tweets within LBs, an instance of which can be seen in figure 16.3.

The tweets are embedded into the LBs and, following Twitter's terms of use, the embedded tweet retains its original Twitter layout. They are thus presented in a different font to the rest of the news text and contain their own

Figure 16.3: Embedded tweet in The Guardian LB (The Guardian 2015a).

follow, respond, re-tweet and like buttons, taken directly from Twitter. They also show the tweeter's profile picture, name and handle (anonymised for privacy in this chapter, not anonymised in the original news text), and each tweet hyperlinks to the original context of the tweet (on Twitter). This hyperlink likely increases perception of the reliability of the tweet as readers have easy access to the original utterance and can check the original wording. Tweets may therefore carry more authenticity than traditional information source quotations. Direct quotations, while presented as verbatim, may not be verbatim, as has been discussed in speech and thought presentation research (see Short, Semino & Wynne 2002; Ikeo 2009). The use of tweets also enhances the newsworthiness of the event by increasing the degree of personalisation as "the event is discursively constructed as having a personal or 'human' face (involving non-elite actors, including eyewitnesses)" (Bednarek & Caple 2017: 55), with which readers are able to connect through Twitter. As readers are provided with direct communication from eyewitnesses and have the option of responding directly to these news actors, readers may feel socially closer to the news event (Cohen, Adoni & Bantz 1990).

16.5 Reader response to sources

Figure 16.4 shows the reader response to the two different kinds of news sources.

Respondents were asked to evaluate the news text as well as the news event. All evaluative statements relating to the news texts, regardless of which

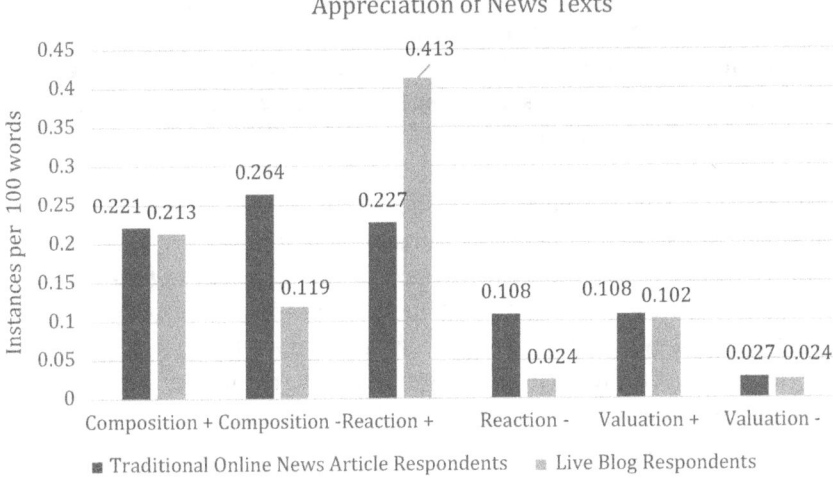

Figure 16.4: Appreciation of news texts by respondents.

question the respondents were replying to, were analysed; these are included in the frequencies in figure 16.4. The figure suggests that positive Reaction was used most by live blog respondents, with the frequency showing the largest difference with the equivalent evaluative category for TONA responses. LB respondents focused these evaluations on quotations and embedded social media as well as the personal stories that were presented by those sources. The TONA respondents, when they did make positive Reaction evaluations, used it similarly to evaluate not only quotations from news actors but also personal stories about news actors as described by the reporters. However, the lower frequency of this evaluative category in TONA responses potentially suggests a less affective evaluation of the presentation of the news content and its text.

Examples (1) and (2) show two instances of how the TONA respondents evaluated the use of personalised stories embedded in the news texts reporting on the Gaza conflict (my emphasis).

(1) I think also (.) the doc- tor eh I think his (2) I can't find where it is now I think it might be below [reading article] yeah I think it's towards the end but yeah I think the doctor's experience is quite eh (.) **strong** as well cause I think he just says about civilian casualties and how horrific can't find it now but I think he uses quite **strong** language about the eh (.) about the scenes so I think they're the main voices

(2) I like that it's taken direct- like not direct quotes but eh (.) it's reporting from there from the area it's not just like an out- **I don't feel like it's an outsider's opinion I feel like it's coming from within the situation** (.) it's like a massacre that's in quotation marks I assume (.) that that's been something that's said about it

In (1), the respondent evaluated a quotation from a doctor working in Gaza. The respondent stated that the doctor's language was "strong", suggesting they found the language powerful. This lexical evaluation in turn suggests that the doctor's quotations were engaging to the respondent. The respondent in (2) stated that the use of quotations and sourcing makes the text "feel like it's coming from within the situation", suggesting that the respondent evaluated the quotations as authentic. This apparent belief in the faithfulness of direct speech is common in relation to written language (Short, Semino & Wynne 2002), with direct speech also shown to increase vividness in perceptions of events (Yao, Belin & Scheepers 2011). The trust in direct sources is also apparent in the final sentence from the example, where the respondent states that someone must have referred to the conflict as a "massacre" as it is in quotation marks.

This apparent trust in quotations was also present in respondents' evaluations of the social media examples used in LB (3 responds to the Gaza conflict reports and example 4 responds to the college shooting specifically):

(3) I think the tweets overall are just (.) they're so **powerful** like you know especially from the civilians' perspective they're so **powerful** for giving you like you know a real a much more real time sense of (.) at the right time (.) a much more like **brutally real** sense of what's going on

(4) this would give you a bit more detail than perhaps you would look for (3) but the way it's sort of integrated all the social media stuff is quite **interesting** (.) you can kind of see lots of different people's opinions all within one news article which you normally can't do

In (3), the respondent referred to the tweets as "powerful", specifying that the tweets from "civilians" were especially engaging. Similar to the evaluations made by TONA respondents, this again suggests that stories told from the perspective of specific individuals and civilians may be more engaging to readers than other parts of the news texts; this interpretation relates to the observation that respondents did not evaluate stories told from journalists' perspectives or authoritative responses such as responses from governments in the same way.

The respondent also evaluated the tweets as "real", an evaluation which was found in half of the LB respondents' evaluations of tweets. This suggests that tweets were perceived as authentic even though neither the respondents nor I were able to confirm the authenticity of these tweets (in the sense of being able to verify the account). The respondent in example (4) evaluated the use of social media more generally, stating that the inclusion of tweets into news texts was "interesting". This echoes findings of Thurman and Walters (2013) that readers appreciate LBs for the range of sources that are included in the news texts.

Both the LB respondents and the TONA respondents used positive Reaction to evaluate the use of different voices within the news texts, with both groups specifically referring to individual news actors presented in the news texts. Both groups, as shown in figure 16.4, used positive Reaction more frequently than negative Reaction. Negative Reaction concentrated on the "factuality" of both news texts and the lack of reporter voice: "the actual writer who kind of did the (.) the summary of it (.) I wouldn't say (.) I heard their voice particularly because it's all very (.) eh (.) **distant** it's **very just factual**". This suggests that personalisation of news stories may increase the use of positive Reaction in respondents' evaluations of the news texts, and its presentation through embedded tweets or direct speech quotations may not be as influential on evaluations of the news text. Respondents seemed to use positive evaluations of what were perceived to be ordinary voices in news texts consistently, regardless of the presentation of these voices.

Contrastingly to the similarities found in evaluations of the news texts, the evaluations of the news events revealed a meaningful distinction between the respondents who read a TONA and the respondents who read an LB (see figure 16.5).

Both groups of respondents used mostly Reaction (consisting of Impact and Quality) in evaluations of the news event, with negative Quality being the most used category. Negative Quality is a sub-category of Reaction, and specifically focuses on whether and how much the evaluator "likes" the target of evaluation (Martin & White 2005: 56). Both TONA and LB respondents referred to personal experiences of news actors when evaluating the news events. The distinction between LB respondents and TONA respondents appears to be in the frequency and intensity of their responses. As shown above, LB respondents used more Reactive evaluations than TONA respondents, with those evaluations focussing on individual news actors and referring to specific experiences of news actors. This included, at times, using a first-person perspective thereby placing themselves in the position of the news actors. TONA respondents on the other hand

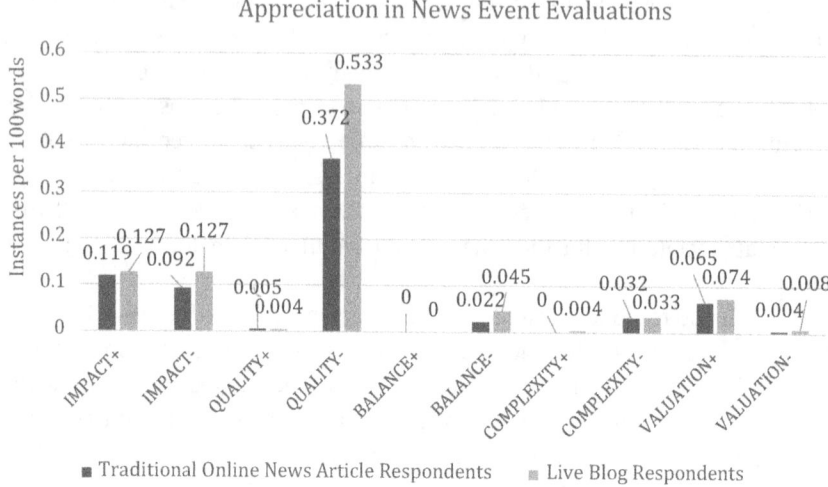

Figure 16.5: Appreciation of news events by respondents.

consistently referred either to groups of people such as "the families" (6, responding to Gaza conflict report), rather than specific individuals (as LB respondents do in examples 7 and 8, responding to Gaza conflict report and college shooting report respectively) or they projected their own feelings onto news actors (5, responding to Gaza conflict report), as opposed to referring directly to experiences of news actors as presented in the news texts as LB respondents did (7 and 8).

(5) I can only imagine it's just absolutely so **terrifying** for (.) eh (.) and they're probably thinking what is being done to help us (.) which is obviously very like for them they'll be you know (.) they'll be there thinking they won't (.) they will be in like unknown (.) they'll be in a state of not knowing what is going to happen and just sort of hoping that some- well something is gonna happen to help these people (.) yes so it's very **scary**

(6) 'I think like me now (.) obviously it's maybe (.) **shocked** (.) and you think about the people and about their families but after this then I'd just carry on with what I was doing so when I'm reading it (.) impact emotionally but then afterwards I would just carry on doing what I was gonna do'

The respondent in (5) stated that the event was "scary", which they connected to the projected personal response to the reported events using the causal conjunction "so" (underlined). The respondent did not refer to a specific point in the TONA. The respondent said they "can only imagine", distancing their response from the experiences of the news actors. In (6), the respondent linked their negative evaluation, "shocked", to non-specific news actors as they stated they would "think about the people and their families" [i.e. those involved in the news event but perhaps not those specifically mentioned]. The respondent evaluated the information about the news actors as engaging while they were reading it, but without having a lasting impact on their life. In both examples, the respondent is projecting their own response onto the situation, rather than empathising directly with the related experiences of specific individuals.

LB respondents on the other hand used negative Quality to refer to specific news actors that were quoted in the LBs, as in (7) and (8), which respond to the Gaza conflict and the college shooting, respectively.

(7) this I think like you know having sources in the area especially civilians like you know the Gaza resident I think seeing his tweets is (.) a pretty **terrifying** like you know breaking my home is shaking right now because of Israeli bombing

(8) I remember there was one guy from New Zealand I think it said (.) who's here doing eh (.) sports scholarship maybe (.) and he'd only been there two weeks eh (.) so (.) yeah it's pretty **horrendous** (1) eh (.) so he (.) there was his account he'd given he was running away with another boy and (.) the other boy he was running with was shot so that's pretty **traumatic**

In example (7), the respondent referred to the tweets of a "Gaza resident", evaluating them as "terrifying". The respondent used a copular construction, X is Y, typical in evaluative statements (Hunston & Sinclair 2000). This evaluation was followed by a shift to first person and present tense, presenting the situation from the perspective of the news actors: "my home is shaking right now". This contrasts to the TONA respondents whose evaluations focused on projections made from their own perspective as readers. Drawing on the tweet, this LB respondent is able to assume the perspective of the news actor, simulating to some extent the presentation of the tweet in the voice of the news actor. In (8), the respondent spoke about a news participant from New Zealand. This account, which the respondent refers to as "his account", was presented as a direct quotation in the LB. They retell details from the account: "he was running away with another boy" and that the student was "here doing [a] sports scholarship". This respondent blurs direct and indirect speech in their retelling: e.g.

starting with the direct speech marker "here", then distancing themselves from the news actor using the indirect speech marker "there" further into the quotation.

To conclude, in the reader response data, the respondents constructed the experiences of ordinary news actors in different ways. In their affective responses to the news events, the LB respondents aligned themselves with the perspectives of specific individuals, while the TONA respondents projected their evaluations onto non-specific news actors, often referring to them as groups. This suggests a distinction in evaluations of sources presented in TONAs through traditional indirect or direct speech as well as the narrator's reports of actions, and sources presented in LBs through foregrounded quotations or embedded social media. Importantly, the latter appeared to elicit stronger or more intense emotional responses which may stay longer with the reader. While the respondents did not evaluate the two kinds of sources differently in their evaluations of the news texts, their evaluations of the news events suggest an implicit difference in the relation between these forms of speech presentation and readers' evaluations of news.

16.6 Perceived authenticity of tweets versus quotations

The respondents provided an overall positive evaluation of how engaging the news texts were. However, the LB respondents used positive Reaction more often than the TONA respondents, suggesting a more positive evaluation of their engagement with LBs than the engagement with TONAs. The use of tweets and different media in the LBs seems to underlie this difference as 44 per cent of positive Impact evaluations by LB respondents, the most used sub-category of Reaction, referred to tweets. The LB respondents evaluated tweets as "real" and often referred directly to tweets or their content as support for their negative Reaction evaluations of the news events. The TONA respondents on the other hand discussed any perceived authenticity less often and did not refer to quotations as making the news event more "real". It should be acknowledged that the relative novelty of tweets in news reports may have made them more salient and perhaps also more likely to be noticed by readers and evaluated by respondents. While this effect may have occurred in this data, it could fade over time as tweets become more common in news reports. This suggests not only that LB respondents did not question the authenticity of the tweets but also that they viewed the tweets as evidence to support the information provided in other updates, whereas quotations were used less often as evidence of authenticity. However, this consideration of direct speech as evidence for news events is not new to digital news texts. Tuchman (1972) found that journalists employ quotations in news texts in the same manner they would employ facts to support their reports. This assumes that quotations can be constructed as factual evidence of participants' emotional states as well as evidence supporting the reported events, an assumption that seems to have been present in most respondents' readings of the LBs, yet less present in respondents' readings of the TONAs.

It is possible that tweets are seen as more authentic than quotations and more closely related to citizen sources (Chouliaraki 2015), although they are in fact often carefully selected by editors and journalists and mostly come from people either familiar to the editors or employed by the editors (Broersma & Graham 2013). Therefore, it is likely that the cause of the difference in evaluations between the LB respondents and the TONA respondents may stem in part from the presentation of the speech in the news texts. As discussed, direct speech in the LBs is foregrounded through layout. Embedded tweets are specifically remarkable given that the embedded tweet retains its original Twitter layout (see figure 16.3), which is obligatory following Twitter's regulations, invoking the experience of reading the tweet in its original context.

16.7 Conclusion

The changing landscape of news reporting in the digital age needs to be considered carefully. It is common to think of new forms of news texts as specific to the digital age and without corresponding news texts, or aspects of news texts, in pre-digital formats. However, many forms of online news reporting are born from the same production methods as pre-digital news texts. TONAs for example are news texts, which are often similar to print news articles apart from the medium. By identifying different online text genres and to what extent these texts are similar to offline texts, like TONAs, or specifically created based on the affordances of the internet, like LBs, research can investigate how the movement towards online texts affects both the text and format as well as the audience responses to these texts. This chapter has shown that even small changes, such as moving from direct quotations to embedded tweets, may have an impact on readers' evaluations of both the news texts and the news events. It shows that transhistorical research can concentrate on short time frames and investigate changes as they occur. Additionally, this chapter highlights the importance of reader response research as the data collected through interviews showed the relation between the different direct speech presentations and the readers' evaluations of the news events and news texts.

Within LBs, sources are foregrounded through layout methods. This is especially true in comparison to the presentation of sources in TONAs, news texts that are based on print journalism. While the presentation may differ between TONAs and LBs, readers do not explicitly evaluate the sources presented in the news texts differently, with both groups of interviewees evaluating the use of sources in both types of news texts as affective and engaging. However, when investigating readers' evaluations of the news events, the difference in speech presentation seemed to have an influence on the respondents' evaluations. Firstly, tweets are perceived as more authentic than quotations. Perhaps the presentation of tweets, through the embedding of its original Twitter-style presentation into the LBs and the hyperlinks to the original context, provide evidence to the reader that the reporter did not alter the reported speech. This type of evidence is not available with quotations, which, while presented through direct speech, still rely on the reporter to report and quote correctly. The fact that readers did not question the sources, and instead used them as evidence for their affective evaluations of the news events, suggest that they may not have been aware of the likely reporter influence in the selection of known or verified tweets (Broersma & Graham 2013).

Secondly, LBs were evaluated more often as affective than were TONAs and the reported news events were evaluated more often as negative when reported through an LB than when reported through a TONA. The respondents linked these evaluations with the inclusion of tweets. This suggests that tweets may be more influential on news event evaluations than traditional quotations. While the impact of tweet source information is inevitably complex; what this chapter has shown is that they can and do play a part in readers' affective evaluations of news events, and that the mechanisms (pragmatic, cognitive) require further research.

It is therefore crucial that readers of news acquire media literacy specific to digital news texts to be able to evaluate digitally native news texts critically. We must consider whether tweets are actually more authentic than quotations, especially considering the anonymity available to web users and the fact that the selection of tweets relies mostly on reporters' contacts (as reporters may struggle to verify other tweeters' identities) and therefore does not automatically include a wide range of "citizen sources". It is also necessary to further investigate what aspect of the presentation of tweets causes the increase in affective evaluations from readers of the news. I have speculated about the foregrounded presentations of tweets, which appear to be related to the readers' affective evaluations of news texts and news events, as well as the hyperlinks contained within the tweets. Most notably though, as the similarities in news text evaluations show, readers may not be aware that their affective responses to tweets are different from their affective responses to quotations within TONAs, suggesting that increasing awareness in audiences is key in developing media literacy in the digital age.

References

Alexa. 2017. The top 500 sites on the web. *Alexa*. http://www.alexa.com/topsites/category/News (accessed 8 January 2018).
Allagui, Ilhem & Johanne Kuebler. 2011. The Arab Spring and the role of ICTs. *International Journal of Communication* 5. 1435–1442.
Allan, Stuart. 2016. Citizen witnesses. In Tamara Witschge, Chris W. Anderson, David Domingo & Alfred Hermida (eds.), *The SAGE handbook of digital journalism*, 266–279. Thousand Oaks: Sage.
Allington, Daniel & Swann, Joan. 2009. Researching literary reading as social practice. *Language and Literature* 18 (3). 219–230.
BBC. 2014a. As it happened: Gaza conflict intensifies. *BBC*. http://www.BBC.co.uk/news/world-middle-east-28391201 (accessed 31 May 2017).
BBC. 2014b. Gaza shelling by Israel leads to deadliest day of conflict. *BBC*. http://www.BBC.co.uk/news/world-middle-east-28389282 (accessed 31 May 2017).
Beckett, Charlie. 2010. The value of networked journalism. *Polis working paper, Department of Media and Communication, London School of Economics & Political Science*. http://www2.lse.ac.uk/media@lse/POLIS/documents/Polis%20papers/ValueofNetworkedJournalism.pdf (accessed 27 June 2018).
Bednarek, Monika. 2006. *Evaluation in media discourse. Analysis of a newspaper corpus*. London: Continuum.
Bednarek, Monika & Helen Caple. 2017. *The discourse of news values. How news organizations create newsworthiness*. Oxford: Oxford University Press.
Broersma, Marcel & Todd Graham. 2013. Twitter as a news source. *Journalism Practice* 7 (4). 446–464.
Bunz, Mercedes. 2010. Google's news experiment Living Stories to go open source. *The Guardian.co.uk*. https://www.theGuardian.com/media/pda/2010/feb/17/digital-media-google-living-stories-open-source (accessed 27 June 2018).
Caldas-Coulthard, Carmen Rosa. 1994. Reporting speech in narrative discourse: Stylistic and ideological implications. *Ilha do Desterro* 27. 67–82.
Chouliaraki, Lilie. 2015. Digital witnessing in war journalism: The case of post-Arab Spring conflicts. *Popular Communication: The international journal of media and culture* 13 (2). 105–119.
Cohen, Akiba A., Hanna Adoni & Charles R. Bantz. 1990. *Social conflict and television news*. Thousand Oaks: Sage.

Crowston, Kevin & Marie Williams. 2000. Reproduced and emergent genres of communication on the world-wide web. *The Information Society* 16. 201–215.

Dörnyei, Zoltán. 2007. *Research methods in applied linguistics*. Oxford: Oxford University Press.

Englebretson, Robert. 2007. Stancetaking in discourse: An introduction. In Robert Englebretson (ed.), *Stancetaking in discourse*, 1–26. Amsterdam: John Benjamins.

Fuoli, Matteo & Hommerberg, Charlotte. 2015. Optimising transparency, reliability and replicability: Annotation principles and inter-coder agreement in the quantification of evaluative expressions. *Corpora* 10 (3). 315–349.

Goźdź-Roszkowski, Stanisław & Susan Hunston. 2016. Corpora and beyond – Investigating evaluation in discourse: introduction to the special issue on corpus approaches to evaluation. *Corpora* 11 (2). 131–141.

Steensen, Steen. 2014. Conversing the audience: a methodological exploration of how conversation analysis can contribute to the analysis of interactive journalism. *New Media & Society* 16 (8). 1197–1213.

Hall, Geoff. 2009. Texts, readers – and real readers. *Language and Literature* 18 (3). 331–337.

Herring, Susan C. 2012. Discourse in web 2.0: Familiar, reconfigured, and emergent. In Tannen, Deborah & Anna Marie Tester (eds.), *Georgetown University Round Table on Languages and Linguistics 2011: Discourse 2.0: Language and new media*. Washington, D.C.: Georgetown University Press.

Hunston, Susan & John Sinclair. 2000. A local grammar of evaluation. In Susan Hunston & Geoff Thompson (eds.), *Evaluation in text. Authorial stance and the construction of discourse*, 74–101. Oxford: Oxford University Press.

Hunston, Susan & Geoff Thompson (eds.). 2000. *Evaluation in text. Authorial stance and the construction of discourse*. Oxford: Oxford University Press.

Ikeo, Reiko. 2009. An elaboration of the faithfulness claims in direct writing. *Journal of Pragmatics* 41. 999–1016.

Khondker, Habibul Haque. 2011. Role of the new media in the Arab Spring. *Globalizations* 8 (5). 675–679.

Leech, Geoffrey & Mick Short. 2007. *Style in fiction: A linguistic introduction to English fictional prose*. Harlow: Pearson.

Lemke, Jay L. 1998. Resources for Attitudinal meaning: Evaluative orientations in text semantics. *Functions of Language* 5 (1). 33–56.

Martin, James R. & Peter R. R. White. 2005. *The language of evaluation. Appraisal in English*. Basingstoke: Palgrave Macmillan.

Miall, David S. 2006. Empirical approaches to studying literary readers: The state of the discipline. *Book History* 9. 291–311.

Miall, David S. & Don Kuiken. 1994. Foregrounding, defamiliarisation, and affect: Response to literary studies. *Poetics* 22. 389–407.

Myrick, Jessica Gall & Bartosz W. Wojdynski. 2016. Moody news: The impact of collective emotion ratings on online news consumers' attitudes toward and memory for content. *New Media & Society* 18 (11). 2576–2594.

Nuttall, Louise. 2017. Online readers between the camps: A text world theory analysis of ethical positioning in *We Need to Talk About Kevin*. *Language and Literature* 26 (2). 153–171.

Peplow, David & Ronald Carter. 2014. Stylistics and real readers. In Michael Burke (ed.), *The Routledge handbook of stylistics*, 440–454. Abingdon: Routledge.

Richards, Keith. 2009. Interviews. In Juanita Heigham & Robert A. Croker (eds.), *Qualitative research in applied linguistics: A practical introduction*, 182–199. Basingstoke: Palgrave Macmillan.

Russell, Adrienne. 2016. Networked Journalism. In Tamara Witschge, Chris W. Anderson, David Domingo & Alfred Hermida (eds.), T*he SAGE handbook of digital journalism*, 149–163. Thousand Oaks: Sage.

Schwartz, Joseph. 2015. Top U.K. media publishers and publications – Ranked for 2015. *Digital Vision*. https://www.similarweb.com/blog/index-top-u-k-media-publishers-and-publications-of-2015 (accessed 27 June 2018).

Semino, Elena & Mick Short. 2004. *Corpus stylistics: Speech, writing and thought presentation in a corpus of English writing*. Abingdon: Routledge.

Short, Mick, Elena Semino & Martin Wynne. 2002. Revisiting the notion of faithfulness in discourse presentation using a corpus approach. *Language & Literature* 11 (4). 325–355.

Tereszkiewicz, Anna. 2014. "I'm not sure what that means yet, but we'll soon find out" – The discourse of newspaper live blogs. *Studia Linguistica Universitatis Iagellonicae Cracoviensis* 131 (3). 299–319.

The Guardian. 2015a. Oregon college shooting: gunman identified as Chris Harper Mercer – As it happened. *The Guardian*. https://www.theGuardian.com/us-news/live/2015/oct/01/shooting-reported-at-oregon-community-college-live-updates (accessed 1 December 2017).

The Guardian. 2015b. "Another mass shooting in America": Oregon killings a grim familiarity for US. *The Guardian*. https://www.theGuardian.com/us-news/2015/oct/01/oregon-umpqua-community-college-shooting (accessed 9 January 2018).

Thompson, Geoff. 2014. Affect and emotion, target-value mismatches, and Russian dolls: Refining the Appraisal model. In Geoff Thompson & Laura Alba-Juez (eds.), *Evaluation in context*, 47–66. Amsterdam: John Benjamins.

Thompson, Geoff & Susan Hunston. 2000. Evaluation: An introduction. In Susan Hunston & Geoff Thompson (eds.), *Evaluation in text. Authorial stance and the construction of discourse*, 1–27. Oxford: Oxford University Press.

Thurman, Neil. 2013. How live blogs are reconfiguring breaking news. In Nic Newman & David A. L. Levy (eds.), *Reuters Institute digital news report 2013: Tracking the future of news*: 85–88. Oxford: Reuters Institute for the Study of Journalism.

Thurman, Neil & Anna Walters. 2013. Live blogging – Digital journalism's pivotal platform? A case study of the production, consumption, and form of live blogs at *Guardian*.co.uk. *Digital Journalism* 1 (1). 82–101.

Thurman, Neil & Nic Newman. 2014. The future of breaking news online? *Journalism Studies* 15 (5). 655–667.

Thurman, Neil & James Rodgers. 2014. Citizen journalism in real time: Live blogging and crisis events. In Einar Thorsen & Stuart Allan (eds.), *Citizen journalism: Global perspectives, volume 2*, 81–95. New York: Peter Lang.

Thurman, Neil & Aljosha Karim Schapals. 2016. Live blogs, sources, and objectivity: The contradictions of real-time online reporting. In Bob Franklin & Scott Eldridge (eds.), *The Routledge companion to digital journalism studies*, 283–292. Abingdon: Routledge.

Tuchman, Gaye. 1972. Objectivity as strategic ritual: An examination of newsmen's notions of objectivity. *American Journal of Sociology* 77 (4). 660–679.

Tuchman, Gaye. 1978. *Making news: A study in the construction of reality*. New York: The Free Press.

Van Peer, Willie. 1983. Poetic style and reader response: An exercise in empirical studies. *Journal of Literary Semantics* 12 (2). 3–18.

Wahl-Jorgenson, Karin. 2012. The strategic ritual of emotionality: A case study of Pulitzer Prize-winning articles. *Journalism* 14 (1). 129–145.

White, Peter R. R. 1997. Death, disruption and the moral order: The narrative impulse in mass-media "hard news" reporting. In Frances Christie & James R. Martin (eds.), *Genres and institutions: Social processes in the workplace and school*, 101–133. London: Cassell.

Yao, Bo, Pascal Belin & Christoph Scheepers. 2011. Silent reading of direct versus indirect speech activates voice-selective areas in the auditory cortex. *Journal of Cognitive Neuroscience* 23 (10). 3146–3152.

Emma Moreton and Chris Culy

17 New methods, old data: Using digital technologies to explore nineteenth century letter writing practices

17.1 Introduction

The sourcing, preservation and documentation of migrant letter collections is gathering pace, with the internet providing a significant new forum for the dissemination of long-hidden archives.[1] Important studies of, for example, English (Gerber 2006), Scottish (Erickson 1972), Irish (Miller 1985; 2008, Miller et al. 2003), Welsh (Conway 1961) German (Kamphoefner, Helbich & Sommer 1988), Swedish (Barton 1990) and Norwegian (Zempel 1991) migration have demonstrated the value of using personal letters to gain a fuller and deeper understanding of both the complex social processes of migration and the conditions and daily lives of the migrants themselves. They have also enriched our understanding of how the form of the letter itself, for migrants more than any other group, "functioned primarily to reconfigure personal relationships made vulnerable by distance" (Elliott, Gerber & Sinke 2006: 17) and to reinforce familial bonds.

Whilst the benefits of uncovering, documenting and analysing historical letter collections are clear, this growing body of research sometimes appears somewhat fragmented. Researchers often work in isolation from one another and their projects evolve independently. Details of letter collections are sometimes difficult to find, and access to resources can be restricted by copyright and intellectual property concerns. This can lead to collections being missed or overlooked and/or the reduplication of work, with letters often being transcribed several times by different projects – projects which have their own research aims and, quite often, their own transcription and markup practices.

---

[1] See, for example: The Mellon Centre for Migration Studies, Ulster American Folk Park Museum (2012-present) *The Irish Emigration Database (IED)*. Available from: http://www.dippam.ac.uk/ied/ [Accessed 1 October 2018]. Immigration History Research Centre, University of Minnesota (2010-present) *Digitizing Immigrant Letters*. Available from: http://ihrc.umn.edu/research/dil/ (accessed 1 October 2018).

Emma Moreton, University of Liverpool, e-mail: Emma.Moreton@liverpool.ac.uk
Chris Culy, Independent Researcher, e-mail: culy@mac.com

There seems to be a good case, therefore, for developing a collaborative, cross-disciplinary approach to working with (migrant) letter collections: the digital humanities (defined here as the use of digital technologies to address humanities research questions), arguably, offers one possible solution. Once digitised in a consistent and formalised way, it is possible for different archives to interconnect and for the letter content to be analysed in a more systematic and replicable way, using, for instance, corpus and visualisation tools that allow us to notice patterns in the data (within and across collections) which we might not have seen otherwise. Additionally, digital tools allow for the easy reanalysis of the data in the future if new questions arise, thus enabling different projects to build on previous research and carry out comparative studies across collections.

Drawing on developments in the field of digital humanities, this chapter uses a combination of qualitative and computational approaches to explore letter writing practices within the context of nineteenth century mass migration from Ireland to America. Our aim is to explore and evaluate the advantages and limitations of digital techniques and methods for the analysis of historical migrant letter collections. In so doing, we hope to show how digital technologies can shed new light on old data in ways which might allow us to better understand and interpret the migrant experience.

The chapter focuses on the letters of two sisters, Annie and Julia Lough, who migrated from Ireland to America in the late nineteenth century. First, a close qualitative reading of the letters is carried out to identify topics in the discourse. Corpus and visualisation tools are then used to examine four topics in more detail, namely: Future Letters (any reference to letters which are going to be sent, or which the author hopes/expects to receive in the future), Previous Letters (any reference to letters which have already been sent or received at the time of writing), Remittance (money orders) and Enclosure (e.g. photographs, gifts, newspaper cuttings etc.). The chapter demonstrates how these features of the letters – often overlooked because of their formulaic nature – are important to our understanding of the migrant experience, providing useful insights into how, through correspondence, vulnerable familial roles and relationships were negotiated, maintained and reinforced.[2] The chapter concludes by considering

---

[2] See, for instance, Plummer's (2001: 55) discussion of what he describes as "dross rate": "Letters are not generally focused enough to be of analytic interest – they contain far too much material that strays from the researcher's concern". Fitzpatrick (1994: 21) observes that oftentimes scholars working with migrant letter collections have "shared the widespread impatience of editors with material deemed 'tedious for the non-specialist,' including 'ritualized pious reflections' and 'endless lists of persons to whom the letter-writer wishes to send his or

the extent to which digital technologies offer new opportunities for the transhistorical study of migrant correspondence more generally.

17.2 The (female) Irish migrant

The post-famine period (circa. 1850s-1920s) was a time that saw a significant increase in female migration from Ireland to America. Economic changes in Ireland, including declining wage earning capabilities due to the deindustrialisation of the Irish countryside, as well as changes in inheritance practices from partible to impartible inheritance systems (in turn, leading to changes in marriage trends), contributed to "a massive post-famine emigration by young, unmarried women" (Miller 1985: 3). As Diner (1983: 10) explains, "in the society created in the wake of the Famine only one son per family could inherit land"; the same son typically entered into matrimony. Additionally, the widespread application of the dowry system meant that only one daughter within a family could realistically expect to marry. Her unmarried sisters had, as Diner puts it, "limited options": "They could remain single in the countryside" with very little chance of work, they could seek employment in cities such as Dublin, or further afield, or they could join the "millions of other young Irish women crossing the Atlantic to seek fortune or family in the United States" (Diner 1983: 12). By the second half of the nineteenth century Ireland had become "a nation characterized by late and reluctant marriage as well as by a massive voluntary exodus" (Diner 1983: 8).

According to Diner (1983: xiv), Irish women differed from other migrant women in several ways. For one, "they were the only significant group of foreign-born women who outnumbered men". Indeed, after 1880, young women constituted the majority of the departing Irish (Miller 1985: 392). However, while female Irish migrants appeared to enjoy a certain level of autonomy and independence – they migrated alone, played an important economic role within the notional family hierarchy, and sought to advance themselves socially – this, Diner argues, "did not mean that that they thought only of themselves". Rather, their actions were largely motivated by "family loyalties" and "a commitment to Irish Catholic culture and to its way of life" (Diner 1983: xiv). The female Irish migrant, then, was required to balance old world traditions with New World ways of life, maintaining relationships with those back home whilst simultaneously integrating into

---

her best regards."' Consequently, what has been viewed as "uninteresting" or "irrelevant" material within these letters has, quite often, simply been omitted (Fitzpatrick 1994: 21).

American society. The letters they wrote home arguably provide insight into how this delicate and complex family dynamic was negotiated and performed.

Previous research which uses Irish migrant letters as a primary data source has typically focused on one of two areas: 1) the language of the letters (these studies have often involved corpus linguistic methods of analysis) and 2) the subject matter of the letters (these studies have generally involved a qualitative reading of the letters). While linguists have been especially interested in exploring the linguistic features of Irish English as well as aspects of language change and variation (see, for instance, McCafferty & Amador-Moreno 2012; 2014; Amador-Moreno & McCafferty 2015; Van Hattum 2014; Montgomery 1995), historians have been more concerned with what the migrants wrote about (see, for instance, Miller 1985; Fitzpatrick 1994). The current study builds on research in both of these areas: linguistics and social history. Similar to Miller and to Fitzpatrick, it begins by examining what the Lough sisters wrote about to see whether similar topics and themes emerge. It then uses computational and visualisation tools to examine four topics in particular, as listed previously: Future Letters, Previous Letters, Remittance and Enclosure to see what these often mundane and formulaic sections of the discourse might reveal about letter writing practices, the communicative function of migrant correspondence, and the ways in which family roles and relationships were constructed through language.

17.3 The Lough letters

The Lough (pronounced /lɒk/) family letters are taken from a much larger body of Irish migrant correspondence collected by Kerby Miller, Emeritus Professor, University of Missouri. Miller himself has explored this wider collection in several pioneering works on Irish migration (see, for instance, Miller 1985, 2008; Miller, Doyle & Kelleher 1995; Miller et al. 2003), and his archive of over 5,000 letters has been referred to by many scholars, including Emmons (1990), Koos (2001), Bruce (2006), Corrigan (1992), Nolan (1989) and Noonan (2011).

The six Lough sisters – Elizabeth, Alice, Annie, Julia, Mary and Maggie – came from a Roman Catholic family in Meelick, in what was then called Queen's County (now County Laois), Ireland.[3] The sisters were daughters of Elizabeth McDonald Lough and James Lough who lived on a small holding consisting of

---

[3] The authors are indebted to Kerby Miller for the information he generously provided relating to the Lough family.

two fields, one of which, according to family legend, was sold to pay for the sisters' passages to America. The Lough family was, according to Miller, not of the lowest class as both parents and daughters were able to write. Apart from Mary and Maggie, all the Lough sisters migrated to America between 1870 and 1884.

There are 99 letters in the Lough collection, the majority of which were written by Annie (39 letters / 20,405 words), the third sister to migrate in 1878, and Julia (35 letters / 12,220 words), the fourth sister to migrate in 1884. This chapter focuses on these two larger collections, which, from hereon in, will be referred to as the ALC (Annie Lough Corpus) and the JLC (Julia Lough Corpus). Obviously, there are issues to do with representativeness when working with private letter collections, as we are unable to account for letters that have been lost, misplaced, or remain undiscovered. Indeed, it is very possible that many more letters were exchanged within the Lough family and their wider social network. Nevertheless, the Lough sisters are representative of the type of female Irish migrant described by Diner; their letters, therefore, offer a good starting point for exploring and understanding the female migrant experience.

Tables 17.1 and 17.2 show how frequently Annie and Julia wrote home and whom they wrote to. Focusing on Annie's correspondence first of all, table 17.1 shows that her earlier letters were addressed to her mother, the first of which was sent in around 1878 (although the letter itself is not dated) from Queenstown, County Cork, Ireland, just before Annie was about to set sail for America. After 1895 (around the time of her mother's death), Annie began writing to her sister, Mary, and the correspondence continued into the late 1920s. Annie wrote to Mary regularly during this 30 to 35 year period, often sending letters at Easter and Christmas, or on the anniversary of a family member's death. Several of Annie's letters are not dated but their content would suggest they were written from 1920 onwards. All but the first letter were sent from Winsted, Litchfield County, Connecticut.

Focusing on Julia's correspondence, table 17.2 shows that 23 of the 35 letters were addressed to Julia's mother, while 12 were addressed to her sister, Mary. Most of Julia's letters (33 out of 35) were sent between 1884 to 1895. Some of the letters are not dated, but their content has allowed them to be placed within an approximate timeframe. Most of the letters dated between 1884, when Julia first migrated, and 1894 were sent from Winsted, Connecticut. In around 1895 Julia relocated to Torrington, Connecticut.

Julia's pattern of letter writing differs quite noticeably from her sister Annie's. Annie's letters are fairly evenly distributed and there are no major gaps in her correspondence. Most of Annie's letters (27 out of 39) were addressed to her younger sister Mary and were sent after their mother's death. In contrast, most of Julia's letters were addressed to their mother. After their

Table 17.1: Overview of the ALC.

	Day	Month	Year	From (location)	Recipient	To (location)	No. Words
1	18	June	–	Queenstown, Ireland	Mother	Meelick, Ireland	356
2	03	March	1890	Winsted, America	Mother & Sister	Meelick, Ireland	480
3	29	October	1891	Winsted, America	Mother	Meelick, Ireland	1055
4	15	December	1891	Winsted, America	Mother	Meelick, Ireland	487
5	23	March	1892	Winsted, America	Mother	Meelick, Ireland	1017
6	30	March	1893	Winsted, America	Mother	Meelick, Ireland	971
7	–	December	–	Winsted, America	Mother	Meelick, Ireland	208
8	–	–	–	Winsted, America	Mother	Meelick, Ireland	645
9	17	March	1895	Winsted, America	Sister	Meelick, Ireland	612
10	18	May	1899	Winsted, America	Sister	Meelick, Ireland	541
11	16	February	1901	Winsted, America	Sister	Meelick, Ireland	394
12	21	September	1901	Winsted, America	Sister	Meelick, Ireland	441
13	10	December	1902	Winsted, America	Sister	Meelick, Ireland	365
14	03	April	1906	Winsted, America	Sister	Meelick, Ireland	431
15	20	June	1906	Winsted, America	Sister	Meelick, Ireland	332
16	30	November	1906	Winsted, America	Sister	Meelick, Ireland	302
17	12	December	1912	Winsted, America	Sister	Meelick, Ireland	632
18	08	December	1913	Winsted, America	Sister	Meelick, Ireland	514
19	11	December	1914	Winsted, America	Niece	Meelick, Ireland	398
20	31	April	1918	Winsted, America	Sister	Meelick, Ireland	664

Table 17.1 (continued)

	Day	Month	Year	From (location)	Recipient	To (location)	No. Words
21	06	May	1918	Winsted, America	Sister	Meelick, Ireland	884
22	14	July	1918	Winsted, America	Sister	Meelick, Ireland	863
23	14	August	1919	Winsted, America	Sister	Meelick, Ireland	857
24	21	March	1920	Winsted, America	Niece	Ireland	469
25	21	March	1920	Winsted, America	Sister	Meelick, Ireland	649
26	07	December	1919/1920	Winsted, America	Sister	Meelick, Ireland	396
27	–	–	–	Winsted, America	Sister	Meelick, Ireland	435
28	31	March	1924	Winsted, America	Sister	Meelick, Ireland	538
29	29	September	1925	Winsted, America	Sister	Meelick, Ireland	237
30	28	March	1928	Winsted, America	Sister	Meelick, Ireland	206
31	18	October	1928	Winsted, America	Sister	Meelick, Ireland	870
32	04	November	–	Winsted, America	Nephew	Ireland	513
33	–	–	–	Winsted, America	Sister	Meelick, Ireland	261
34	–	–	–	Winsted, America	Sister	Meelick, Ireland	400
35	–	–	–	Winsted, America	Sister	Meelick, Ireland	489
36	–	–	–	Winsted, America	Sister	Meelick, Ireland	476
39	–	–	–	Winsted, America	Sister	Meelick, Ireland	207
38	–	–	–	Winsted, America	Sister	Meelick, Ireland	307
39	01	December	1919	Winsted, America	Sister	Meelick, Ireland	503

Table 17.2: Overview of the JLC.

	Day	Month	Year	From (location)	Recipient	To (location)	No. Words
1	27	September	1884	Queenstown, Ireland	Mother	Meelick, Ireland	40
2	–	–	1884	Ireland or England	Mother	Meelick, Ireland	98
3	20	December	1884	Winsted, America	Sister	Meelick, Ireland	519
4	–	–	1884–1894	Winsted, America	Mother	Meelick, Ireland	190
5	–	December	1888	Winsted, America	Mother	Meelick, Ireland	342
6	03	November	1889	Winsted, America	Mother	Meelick, Ireland	444
7	02	December	1889	Winsted, America	Mother	Meelick, Ireland	436
8	–	–	1889–1890	Winsted, America	Mother	Meelick, Ireland	487
9	–	–	1889–1894	Winsted, America	Mother	Meelick, Ireland	259
10	09	March	1890	Winsted, America	Mother	Meelick, Ireland	463
11	10	August	1890	Winsted, America	Mother	Meelick, Ireland	366
12	–	December	1890	Winsted, America	Mother	Meelick, Ireland	350
13	18	January	1891	Winsted, America	Sister	Meelick, Ireland	348
14	25	January	1891	Winsted, America	Mother	Meelick, Ireland	351
15	30	March	1891	Winsted, America	Mother	Meelick, Ireland	225
16	18	October	1891	Winsted, America	Mother	Meelick, Ireland	317
17	14	December	1891	Winsted, America	Mother	Meelick, Ireland	300
18	11	May	pre-1892	Winsted, America	Mother	Meelick, Ireland	400
19	01	September	1892	Winsted, America	Mother	Meelick, Ireland	396
20	–	–	1892–1893	Winsted, America	Mother	Meelick, Ireland	321

Table 17.2 (continued)

	Day	Month	Year	From (location)	Recipient	To (location)	No. Words
21	21	March	1893	Winsted, America	Sister	Meelick, Ireland	423
22	–	May	1893	Winsted, America	Mother	Meelick, Ireland	305
23	–	July	1893	Winsted, America	Mother	Meelick, Ireland	340
24	03	September	1893	Winsted, America	Mother	Meelick, Ireland	356
25	10	October	1893	Winsted, America	Mother	Meelick, Ireland	334
26	–	December	1893	Winsted, America	Mother	Meelick, Ireland	451
27	25	March	1894	Torrington, America	Sister	Meelick, Ireland	183
28	24	May	1893–1894	Torrington, America	Sister	Meelick, Ireland	477
29	–	–	1889–1894	Torrington, America	Sister	Meelick, Ireland	354
30	04	June	1894	Winsted, America	Sister	Meelick, Ireland	736
31	–	November	1895	Winsted, America	Sister	Meelick, Ireland	469
32	08	July	1895	Queenstown, Ireland	Sister	Meelick, Ireland	44
33	–	August	1895	Torrington, America	Sister	Meelick, Ireland	416
34	17	March	1919–1920	Torrington, America	Sister	Meelick, Ireland	331
35	09	November	1927	Torrington, America	Sister	Meelick, Ireland	349

mother's death, Julia wrote somewhat sporadically to Mary and there was a 24-year gap in Julia's writing between letter 33 (sent in 1895) and letter 34 (sent in 1919–1920). Overall, Annie tended to write longer letters than Julia with an average word count of 523 (versus 349 for Julia). Additionally, Annie's letters were more varied in length than Julia's.

17.4 Topic identification

To prepare the letters for analysis they were first transcribed and saved in Plain Text format. While automated semantic taggers provide a useful overview of the content of a corpus, they can sometimes miss more subtle topics and themes in the discourse. A trial study using *Wmatrix* (Rayson 2009) as a starting point, for example, showed that it was sometimes difficult to ascertain those sections of the discourse that were describing, for instance, homesickness, which is often expressed indirectly or through the use of metaphor. Unsurprisingly, there is no specific semantic domain for homesickness in the UCREL semantic tagset. This meant that it was necessary to look for semantic domains that might indicate expressions of homesickness in the discourse. Obvious domains might be *E1+ Emotional* or *E4.1- Sad*, or perhaps *N2.2- Distance: Far*; however, descriptions of remembering, forgetting and dreaming are also typically used by the Lough sisters in the context of describing feelings of homesickness – something which could only be identified through a contextualised reading of the correspondence. As such, a close reading of the letters was necessary to identify sequences in the discourse that appeared to be lexically related to see what topics emerged.

The topics were then annotated following eXtensible Markup Language (XML) conventions (XML will be explained in further detail later in the chapter). The section below, for example, is about education and is marked with the opening tag <education> to show where this section begins and the closing tag </education> (with forward slash) to show where it ends, as follows:

> <education>I hope you keep them to school all you can when they grow bigger you can not send them very well I suppose there are not many of the nuns alive now that was there when I went to school we call them Sisters here I think we have 15 or more of them here they have a very nice convent they go to Mass with the school children and go see the sick we have two other schools besides publick schools that is for any one wishes to go there and there is a High school also</education> (ALC, 10 December 1902).

In cases where the discourse could be interpreted in more than one way, two or more tags were assigned. This meant that a section could be said to be about just one topic, or it could be said to be about a number of topics. In the example above, where the text is annotated with the tags <education></education>, an alternative interpretation might be the topic "Ireland and America" (any reference to life in Ireland and/or America). In this situation, the annotation is as follows:

> <education><IrelandAmerica>I hope you keep them to school all you can when they grow bigger you can not send them very well I suppose there are not many of the nuns alive now that was there when I went to school we call them Sisters here I think we have 15 or

more of them here they have a very nice convent they go to Mass with the school children and go see the sick we have two other schools besides publick schools that is for any one wishes to go there and there is a High school also</IrelandAmerica></education>
(ALC, 10 December 1902).

Additionally, it is possible for one or more topics to be embedded within another main topic. In the example below, for instance, the main theme is work; however, within this section Annie makes a comment regarding attitudes towards work in Ireland versus America, so the tag <IrelandAmerica> has been embedded within <work>, as follows:

<work>is Maggie home yet or is she going to stay home all winter idle spending her money and weering out her nice clothes I think she is very foolish for her self she had ought to stay in a good place when she had one she wont get one like it for a while again I wonder she comes home to stay there now <IrelandAmerica>she ought to be working for herself and considering the wey things are at home now what she would do if she was here no one ever thinks of staying a week away from work unless they were sick or out of work</IrelandAmerica></work>
(ALC, 15 December 1891).

Tagging for topics allowed us to get a sense of what the sisters wrote about – their preoccupations, perceptions and experiences. It also allowed us to extract all instances of a particular topic to explore how language is used within that specific context.

Table 17.3 lists the topics that were identified in the ALC and JLC, organised alphabetically, while figure 17.1 shows the same information represented visually. While the topic categories were developed from scratch (i.e. we did not approach the data with any preexisting ideas about what we expected to find), most of the topics identified can be mapped onto Fitzpatrick's (1994: 643–649) thematic index.[4] There are, however, a few differences, namely: a distinction is made between the topics Memories and Recollections and there is a separate category for Homesickness. Additionally, there are separate categories for Future Letters and Previous Letters and a distinction is made between remittances and other types of enclosure. Finally, the topics Postal System, World War I, Reassurance and Identity are evident in the Lough letters, but these categories do not appear in Fitzpatrick's index. As with most qualitative approaches to topic identification, the process is largely a subjective and intuitive one. However, through tagging the topics (thereby making transparent our reading of the letters) it is possible for other researchers to build on and/or challenge our interpretation of the discourse. Indeed, one of the benefits of using XML markup to annotate the letters is that it

---

[4] Fitzpatrick (1994), analysing 111 letters from/to Irish migrants in Australia, identified around 140 main themes and almost 250 sub-themes within his letters.

Table 17.3: Topics in the ALC and JLC, listed alphabetically.

ALC topics	Freq.	Av. p/letter	Word	%	JLC topics	Freq.	Av. p/letter	Word	%
Childbirth	1	0.03	92	0.45	Daily life	8	0.23	320	2.62
Death	18	0.46	1712	8.39	Death	9	0.26	691	5.65
Education	6	0.15	255	1.25	Education	2	0.06	53	0.43
Enclosure	49	1.26	1354	6.64	Enclosure	17	0.49	699	5.72
Family and friends	82	2.10	8149	39.94	Family and friends	58	1.66	4255	34.82
Future letters	86	2.21	1580	7.74	Future letters	41	1.17	642	5.25
Health and illness	25	0.64	1197	5.87	Health and illness	24	0.69	563	4.61
Homesickness & separation	7	0.18	230	1.13	Homesickness & separation	28	0.8	737	6.03
Identity	1	0.03	9	0.04	Identity	6	0.17	234	1.91
Ireland and America	59	1.51	4517	22.14	Ireland and America	66	1.89	2269	18.57
Marriage	6	0.15	274	1.34	Migration	1	0.03	136	1.11
Migration	7	0.18	453	2.22	News event	10	0.29	476	3.90
News event	12	0.31	800	3.92	Previous letters	49	1.4	1186	9.71
Postal system	4	0.10	129	0.63	Recollections	31	0.89	978	8.00
Previous letters	71	1.82	1681	8.24	Religion	48	1.37	1854	15.17
Reassurance	5	0.13	231	1.13	Remittance	16	0.46	539	4.41
Recollection	39	1	1274	6.24	Reunion	10	0.29	213	1.74
Religion	17	0.44	961	4.71	Transportation	1	0.03	60	0.49
Remittance	15	0.38	438	2.15	Weather and seasons	31	0.89	774	6.33
Reunion	6	0.15	152	0.74	Work	23	0.66	885	7.24
Transportation	1	0.03	69	0.34					
Weather and seasons	15	0.38	616	3.02					
Work	27	0.69	823	4.03					
World War I	4	0.10	396	1.94					

Freq. = shows the number of times this topic occurs within the corpus / Av. p/letter = shows the average number of times this topic occurs per letter / Word = shows the number of words attributed to this topic / % = shows what percentage of the corpus is attributed to this topic.

becomes possible for other researchers to comment on this annotation and to add their own layers of interpretative markup. The markup process can thus become a collaborative effort with each iteration being fully explained and documented within the markup itself.

The "Freq." column shows how often the topics occurred across all letters and the "Av. p/letter" column gives the average frequency of a topic per letter.

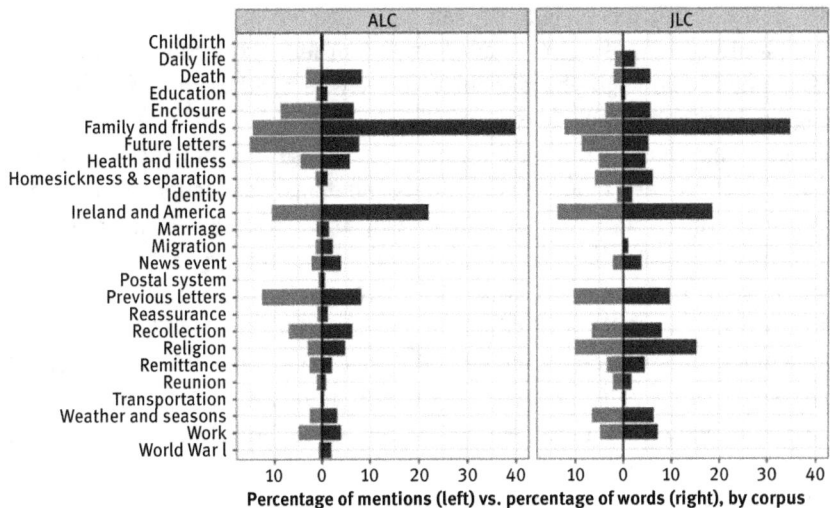

Figure 17.1: Topics as proportion of mentions vs. proportion of words, by corpus.
Source: Full colour renderings of these visualisations can be found at chrisculy.net

Of course, it is possible that a topic may be mentioned several times in the same letter, or it may not be mentioned at all. Counting the number of times a topic occurs thus offers only one way into the letters. Counting the number of words attributed to each occurrence of a particular topic, on the other hand, arguably provides a more accurate reflection of the content of a letter, or a letter collection (i.e. it tells us what percentage of the letter or letter collection was spent discussing health, education or work, for instance). The "Word" column, therefore, provides the raw word count for each topic while the "%" column shows what percentage of the corpus was attributed to that particular topic.

Tagging the letters for topics, placing the letters in a digital frame, arguably allows the researcher to look more objectively at the spread of topics within and across collections, thereby encouraging a more neutral analytic approach. What is perhaps striking about table 17.3, for example, is how rarely topics like Migration, Work and Education seem to crop up, even though these topics are precisely the ones many researchers on migrant letters have focused on (e.g. Koos 2001; Miller 1985; Miller, Doyle & Kelleher 1995). Instead, the far greater focus of both Annie's and Julia's letters is on Family and Friends (82 occurrences (39.94% of the overall content) in the ALC and 58 occurrences (34.81%) in the JLC), as well as the subtle national comparisons identified under Ireland and America (59 occurrences (22.14%) in the ALC and 66 occurrences (18.57%) in the JLC). It is perhaps unsurprising that these are the two most frequent topics in the Lough sisters' letters given the context in which they wrote; however it would be interesting to compare different letter collections, taking into consideration sociobiographic variables, to see whether these topics are typical of migrant correspondence more generally.

Other topics, meanwhile, feature heavily because they provide a recurring structure to the letters, reflecting the rituals and demands of letter writing itself. For instance, the topics Future Letters, Previous Letters and Enclosure are a significant part of Annie's and Julia's correspondence (and, arguably, correspondence more generally; see Fitzmaurice 2012, 2015). Table 17.3 shows that although these topics have very high frequencies (i.e. they may be mentioned several times in each letter), they only take up a small percentage of the overall discourse (7.74%, 8.24% and 0.24% in the ALC and 5.25%, 9.71% and 5.72% in the JLC). In other words, these tend to be short, often formulaic sections, which occur within most letters.

The following sections use digital humanities techniques to examine these topics (as well as the topic Remittance, a specific type of enclosure) in more detail. Whilst these topics may not be very rich in terms of their content, they can provide useful insights into how transatlantic relationships were structured, reinforced and maintained through correspondence. First, we annotate the topics for information regarding the participants involved. We then analyse the topics across the letters using a combination of numerical and visual presentations. The visualisations allow us to identify patterns and trends across the letters, which would be more difficult to notice through reading alone. The analyses were done using a combination of manual and automatic methods through a variety of tools. Most of the counting was done automatically using programs we developed in Python 3, though the counting of the interactants was done manually. Percentages were calculated in spreadsheets, while all of the visualisations were created with the R programming language using the ggplot2 package (Wickham 2016). Finally, we evaluate the use of digital humanities tools for exploring topics and themes in the discourse.

There are two interesting aspects of the topics that we can see from the visualisation in figure 17.1. The first aspect is that a few topics show a large difference between their percentage of mentions as a topic and the percentage of words they occupy. For example, occurrences of Family and Friends are 10–15 % of the topic instances, but they take about 35–40% of the total words in the letters. In other words, a disproportionate amount of the content of the words is taken up by the topic Family and Friends. Ireland and America shows a similar, if less striking pattern.

The second interesting aspect of the topics is seeing the similarities and differences between the two corpora. While overall the distributions of the topics are similar in the two corpora, there are striking instances of topics that occur (primarily) in one corpus or the other. For example, ALC contains Education, Marriage, and Reassurance, while JLC does not but does contains Daily Life and Identity.

17.5 Using XML markup to capture information about participants

Having identified and annotated the different topics in the *ALC* and *JLC*, the next stage was to capture information about the participants involved. In other words, who was expecting a letter from whom? Who had received a letter from whom? And who was sending/receiving enclosures and remittances? To do this, each instance of the topics Future Letters, Previous Letters, Remittance and Enclosure was annotated for person information, following XML conventions.

We have already seen how XML was used to tag topics in the data. It is worth at this point looking in more depth at what XML annotation involves. There are various applications of XML.[5] For this project, we referred to the *Text Encoding Initiative (TEI) Guidelines* when carrying out the encoding process. (The TEI provides a set of guidelines as well as a markup language for encoding texts in the humanities and is considered the de facto standard.) As an application of XML, TEI markup language must do certain things for it to be XML compliant – that is, it must obey certain rules for it to be considered well-formed. Those rules (as explained in the *TEI Guidelines*) are summarised below:
1. A tag (in the form of angle brackets <>) must explicitly mark the start and end of each *element*. Elements represent the structural components of a text, such as the body, paragraphs and line breaks. Elements of one type (say, a paragraph) may be embedded within elements of another type (the body, for instance).
2. There must be a single element enclosing the whole document: this is known as the root element.
3. Each element apart from the root element must be completely contained by another element; elements cannot partially overlap one another.
4. In addition to elements, there are *attributes*. Each element can possess one or more attributes. The TEI describes attributes as "information that is in

---

[5] See, for instance, the MEI (Music Encoding Initiative) available from: http://en.wikipedia.org/wiki/Music_Encoding_Initiative (Accessed 1 October 2018); and the MathML (Mathematical Markup Language) available from: http://en.wikipedia.org/wiki/MathML (Accessed 1 October 2018).

some sense descriptive of a specific element occurrence but not regarded as part of its content" (TEI Consortium 2008: xlii).
5. Other key characteristics of well-formed XML are the case-sensitivity of tag names and the fact that special reserved characters ("<" and "&") must be "escaped" with entity references.[6]

In the example below, for instance, a letter by Julia Lough to her Mother, the opening tag <futureLett> and closing tag (with forward slash) </futureLett> tell us that this section of the discourse is concerned with the topic Future Letters. The information contained within the <interaction></interaction> tags provides more details regarding who is sending (role type: from) and who will receive (role type: to) this future letter. The unique identifiers LoughPers_003 and LoughPers_006 used in the @key attribute tell us that in this occurrence of Future Letters Julia is referring to a letter that Annie is going to write to their Mother (Elizabeth McDonald Lough).

(1)   <futureLett>
        <interaction>
            <role type="from" key="LoughPers_003" name="Annie Lough"/>
            <role type="to" key="LoughPers_006" name="Elizabeth McDonald Lough"/>
        </interaction>
        I think she is going to write home before Christmas
      </futureLett>

                                    JLC, 2 December 1889, Julia to her Mother

The unique identifier is used to create an association between the <persName> element and the @key attribute in the markup and the corresponding <person> element and @xml:id attribute located in a separate personography file, containing all known information about that particular participant (their maiden and married names and nicknames, their date of birth, occupation, educational background,

---

[6] Certain characters cannot be used within XML because they have special meanings. These include the ampersand (&), "double quotes", 'single quotes' and <angle brackets>. Many of the Lough letters contain, for example, the ampersand in the main body of the text, so these characters need to be "escaped" with a predefined entity reference as follows: &. For more on entity references see: *TEI by Example* (2004) available from: http://www.teibyexample.org/modules/TBED00v00.htm?target=xmlgroundrules (Accessed 1 October 2018).

places of residence etc., as well as their relationship to other participants in the corpus). See (2–5) for examples of how the topics were annotated for participants.

(2) <futureLett>
    <interaction>
        <role type="from" key="LoughPers_004" name="Julia Lough"/>
        <role type="to" key="LoughPers_005" name="Mary Lough"/>
    </interaction>
I wonder why Mary never writes to me for herself I have been expecting a letter from time to time but I suppose she has too much to take up her time now
</futureLett>

                          JLC, 1 Sept 1892, Julia to her Mother
                        [i.e. Julia is expecting a letter from Mary]

(3) <previousLett>
    <interaction>
        <role type="from" key="LoughPers_004" name="Julia Lough"/>
        <role type="to" key="LoughPers_006" name="Elizabeth McDonald Lough"/>
    </interaction>
I received all your letters. I was so surprised to get a letter in your own dear hand writing. I think you done just splendid it was a very nice letter and I am very thankful to you I shall always treasure it as the only letter I ever received from my dear mother and will often read it. I assure you I did not cry so much in a long time as when I read your letter but I do think you ought to often write and not say that is your last
</previousLett>

                        JLC, 9 March 1890, Julia to her Mother
                    [i.e. Julia received a letter from her Mother]

(4) <enclosure>
    <interaction>
        <role type="from" key="LoughPers_005" name="Mary Lough"/>
        <role type="to" key="LoughPers_004" name="Julia Lough"/>
    </interaction>
so you do not know how much I felt when I looked upon your face again if only in a picture it is a very poor picture and I always considered you good looking and if it was done decent it would be a good picture Lizzie and Nan said they would never know you but I should I noticed in particular how

nice your hands looked and you had flowers under the side of your hat. I am very thankful to you I am sure you had trouble to get it
</enclosure>

JLC, 4 June 1894, Julia to Mary
[i.e. Mary sent an enclosure to Julia]

(5) <remittance>
    <interaction>
       <role type="from" key="LoughPers_004" name="Julia Lough"/>
       <role type="to" key="LoughPers_006" name="Elizabeth McDonald Lough"/>
    </interaction>
I am sending you one pound and five shillings to get two masses said for fathers and Mothers souls I suppose you can include both. The one pound is your xmas present and let me know will the five shillings pay for the two masses
    </remittance>

JLC, n.d. November 1894, Julia to Mary
[i.e. Julia sent a remittance to Mary]

Once annotated in this way it is possible to extract topic and participant information so as to analyse differences in letter writing practices between the two sisters.

17.6 Analysing differences in letter writing practices

Table 17.4 provides an overview of the number of occurrences of each topic, Future Letters, Previous Letters, Remittance and Enclosure, across all letters in the ALC and JLC.

Table 17.4: Frequency summary.

	ALC	Av p/letter	JLC	Av p/letter
futureLett	87	2.23	42	1.20
previousLett	71	1.82	49	1.40
enclosure	49	1.26	16	0.46
remittance	14	0.36	14	0.40

Some of the letter writing patterns and practices as they emerge over the course of the correspondence are highlighted more clearly in the following charts. In figure 17.2, we have the distributions of the topics in each of the two corpora. One of the striking things we can observe is how much more Annie talks about enclosures than Julia does. There are also strong differences between the two sisters with respect to remittances, though for both of them the topic is much less common than the other three. On the other hand, their patterns for previous and future letters are broadly similar, with more mentions of future letters early in the sequences.

In figure 17.3, we have the same information as in figure 17.2, but viewed from the perspective of the authors. Here we can see that Annie's discussion of these four topics is much denser than Julia's. Annie almost always mentions several topics in a letter, and very often touches on all four topics. Julia, on the other hand, typically mentions just one or two of the topics. While this could be connected to Annie's longer more varied writing in general, there is no a priori reason why these particular topics and should be so much denser in Annie's letters.

In figures 17.4 and 17.5, we have the same information as in figures 17.2 and 17.3, but showing the topics in relation to the length (in words) of the letters. There is not much difference here, except that a couple of longer letters by Julia diminish the prominence of certain topics. For example, looking at figure 17.5, the five instances of futureLett in letter three are similar in proportion to the three instances of futureLett in letter five, simply because letter three is longer than letter five (519 words vs. 342 words). While these differences are small and the exception rather than the rule (and seemingly more common for the JLC corpus), they are worth noting in passing.

Using the markup described in section 17.5, we were then able to look more closely at the interactants, i.e. the people being talked about in Annie's and Julia's letters. Figure 17.6 gives an overview of the patterns of interactants. Each subchart shows the patterns for the "to" interactant labelled at the top of the subchart, with the corresponding "from" interactants in the rows. The numbers of mentions in Annie's letters are indicated by the size of the circles, while triangles indicate the number of mentions in Julia's letters.

Most obviously, we see that the combinations of interactants is restricted (e.g. only Annie refers to Friend; only Annie, Mother and Julia refer to NN=nieces and nephews, etc.). However, there are two more subtle observations that we can make. First, both corpora have the same combinations of interactants (i.e. at every line intersection in the chart we have both a circle for ALC and a triangle for JLC). This means that not only are Annie and Julia talking about the same

348 —— Emma Moreton and Chris Culy

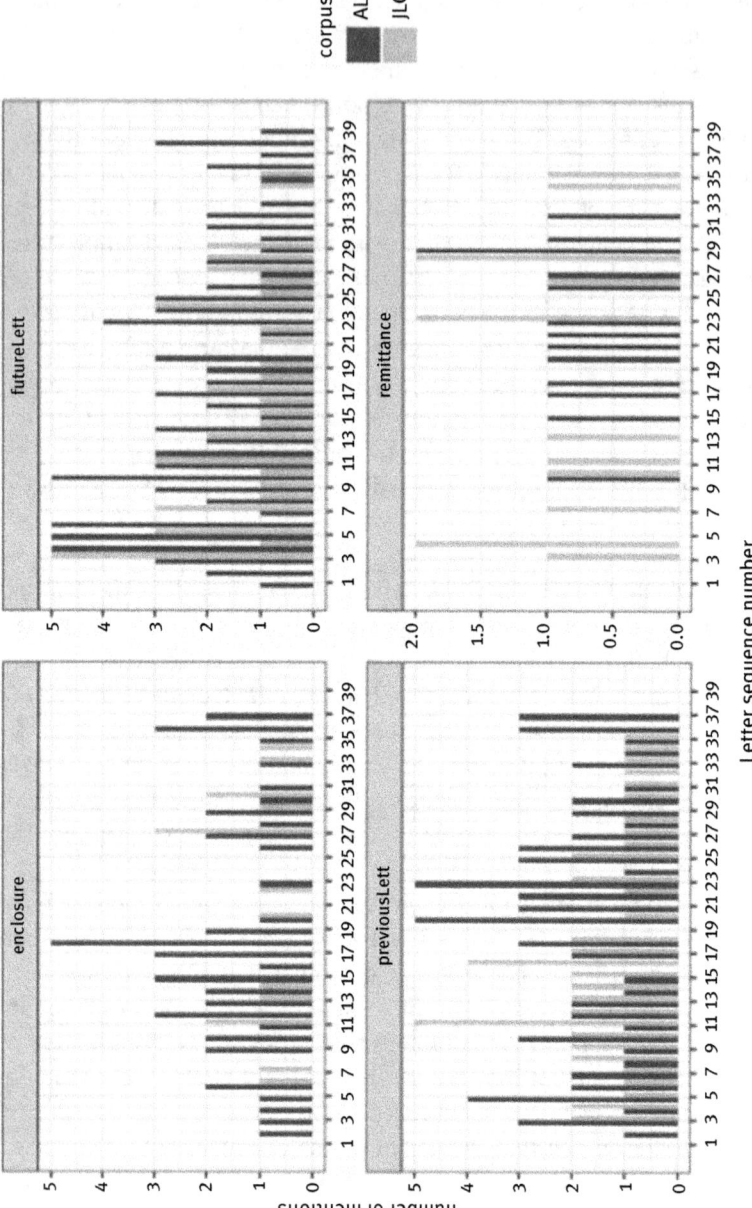

Figure 17.2: Absolute frequency of selected themes in ALC and JLC, grouped by theme.

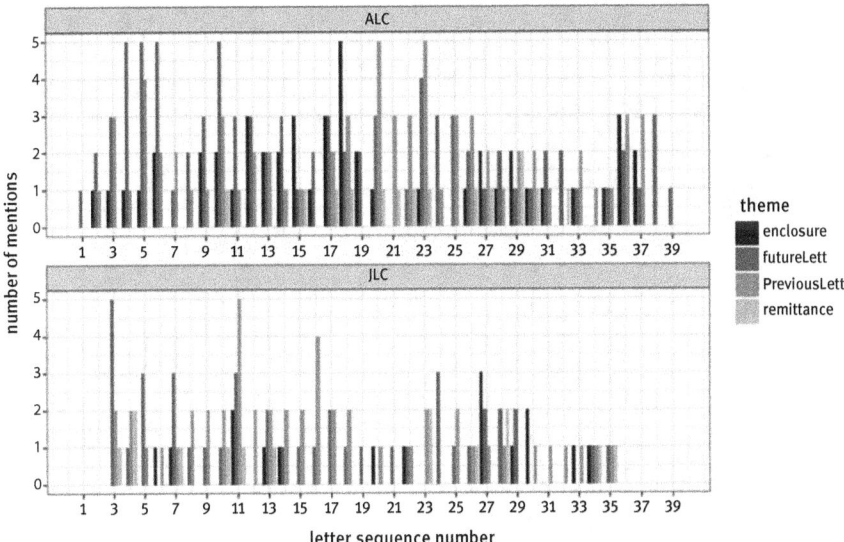

Figure 17.3: Absolute frequency of selected themes in ALC and JLC, grouped by author.

interactants, but the interactants have the same to and from roles in both corpora. The second subtle observation is that Annie and Julia talk about the interactants in roughly the same proportions, with the natural exception that each talk about themselves more than about others.

17.7 A closer look at the topics Future Letters and Previous Letters

Digital humanities techniques (annotating the Lough letters for topics and personography information as well as using computational and visualisation tools to extract metadata and present it in different ways and from different viewpoints) have allowed us to identify potentially interesting features of the letters.

Overall Annie's discussion of the four topics (Future Letters, Previous Letters, Remittance and Enclosure) is a lot denser than Julia's. Additionally, whereas Annie seems to cover all four topics in each letter, Julia may cover just one or two. While Annie sent significantly more enclosures (typically newspaper cuttings) than Julia, both sisters sent remittances. There are, however, some differences in the spread of these remittances over the course of their correspondence. Julia, for instance, consistently sent remittances to her mother

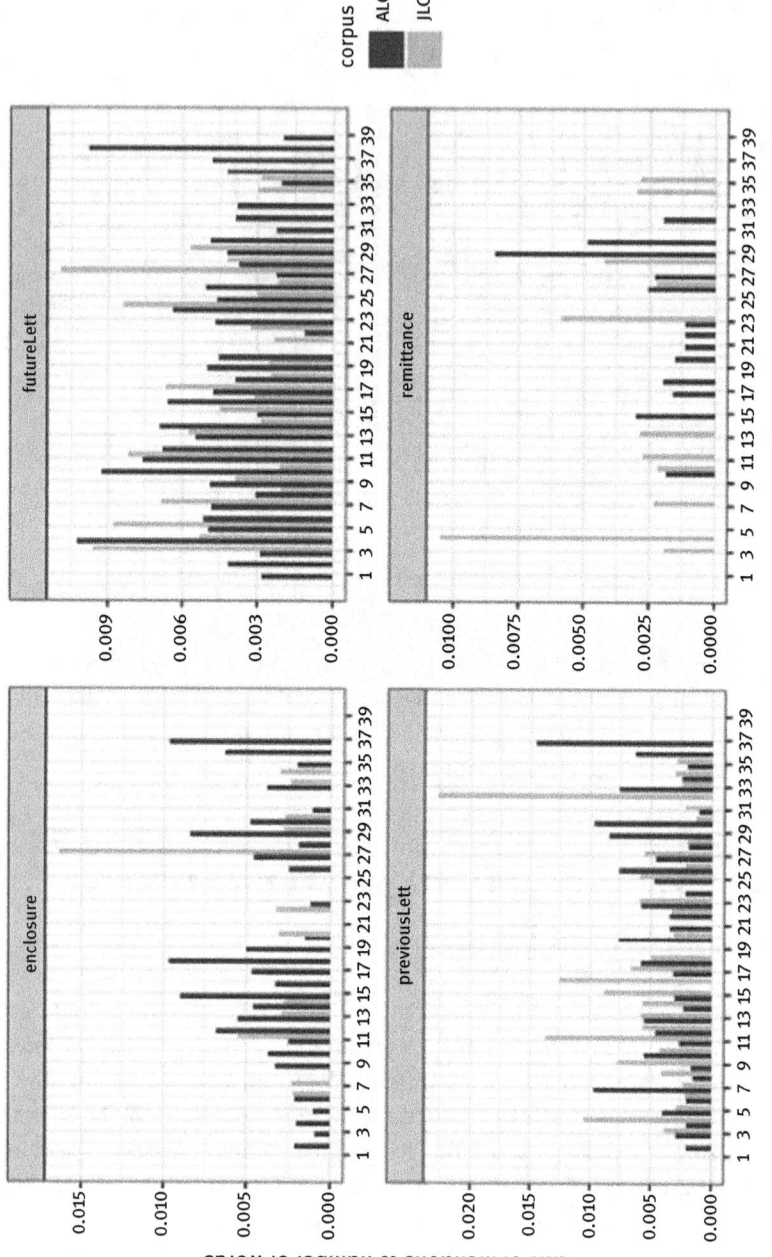

Figure 17.4: Relative frequency of selected themes in ALC and JLC, grouped by theme.

17 New methods, old data — 351

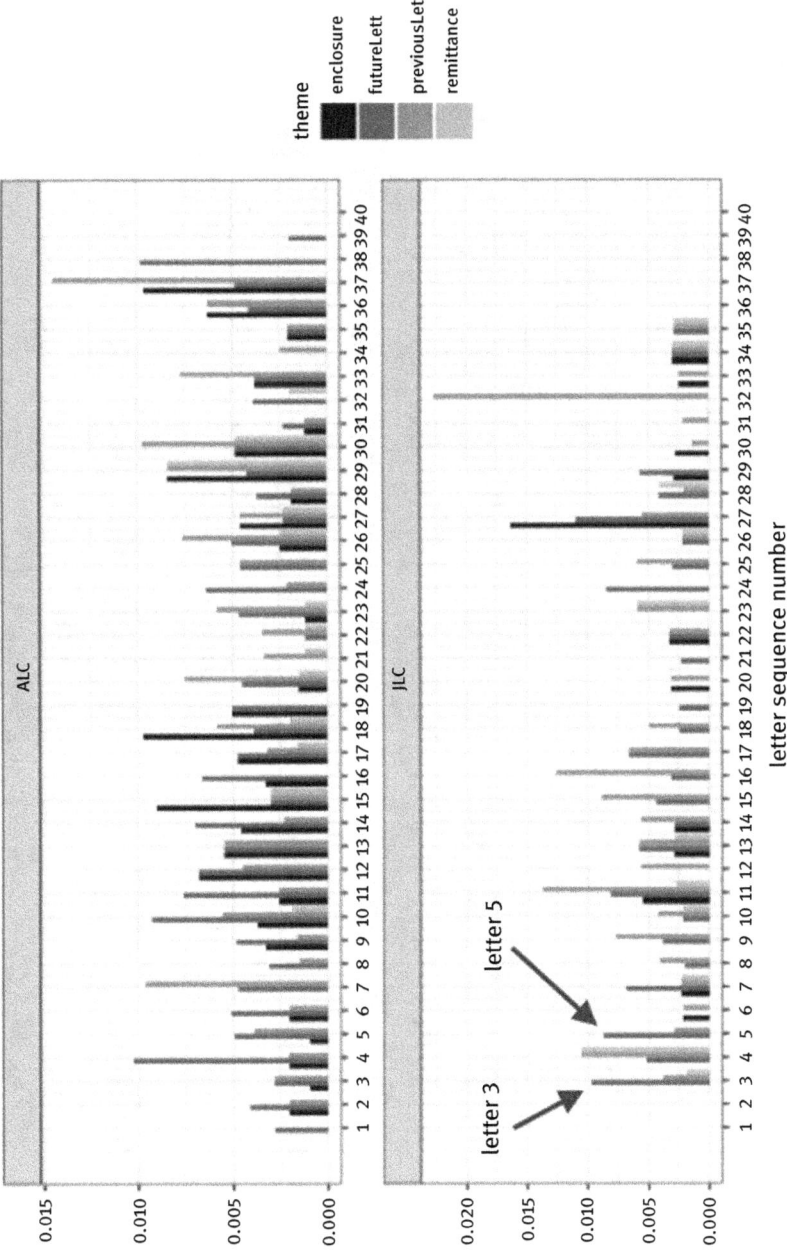

Figure 17.5: Relative frequency of selected themes in ALC and JLC, grouped by author.

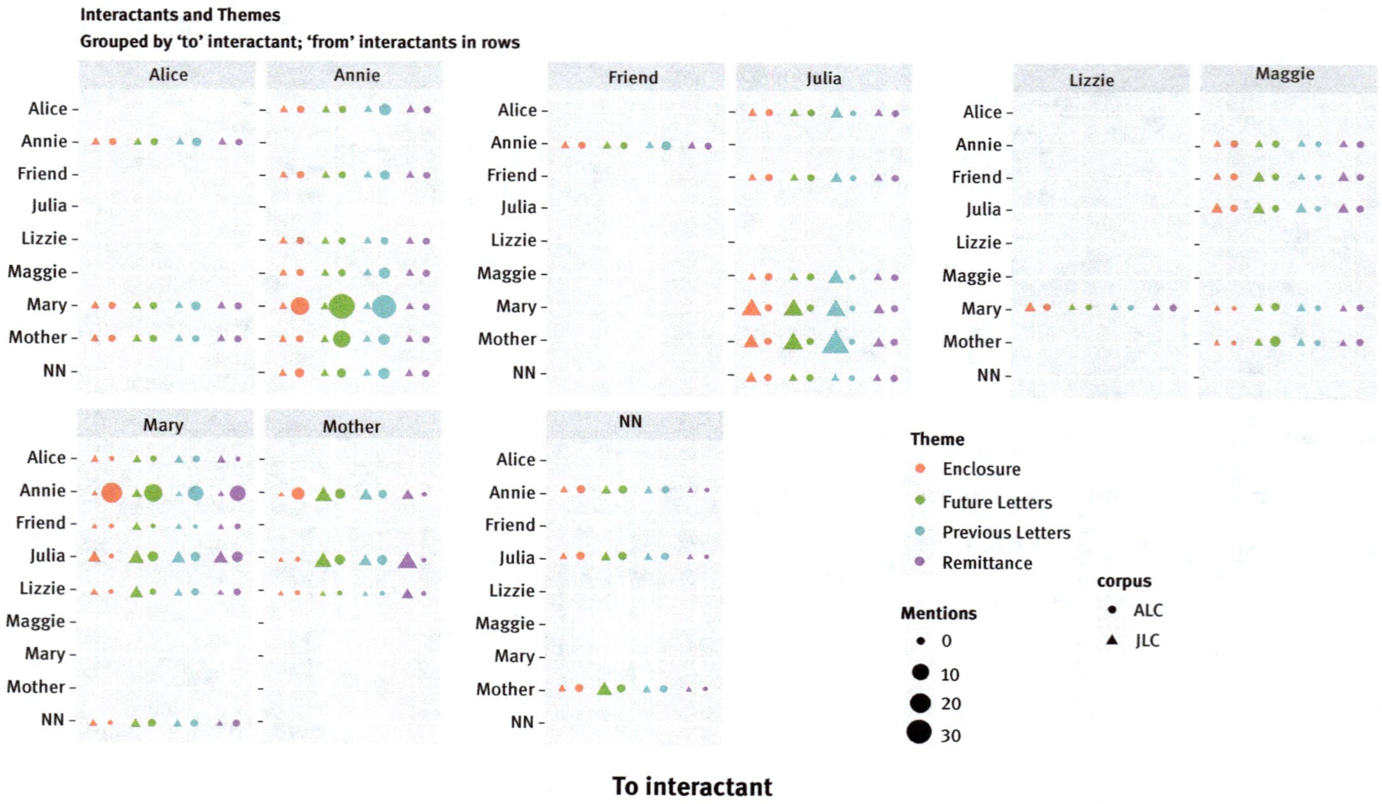

352 — Emma Moreton and Chris Culy

Figure 17.6: Interactants and themes in the corpora (circles are for ALC, triangles for JLC).

earlier on in her correspondence. The remittances then stopped for some time (possibly because these were Julia's childrearing years). In her later letters (after her mother's death), the remittances continue, this time to her younger sister, Mary. Annie, in contrast, primarily sent remittances to her younger sister, Mary, regularly and without any significant gaps.

Both Annie and Julia frequently talk about future and previous letters in their correspondence, with both sisters tending to write more about future letters (letters which they plan/hope to send/receive) in their earlier correspondence. In her later correspondence, Annie (unlike Julia) talks in some depth about previous letters she received.

A closer look at the interactants involved in the four topics shows that both sisters corresponded with, and wrote about, the same individuals – typically family members in Ireland and America. However, in the context of writing about previous and future letters, Annie tended to refer to a wider network of people. In other words, while Julia tended to focus on letters sent between her and her mother (*I received your letter, I will write soon*), Annie was more likely to write about letters that her Mother and Sister received or can expect to receive from other family members. Given that Annie mainly wrote to her younger sister Mary, while Julia mainly wrote to her mother, our initial findings could suggest that different letter writing practices reflect different familial roles. Indeed, a closer look at the language of the topic Future Letters (using the corpus tool *Sketch Engine* (Kilgarriff & Kosem 2012)) showed that Annie tended to use more direct (*write soon*) and indirect commands (*I hope you will write soon*) when referring to future correspondence. In contrast, Julia (mainly writing to her mother) was less likely to instruct the recipient to write a letter. Rather the pattern *I will write soon* is most typical in Julia's letters.

Table 17.5 shows the most frequent lemmas within the topic Future Letters in both the ALC and JLC. A closer look at the lemma WRITE (which occurs more than twice as often in the *ALC* when compared with the JLC) revealed that it is typically used in the following structures in the ALC:

(6) when you write + infinitive (as in, *when you write + let me know how are they, remember me to her, tell Lizzie she must write to me, let me know if old Mrs Cassen is deed yet*) (19 occurrences)

(7) *I hope you will write* (as in, *I hope you will write her often*) (15 occurrences)

(8) and write + adverb/noun phrase (as in, *and write soon to me, and write a longer letter next time*) (7 occurrences)

Table 17.5: Most frequent lemmas in the topic Future Letters in the ALC and JLC.

ALC		JLC	
Lemma	Freq.	Lemma	Freq.
you	134	I	74
I	85	be	66
and	74	you	66
write	72	to	57
to	63	write	37
will	59	and	32
me	50	will	29
be	46	she	25
hope	42	have	23
soon	39	letter	21
all	35	a	21
know	28	the	21
send	28	all	19
the	27	not	17
let	27	hope	16
when	26	me	16
a	25	well	16
from	23	from	14
get	21	her	14
how	20	when	13
time	19	it	12

(9) *I will write* (as in, *I will write again by Christmas* or *I will write to you soon again*) (7 occurrences)

Julia, in contrast, typically uses the lemma WRITE in the structure *I/she + will + write* (9 occurrences) and *I/she + is going to write* (6 occurrences), with 5 occurrences referring to the process of learning to write (as in, *she is not able to read or write yet*). Only 5 of the 37 instances of the lemma WRITE in the JLC instruct the recipient of the letter (*you*) to write. In short, while both sisters refer to future letters in their correspondence, Annie is much more likely to be instructing or directing the recipient to write, whereas Julia is more likely to be confirming and reassuring the recipient that she will write again soon.

Finally, a keyword search of the topics Future Letters and Previous Letters in both the ALC and JLC revealed a noticeable amount of emotive language. Both sisters express anxiety over not receiving a letter (*I am very anxious to hear from Mary I hope to get good newes from her* (ALC)), they write about crying at the sight of a letter from home (*I assure you I did not cry so much in a long time as when I read your letter* (JLC)), and they write about feelings of happiness upon hearing news about loved ones (*I am very happy to hear from you and to hear you are in the enjoyment of good health* (JLC)). Whilst these topics may appear on the surface to be rather formulaic in nature (*I hope you will write* is the most common n-gram in the topic Future Letters in both corpora, for instance) their function is, arguably, much deeper than that: these topics reassure the recipient that they are missed and thought about and as such perform a key role in maintaining familial relationships.

17.8 Conclusion

This chapter set out to explore the use of digital humanities techniques for examining letter writing practices in the context of nineteenth century mass migration from Ireland to America. Specifically, our aim was to explore how digital/visualisation tools (i.e. new methods) can help us to notice patterns and trends in old data. Whilst our findings may not be entirely surprising and/or revealing, through repeating the process we have described here it may be possible to see whether our observations are typical (or not) of other letter collections.

There are two aspects of digital methods used here, XML markup and visualisation, each of which provides certain benefits. The XML markup is a way of providing annotations which has several advantages over non-digital markup. One advantage is that it is easy to have detailed, overlapping annotations, such as a topic within a topic. Another advantage is that it is easy to check for consistency of the annotations. A third advantage of digital markup is that it is easy to tally the various annotations for further analysis, including input to the visualisations.

The complex visualisations are made possible not only by having the digital data, but by the existence of high-level tools that allow for their rapid creation, which in turn facilitates exploration of the data in various ways. Visualisations enable analysts to discover patterns that we might not have otherwise noticed, or even thought to look for, such as the similarity of the roles of the interactants in ALC and JLC shown in figure 17.5. Visualisations also allow researchers to communicate patterns they have discovered, and enable others to discover new patterns. Of course, any visualisation embodies assumptions and perspectives, and the visualisations presented here are no different: they were chosen from a variety of alternatives to highlight certain aspects of the data and to communicate certain ideas.

In short, both methods (markup and visualisation) allow us to analyse the Lough letters in ways that would have been extremely difficult to do in a non-digital fashion. The use of digital methods allows for quick, detailed exploration of the letters. For example, the charts in figures 17.2–17.5 took minutes to prepare digitally from the calculated counts, not hours. It is also very easy to change perspectives, such as from the counts in figures 17.2 and 17.3 to the ratios in figures 17.4 and 17.5. In addition, using digital annotations allows for different future analyses without having to re-annotate the letters. Of course, since this corpus is relatively small, all of the work here *could* have been done manually, at a much greater cost in time and effort. However, for larger corpora, it simply would not be feasible to conduct these kinds of studies without digital methods.

Digital methods are not a panacea, of course. For this study, the annotation of themes had to be done manually, since there are no digital tools for the task. Digital analysis tools typically depend on the existence of large annotated corpora similar to the one to be analysed, and there are no corpora of immigrant letters annotated for these themes, or even similar themes. In addition, the algorithms that digital tools use for "topic modelling", such as term-frequency / inverse document frequency (TF/DIF, Spärk Jones 1972) and latent Dirichlet allocation (LDA, Blei et al. 2003) operate at the level of words or short phrases. The construction of more abstract themes such as "future letters" over stretches of text are currently not possible without human intervention. At this point, we can only speculate whether automatic theme analysis will ever be possible for corpora such as the one studied here. Our view is that certain aspects will be possible to annotate automatically, aspects which occur in other, larger corpora (e.g. death, religion, weather, etc). However, more narrow topics (e.g. future letters, Ireland and America) may be more difficult.

Analysing the interactants in a corpus such as the Lough letters using "information extraction" is also not currently possible, due to the limited scope of the techniques. While further discussion is beyond the scope of this paper, we believe that information extraction is a promising area for exploration of interactants, via a combination of manual annotation of the themes along with automatic annotation of interactancts with those themes.

The results presented in this chapter are provided as an illustrative guide to the kinds of insights and findings made available by these methods. The next step will be to carry out similar studies across other collections to see the extent to which the Lough letters reflect letter writing practices of other migrant families and groups. For example, do male and female migrants tend to write as frequently and about similar topics? Do they send similar numbers of remittances and enclosures? Are the topics Future Letters and Previous Letters prevalent across other migrant letter collections, and to what extent do letter writing practices (such as those described in this chapter) reflect different familial roles? Whilst identifying topics and themes in the discourse is a largely subjective process, the use of digital markup makes that process transparent, allowing others to build on, contribute to and challenge the various categories. The process of topic identification (and the resultant analysis of those topics) thus becomes a collaborative process and opens up the possibility for cross disciplinary discussion.

References

Amador-Moreno, Carolina. P. & McCafferty, Kevin. 2015. "Sure this is a great country for drink and rowing at elections": Discourse markers in the *Corpus of Irish English Correspondence, 1750–1940*. In Carolina P. Amador-Moreno, Kevin McCafferty & Elaine Vaughan (eds.), *Pragmatic markers in Irish English*, 270–291. Amsterdam: John Benjamins.

Barton, H. Arnold. 1990 *Letters from the promised land: Swedes in America, 1840–1914*. Minneapolis: University of Minnesota Press.

Blei, David M., Andrew Y. Ng, Michael I. Jordan, Michael I & John Lafferty. 2003. Latent Dirichlet allocation. *Journal of Machine Learning Research* 3. 993–1022.

Bruce, Susannah Ural. 2006. *The harp and the eagle: Irish-American volunteers and the Union Army, 1861–1865*. New York: New York University Press.

Conway, Alan. 1961. *The Welsh in America: Letters from the immigrants*. Minneapolis: University of Minnesota Press.

Corrigan, Karen. P. 1992. I gcuntas De muin Bearla do na leanbhain': Eisimirce agus an Ghaeilge sa naou aois deag. In Patrick O'Sullivan (ed.), *The Irish world wide*, 143–161. Leicester: Leicester University Press.

Diner, Hasia R. 1983. *Erin's daughters in America*. Baltimore: Johns Hopkins University Press.

Elliott, Bruce. S., David A. Gerber & Suzanne. M. Sinke (eds.). 2006. *Letters across borders: Epistolary practices of international migrants*. Basingstoke: Palgrave Macmillan.

Emmons, David. M. 1990. *The Butte Irish: Class and ethnicity in an American mining town, 1875–1925*. Urbana: University of Illinois Press.

Erickson, Charlotte. 1972. *Invisible immigrants: The adaptation of English and Scottish immigrants in nineteenth-century America*. London: Weidenfeld & Nicolson.

Fitzmaurice, Susan. 2015. Aristocratic Letters. In Anita Auer, David Schreier & Dominic Watt (eds.), *Letter writing and language change*, 156–184. Cambridge, UK: Cambridge University Press.

Fitzmaurice, Susan. 2012. Sociability: Conversation and the performance of friendship in early eighteenth century letters. In Ulrich Busse & Axel Hübler (eds.), *The meta-communicative lexicon of English now and then: A historical pragmatics approach*, 21–43. Amsterdam: John Benjamins.

Fitzpatrick, David. 1994. *Oceans of consolation: Personal accounts of Irish migration to Australia*. Cork: Cork University Press.

Gerber, David. A. 2006. *Authors of their lives: The personal correspondence of British immigrants to North America in the nineteenth century*. New York: New York University Press.

Kamphoefner, Walter. D., Wolfgang Helbich & Ulrike Sommer (eds.). 1988. *News from the land of freedom: German immigrants write home*. Ithaca: Cornell University Press.

Kilgarriff, Adam & Iztok Kosem. 2012. Corpus tools for lexicographers. In Sylviane Granger & Magali Paquot (eds.), *Electronic lexicography*, 31–56. Oxford: Oxford University Press.

Koos, Greg. 2001. The Irish hedge schoolmaster in the American backcountry. *New Hibernia Review* 5. 9–26.

McCafferty, Kevin & Carolina P. Amador-Moreno. 2012. "I will be expecting a letter from you before this reaches you": A corpus-based study of *shall/will* variation in Irish English correspondence. In Marina Dossena & Gabriella Del Lungo Camiciotti (eds.), *Letter writing in late modern Europe*, 179–204. Amsterdam: John Benjamins.

McCafferty, Kevin & Caroline P. Amador-Moreno. 2014. "If you write soon I shall get it & will reply at once": The spread of first-person future *will* in Irish English. *English Language and Linguistics* 18. 407–429.

Miller, Kerby. A. 2008. *Ireland and Irish America: Culture, class, and transatlantic migration*. Dublin: Field Day.

Miller, Kerby. A. 1985. *Emigrants and exiles: Ireland and the Irish exodus to North America*. Oxford: Oxford University Press.

Miller, Kerby. A., David. N. Doyle & Patricia Kelleher. 1995. For love and liberty: Irish women, migration and domesticity in Ireland and America, 1815–1920. In Patrick O'Sullivan (ed.), *The Irish world wide*, 54–61. Leicester: Leicester University Press.

Miller, Kerby. A., Arnold Schrier, Bruce D. Boling & David N. Doyle. 2003. *Irish immigrants in the land of Canaan: Letters and memoirs from colonial and revolutionary America, 1675–1815*. Oxford: Oxford University Press.

Montgomery, Michael. B. 1995. The linguistic value of Ulster emigrant letters. *Ulster Folklife* 41. 26–41.

Nolan, Janet. A. 1989. *Ourselves alone: Women's emigration from Ireland, 1885–1920*. Lexington: University Press of Kentucky.

Noonan, Alan. J. M. 2011. "Oh those long months without a word from home": Migrant letters from mining frontiers. *The Boolean*, 129–135. Cork: University College Cork.

Plummer, Ken. 2001. *Documents of life 2: An invitation to a critical humanism*. London: SAGE Publications.

Rayson, Paul. 2009. *Wmatrix*. Lancaster: Lancaster University. Available at: http://ucrel.lancs.ac.uk/wmatrix/ (accessed 22 July 2019).

Spärck Jones, Karen. 1972. A statistical interpretation of term specificity and its application in retrieval. *Journal of Documentation* 28 (1). 11–21

Van Hattum, Marije. 2014. "Queensland for rver & Augus un ballybug go braugh": The expression of identity in nineteenth-century Irish emigrant letters. In David Evans (ed.), *Language and identity: Discourse in the world*, 105–122. London: Bloomsbury.

Wickham, Hadley. 2016. *ggplot2: Elegant graphics for data analysis*. New York: Springer-Verlag.

Zempel, Solveig. 1991. *In their own words: Letters from Norwegian immigrants*. Minneapolis: University of Minnesota Press.

Elisabetta Adami
18 Transhistoricizing multimodality: Reflections on the how-to

By looking at the multimodality of different texts as well as the contexts and practices of production and engagement with them, from pre-print times through to early printing and up to online news texts, the chapters in this section offer three possibilities of transhistorical investigation. They (1) apply contemporary theories/analytical frameworks to investigate past practices (Moore), (2) trace similarities between past and contemporary practices (Thompson & Collins), including those that co-exist on the same online platforms (van Driel), and (3) re-interpret past practices through the lens of new digital technologies (Moreton). Reading them one after the other made me think that we need ways to integrate all three takes, if we want to factor in "time", in its multiple timescales (and along with space), in our understanding of the multimodality of human communication and its relations with "the social", in and beyond the digital realm. The question, to me, is one of method, i.e. "how do we do that?"

Back in 2007, when I was trying to make sense of my PhD subject matter, i.e., videos replying to other videos on the (at that time fairly new) YouTube platform, Gunther Kress[1] had a supervision meeting with me at a café outdoor table in Russell Square, in London. I was telling him about my struggle to explain this new form of interaction by means of videos through any of the theories I knew, such as coherence/cohesion (Halliday & Hasan 1976), Relevance (Wilson & Sperber 2004), Gricean principles (Grice 1975), and all theories that define successful communication in terms of making oneself understood and understanding what the other intends to mean. Not far from us in the square, there was a group of youth freestyling in a circle, taking turns at stepping in the centre to perform their dance moves. Gunther pointed at them saying that

---

[1] This piece was written months before Gunther Kress' sudden death in June 2019. I sent him the draft asking for his opinion, and he emailed back promptly, very pleased with it. In his usual, never feigned, humble attitude, he wrote that he did not remember contributing much in that particular occasion but that he remembered very fondly our discussions during my time in London. Timescales enter in this too, as I would have never imagined that, by the time of this publication, this piece would be re-signified as my very little tribute to his memory and the profound impact he had – and will continue to have – on my thinking.

Elisabetta Adami, University of Leeds, Centre for Translation Studies, Leeds,
e-mail: e.adami@leeds.ac.uk

he thought my YouTube "stuff" was more similar to the kind of social interaction that those freestylers were having; it followed principles of social organization that differed from those for which traditional linguistic theories had been developed. That observation was a light-bulb moment for me in many respects.[2] The one that I believe is relevant to my "how-to" question is the use of analogy as a methodological tool. From that occasion I've learnt that the farthest the phenomena apparently are (as in the case of a group freestyling in a park and one video replying to another), the more insightful the analogies.

Often, the chapters in this section use analogy as a method, to relate past and present resources, texts, media, and practices. To use it as a method, we need to refine and integrate the notion in two respects. Firstly, in conceptual terms: analogy (as the basis of metaphor) is selective; to use it as a method, we need to unpack the metaphor (see Lakoff & Johnson 1980), and we need to spell out not only what we select (i.e., the "criterial aspect" in Kress 1993: 172) but also what we rule out when describing/explaining one phenomenon in terms of another. Put simply, analogy as a method needs to map both similarities *and* differences. Secondly, comparison is not enough; we need heuristic tools that enable not only a tiered analysis of a phenomenon in the terms of another (analogy), but also, if we conceive of timespace in its complexity, a layered analysis of the effects of one onto the other.

To underpin such a method, I'll propose three conceptual triplets. As a first, I think it is useful to draw on three key concepts of Social Semiotics (Hodge & Kress 1988; Kress 2010; van Leeuwen 2005), i.e., *affordances, provenance*, and *power*. *Affordance* labels the social and material constraints and possibilities of a resource. *Provenance* labels the meaning potentials of a resource imported into a new context by virtue of the social values that derive from its past uses in other contexts. *Power* points to the social relations among participants that are both reflected in and shaped by a representation. While I have used these notions in my research to make analogies (and differences) among relatively coeval communicative phenomena (but see all of Kress' work for applications across time), the chapters in this section made

---

2 It was one of the many discussions we had that year while we were reflecting on what would later become a notion of communication in terms of prompt-response, in my PhD thesis (Adami 2009) and in Gunther's book (Kress 2010), with me reaching the conclusion that video-interaction was paradigmatic of contemporary principles of communication, with successful communication no longer defined by mutual understanding of the interactants' intended meanings, but by individualized participation in chains of semiosis producing compatible effects that fulfilled the interactants' diverse interests.

me think about how to use them transhistorically, to map similarities and differences between past and present, integrated with the effects of the past nested into the present. As a second triplet, the three notions need to be applied to *modes* (as technologies for representation), *media* (as technologies for designing, producing and distributing them) and *genres* (as entextualisations of social practices/relations). The third triplet concerns the variables that need to be considered at each and all levels, i.e. *materiality, socio-cultural availability*, and sign-makers' *agency*.

Mapping affordances, provenance and power onto modes, media and genres, in respect to materiality, socio-cultural availability, and sign-makers' agency across time and space, will enable a fine-grained transhistorical investigation, both in terms of similarities *and* differences, and of effects, in sign-making practices and their social significance. Such a method involves asking:

1. Affordance: What did, e.g., the colour red, the manuscript as a medium, that given genre, afford sign- and meaning-makers to achieve (function), similarly and differently (in function-form combinations) than, say, a Facebook post, because of the materiality, social availability and the individual's creativity (of/in resources, media and genres)? Answering this question involves a comparative take (along the lines of Thompson & Collins' chapter). However, as I understand it after reading this section, a transhistorical perspective goes beyond considering past and present as discrete; thus comparison needs to be integrated by something else; hence:
2. Provenance: What meaning potentials did the use of that resource in the medium and genre have, by virtue of the traditions of use in other (previous) contexts at that time, and how have these meanings been imported (hence transformed) across time and space in similar/different function-forms associations on Facebook, by virtue again of materiality, social availability and individual agency? Answering this question (perhaps along the lines of van Driel's chapter) involves tracing trajectories in which the past enters the present, and, possibly, that look back at the past through the novel insights of the effects that we can observe in the present. Effects are never only "textual" or "semiotic"; they are eminently social (and possibly also psychological, affective and cognitive); hence:
3. Power: What do the sign-making practices as identified above tell us in terms of who could (not) produce and engage with these resources, media and genres through which forms of social organisation; how are these similar/different now; and how do (changes in) past social semiotic organisations affect the present ones (as well as how does what we know of today's social semiotic landscapes shed light onto those of the past)?

The materiality and sociality of production and engagement with texts has dramatically changed, beyond what was known as the "age of mechanical reproduction" (Benjamin 1936), given that anybody with access to a digital device can now (re)produce them. Today we have several millions (billions?) of people using digital technologies to communicate through videos, songs, pictures, writing and speech across the world; this, in numbers, availability and circulation, is possibly more comparable to people's face-to-face interactions, singing or dancing in the Middle Ages, than to the material and social constraints/possibilities of the closed literate circle of manuscript scribes and readers of those times. Something has definitely changed, because societies have changed, and this always reflects into the semiotic. Yet, as the chapters show, not everything in the digital age is new; printing could be seen in many respects as a brief (yet highly effect-bearing) parenthesis in the history of humans using some supports to "leave meaningful marks"; and refining methods for a transhistorical investigation of communication through analogy can help us understand deeply the specificities of contemporary practices, where they come from and where they are heading (in scary and puzzling times of big data, fake news and social control through machine-generated algorithms), as well as to trace the common human principles of communication, which may shed more or new light onto what it means to be (and possibly stay) human.

References

Adami, Elisabetta. 2009. Video-interaction on YouTube: Contemporary changes in semiosis and communication. Verona: Universita' degli studi di Verona PhD thesis. DOI: 10.13140/RG.2.2.35784.88328, https://www.researchgate.net/publication/337441221_Video-Interaction_on_YouTube_Contemporary_Changes_in_Semiosis_and_Communication_Adami_Elisabetta_2009_PhD_Thesis_Universita_degli_Studi_di_Verona (accessed 26 February 2020).

Benjamin, Walter. 1936. *The work of art in the age of mechanical reproduction*. New York: Random House.

Grice, H. Paul. 1975. Logic and conversation. In Peter Cole & Jerry L. Morgan (eds.), *Syntax and semantics*, 41–58. New York: Academic Press.

Halliday, Michael A.K. & Ruqaiya Hasan. 1976. *Cohesion in English*. Harlow: Longman.

Hodge, Robert & Gunther Kress. 1988. *Social semiotics*. Cambridge, UK: Polity Press.

Kress, Gunther. 2010. *Multimodality. A social semiotic approach to contemporary communication*. Abingdon: Routledge.

Kress, Gunther. 1993. Against arbitrariness: The social production of the sign as a foundational issue in critical discourse analysis. *Discourse & Society* 4. 169–191.

Lakoff, George & Mark Johnson. 1980. *Metaphors we live by*. Chicago: University of Chicago Press.

van Leeuwen, Theo. 2005. *Introducing social semiotics*. Abingdon: Routledge.

Wilson, Deirdre & Dan Sperber. 2004. Relevance theory. In Lawrence Horn & Gregory Ward (eds.), *The handbook of pragmatics*, 607–632. Oxford: Blackwell.

Ana Deumert
Postscript

You say you want a revolution? Histories and futures of researching the digital, a view from the south

19.1 Histories

It appears that we – as social scientists, sociolinguists, internet and digital media scholars – have reached a point in time where we wish to reflect on the history of contemporary communication and information technologies: the so-called "new media" are no longer "new", but have become an integral part of many lives. The present volume – based on a seminar that took place in 2016 – is evidence of this trend. In 2017, the journal *Internet Histories: Digital Technology, Culture and Society* was inaugurated, speaking further to the need of establishing a historical perspective in the broad field of "digital media studies" (Brügger et al 2017). In the same year, Goggin and McLelland (2017) published the *Routledge Companion to Global Internet Histories*. The volume includes chapters on the history of technosociality and digital cultures, the evolution of the internet in diverse locales (e.g. Brazil, Bhutan, France, Israel, Japan, Mexico, Taiwan), the histories of particular genres (e.g. BBS, blogging, online advertising), and the emergence of digital publics. In 2018, Brügger and Milligan published the *SAGE Handbook of Web History*, exploring the methodological questions that underpin web-historiography as well as the rise of platforms such as Wikipedia and Facebook, vernacular creativity, trolling and sound archives. In addition, tools such as the *Way-Back-Machine* (created in 2001) allow one to browse – study and appreciate – the internet-as-archive. Digital media, one might argue, call for historical investigation: the actions we perform online leave traces and create archives. Facebook regularly reminds us of things we did a year or two ago, and unless we delete our WhatsApp chats, they stay with us, can be searched and revisited (by ourselves or by anyone with access to our data). It is the archival nature of digital communication that

Note: I would like to thank the editors for the invitation to write this postscript, and the privilege to read the volume ahead of print. And I would like to thank my students for discussing their views on digital media with me in class and outside of class.

Ana Deumert, University of Cape Town, School of African and Gender Studies, Anthropology and Linguistics, Cape Town, e-mail: ana.deumert@uct.ac.za

https://doi.org/10.1515/9783110670837-024

allowed Cambridge Analytica to mine large amounts of data for political ends, and to influence political decision-making across the globe (Laterza 2018; Nyabola 2018).

At the same time the internet has the potential for impermanence. This ephemerality is exploited by applications such as Snapchat, Telegram, CoverMe and Wickr. Messages sent on these applications self-destruct and do not get archived. Yang and Wu (2018) further note that "websites everywhere have come and gone", and that work on the history of the internet should also include how people remember websites that have disappeared. Similarly, people have memories about how they used to engage with technologies that are now obsolete (such as Blackberry messenger), or how they moved from emoticons to emojis, changed their spelling habits, or adopted voice notes. That media memories can have emotional pull becomes evident when I ask students – as part of my lectures in historical sociolinguistics – to remember their first mobile phone: it is not just the memory of an object, but of an "evocative object"; that is, an object that evokes emotion, that becomes a companion to our life (Turkle 2007). Bringing back the memory of one's first feature phone, looking up images of it online, or remembering playing "snakes" on an old Nokia, is an experience that is saturated with affect.

Taking history into account and recognizing the myriad links between past-present-future is a topic that I have explored over the past few years, drawing on the broad field of southern or decolonial theory (see, e.g., Deumert 2018). But perhaps, a keen awareness of continuities – especially colonial/modernist continuities and persistent structures of inequality and injustice – can close our mind as well: it makes it difficult to see change, transformation, and perhaps even revolution. In this postscript, I will not discuss the rich analyses that are provided by the contributors to this volume; this was done beautifully by the commentators, as well as by the editors (who provide insightful introductions to each section). Rather I want to reflect on the "big" question of continuity and change, as well as what we might be missing if we restrict our work to particular geographical regions and languages (in this case Europe and English).

19.2 Ancestors

In 2014, in the introductory chapter to *Sociolinguistics and Mobile Communication*, I reflected on the question of novelty and theory: do we, as linguists and semioticians, need to formulate new theories about language in response to the far-reaching changes that have happened in the field of information and communication technologies since the 1980s? Perhaps for some the answer might be a "yes": too much has changed, especially in the past ten years, and our theories of language and social life are lagging behind, unable to explain the complexities of the digitally mediated present (and perhaps also unable to imagine the possibilities of digital futures). For others – such as myself and the editors of this volume – a careful and critical "rethinking" of existing theories is required; that is, we need to pay attention to continuities and discontinuities, to what is new, and to what remains of the old.

In 2014, I wrote about our "ancestors": scholars of language and semiotics (such as Humboldt, Sapir, Bakhtin, and Derrida) whose work on languaging (language-as-doing), heteroglossia, citationality and linguistic creativity remains meaningful to our contemporary engagement with communication and meaning-making. By drawing on a specific group of scholars – scholars who one might call post-structuralist (if such a label is necessary) – I made a particular argument. Namely, that even though we might not need "new" theories, we nevertheless need a "new" orientation to language: an orientation that moves away from structuralism (which has been dominant in linguistics and sociolinguistics throughout the twentieth century), and towards an understanding of language and communication as emergent, as first-order experience, which – only later and through discursive agency – sediments into second-order concepts and categories (see, e.g., Pablé & Hutton, 2015, drawing on work in integrational linguistics; for a critique of structural linguistics as a modernist-colonial project see Veronelli 2015; Deumert & Storch forthcoming).

Such a re-orientation of linguistics also includes paying attention to "assemblages": entanglements of the human and the non-human. This tradition has been referred to as post-humanism in the literature, and is a fairly new topic for most linguists and sociolinguists (Pennycook 2018; and see Sealey, this volume). Yet, work on human/non-human relations has a long tradition in Indigenous thought and scholarship, a tradition that is often ignored. Thus, when the Indigenous scholar Zoe Todd attended a lecture by Bruno Latour – one of the scholars who has spearheaded posthumanist approaches in the social sciences – she was surprised (and also not surprised) that his lecture did not reference any of the Indigenous scholars, scholars who have spoken about assemblages long before the Western academy recognized their existence. She writes:

> I waited through the whole talk, to hear the Great Latour credit Indigenous thinkers for their millennia of engagement with sentient environments, with cosmologies that enmesh people into complex relationships between themselves and *all* relations, and with climates and atmospheres as important points of organization and action. I waited ... waited to hear a whisper of [these] lively and deep intellectual traditions ... It never came. (Todd 2016: 6–7)

Asking about our ancestors also links to calls to de-westernize media studies (Park & Curran 2000), including sociolinguistic studies of media communication. To de-westernize media studies is not merely a quest to include more global examples and studies, but implies, as noted by Shome (2016), the adoption of a postcolonial or decolonial perspective. She argues for a "*postcolonial interruption*" (her emphasis); that is, to recognize the invisibility of the global south in studies of media usage, media coverage, and – importantly – media theory. The editors of this volume call on scholars to work towards establishing a *transhistorial* perspective. I would like to expand on this and suggest that future work should be *translocal* as well as *transhistorical*, moving – deliberately and decisively – beyond the canon of northern scholarship and northern experiences of digital media.[1]

19.3 Revolutions (First Take)

Even though I remain wary of narratives of rupture and revolution with regard to digital technologies, I do find them to be cautiously inspiring. The narrative of a communication revolution has been most explicitly articulated by Crystal (2004). He argues that we are witnessing a "language revolution", and find ourselves at the beginning of "a new linguistic era"; an era characterized (i) by the rise of English as the first truly global language (leading to the formation of many Englishes), (ii) by accelerated loss of linguistic diversity and, finally, (iii) by the arrival of digital media. He notes:

> I do not believe that "revolution" is too strong a word for what has been taking place. A "revolution" is any combination of events which produces a radical shift in consciousness or behaviour over a relatively short period of time, and this is what has happened.
> (Crystal 2004: 20)

While working on this postscript, I showed Crystal's assessment to some of my postgraduate students and asked: "What do you think, was the internet a revolution? Is he correct?" They didn't hesitate: "Definitely!! It changed everything!!" It

---

[1] I follow Santos (2014) in approaching "the south" and "southern theory" as a space of distinctive experience and intellectual production, not merely as a geo-political space. The south, in this broader sense, can also be found in the global north, just as the north can be found within the global south. For example, African American ghettos within cities in the USA would be examples of "the south in the north" (and the black radical tradition is therefore an example of southern theory); expensive private schools and wealthy suburbs in South Africa are examples of "the north in the south".

is important to note that they didn't associate the "revolution" with a particular application or platform, but consistently with hardware: the smartphone.

So what "has been taking place", producing "a radical shift in consciousness or behaviour"? Firstly, digital media have become omnipresent in the global north and in parts of the global south. Many of us are now, as argued by the psychologist Turkle (2011), tethered to our devices (especially smartphones), creating technologically-mediated – and affectively experienced – human/non-human assemblages. Secondly, new forms of writing and meaning making have emerged. While there exist, as shown in this volume, important "objective" continuities with earlier communicative practices, these practices are often *experienced* – "subjectively" – as novel and creative. One could easily add a thirdly (new forms of political engagement, new ways of doing politics), fourthly (new forms of sociability, and its opposite, i.e. new forms of doing hate), and so forth (see also McCulloch 2019, whose *Because Internet* is a celebration of this experiental "newness").

I am much in favour of revolutions (especially political ones that aim to bring about social justice, political equality and decolonization), but I also believe that we need to be careful with our terminologies. Selbin (2010: 13) reminds us that "[p]eople across the world and throughout time have their own understanding of revolution, rooted in the stories we tell". When I think about revolutions, I think about Haiti and Russia, but also about the Zapatistas and their on-going struggles in Mexico; I think about the history and present of the ANC's National Democratic Revolution in South Africa. I might also think of Cuba or Venezuela, or of the failed revolution in Germany. In other words, I think – first and foremost – of political revolutions, of dramatic and passionate upheavals that are led by people, that have people at their centre, and that tend to demand sacrifices and a deep commitment from people.

Talking about an "internet revolution" means that one adopts quite a different perspective: not only people can be agents of change, but also scientific discoveries and technologies. Thus, one might speak, for example, of the *Copernican revolution* (which put the sun, and not the earth, at the centre of the universe),[2] and Kant (1998 [1782]: 108) argued in the preface to the second edition of the *Critique of Pure Reason* that scientific discoveries can usher in "*a revolution* in the way of thinking" (my emphasis). Two centuries later, this observation was at the core of Kuhn's (2012 [1962]) magisterial *Structure of Scientific Revolutions*, where he writes: "during revolutions scientists see new

---

2 Interestingly, Copernicus' work (*De revolutionibus orbium coelestium*, 1543) makes use of an older meaning of "revolution", objects that "revolve" around one another. It was reinterpreted

and different things when looking with familiar instruments in places they have looked before" (p. 428). Engels was one of the first scholars to apply the idea of "revolution" to technological, rather than political or scientific, change. He noted in *The Condition of the Working Class in England* (1969 [1845]), that one cannot understand historical change if one does not pay attention to technological change. He then discusses, *inter alia*, the invention of the steam engine, which started "an industrial revolution, a revolution which at the same time *changed the whole of civil society*" (Engels 1969 [1845]: 33; my emphasis). With regard to communication technologies, Eisenstein's *The Printing Press as an Agent of Change* (republished as *The Printing Revolution in Early Modern Europe*, 2005 [1983]), expresses a version of Engels' argument. Inspired by McLuhan's (1962) *Gutenberg Galaxy: The Making of Typographic Man* as well as Williams' (1961) *The Long Revolution*, she argues that the printing press started a socio-cultural revolution. Aspects of Eisenstein's argument are echoed by Anderson (1983) in *Imagined Communities*. He argues that the origins of European nationalism – creating nation states and "inventing" languages – were closely tied to the emergence of print capitalism. In these cases "revolution" does not describe a sudden rupture and upheaval, but rather a process of fundamental and irreversible change, a process that includes a sense of speed, but that unfolds over time. It is thus unlike the dramatic and sudden change brought about by many, but not all, political revolutions.

Considering the history of "revolution" as an analytical and descriptive term, it seems to me that Crystal and my students are right: the idea of a revolution is worth considering. This is not to argue against the presence of the transhistorical continuities. Rather the term encourages us to simultaneously look for discontinuities, to that which is new. I want to end this section with a number of questions: Did the revolution start with the printing press which allowed for the mass circulation of reading material, and created new types of reading publics? Did the effects simply continue throughout the centuries, shifting and twisting here and there, but basically following the same trajectory, moving from print media to digital media? Or is the shift from book to smartphone more substantial, and requires more careful reflection? What is the role of capitalism and commodification in this process, turning words and other forms of signification into a commodity, assigning them an exchange value? And if we agree that we have seen some kind of revolution, what does this mean for

---

as a "revolution" in the modern sense (i.e. as a transformation of how we think about the world and our place in it) by Kant.

Labov's (1972) uniformitarian principle? Maybe, sometimes, the past is another country after all?

19.4 Materialities

Considering questions of "revolution" – recognizing continuities and discontinuities, habit and disruption – is not to argue for technological determinism. The concept of assemblages, mentioned above, makes this impossible: we are never looking at one thing or the other, but always at complex entanglements of the human and the non-human. However, I want to suggest that Crystal, Kant, Kuhn, Engels, Eisenstein and Anderson are nevertheless limited in their analysis, and that this limitation is symptomatic of much theory-from-the-global-north: Kant, Kuhn, Engels, Eisenstein and Anderson focus on Europe, and Crystal on English. Yet, the repercussions of revolutions – and even smaller upheavals – resonate around the globe, and are discussed in many languages.

Consider the instrustrial revolution. Engels locates it firmly in nineteenth century England. Yet, as Williams (1944), Sheridan (1969), Beckford (1999 [1972]) and Higman (2000) have shown, the industrial revolution would not have been possible without the "sugar revolution" in the Caribbean. It was the plantation economy, especially sugar production, which started mercantile capitalism and injected much needed cash into the British and French economies in the seventeenth and eighteenth centuries (see also Davis et al. 2019 on the *Plantationocene*, a term that foregrounds the role of the plantation in the making of the modern world, including the twenty-first century current ecological crisis). Higman (2000: 213) summarizes the effects of the "sugar revolution" as follows:

> [I]t generated a massive boost to the Atlantic slave trade, provided the engine for a variety of triangular trades, altered European nutrition and consumption, increased European interest in tropical colonies, and ... contributed vitally to the industrial revolution.

To neglect the global south – the majority world – remains common practice. However, without the resources of the global south there would not have been an industrial revolution, nor would we have mobile phones and computers.

This text was written on an Apple Inc. laptop. Yet, it was not produced in the United States where Apple Inc. has its headquarters, and where its stock market value is assessed. Instead, complex forms of transnational labour and labour exploitation were involved in the creation of my laptop before I purchased it, and Apple Inc. could profit from its sale. The computer in front of me (just like the mobile phone that I keep next to me) are complex political-economic assemblages that stretch from the United States (where profit is made) to West Africa (where cobalt and other minerals are mined), to Asia (where the parts are assembled), to South Africa (where I am writing this text), and finally to one of the many places in the global south where toxic e-waste is handled (Fuchs 2015). This assemblage of transnational connections is not innocent, it is one of capitalist violence: the mining industry in West Africa is highly exploitative, bordering on modern-day slavery and utilizing various forms of forced labour; the manufacturing industry in China is equally exploitative, as documented, for example, in the case of Foxconn, which assembles Apple Inc. products. And once I discard my laptop and purchase a new one, the e-waste that has been produced will be sent to countries such as India, where discarded devices from across the globe are dismantled so that metals and minerals can be extracted and recycled. This work is extremely hazardous, "releasing clouds of dust filled with toxins" (Shome 2016: 252), and destroying the health of those involved. And then, there are also the software producers, who make it possible for me to use my laptop, whose code creates the applications that I then use to create new texts. In the past software development was usually well paid and software developers were described as a "labour aristocracy". This, however, has changed and software development is increasingly outsourced to workers around the globe, workers who have been described as "badly paid and highly stressed" (for a detailed discussion of the political economy of hardware and software production, see Fuchs 2015; Parikka 2015).

Commenting on the "sugar revolution" in the Caribbean, Sheridan (1969: 25) notes: "it is ironical that after contributing so markedly to the progress of Northerners ... the people of the tropics are today in an economically inferior condition". One can say the same about digital capitalism: those who mine minerals, assemble smartphones and computers, and recycle discarded hardware enable digital connectivity for those in the global north (and affluent parts of the global south), but themselves have no or limited access to these technologies. Global statistics are helpful when we try to understand access and use: at the end of 2018, close to four billion people were online (ITU 2018). This is just over 50 percent of the global population. Is this a glass half full or half-empty? If digital media and the internet were indeed a revolution, then it was one which affected people differently in different locales: it was global (since there is no part of the world which is outside of the digital economy), yet unequal. In high-income countries around 80% of the population are online, compared to 45% in "developing nations" and around 20% in "least developed nations". In Africa, the continent from which I write, roughly one-quarter of people are online. It is important to remember that these inequalities are heavily racialized: white people have more access than black people. Capitalism is not neutral, its exploitation and destruction does not affect everyone equally. Rather, it is realized as racial capitalism, embedded in a fundamentally racist world system (on decolonization, racism and digital divides see Moyo 2018).

I have argued elsewhere (Deumert 2014) that digital social inequalities – and their racialized foundations – matter to the questions sociolinguists ask. The limited access to digital media in the global south means that many of the hopes invested in these technologies have not materialized. The "participatory [digital] culture" envisaged by Jenkins (e.g. Jenkins et al. 2015), might exist in Britain or Sweden, but not in Mali or Sudan, where traditional *oramedia* – song, dance, music – remain central to cultural and political engagement (Salawu 2015). With regard to language one of the hopes invested in digital communication was that multiple languages could flourish in diverse reading and writing spaces (since digital media cut down production costs and allow for the creation of texts in a variety of languages, see Prado 2012). Yet, currently, those areas of the world that show the greatest linguistic diversity are also the areas where digital access is most limited. In addition, language use online is shaped not only by present-day socio-economic realities (access and lack thereof), but also by historical patterns of literacy/illiteracy and language dominance in society. Thus, languages that have established written traditions, and/or are languages that are taught in the school system are frequently favoured by multilingual users. In the former colonies, this means that English, French and Portuguese retain high visibility, both online and offline (Deumert & Lexander 2013). Thus, the internet and associated networking applications might be potentially "revolutionary" technologies, but they reflect and reproduce historical continuities of structural inequality, reinforcing the imbalances, silences and marginalizations that define the global world system. Maybe they are not revolutionary at all?

19.5 Futures (Revolution Second Take)

Talking about histories links to imagined futures, and often the past shapes the futures one can imagine. Marx (2008 [1852]: 1) writes in the *Eighteenth Brumaire of Louis Bonaparte* about the past shaping the present, even in the aftermath of a revolution:

> At the very time when men appear engaged in revolutionizing things and themselves, in bringing about what never was before, at such epochs of revolutionary crisis do they anxiously conjure up into their service the spirits of the past, assume their names, their battle

cries, their costumes to enact a new historic scene in such time-honoured disguise and with such borrowed language.

It was with "Roman costumes" and "Roman phrases" that the revolutionaries of 1789 achieved the "task of their time: the emancipation and establishment of modern bourgeois society" (Marx 2008 [1852]: 1). Sometimes continuities across time hide discontinuities from sight.

In his 1998 review of the history of the internet, Rosenzweig notes: "The future remains uncertain. But it is clear that any history of the Internet will have to locate this story within its multiple social, political and cultural contexts" (Rosenzweig 1998: n.p.). He continues to describe the internet as an emerging "meta-medium" that "combines aspects of the telephone, post-office, movie theater, television set, newspaper, shopping mall, street corner, and a great deal more". This is the story of what is known as "convergence" in media studies, referring to a complexity of media functions at one's fingertips; a complexity that one might indeed call "revolutionary".

In previous writings (e.g. Deumert 2019) I have cited an unattributed adage that has made its rounds on the internet since 2015. This adage is helpful when reflecting on the idea of revolution: "If it is inaccessible to the poor it's neither radical nor revolutionary". This is an important caveat when thinking about revolution: is the revolution that Crystal and others have written about a bourgeois revolution? A revolution that remains fundamentally exclusionary, paving the way for a new type of capitalism? Do we need a working-class revolution when it comes to media usage? And what would such a revolution look like? Fuchs (2015: 304ff.) uses the terms "proletariat" and "working class" to distinguish between the objective and subjective dimensions of class formation under capitalism. The proletariat, in Fuchs' interpretation, is a "not-yet-politically-organized", "not-yet-united" and "not-yet-conscious group" of exploited labour.[3] Their media use happens under conditions of scarcity with people making the most of limited resources, but ultimately arranging themselves within the structures of digital

---

[3] Fuchs' usage differs from Marx and Engels, who use the two terms largely as synonyms in the *Communist Manifesto* (1848), e.g. *die modernen Arbeiter, die Proletarier*, "the modern workers, the proletarians"; *das Proletariat, die Klasse der moderen Arbeiter*, "the proletariat, the class of the modern workers". However, Fuchs follows Marx and Engels in emphasizing the process of conscientization: the proletariat moves from mere existence (not-yet-politically organized etc.) to becoming a "revolutionary class". (http://www.mlwerke.de/me/me04/me04_459.htm). When talking about the proletariat or the working class we should also keep in mind that the first "modern workers", as theorized by Marx and Engels, did not emerge in England, but in the plantation colonies (James 2001 [1938]). Thus, the first modern workers were black.

capitalism. Working-class media, on the other hand, would be quite different: it would be a political-utopian project that challenges the logic of capitalism. The working class, from a Marxist perspective, is conscious of its own position within a system of exploitation, and works actively towards the end of class society and, with regard to digital media, against the exploitative system on which digital capitalism is built. The aim would be the development of a commons, accessible to all and owned by those who produce it, i.e. the workers (miners, factory workers, e-waste recyclers, software developers and everyone who contributes their digital labour by creating content). Wouldn't this be a real revolution, transforming society from the bottom-up rather than enabling a particular group while keeping the exclusionary and exploitative system of capitalism intact? Making digital media available to everyone and creating a true digital commons? Can the bourgeois revolution become a working-class revolution? Can it become a decolonial revolution that spans the globe? If internet access would be a right (as it is already in some countries), perhaps then – with everyone in the world connected and able to use digital media (if they wish) – the scale of reading/writing as well as engaging multimodally will rise to a true mass literacy movement, to multiple voices "writing back" to the centres of power in a multitude of languages, challenging the enduring legacies of colonialism and the coloniality of the present. And perhaps then we will see more ruptures – also in language and signification – than continuities.

References

Anderson, Benedict. 1983. *Imagined communities. Reflections on the origin and spread of Nationalism*. London: Verso.
Beckford, George L. 1999 [1972]. *Persistent poverty: Underdevelopment in plantation economies of the Third World*. Mona, University of the West Indies: Canoe Press.
Brügger, Niels, Gerhard Goggin, Ian Milligan & Valérie Schafer. 2017. Introduction: Internet histories. *Internet Histories* 1. 1–7.
Brügger, Niels & Ian Milligan. (eds.) 2018. *The SAGE handbook of web history*. Los Angeles: Sage.
Crystal, David. 2004. *The language revolution*. Cambridge, UK: Polity.
Davis, Janae, Alex A. Moulton, Levi Van Sant & Brian Williams. 2019. Anthropocene, capitalocene ... plantationocene?: A manifesto for ecological justice in an age of global crises. *Geography Compass* 13. e12438.
Deumert, Ana. 2014. *Sociolinguistics and mobile communication*. Edinburgh: Edinburgh University Press.
Deumert, Ana. 2018. Mimesis and mimicry in digital writing. Towards a postcolonial aesthetics. *Language Sciences* 65. 9–17.

Deumert, Ana. 2019. Revolutions and digital technologies. *Diggit Magazine*, https://www.dig gitmagazine.com/column/revolutions-working-class-media (accessed 24 August 2019).

Deumert, Ana & Kristin V. Lexander. 2013. Texting Africa: writing as performance. *Journal of Sociolinguistics* 17. 522–546.

Deumert, Ana & Anne Storch, Forthcoming. Introduction: Colonial linguistics, then and now. In Ana Deumert, Anne Storch & Nick. Shepherd (eds), *Colonial and decolonial linguistics, knowledges and epistemes*. Oxford: Oxford University Press.

Eisenstein, Elizabeth. 2005 [1983]. *The printing revolution in Early Modern Europe*, 2nd edn. Cambridge, UK: Cambridge University Press.

Engels, Friedrich. 1969 [1845]. *The condition of the working class in England*. Moskow: Panther Books.

Fuchs, Christian. 2015. *Digital labour and Karl Marx*. New York: Routledge.

Goggin, Gerhard & Mark McLelland. 2017. *Routledge companion to global internet histories*. Abingdon: Routledge.

Higman, Barry W. 2000. The sugar revolution. *Economic History Review* 53: 213–236.

ITU [International Telecommunications Union] 2018. *Measuring the Information Society*. Two volumes. Geneva: ITU.

James, Cyril L.R. 2001 [1938]. *The Black Jacobins. Toussaint L'Ouverture and the San Domingo Revolution*. London: Penguin.

Jenkins, Henry, Mizuko Ito & danah boyd 2015. *Participatory culture in a networked era: A conversation on youth, learning, commerce, and politics*. Oxford: John Wiley & Sons.

Kant, Immanuel. 1998 [1782]. *Critique of pure reason*. Edited by Paul Guyer & Allen W. Wood. Cambridge, UK: Cambridge University Press.

Kuhn, Thomas. 2012 [1962]. *The structure of scientific revolutions*. 50th anniversary edition, with an introduction by Ian Hacking. Chicago: University of Chicago Press.

Labov, William. 1972. *Sociolinguistic patterns*. Philadelphia: University of Philadelphia Press.

Latzera, Vito. 2018. Cambridge Analytica, independent research and the national interest. *Anthropology Today* 34. 1–3.

Marx, Karl. 2008 [1852]. *The Eighteenth Brumaire of Louis Bonaparte*. New York: Cosimo.

McCulloch, Gretchen. 2019. *Because Internet: Understanding the new rules of language*. New York: Riverhead Books.

McLuhan, Malcolm. 1962. *Gutenberg Galaxy*. The making of typographic man. Abingdon: Routledge.

Moyo, Last. 2018. Rethinking the information society: a decolonial and border gnosis of the digital divide in Africa and the Global South. In Massimo Ragnedda & Glenn W. Muschert (eds), *Theorizing digital divides*, 134–147. Abingdon: Routledge.

Nyabola, Nanjala. 2018. *Digital democracy, analogue politics: How the internet is transforming politics in Africa*. London: Zed Books.

Pablé, Adrian & Christopher Hutton. 2015. *Signs, meaning and experience. Integrational approaches to linguistics and semiotics*. Berlin: De Gruyter Mouton.

Park, Myung-Jin & James Curran. 2000. *De-Westernizing media studies*. London: Routledge.

Parikka, Jussi. 2015. Dust and exhaustion: the labor of media materialism. *CTheory*. http://journals.uvic.ca/index.php/ctheory/article/view/14790/5665 (accessed 26 August 2019).

Pennycook, Alastair. 2018. *Posthumanist applied linguistics*. Abingdon: Routledge.

Prado, Daniel. 2012. Language presence in the real world and in cyber space. In Laurent Vannini & Hervé Le Crosnier (eds.), *NET.LANG. Towards the multilingual cyberspace*, 35–52. Caen: C&F éditions.

Rosenzweig, Roy. 1998. Wizards, bureaucrats, warriers and hackers: Writing the history of the internet. *American Historical Review* 103. 1530–1552.
Salawu, Abiodun. 2015. Oramedia as a vehicle for development in Africa: The imperative for the ethical paradigm of development. *Journal of Sociology and Social Anthropology* 6. 209–216.
Santos, Boaventura de Sousa. 2014. *Epistemologies of the South: Justice against epistemicide*. Boulder, C.O.: Paradigm.
Selbin, Eric. 2010. *Revolution, rebellion, resistance. The power of story*. London: Zed Books.
Sheridan, Richard B. 1969. The plantation revolution and the industrial revolution, 1625–1775. *Caribbean Studies* 9. 5–25.
Shome, Raka. 2016. When postcolonial studies meets media studies. *Critical Studies in Media Communication* 33. 245–263.
Todd, Zoe. 2016. An indigenous feminist's take on the ontological turn: "Ontology" is just another word for colonialism. *Journal of Historical Sociology* 29. 4–22.
Turkle, Sherry. 2007. *Evocative objects. Things we think with*. Cambridge, MA: MIT Press.
Turkle, Sherry. 2011. *Alone together: Why we expect more from technology and less from each other*. New York: Basic Books.
Veronelli, Gabriela A. 2015. The coloniality of language: Race, expressivity, power, and the darker side of modernity. *Wagadu: A Journal of Transnational Women's & Gender Studies* 13. 108–131.
Williams, Eric. 1944. *Capitalism and slavery*. Chapel Hill: University of North Carolina Press.
Williams, Raymond. 1961. *The long revolution*. London: Chatto & Windus.
Yang, Guobin & Shiwen Wu. 2018. Remembering disappeared websites in China: Passion, community, and youth. *New Media and Society* 20. 2107–2124.

Index

Abridging 241, 242, 250
Academic article(s) 6, 149–151, 153–157, 158, 160, 161
Academic value 154, 160, 162
Acrostics 212, 214–216, 224
Action systems 26, 27
Actions 21
Affordances 6, 47, 158, 297, 299, 323, 360, 361
Agency 361
Aggression 47, 49
Algorithms 18, 22–25, 30–33, 362
Alpine Club 94
Ambient affiliation 133
Anachronism 81, 83
Analogy 360
Anglicisation 176, 184
Anglicised spellings 185
Annotation 275
– automated annotation 356
– manual annotation 356
– markup 329, 347, 356, 357
Anthropocentrism 87, 104, 108, 164–166
Anxieties 302
Apple Inc. 369, 370
Appraisal framework 312
– affective evaluations 324, 325
– appreciation 312
– negative quality 319, 321
– negative reaction 319
– positive reaction 319, 322
– reaction 319
Assemblage 19, 23, 164, 166, 365, 369, 370
– assemblage theory 164
Audience(s) 154, 156, 157, 161, 162
Austin, J.L. 25
Authorship
– auctor model of authorship 266
– collaborative authorship 154, 159, 162, 258, 264, 282, 289, 296, 302, 340, 357
– medieval authorship 267
– solo authorship 289
Automated semantic taggers 338

Berners-Lee, Tim 20
Black box 25, 33
Blank space 194, 195
Blended data 58
Blogs 157
Boldface 295. *See also* Typeface
Book history 171
Book of Common Prayer 134
Borrowings 175, 186, 189, 191
Burgh laws 193, 194

Cambridge Analytica 17, 33, 364
Capitalisation 200, 223, 224
CB radio 92
Chancery 291
Chirographic 183
Choose your own adventure books 286
Citation 156, 157, 160
Citizen sociolinguistics 9, 131, 136, 138, 143, 144
Citizen sources 308, 323, 324
Citizen witnesses 307. *See also* Citizen sources
Clickbait 30
Cloud-based file-sharing platforms 159
Code-switching 212
Colophon. *See* Print, Colophon
Colour 295
Column layout 274
Communal practices 292
Communicative repertoire(s) 6, 7
Comparative approach 9, 55, 56, 60
Composition practices 289
Conduct books 9, 201
Context(s) 14, 21, 24, 25, 28–30, 55, 57–60, 94, 164, 359
– context collapse 162
– contextual breadth 57
Contextualisation 57, 58
– contextualisation cues 57, 58, 74, 75
Continuities 1, 2, 4, 9, 14, 15, 55, 56, 75, 87, 364, 365, 367–369, 371–373
– discontinuities 365, 368, 369, 372

378 — Index

Contrastive approach. *See* Comparative approach
Convergence 372
Copying 266
Corpus analysis 9, 59, 64, 82, 259, 330
Correspondence 2, 7, 9, 15, 55, 62–64, 73–75, 115, 150, 151, 155, 157, 162
– Irish migrant letters 332
– letter writing practices 76, 330, 342, 347
– migrant letter collections 329, 357
Courtesy 15, 41
Cross-modal practices 158
Cursor 298

Data 262
– data doubles 31, 32
– data visualization 157
Decolonial theory 364, 366
Decorated initial 284
Deictics 101, 106, 273
Democratization of publishing 298
Diachronic and synchronic research 38, 39, 52, 59
Diachronic reading 60
Digital
– digital capitalism 372, 373
– digital commons 373
– digital communication 42, 281
– digital divide 371
– digital fiction 282
– digital humanities 9, 330, 342, 349
– digital media 56–58, 60, 67, 289, 293
– digital methodologies 259
– digital practices 302
– digital publics 363. *See also* Networked publics
– digital scholar 149–153
Direct commands 353
Directionality 102
Discernment 41
Discourse(s) 86, 164–166
– discourse about and in motion 89, 107
– discourse analysis 133, 164
– discourse communities 204
– discourse management 174
– discourse structuring 180, 183

– discourse-in-motion 90, 91, 98, 99, 165
– discursive concept 82
– discursive connectors 271
Disruptive practices 292
Distributional semantics 81

Effort of processing 301
Elizabeth I, Queen 86, 112, 114–117, 119–121, 125, 126
Email(s) 4, 6, 38, 154, 159, 162
Embedding
– embedded pictures 307
– embedded tweet 314, 315, 319, 323
Embodiment 29, 291, 293
Emic 201, 208
Emoji(s) 58, 62, 144, 170, 364
Emotional outsourcing 307
Emotionality 307
Emotive language 354
English language practices 2–3, 5, 8, 55
Entextualisation 234
Ephemerality 364
Epigraphs 241
Episode boundary marker 216
Epistemology 27
Epistles 38
Epitexts 232, 233, 237
Epithet 142, 148
Erasure 289
Ethnography
– linguistic ethnography 152
– virtual ethnography 131
Etic 201, 208
Etiquette 43, 44
Evaluative language 312
E-waste 370, 373
Expertise 104
Expository 282, 294
EXtensible Markup Language (XML) 338, 343
External authorities 212

Face theory 44
Facebook 6, 17, 18, 21, 22, 27, 30, 33, 132, 136, 140, 143, 361, 363
– Like 17, 18
– wall event 132

Faithfulness 318. *See also* Reporting
Fake news 124
Familial roles 353
Figure and Ground *See* Graphical analysis, Figure and Ground
Flexibility 276
Fluidity 261, 281, 299, 302
Font(s) 255, 283, 291, 293, 314
– font choice 264
– font size 180, 183, 184, 206, 209, 214, 215, 216, 218, 220, 264, 276, 294, 295, 314
– italic 206, 216, 220, 221, 224, 239
– olde English font 295
– serif and san serif font 293
– weight 293, 294
Footing 58, 74
Footnotes 237, 245, 249, 255
Forensic linguistics 292
Format(s) 204, 208, 210, 224. *See also* Layout
Formulaic language 194, 330, 342, 355

Gender 96, 116, 117, 119
Genre(s) 87, 150, 151, 154, 155, 158, 160–162, 361, 363
– reproduced genre 306
GIFs 170
Global north, the 366, 367, 369, 370
Global south, the 363, 366, 367, 369–371
Goffman, Erving 29, 44
Gold leaf 296. *See also* Illumination(s)
Google 20, 21, 26, 27, 30, 33
– Google Docs 282, 289
Gothic 284, 291, 293. *See also* Typeface, Blackletter
Graphical analysis 263
– domain of visual elements 263
– figure and ground 97, 107, 263, 274, 275
– rationalization of a surface 263
Greeting 2
Gricean maxim of quality 299

Habitus 59
Handwriting 289, 291
Hashtag(s) 141, 143–145, 148
– #RIP 129–145
Herring's three-way model 5, 7, 130, 145, 306
Historical pragmatics 40, 41, 52
Historical depth 57
Historical linguistics 253, 281
Historicisation 15, 38–42, 45, 47, 52, 53
– historically-grounded interpersonal interactional approach 38, 39, 52
– interactional historicisation 40, 42, 44
– lexical historicisation 40, 41
Historicism 83
Historicity 40, 53
History writing 255, 264
Home page 225
Human 21, 33, 56, 86, 98, 107, 362, 365, 369
– human communication 1, 8, 14, 56, 87, 108, 359
– non-human 19, 33, 87, 165, 365, 369
Human-algorithm communication 19, 22, 28. *See also* Interaction, human-algorithm interaction
Hyperlinks 6, 296, 297, 307, 309, 316, 324, 325

Ideational meaning 284, 312
Identities 24, 25, 28–32, 72, 75, 76, 164
– identity types 29
– online identities 162
– professional identity 157
Ideologies 9, 115, 170
– functional efficiency 70
– ideological antiquarianism 192
– ideology of print 291
– ideology of standards 61, 76
– language ideologies 55, 73
– media ideologies 7
Illumination(s) 268, 276, 298, 296
Image 264
– drawings 99, 102, 103
– illustration 206–208, 221, 222, 224, 236, 274, 284, 289
– image alteration 104
Imagery 283, 298
Immediacy 93

Implicature 14, 25, 27
Imprint 206. *See also* Print, Colophon
Index(es) 237, 241–243, 245, 249
Indigenous scholarship 365
Inferencing 18, 21–25, 27, 28, 30
Information 17, 18, 24, 26, 28, 30, 33, 262
– information design 9, 258, 261–264, 268, 269, 272, 273, 275, 276, 277, 356
– information studies 262
Initialism R.I.P. 86
Instagram 144, 145
Interaction 300
– human-algorithm interaction 7, 14, 15
– human-computer interaction 22
– interactional phenomena 38, 53
Interactivity 105, 106
Internet meme 170
Internet 5, 47
– history of the internet 363, 364, 372
Interpersonal 312
Intertextuality 96, 253, 297
Interview
– day-in-the-life interview 153
– techno-biographic interview 15, 152, 153
– walk-around interview 153
Inverted-pyramid structure 306
Iteration, practices of 289

Journal articles *See* Academic articles
Journalism
– affective journalism 307
– citizen journalism 306
– digital journalism 306, 307
Juxta Commons 174, 184, 185, 187

Keyword 354
– keyword project 81
Knowledge 262
Kress, Gunther 359, 360

Language of mourning 129, 130
Latin 8, 173–176, 179, 183, 186, 187, 189, 190, 192, 193, 206, 212
Legal
– legal commonplace books 243

– legal discourse 174, 195
– legal scribes and clerks 178
– legal terms 179
– legal texts 9, 175, 186
– Scottish burgh laws 173, 178
Layout 174, 178, 206, 208, 212, 215, 224, 268, 308, 324, 327
Letters. *See* Correspondence
Lexis
– lexical co-occurrence 83
– lexical evaluation 312, 318
– supralexical 82
Liminality 39, 43
Limning. *See* Illumination(s)
Linearity 1, 286, 287, 299
– non-linearity 199, 261
Linguistic diversity 366, 371
Linguistic DNA 81
Links 283
Literacies 2, 68, 70, 76, 203
– academic literacies 150, 161
– digital literacies 33, 149, 286
– literacy studies 152
– media literacies 324, 325
Litterae notabiliores 193
Live blogs (LBs) 9, 306-325
Location(s) 89, 92, 93, 96–98, 101–103, 105–107, 165
– location-sharing 93, 107
– self-location 89, 90, 91, 107
Locative function of new media 101

Manicules 298
Manuscript(s) 6, 8, 9, 362
– manuscript culture 289
– manuscript layout 262
– manuscript page 274
– medieval manuscript production and consumption 281
Map(s) 99–103
Margins 274, 284
– marginalia 255, 275, 276, 297
Material objects 170
Materiality 361, 362
McLuhan, Marshall 1, 8, 173, 177, 368

Media
- mainstream media 86, 120–122, 125, 126, 132, 139, 140
- media ecologies 4
- mediascape 7, 156
- new media 3, 4
- old media 4
- online news articles 306, 309
- social media 8, 86, 87, 112, 124, 126, 132, 137, 139, 143, 145, 157, 162
- working-class media 373

Mediatisation 121, 124
Membership Categorization Analysis 18, 31, 32
Metacommentary 15, 52, 73, 101, 132, 141, 144
Metadata 20
Metalanguage 94, 101, 106
Metalexemes 46, 48, 49
Metalinguistic evidence 72
Metaphor 118, 360
Metrolingualism 59
Micro-coordination 89, 92, 94
Microanalysis 108, 201, 208–210
Microgenetic context 150
Microsoft Word 289
Migration
- female migration 331, 333
- Ireland to America 330, 331
- nineteenth-century mass migration 330

Mise-en-page 178, 179, 204, 205, 268
Mobile phone(s) 4, 62, 89, 92, 96, 103, 364
- mobile messaging 86, 90–92, 94, 97, 100, 102, 106, 107

Modality 299, 300, 302
- dependence 301
- low modality 298, 301
- modality markers 291

Modes 361
MOOD (microanalysis of online data) 14
Moralising metadiscourse 48
Motion 90–93, 95, 98, 101, 106
- motion verbs 106

Mourning 9, 86, 129, 134, 135, 139–141, 143–145

- online mourning 129, 130, 140, 144

Multimedia 6
Multimodality 3, 99, 101, 108, 154, 157, 158, 170, 199, 220, 226, 281, 359
- multimodal discourse analysis 283

Musical scores 99

Networked publics 129, 133, 143, 144
News websites 6, 225, 282, 359. *See also* Media
Newspaper readership 282
Non-verbal texts 96, 114, 115. *See also* Multimodality
Novelty 322

Old Bailey, Proceedings of 254
Ontogenetic development 150
Ontology 164
Oramedia 371
Ordinatio 174, 178, 179, 193, 268, 269
Orthography 55, 60, 283. *See also* Spelling

Page structure 283. *See also* Layout
Pagination 205
Paraph marks 271
Paratext 171, 200, 232, 237, 240–241, 249, 250, 253, 268, 269, 275, 289
- paratext theory 9

Performativity 25, 26
Peritext 232, 237
Personal letters 329. *See also* Correspondence
Personalisation 319
Photographs 103
Phylogenetic or evolutionary development 150
Politeness 15
- impoliteness 43
- positive politeness 293

Political leadership 9
Polymedia 6, 7
Postcards 2, 62
Postcolonial interruption 366
Post-humanism 365
PowerPoint 158

382 — Index

Practices 150–152, 154, 155, 157–159, 161, 359
Pragmatic markers
– visual pragmatics markers 200, 201, 212, 226
Pragmatics 8, 9, 14, 19, 22, 25, 33, 38–40, 42, 52, 57
– addressivity 148
– algorithmic pragmatics 14, 15, 19, 23, 25, 33
– analogue pragmatics 19, 22, 23
– contrastive pragmatics 42
– cyberpragmatics 19
– diachronic pragmatics 38, 59
– historical pragmatics 3, 40, 53, 58, 60, 83, 174, 199
– pragma-historical linguistics 58
– pragmaphilology 58, 59, 199, 201, 226
– pragmatic domains 200
– pragmatic features 45
– pragmatic functions 210
– pragmatics on the page 170
– sociopragmatics 41
– synchronic pragmatics 38
– visual pragmatics 9, 199, 226
Prefaces 237–241, 244, 255
Preferential forms 67, 71
Presentism 15, 80, 83
Print 1, 6, 76, 177, 178, 183, 195, 261, 264, 276, 293, 302
– colophon 202, 206, 216, 218, 244
– consistency of print 262, 266, 299
– licencing 235
– print culture 266
– printed books 289
– printers 6, 195, 200, 201, 202, 203, 205, 212, 221, 235
– printing 150, 161, 170, 174, 176, 178, 186, 187, 216, 265, 359, 362, 368
– printing house 202
– printing press 173, 174, 291
– printing press fonts 292
Printers' devices 226. See also Print, Colophon
Prologues. See Prefaces
Promotion 232, 240, 247, 249, 250
Provenance 360, 361

Publisher(s) 202, 221
Punctuation 194, 200
– subpunction 289
Python 342

Quality 299
Quires 204
Quora 131, 132, 138
Quotation(s) 258, 307, 309, 314, 315, 317, 323, 324

R programming language 342
R.I.P. (Rest in peace) 29, 129–145, 148
– #RIP 129–145, 148, 165
Radio 6
Reactions 21
Reader processing
– bottom-up processing 301
– top-down processing 301
Reading
– close reading 338
– medieval reader 287
– reader response 253, 309, 310, 324
– reading path 286
– reception 261
– recursive reading process 287
Reappropriation 233
Reception. See Reading, reception
Register 74, 122, 129, 130, 145, 151, 176, 261
Relevance 29
Religion
– religious discourse 134, 141
– religious imagery 237
Remediation 3, 5–7, 9, 91, 129, 174, 177, 183, 194, 281, 295, 299
Reported speech. See Reporting
Reporting
– direct quotations 323
– direct speech 308–309, 314, 318, 321–324.
– direct writing 308.
– indirect language 321, 322
– reported speech 308, 322, 324
– reporting clauses 314
Reverse-chronological structure 306
Revolution 363, 364, 367–369, 372, 373
– communication revolution 366

– internet revolution 367
– sugar revolution 369, 370
Rhetoric 4
– visual rhetoric 281, 283, 284, 299
Ritual 15, 43, 44, 47, 49, 56, 137
– interactional ritual 39
– interactional ritual analysis 47
– ritual language 134, 138, 141, 143, 144
– shaming ritual 48
Royal arms 237
Rubrication 180, 181, 269, 271, 276, 283, 284, 296–298
Rubrics 181, 193
Ruling 274

Scots 174, 176, 179, 184–186, 189–191, 194
– Scots borrowings 175
– Scots laws 176
– Scots scribes
– Scots vernacular 170
Scribal practices 293
Scribe(s) 180, 186, 189, 266, 292, 299
– scribal legibility 298
– scribal tradition 274
Scripts 291
Self-fashioning 9, 112, 114, 118, 120, 122, 124, 125
Self-positioning 102
Semantic domains 338
Semiotic resources 74, 94, 106, 170, 295
Sensory experiences 98, 99, 101, 102, 107
Shaming 45–49, 51, 52
– medieval shaming 15, 46, 47, 49
– online shaming 15, 39, 44, 45, 47, 49
– public shaming 44
– slut shaming 46
Sharing 129, 144
– ecstatic sharing 129
Skype 159
Smartphone 367, 368. *See also* Mobile phone
Smiley. *See* Emoji(s)
SMS text messaging/es 2, 4, 6, 15, 55, 60, 62, 64, 71, 74–76
Social Semiotics 360
– socio-cultural availability 361
Sociocultural framework 149

– socio-cultural development 150
Sociolinguistics 3, 8
Space 89, 90, 92, 93, 96, 98, 101, 102, 106, 107
– space management 183
Speech act(s) 14, 18, 25
Speech(es) 5, 15, 17, 55–56, 60, 71–72, 74–75, 115, 116, 118, 119, 122, 184, 186, 187, 200
Spelling
– abbreviation 2
– acronym 141, 142
– consistency 56, 67, 68, 70, 71, 74–76,
– digital media spelling 60, 76
– exceptional respellings 74, 76
– epistolary spelling 63, 64
– extended orthographic palette 61, 75
– eye dialect 74
– g-dropping 72
– homophone 71, 73
– initialism 130, 134
– intra-speaker variation 70
– manuscript and print spelling 72
– new media spelling 15
– non-standard spelling 75, 76
– regular respellings 75
– respelling 4, 55, 58, 61–63, 70–73, 76
– SMS spelling 61–64, 68, 71, 73, 75, 76
– sociolectal orthographic variation 71
– spelling variants 68, 71, 177
– Spelling variation 55, 60, 63, 71, 72, 74, 76, 177, 264, 266, 276
– standard spelling 74
Spoken styles 263
Standard 63, 67, 73–76
– a-Standard 74, 76
– discourse standardisation 194
– standardisation 55, 195
– standardness 67, 73
Strikethroughs 289
Structural markers 216
Subjunctive 142
Surveillance 23
Swales, John 149, 151, 157

Tables 237
Tables of contents 237, 239, 240, 268

Tag 144, 343, 339
Tapinosis 122
Tay 23
Technological determinism 108, 109, 369
TEI (Text Encoding Initiative) 343
Telegrams 62
Telephone 4, 6
Television 4
Text message. *See* SMS text messaging
Text 94, 114, 115, 121, 154, 155, 362
– digital text 276, 297
– digital textuality 265
– text type 154, 156
– textual experience 281
– textual instability 264
– textual organization 284
– textual promotion 233
– textual stability 258, 265, 266
– textual transmission 174, 264
– textual uniformity 1
– verbal text 115
The Law Students' Library 248
Title page(s) 206, 207, 216, 218, 220, 221, 224, 225, 236–243, 245
Todd, Zoe 365
Topics 330, 341, 342, 349, 354, 355, 357
– topic identification 339, 357
– topic modelling 356
Text trajectory(ies) 9, 170, 171, 233, 250, 361
Transcription 329
Transhistorical approach(es) 1, 2, 3, 4, 7–9, 14, 15, 55–60, 63, 75, 76, 89–91, 107, 359, 361, 362, 366
Translation 176, 193
Translocal 366
Transmedia 130, 131, 158
Transmission(s) 175, 178–180
Travel writing 90, 91, 92, 93, 95, 96
– Alpine travel writing 86, 89–109
Trump, Donald 17, 23, 86, 112, 113, 120, 121, 123–126
Twitter 5, 8, 23, 122–124, 126, 131, 133, 134, 140, 141, 144, 157, 258, 308, 309, 315, 316, 318, 319, 321–325
Typeface(s) 205, 208

– blackletter 205, 206, 208–210, 212, 215, 224, 227, 239, 243, 293, 294
– comic sans 7
– roman 205, 206, 209–212, 214–216, 220, 221, 224, 239, 243
– typeface switching 170, 224
Typesetter 184
Type-size 314. *See also* Font, font size
Typography 237, 283
– typographic image 291

Uniformitarian principle 15, 55–57, 80, 83, 282, 369
Usenet 5
User comments 6
Utterances 199, 200, 204

Verbatim 308, 316
Vernacularisation 174
Video 300, 301
Visual. *See also* Multimodality
– visual aspects 199
– conservatism 211
– discourse 174, 178–180, 183, 186
– features 3
– format 195
– layout 263
– organisational strategies 179
– practices 3
– strategies 183
– structural devices 215
– structuring 180
– synthetic personalization 293
Visualisations 342, 355, 356
– visualisation tools 330, 332, 355
Visuality 253
Vividness 318
Voice 122–124
Vygotsky, Lev 149, 150

Way-Back-Machine 363
Wayfinding 263, 268, 269, 276
Web
– pragmatic web 14, 19, 21, 22, 33, 80
– semantic web 20

– syntactic web 20
– web 1.0 5
– web 2.0 5
– web 4.0 21
WhatsApp 4, 86, 90, 92, 95, 96, 98, 106, 108, 363
Wiki 7
Wisdom 262
Writing
– academic writing practices 86, 87, 149, 152, 154, 155, 161, 162
– digital writing practices 281, 289
– writing and reading practices 275, 281

– written language 4, 64, 157, 261, 264, 318
– writing practices 152
– written styles 263
– writing technology 291

XML (eXtensible Markup Language) 339, 355
– attribute 343
– element 343
– unique identifier 344

Youth Abbeys 46, 49, 51, 52
YouTube 7, 23, 359, 360

www.ingramcontent.com/pod-product-compliance
Lightning Source LLC
Chambersburg PA
CBHW051555230426
43668CB00013B/1859